W9-BZY-386

MICROSOFT WINDOWS XP & OFFICE

KILLER TIPS

Microsoft® Windows® XP and Office®

KILLER TIPS

COLLECTION

MICROSOFT® WINDOWS® XP AND OFFICE® KILLER TIPS COLLECTION

PUBLISHED BY
New Riders
1249 Eighth Street, Berkeley, CA 94710
800-283-9444 • 510-524-2178 • 510-524-2221 (fax)

New Riders is an imprint of Peachpit, a division of Pearson Education.

Copyright © 2006 by Kelby Corporate Management, Inc.

FIRST EDITION: November 2005

All rights reserved. No part of this book may be reproduced or transmitted in any form, by any means, electronic or mechanical, including photocopying, recording, or by any information storage and retrieval system, without written permission from the publisher, except for inclusion of brief quotations in a review.

Composed in Myriad, Trebuchet, and Helvetica by NAPP Publishing

Trademarks

All terms mentioned in this book that are known to be trademarks or service marks have been appropriately capitalized. New Riders cannot attest to the accuracy of this information. Use of a term in the book should not be regarded as affecting the validity of any trademark or service mark.

Microsoft, Windows, and Office are either registered trademarks or trademarks of Microsoft Corporation in the United States and/or other countries.

Warning and Disclaimer

This book is designed to provide information about Windows XP and Office 2003 tips. Every effort has been made to make this book as complete and as accurate as possible, but no warranty of fitness is implied.

The information is provided on an as-is basis. The authors and New Riders shall have neither liability nor responsibility to any person or entity with respect to any loss or damages arising from the information contained in this book or from the use of the discs or programs that may accompany it.

ISBN 0-321-37462-2

Note: This edition is a collection of the following books:
Windows XP Killer Tips (ISBN 0-7357-1357-X)
Microsoft Office 2003 Killer Tips (ISBN 0-7357-1437-1)

9 8 7 6 5 4 3

Printed and bound in the United States of America

www.newriders.com
www.peachpit.com
www.scottkelbybooks.com

Microsoft® Windows® XP and Office®
KILLER TIPS
COLLECTION

Thank you for purchasing the *Microsoft Windows XP and Office Killer Tips Collection*. By combining two books into one, you save money and learn the best tips for Windows XP and Office in the same book.

Windows XP Killer Tips is the first book in this combined volume, with the index for the book following immediately after the text. This is followed by *Microsoft Office 2003 Killer Tips*, with its index following immediately after the text, as well.

Windows® XP KillerTips

Kleber Stephenson

WINDOWS XP® KILLER TIPS

**The Windows XP
Killer Tips Team**

EDITOR
Barbara E. Thompson

TECHNICAL EDITOR
Tommy Maloney

PROOFREADER
Richard Theriault

PRODUCTION EDITOR
Kim Gabriel

PRODUCTION
**Dave Damstra
Dave Gales
Ted LoCascio
Margie Rosenstein**

COVER DESIGN AND
CREATIVE CONCEPTS
Felix Nelson

SITE DESIGN
Stacy Behan

The New Riders Team

PUBLISHER
David Dwyer

ASSOCIATE PUBLISHER
Stephanie Wall

EXECUTIVE EDITOR
Steve Weiss

PRODUCTION MANAGER
Gina Kanouse

PROJECT EDITOR
Jake McFarland

PROOFREADER
Gloria Schurick

PRODUCTION
Wil Cruz

PUBLISHED BY
New Riders

Copyright © 2003 by Kleber Stephenson

All rights reserved. No part of this book may be reproduced or transmitted in any form, by any means, electronic or mechanical, including photocopying, recording, or by any information storage and retrieval system, without written permission from the publisher, except for inclusion of brief quotations in a review.

Composed in Myriad, Trebuchet, and Helvetica by NAPP Publishing

Trademarks
All terms mentioned in this book that are known to be trademarks or service marks have been appropriately capitalized. New Riders cannot attest to the accuracy of this information. Use of a term in the book should not be regarded as affecting the validity of any trademark or service mark.

Windows is a registered trademark of Microsoft Corporation.

Warning and Disclaimer
This book is designed to provide information about Windows XP tips. Every effort has been made to make this book as complete and as accurate as possible, but no warranty of fitness is implied.

This information is provided on an as-is basis. The authors and New Riders shall have neither liability nor responsibility to any person or entity with respect to any loss or damages arising from the information contained in this book or from the use of the discs or programs that may accompany it.

ISBN 0-7357-1357-X

Printed and bound in the United States of America

www.newriders.com
www.windowsxpkillertips.com

For my wonderful wife, Debbie

and amazing children, Jarod and Jenna

ACKNOWLEDGMENTS

This book would never have been possible if it weren't for the support and understanding of my family and friends. I simply couldn't have done it without them. I'm so grateful to everyone. Thanks!

I first want to thank God, Jesus Christ; my life has been so wonderfully blessed and I feel Him in my life every day. Thanks for always being there for me and always listening to my prayers. Next, I want to thank my wife, Debbie. You're simply the most beautiful woman I've ever seen; you have the most amazing smile. You're my best friend, a fantastic mother, and you completely crack me up (all the time). I still can't believe that I was lucky enough to marry you. I love you more every day.

I also want to thank my children, Jarod and Jenna. Just thirty seconds with you guys and I realize how great my life truly is. You make every single day better. I'm so proud of both of you; you're definitely my greatest accomplishment. Jarod, you're so confident and self-assured, and the most interesting person I've ever met. There's no one I'd rather just hang out with. Jenna, you have your mother's beauty and even at age two, you're already so charming and sweet that you preoccupy everyone in a room and immediately steal their hearts. You stole mine the moment you were born. Thanks guys, for reminding me when I'm ignoring you and for not letting me get away with it.

Thanks also to my parents, Kleber and Barbara. I don't have enough pages in this book to express my gratitude for my mother. I wish everyone could have a mother as wonderful, as caring, and as giving as she is. Everything that's good in me I got from her. And Dad, thanks for showing me that there's no substitute for enthusiasm, and for the mantra, "It just doesn't get any better than this!" I agree Dad—it doesn't. And to the best sisters anyone could ever have: Cheryl, Kalebra, Julie, and Heidi; the four of you make our family great. I'm completely blown away to see how successful you've all become. You're all incredible! Thanks for your support and encouragement!

I also want to thank my grandmother, Reverend Ethel Trice—the most influential person I've ever known. She'd always get me to follow the right path even though I was determined not to. She taught me that I could do anything. She's no longer with us, but the world's a much better place because she was once with us. I miss her.

In addition, I'd like to express my tremendous appreciation and gratitude for my staff at Medical Assisted Services and U.S. Diginet—a fantastic team that gives its best each and every day. Everyone should be so fortunate to work with such a great group of people.

Of course, a very special thanks to Scott Kelby—you're simply the coolest, and an inspiration. And to my sister Kalebra. Ever since we were little kids hanging out in the trees in our backyard hoarding candy and cracking jokes, I've thought you were the greatest, and I still think you're the greatest. I'd like also to thank everyone at KW Media Group, especially Barbara Thompson, Felix Nelson, Tommy Maloney, Kim Gabriel, Dave Damstra, Dave Gales, and Margie Rosenstein. I couldn't possibly imagine a better production team to work with. All of you made producing this book seem effortless.

Finally, I'd like to thank my "PC Posse" (people who know a lot more about computers than I do), especially Steve Iverson and Larry Brown. I've known Steve for more than a decade, and he's taught me more about computers (by fixing my screw-ups) than anyone I've ever known. Larry, you're scary (couldn't resist); if the Government knew about you, you'd either be working for them, or you'd be in jail.

Again, many, many thanks to everyone!

ABOUT THE AUTHOR

Kleber Stephenson

Kleber is President of U.S. Diginet—Interactive Communications, an award-winning, full-service provider of Internet solutions, integrated strategy consulting, and secure, stable hosting environments for growing e-business enterprises.

Kleber is also President of Medical Assisted Services, Inc., a Florida-based medical company with several divisions, providing diagnostic testing services, pain-management solutions, and durable medical equipment to Physicians and healthcare professionals throughout the US.

Kleber is also a contributing technology reviewer for *Mac Design Magazine* and *Photoshop User*, and he has more than a decade of experience analyzing and implementing business computing infrastructures based on the Windows platform. Through his existing businesses, Kleber designs and develops real-world network and administrative solutions based on Microsoft technologies and the Windows OS architecture.

Kleber lives in the Tampa Bay area of Florida with his wife, Debbie, his son, Jarod, and his daughter, Jenna.

FOREWORD by Scott Kelby

As Editor for the Killer Tips series, I'm excited to not only bring you another Killer Tips book, but I'm particularly excited to introduce you to an author who is going to take you to a whole new level of speed, efficiency, productivity, and sheer un-adulterated out-and-out fun using Windows XP. (I just realized that when you put the words "sheer" and "unadulterated" together, it sounds kind of dirty, but it's not meant to be. That comes later.) But first, a little background on this book and why it's different from every other Windows book out there.

The idea for this type of book came to me one day when I was at the bookstore, browsing in the computer section, when I thought to myself, "Man, these authors must be making a ton of money!" No wait, that wasn't what I was thinking (it's close, mind you, but not exactly). Actually, I was standing there flipping though the different books on Adobe Photoshop (I'm a Photoshop guy at heart). Basically, what I would do is look for pages that had a tip on them. They're usually pretty easy to find, because these "rich book authors" usually separate their tips from the regular text of the book. Most of the time, they'll put a box around the tips, or add a tint behind them, maybe a Tip icon—something to make them stand out and get the readers' attention.

Anyway, that's what I would do—find a tip, read it, and then start flipping until I found another tip. The good news—the tips were usually pretty cool. You have to figure that if an author has some really slick trick, maybe a hidden keyboard shortcut or a cool workaround, they probably won't bury it in blocks of boring copy. No way! They'll find some way to get your attention (with those boxes, tints, a little icon, or simply the word "Tip!"). So, that's the cool news—if it said tip, it was usually worth checking out. The bad news—there were never enough tips. Sometimes they'd have five or six tips in a chapter, but other times, just one or two. But no matter how many they had, I always got to the last chapter and thought, "Man, I wish there had been more tips."

Standing right there in the bookstore, I thought to myself, "I wish there were a book with nothing but tips: hundreds of tips, cover-to-cover, and nothing else." Now *that's* a book I'd go crazy for. I kept looking and looking, but the book I wanted just wasn't available. That's when I got the idea to write one myself. The next day I called my editor to pitch him the idea. I told him it would be a book that would be wall-to-wall, nothing but cool tips, hidden shortcuts, and inside tricks designed to make Photoshop users faster, more productive, and best of all, to make using Photoshop even more fun. Well, he loved the idea. Okay, that's stretching it a bit. He *liked* the idea, but most importantly, he "green-lighted it" (that's Hollywood talk—I'm not quite sure what it means), and soon I had created my first all-tips book, *Photoshop 6 Killer Tips* (along with my co-author and good friend, *Photoshop User* magazine Creative Director Felix Nelson).

As it turned out, *Photoshop 6 Killer Tips* was an instant hit (fortunately for me and my chance-taking editor), and we followed it up with (are you ready for this?) *Photoshop 7 Killer Tips*, which was an even bigger hit. These books really struck a chord with readers, and I like to think it was because Felix and I were so deeply committed to creating something special—a book where every page included yet another tip that would make you nod your head, smile, and think "Ahhh, so that's how they do it." However, it pretty much came down to this: People just love cool tips. That's why now there are also *Dreamweaver MX Killer Tips* and *QuarkXPress 6 Killer Tips* books.

So how did we wind up here, with a Killer Tips book for an operating system? Well, there was an intermediate step: Last year I wrote *Mac OS X Killer Tips* for Macintosh users switching over to Apple's new UNIX-based operating system. It turned out to be such a big hit; it actually became "biggety-big" (a purely technical term only used during secret book-publishing rituals).

So creating a Windows XP Killer Tips book was a natural. The only problem is that I'm really a Photoshop guy and for this book to surpass the Mac book's "biggety-bigness," it would take a pretty special author. It would take a person who was an absolute Windows XP expert (with a giant über-brain), who has professional writing experience, a great sense of humor, and a casual, conversational writing style. This person would have to have a keen sense for uncovering those inside tips that the pros use to get twice the work done in half the time. They'd have to be one of those people who don't do anything "the hard way," and they'd have to know every timesaving shortcut, every workaround, and every speed tip to make something different, something special, and the only book of its kind in a very crowded Windows XP book market.

Here's the thing: I knew just the guy—Kleber Stephenson. I chose him for one simple reason: the similarity of his first name to my last name. Heck, it's almost the same name (Kleber Kelby. See what I mean?) That was enough for me. Okay, that's actually not the reason at all (just a lucky coincidence). I chose Kleber because he fit every criterion I had set for the ideal Killer Tips author. First, he totally "gets" the Killer Tips concept because just like me, he's a tip hound—a tip junkie (if you will). Second, I've always enjoyed his writing style, humor, the completeness of his research and attention to detail, and how he really immerses himself in a project. Third, like me he's a die-hard Tampa Bay Bucs fan. Fourth (and perhaps most important), he knows more Windows tips and has a better understanding of the Windows Operating System than anyone I know. Period. That's why, when we decided to do the book, I called him first, and honestly if he had decided to pass on the project, you wouldn't be reading this book now, because he was *so* the right person to do this book that I didn't have another person in mind as a backup plan. I wanted Kleber, and if I couldn't get him, I'd shelve the idea and move on to another project. That's how strongly I felt that he was the right person for the job, and I'm absolutely delighted that you're holding his book right now. Kleber has really captured the spirit and flavor of what a Killer Tips book is all about, and I can tell you this—you're gonna love it!

I can't wait for you to "get into it," so I'll step aside and let him take the wheel, because you're about to get faster, more efficient, and have more fun using Windows XP than you ever thought possible.

All my best,

Scott Kelby
Series Editor

CHAPTER 1 2
Windows…Wide Open
Get the Most Out of Windows XP

Two Clicks Are Too Much 4
That Picture Suits Me 4
May I See a Menu Please? 5
Give the True Gift of Love…Share Your Computer 5
Not Sure About a File? Just Drop It 6
Another Way to Maximize and Restore Windows 6
Minimize Using the Taskbar 7
Close Using the Taskbar.. 7
Don't Just Maximize Your Windows—Go Full Screen 8
Manually Resize a Window 8
Resize a Maximized Window 9
Change Which App Opens a File 9
You Can Make It Smaller if You Squeeze It...................10
Make Room! Compress Folders and Directories 10
Change Your Views...11
Nice View! I Think I'll Save It....................................11
Want More Toolbar Buttons? Who Can Blame You? 12
Toolbars Getting Crowded? Shrink the Icons 12
Organize Icons on Your Toolbar 13
Keep 'em Separated 13
What Are Those Little Black Arrows on My Toolbar?.......14
Toolbars a Mess? Get Back Your Defaults....................14
Finally! Toolbars the Way You Like Them 15
Links…The Ultimate Toolbar 15
Add New Folders to the Links Toolbar 16
Rearrange the Links Toolbar Icons..............................16
They're Icons; You Can Change 'em 17
Removing the Links Toolbar Icons...............................17
Anti-Scroll Tip—Right-Mouse-Click 18
Anti-Scroll Tip—Use the Keyboard 18
Wheel Mouse Scroll Tip—Adjust the Wheel 19
Serious Folder Power 19
Applying Folder Templates 20
That's Better Than an Icon 20
What are Those Little Black Arrows on My Task Panes? 21
Remove the Task Panel 21
Use Filmstrip View to Browse Pictures 22
The Not-So-Obvious Power of Filmstrip View 22
Open Folders in Different Windows.............................23
Hmm, It Needs Its Own Window................................23
Instantly View a File's Details 24
Don't Like Toolbars? Don't Use 'em...........................24

TABLE OF CONTENTS

Browse the Web From Any Window 25
Find Files Using the Address Bar.................................25
Pop-Up Taskbar Buttons 26
View Status Bar on Windows.......................................26
Screen-Saver Safe 27
Control the Control Panel 27
Side-by-Side 28

CHAPTER 2 30
Have It Your Way
Customize Windows XP

Ground Control…We Have Icons 32
It's A-to-Z for the All Programs Menu 32
Don't Like the New Start Menu? Change It Back 33
More Programs on the Start Menu 33
"Pin" Programs to the Start Menu 34
Scroll Your Programs Instead.....................................34
My, My, My…We Get It...35
The Internet on Your Taskbar 35
Taskbar Web Pages..36
Launch Apps from the Address Bar 36
Favorites All the Time 37
Floating Toolbars? Cool!...37
Quick! Launch It 38
Quick Launch Your Favorite Apps 38
Moving Quick Launch Icons 39
One-Click Search...39
Taskbar…On the Move 40
Stretch! Ah, That's Better 40
Peek-a-Boo with the Taskbar 41
Hide the Taskbar Manually 41
A Desktop You Can Always See 42
Make Some Room: Stack 'em 42
Huddle Up, Group Your Buttons....................................43
Speed Tip: Close a Group at Once.................................43
If I'm Not Using 'em, I Don't Want to See 'em 44
You've Been Notified…You've Got to Go 44
Pump Up the Volume 45
Do You Need the Time? 45
Work Out of Your Briefcase.......................................46
It's Time for a Change 46
I Prefer Solids 47
It's Not a Theme Park, But It's Close............................47
Create Custom Themes...48
Appearing Live on Your Desktop…Your Favorite Web Page...........48

A Refreshing Desktop 49
Add Cool Web Stuff to Your Desktop 49
Animate Your Desktop 50
Lock Web Items 50
Change Your Pointer Scheme 51
It's Not Easy Lookin' This Good 51

CHAPTER 3 52
Cruisin'
Navigating Windows XP

It All Happens Here…Get There Quickly 54
A Different Default View 54
Turn Any Window into Explorer 55
Instantly Explore Any File 55
Can't See It? Doesn't Matter 56
Just Type Its Name 56
It's All About the Details 57
Making the Details Fit 57
Let's Sort This Out 58
Rearrange Columns in Details View 58
Using the Keyboard to Navigate Views 59
Windows a Mess? Group 'em 59
I'm Feeling a Little Blue; I'm Compressed 60
Find Your Hidden Files 60
Where Am I? 61
Where Am I? (Another Way) 61
No Go 62
Delete This! 62
Taking Out the Trash 63
Oops! I Didn't Want to Delete That 63
Navigate Windows Without the Mouse 64
Navigate Menus Without the Mouse 64
Save It Where Ya Want It 65
Quick Save 65
Instantly Save to a New Folder 66
Single Click? Don't Overwrite 66
I Don't Think I'll Save After All 67
Resize Open/Save Dialog Box 67
You Can Cut and Paste from Here 68
Show File Extensions 68
Be Choosy with Extensions 69
System Properties in a Click 69
You Can Always Go Back 70
Moving Files Using the Tasks Pane 70

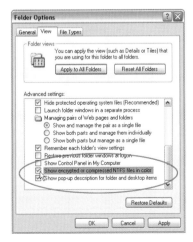

TABLE OF CONTENTS

CHAPTER 4 72

An American Icon

Working with Icons in Windows XP

Send Shortcuts to the Desktop 74
Move Folders 74
Drag-and-Drop Shortcuts 75
Drag-and-Drop Copies 75
Can't Make Up Your Mind? Give Yourself Options.....................76
Create Shortcuts from the Start Menu 76
Create a Shortcut for Just About Anything..................................77
Don't Forget the Shortcut's Shortcut Menu 77
I Know It's a Shortcut 78
Change a Shortcut's Icon 78
Change a Folder's Icon 79
Don't Like Your New Icon? Change It Back 79
Make Your Own Icons 80
Arrange Your Icons 80
Keep Your Icons in Line 81
Adjust Icon Spacing 81
Where Are My Desktop Icons?..82
Change Default Desktop Icons 82
Super-Size 'em 83
Create a New Folder 83
Add Comments to Your Shortcut Icons 84
Locate a Shortcut's Target 84
That's a Long File Name..85
Turn on the Thumbnails 85
Select Everything in a Folder..86
Click-and-Drag to Select Icons 86
Select Almost Everything 87
Select Continuous/Noncontinuous Files 87

CHAPTER 5 88

The Fast and The Furious

Windows XP Speed Tips

Dragging Files to the Recycle Bin When It's Hidden 90
A Quicker Way to Rename 90
Undo Renaming Mistakes 91
e-Mail Attachments from Just About Anywhere 91
Cool! Toolbar Drives..92
Making Favorites a Real Favorite 92
Speed-Launch Your Favorite Apps 93
Not Just No; No To All 93
Open Multiple Files at the Same Time...94

Show the Desktop Fast; Restore It Even Faster 94
Shortcut to Shut Down 95
Switch 'em Out and Lock 'em Up 95
A Useful Power Button? 96
Quick Quitting 96
Instantly Resize Columns in Detail View 97
Quickly Expand Folders.. 97
Don't Forget Me, I'm Special 98
Launch Favorite Apps at Startup 98
One-Click Properties 99
Toggle Open Items on the Taskbar 99
You Can Be Choosy when Opening Files.................................. 100
Delete an Open Folder? 100
Create a Shortcut of an Open Folder 101
Open an Open Folder's Shortcut Menu 101
You Don't Have to See It to Move It 102
You Don't Have to See It to Move It (Take 2)............................ 102
Selectively Group Open Windows on the Taskbar...................... 103
Copy and Delete at the Same Time 103
It's Outta Here!.. 104
I Didn't Want to Drag That 104
Close a Group of Windows with One Click................................ 105
Close a Group of Windows with One Click
    (But Leave the Active Window Open) 105
Minimize All Windows at Once 106
Didn't Mean to Move It? Undo It... 106
A Faster Way to Search Folders 107
Delete the Entire Word... 107

CHAPTER 6 108
We Will Rock You
Rockin' Windows Tips

Rename 'em All at Once... 110
It's Show Time! 110
Cool Custom Screen Savers 111
Don't Stand by, Hibernate 111
Let Windows Do the Talking 112
Give the Scraps to Your Desktop 112
Drag-and-Drop Drives 113
Personalize the All Programs Menu... 113
I'm Really Good at Checkers 114
Right-Click Print 114
Grandma's Gettin' a Fax 115
Just Go Home 115
Search the Web at Any Time, from Any Place........................... 116

TABLE OF CONTENTS

Install Fonts Without Installing Them 116
No Adobe Type Manager? No Problem 117
Preview Installed Fonts 117
Associate Files with Multiple Apps 118
"Send To" Anywhere You Want 118
Folder Icons? 119
Hidden Apps—Chat with People on Your Network 119
Hidden Apps—Create Self-Installing Packages 120
Hidden Apps—Custom Characters 120
Hidden Apps—What Happened to NetMeeting? 121
Capture Me if You Can.. 121
Save That Pop-Up... 122
Open Several Apps at Once 122
Create a New File Without Launching Its Program........................ 123
Top-Secret, Invisible Folders 123
Do You Have the Correct Time? 124
Little Help Please 124
See Clearly with ClearType 125
Super-Fast Media Previews... 125
Save Streaming Media 126
Keep 'em Out of Your Folders... 126
Print Photo Sheets 127
Order Prints Online 127
Toggle Display of File Names in Filmstrip/Thumbnails View 128
Drag-and-Drop Previews.. 128
Disguise Your Files 129

CHAPTER 7 130
Play That Funky Music
Windows Media Player 9 Tips

Skin Deep 132
Shed Your Skin 132
Love That Skin 133
Anchors Away 133
Get Funky 134
Maximize the Funk... 134
I Need More 135
Drag, Drop, Play 135
Custom Color 136
Alvin? Is That Alvin? 136
Play It Even Faster 137
What's Your EQ?... 137
Super-Fast Playlists 138
Shortcut to Playlists.. 138

Add from Anywhere 139
Add 'em All at Once 139
It's Automatic 140
Give It One Star 140
Built-In Power Sorting 141
Let's Sort It Out 141
Surprise Me 142
Queue-It-Up 142
It's Mini-Player! 143
Mini-Player's Mini Info 143
Mini-Funk 144
Play It Again 144
It's a Control Thing 145
It's Worth Waiting For 145
Make It Right 146
Gettin' Geeky 146
I'll Tell You Where to Look 147
Can't Take the Highs and Lows 147
Level the Playing Field 148
Can You Relate? 148
Sing Along 149
WOW! 149
You Can Find It from Here 150
It's All in the Name 150
This Isn't Going Anywhere 151

CHAPTER 8 152

It's a Small World

Explore Your World with Internet Explorer

Don't Type Your URLs 154
Back and Forth in a Flash 154
Back and Forth Using the Keyboard 155
You Should Know Your History 155
Quick Favorites 156
Drag-and-Drop Favorites 156
That Makes No Sense 157
Folders for Favorites 157
Never Organize Favorites 158
Home's a Drag 158
Speed Search 159
I Want a New Window 159
Like It? Send It to a Friend 160
Don't Just Send It; Archive It 160
Erase Your History 161
Cover Your Tracks 161

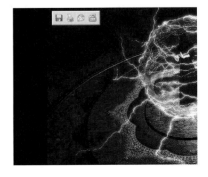

TABLE OF CONTENTS

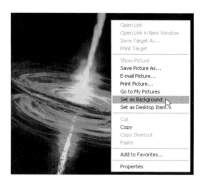

Cover Your Tracks Automatically..162
Master of Disguise..162
I Don't Need That Much Space..163
Power Search...163
Super-Fast Browsing..164
View It Offline...164
Take It a Step Further..165
Quick Save Web Graphics...165
Make It Your Background..166
Clearing Passwords..166
Who's Related?..167
Smart Printing...167
You Don't Have to See It to Save It..168
Send It to Your Desktop..168
Tab Your Way Through Forms..169
One-Click Favorites..169

Chapter 9 170
Come Together
e-Mail Made Easy

I Just Want to Start Up..172
You've Got a New Mail Sound..172
Go Directly to Your Inbox...173
Read It, But Leave It..173
Group 'em...174
Add New Members...174
Bcc Is Better..175
Right-Click to e-Mail..175
Manage Your Mail..176
What's the Subject?..176
Flag It 177
Yep, We Received It 177
Shortcut to Your Best Friend..178
Personal Phone Book...178
Sign It and Forget It...179
Did You Get My Message?..179
Snag That Stationery...180
I Can't Get Enough...180
Do-It-Yourself Stationery..181
Things To Do...181
Move Messages Quickly..182
Drag-and-Drop to Edit..182
Can't Spell?..183
Teach It to Spell..183
Just Show Me New Messages 184

That's the Font for Me...184
No Mail from You..185
Check e-Mail Continuously...185
Got Mail? Your Notification Area Knows....................................186
Quick Add Contacts...186
Who's Online?...187
Say "Hey" Instantly..187
Too Racy? Turn It Off...188
Drag-and-Drop Attachments...188
Create a vCard..189
Give Me Directions...189
Messenger—Are You There?...190
Messenger—Give Me a Break..190
Messenger—Drag-and-Drop to Send..191
Messenger—.NET Alerts..191
Messenger—You're Blocked..192
Messenger—Super-Fast Groups..192
Messenger—Quickly Add Contacts to Groups..........................193
Messenger—What Did They Say?..193
Messenger—Send Messages from the Taskbar.........................194
Messenger—Make It a Party..194
Messenger—Get Rid of Pop-Ups in a Hurry.............................195

Chapter 10 196
It's a Wrap
Movie Making with Windows Movie Maker 2

Super-Size the Storyboard...198
Trimming Made Easy..198
Un-Trim Your Clips...199
Trim a Picture..199
Quickly Rearrange Clips 200
Create Title Effects 200
Quick-Change Title Text 201
Snag a Still Shot 201
Freeze Frame..202
Audio Only...202
Get Rid of the Audio..203
AutoMovie..203
Add Background Music...204
Narrate Your Movies..204
Getting' Geeky with Transitions..205
Cross-Fade Clips...205
Double Time...206
Getting Precise with the Timeline...206
Back to the Beginning 207

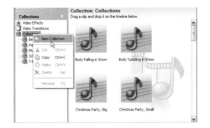

TABLE OF CONTENTS

Quick Fades 207
Don't Split My Clip 208
Do-It-Yourself Clips 208
Share Your Clips 209

Chapter 11 210
Hacked Off
Those Annoying Things You Do

Yes, I Really Want to Delete 212
I Know, I Installed It 212
Stop Printing 213
Don't Report Me 213
A Less-Friendly Search... 214
I'll Update Myself 214
No More Pop-Ups 215
Bigger, Smaller…They're the Same.............................. 215
I'm Distracted.. 216
Why Would I Want to Restart?..................................... 216
Beat Your CD Player to the Punch............................... 217
Why Can't I Drag-and-Drop It? You Can, But It's Weird 217
Scientific Calculator?... 218
Annoy Others—Freaky Desktop................................... 218
Annoy Others—My Documents Are Gone! 219
Annoy Others—Nothing But Shortcut Menus 219
Annoy Others—Can You See Me Now? 220
Annoy Others—Shut Down at Startup.......................... 220
Annoy Others—Launch Everything at Once................... 221

Chapter 12 222
Doh!
Troubleshooting…Smash Forehead on Keyboard to Continue

Three-Finger Salute 224
Where's My ScanDisk?.. 224
Knowledge Can Make You Smarter 225
Am I Connected? 226
Give It a Boost 226
Feeling Sluggish? 227
We're Compatible 227
It Could Be Hung Up.. 228
Save Searches 228
Help and Support Favorites.. 229
I Can't Move My Toolbars 229
I Wish I Could Go Back 230
Protect Files from System Restore 231

Don't Just Click OK...231
Save the Blue Screen of Death 232
How Much Space Do I Need?..............................233
Trash the Garbage...233
Prefetch?..234
10% Is Too Much 234
Stay Up to Date with Update 235
I Forgot My Password, Now What? 235
What's the Process?...236
Special Events 236
I'm a Network Guru 237

Chapter 13 238
Feeling Fearless?
Windows XP Registry Hacks

Back Up Your Registry 240
Registry Favorites 240
I Prefer Trash 241
It's All in the Name 241
Speedier Menus 242
I Don't Need the Arrows 242
Start Without Me 243
I've Got a Tip for You 244
My Media Player 244
Outlook Express Should Start Here.....................245
Control the Control Panel 245
Hack IE's Title Bar 246
How About Outlook Express' Title Bar?...............246
Friendly Trees Aren't Friendly at All....................247
You've Been Infected! 247
You Can't Notify Me...248
Grouping, My Way 249
"Shortcut to" Nowhere 250
Not-So-Recent Documents..................................251
Who Are You? 252
No Access 253
Hyper-Trash..254

Index 256

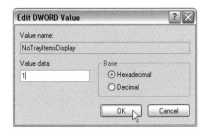

Windows...
Wide Open

GET THE MOST OUT
OF WINDOWS XP

Ah, the beginning, the first chapter of my first book. And you're actually reading the chapter description for the first chapter of

Windows...Wide Open

get the most out of windows xp

my first book! That's just so cool! But you're probably already getting bored with this whole first-chapter-description thing and want to jump right into the tips. I can't really blame you (actually I can, but I won't). This book's loaded with great tips and I'm not just saying that because I wrote it. No, really, I'm not. Okay, I guess I am. But cut me a little slack, as this book was extremely tough to write. All right, it wasn't extremely tough. It wasn't like pulling-an-airplane-with-my-teeth tough, but it wasn't super-easy either. Anyway, this chapter's mostly about windows, folders, and toolbars, and is there anything more exciting than windows, folders and toolbars? Well just maybe having you read the chapter description for the first chapter of my first book. That's just so cool!

TWO CLICKS ARE TOO MUCH

It just makes sense that if you can do the same thing in Windows with a single click of the mouse that you can do with two clicks, you'd take the shorter route, right? To take this one-click path, click Start, click My Computer, click Tools on the Menu Bar, and click Folder Options (Start>My Computer>Tools>Folder Options). Now click the General tab in the dialog box, choose Single-click to open an item (point to select), and then click OK. This makes everything in Windows exactly one click faster.

THAT PICTURE SUITS ME

It's actually kind of cute that Windows requires you to associate your User Account with a picture—okay, not really. Since Microsoft didn't give you an easy way to turn off this feature, you might as well find a photo that suits you. To do this, click Start and then click the picture next to your name at the top of the Start menu. This opens the User Accounts window where you can select a new picture or browse your hard drive for something different (if rubber ducks and soccer balls aren't for you). After you've made your selection, click Change Picture and you're done.

MAY I SEE A MENU PLEASE?

By default, Windows lists many of the Start menu items, such as the Control Panel, as links. This means that when you click the item, a new window opens. You can, however, view these items as menus instead. For example, if you want to view the Control Panel as a menu, then right-click Start and click Properties on the Shortcut menu. Next, click the Start Menu tab in the dialog box and choose Customize Start Menu. Now, click on the Advanced tab. Under Start Menu Items, locate the Control Panel item, click Display as a Menu, and then click OK. Now, when you point to Control Panel, a menu will pop up listing its contents.

 GIVE THE TRUE GIFT OF LOVE...SHARE YOUR COMPUTER

I know what you're going to say—sharing your computer is about as much fun as sharing your toothbrush. But since you're gonna have to do it, why not avoid some of the pain and create User Accounts? There are tons of advantages to this, the most obvious being that users get to personalize Windows to their own tastes, and you get to protect your important documents. So when you're ready, click Start and open the Control Panel. Next, click the

User Accounts icon, click Create a New Account, and follow the setup instructions. You'll be asked to provide a name for the new user and to pick the account type. After you've answered these questions, click Create Account.

 ## NOT SURE ABOUT A FILE? JUST DROP IT

UltraDev

Hmm...File

Microsoft File
Word

Adobe
Photosh...

Every once in a while you'll get an odd file. You just can't tell what kind of file it is and there's no program associated with it. Here's a way to try to find a program that can open it: Drag-and-drop the file onto different programs' icons. If the program can open the file, then the App will launch to display the file. If the program can't open the file, then the "unavailable" cursor pops up.

 ## ANOTHER WAY TO MAXIMIZE AND RESTORE WINDOWS

Instead of struggling to click the Maximize or Restore buttons on a window's Title Bar—you know, the square buttons about the size of a mini Chiclet—try this. Double-click the window's Title Bar to maximize the window. To restore the window, double-click the Title Bar again.

MINIMIZE USING THE TASKBAR

Next time you're minimizing a
window, use the Taskbar. Instead of
going for the Chiclets on the Title

Bar, try clicking the window's Taskbar button, which will minimize the window. Click the
Taskbar button again to restore the window. Try doing this really fast for a nice strobe effect!

 CLOSE USING THE TASKBAR

Sticking with this whole Chiclets thing—there's also a way to
avoid them when closing a window. Right-click the window's
Taskbar button and click Close on the Shortcut menu.

DON'T JUST MAXIMIZE YOUR WINDOWS—GO FULL SCREEN

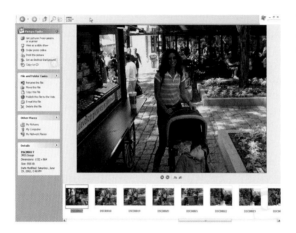

When you need a really big window, don't just maximize it: Go full screen! To view a window full screen, hold down the Ctrl key and double-click the window's Title Bar—or when the window's active, press the F11 key at the top of your keyboard—to get the biggest window possible.

 MANUALLY RESIZE A WINDOW

Scroll your mouse to any edge of a window's four sides until you see the vertical or horizontal resize cursors. The arrows tell you which way you can drag the window's border. When the cursor pops up, click-and-hold with your mouse, and drag to resize the window. If you want to resize two sides at once, you can grab any of the four corners of a window the same way and drag to make your window instantly smaller or larger.

RESIZE A MAXIMIZED WINDOW

To resize a maximized window, scroll your mouse over the middle button (it looks like two stacked boxes) located top-right on the window's Title Bar button (see image). This is the Restore Down button. If you hold your mouse over the button for a moment, a description of the button will pop up. Click the Restore Down button and this decreases the size of your window without minimizing it. Now, you can adjust the window to any size you like.

 CHANGE WHICH APP OPENS A FILE

You use Windows Media Player to open your music files (MP3s, WAVs, etc.), and you like it that way. Well, you've just downloaded and installed a new music player and suddenly your MP3s are opening in your newly installed player, not in the Windows Media Player. What's up with that? Wait, don't start uninstalling software; there's an easier way to get your music files back. Right-click the icon of any MP3 file and click Properties on the Shortcut menu. Then, click the General tab in the dialog box and click Change. On the Open With dialog box, scroll the Recommended Programs, click Windows Media Player, and click OK. Now, click OK on the General tab. Whew, that's better! Use this same technique to associate programs with any file type.

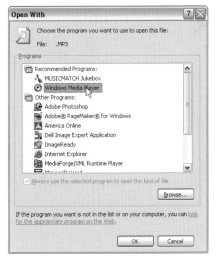

 YOU CAN MAKE IT SMALLER IF YOU SQUEEZE IT

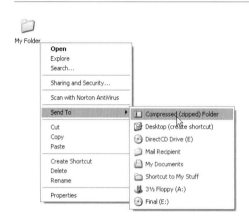

Windows XP makes it easier than ever to compress or zip files. This is especially handy when you want to e-mail a folder containing several files (compressing a file can make it considerably smaller, and thus faster to e-mail) or to protect and store data. To compress a file or folder, right-click the file you want to compress, point to Send To and click Compressed (Zipped) Folder on the Shortcut menu. Windows will immediately create a new compressed folder in the same location as the source file. You'll be able to identify the new compressed folder by a little zipper on the folder's icon.

 MAKE ROOM! COMPRESS FOLDERS AND DIRECTORIES

If you have folders or directories that contain many large files, compress them. Not only does this save a ton of space, but you can also work with compressed folders the same way as any other folder. Right-click your folder and click Properties on the Shortcut menu. Next, click the General tab in the dialog box, then click Advanced Attributes. Check Compress Contents to Save Disk Space, then click OK.

CHANGE YOUR VIEWS

Windows XP offers new and improved ways to view files, and it's easy to find the view that works best for you. From an open window, click Views on the Standard Buttons Toolbar. You'll have several views available to you. Click each view to see how it affects your files. You can set views differently for folders, so play around with them until you find the best view for your folder. For instance, you'd probably want to view a folder containing photos differently than you would a folder containing documents.

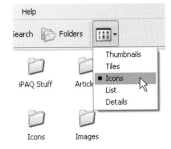

 ## NICE VIEW! I THINK I'LL SAVE IT

Okay, you've found the perfect folder view. The view just seems to work for everything. Wouldn't it be nice if you were able to apply that view to all your folders with just a click of the mouse? Well, you can't. It's impossible (just kidding).

To give all your folders the same view, open the folder with the view that you want to apply to them and, on the folder's Menu Bar, click Tools>Folder Options. Next, click the View tab in the dialog box and choose Apply to All Folders. You'll be asked to confirm your request. Click Yes, and now all the folders on your computer will have the same view.

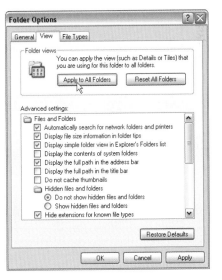

 WANT MORE TOOLBAR BUTTONS? WHO CAN BLAME YOU?

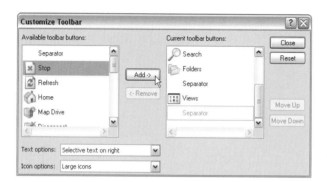

Hey, who doesn't want more buttons? They're cute. Get it, cute as buttons (sorry, that was bad!). Here's how you can quickly customize your Toolbar with all kinds of useful and cute buttons (I just can't leave it alone). To check out all of the Toolbar buttons available to you, right-click the Standard Buttons Toolbar and click Customize on the Shortcut menu.

Simply scroll the Available Toolbar buttons on the left side of the dialog box. When you find a button that you want to add, click to highlight it, and then click Add (in the center of the dialog box). You'll see that the button now appears in the Current Toolbar Buttons on the right of the window. When you're finished, click Close.

 TOOLBARS GETTING CROWDED? SHRINK THE ICONS

What are you going to do now that you have every single available button on your Toolbar? The answer is: Shrink 'em. Right-click the Standard Buttons Toolbar and click Customize on the Shortcut menu. Next, select Small Icons from the Icon options drop-down menu (see image) and click Close. Look at all that room! I think I need more buttons!

ORGANIZE ICONS ON YOUR TOOLBAR

This is really kind of clunky. (Is clunky a word?) Anyway, if you want to change the order of your Toolbar buttons, right-click the Standard Buttons Toolbar and click Customize on the Shortcut menu. On the right of the dialog box, click in the Current Toolbar Buttons window to highlight the button that you want to move. Now, use the Move Up and Move Down but-

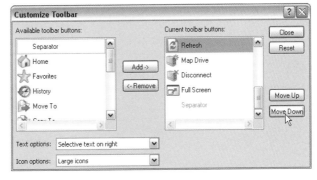

tons (on the right) to change the order of the buttons, and click Close. Wouldn't it be nice if you could just grab the Toolbar buttons with your mouse and drag them where you want? (Hmmmm...In case anyone from Microsoft is reading this book: Wouldn't it be nice if you could just grab the Toolbar buttons with your mouse and drag them where you want?)

 KEEP 'EM SEPARATED

You can also organize your buttons into groups—sort of—by putting a separator between similar buttons to help make them a little easier to locate. Right-click the Standard Buttons Toolbar and click Customize on the Shortcut menu. Scroll the Available Toolbar buttons (on the left side) until you see a button named—you guessed it—Separator. Click to highlight it and then click Add. Now move the Separator up or down to position it and click Close.

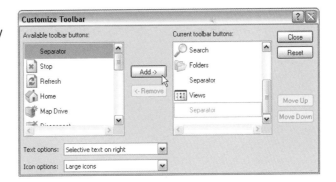

WHAT ARE THOSE LITTLE BLACK ARROWS ON MY TOOLBAR?

When your window's Toolbar is too short to display all your Toolbar buttons, you'll see two little black arrows to the right of the Toolbar. These arrows tell you that you have additional buttons on the Toolbar. Clicking the arrows will display a menu of the unseen buttons. You can also stretch your window, making the Toolbar larger until you no longer see the arrows.

TOOLBARS A MESS? GET BACK YOUR DEFAULTS

Okay, you've been playing with your Toolbars for hours when you realize that the only thing you've accomplished is a big mess. There's a way to get you quickly back to normal. Right-click the Standard Buttons Toolbar and click Customize Toolbar on the Shortcut menu. Under Close, to the right, you'll find the Reset button. Click Reset and the Standard Buttons Toolbar goes back to its default setting.

FINALLY! TOOLBARS THE WAY YOU LIKE THEM

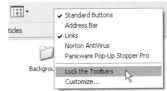

It's inevitable. You finally get your Toolbars set up just the way you like them when suddenly your four-year-old comes flying by, knocks your arm and BAM! Toolbars all over the place. When this happens, there's a way to keep from having to start over—lock 'em.

When you have your Toolbars set up, right-click any Toolbar, and click Lock the Toolbars on the Shortcut menu. Now, not even a nuclear blast will move them. Of course, if you ever do want to move them again, just right-click any Toolbar and deselect Lock the Toolbars on the Shortcut menu.

LINKS...THE ULTIMATE TOOLBAR

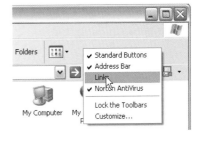

You know what would make a great Toolbar? One where you could put your favorite Apps and documents so that you could open them from any window at any time. Guess what? You can and here's how: Click Start, then My Computer. Now right-click the Standard Buttons Toolbar and then click Links on the Shortcut menu. You now have the Links Toolbar on your windows (the same Links Toolbar that's in Internet Explorer). *Note:* Make sure that Lock the Toolbars is not checked. Click on it to deselect it if it is.

The really cool thing about the Links Toolbar is that it's completely customizable—try this: Navigate to your favorite App and drag-and-drop its icon to the Links Toolbar. You just created a shortcut. Do this again and again for as many Apps as you want to appear on the Toolbar.

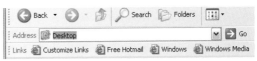

ADD NEW FOLDERS TO THE LINKS TOOLBAR

To keep your shortcuts better organized on the Links Toolbar, you can create folders to hold them. From an open window's Menu Bar, click File, point to New, and then click Folder to create a new folder in the window. Rename the folder to whatever you like. Next, while holding down the Ctrl key, drag-and-drop the folder onto the Links Toolbar. Instead of creating a shortcut to the new folder, you just created a copy of the folder on the Toolbar. Delete the new folder from the window (not the Links Toolbar), as you don't need it anymore. Now you can start dragging-and-dropping shortcuts to the folder instead of directly onto the Toolbar.

 REARRANGE THE LINKS TOOLBAR ICONS

After you have your folders and shortcuts on the Links Toolbar, you can easily rearrange them in any order you want. Just click-and-hold, then drag-and-drop them onto the Toolbar in any order. (If only the Standard Buttons Toolbar was this friendly.)

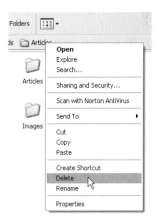

 ## THEY'RE ICONS; YOU CAN CHANGE 'EM

If you want to change your Links Toolbar folders or shortcuts to different icons, go right ahead. Just like any other folder or shortcut, you can change them to whatever you like. Here's how: Right-click the folder or shortcut on the Links Toolbar and click Properties on the Shortcut menu. If it's a shortcut's icon you're changing, click the Shortcut tab in the dialog box, then click Change Icon. Select a new icon then click OK. If you're changing a folder's icon, click the Customize tab, click the Change Icon button, then select a new icon, and click OK.

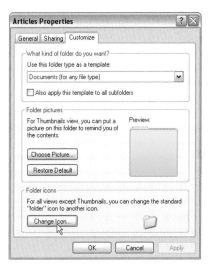

 ## REMOVING THE LINKS TOOLBAR ICONS

If you want to remove a folder or shortcut from the Links Toolbar, click-and-hold, then drag it to the Recycle bin. You can also right-click the shortcut and click Delete on the Shortcut menu.

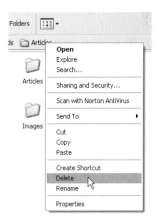

 ANTI-SCROLL TIP—RIGHT-MOUSE-CLICK

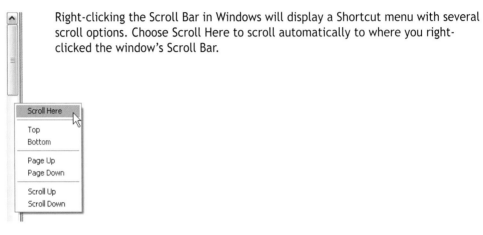

Right-clicking the Scroll Bar in Windows will display a Shortcut menu with several scroll options. Choose Scroll Here to scroll automatically to where you right-clicked the window's Scroll Bar.

 ANTI-SCROLL TIP—USE THE KEYBOARD

The next time you're scrolling away inside Windows, try using your keyboard instead. The Page Up and Page Down keys do exactly that—move the window's page up or down. Use the Home key to jump back to the top of a window, and the End key to zip to the bottom.

WHEEL MOUSE SCROLL TIP—ADJUST THE WHEEL

If you own a wheel mouse, then you can control how many lines your mouse will scroll when you turn the wheel. Click Start and open the Control Panel. Next, click the Printer and Other Hardware icon then the Mouse icon. (*Note*: This is in Category view, not Classic view.) Click the Wheel tab in the dialog box, change the number of lines your mouse will scroll with each turn of the wheel, and then click OK.

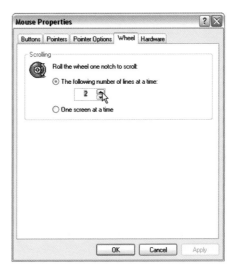

 ## SERIOUS FOLDER POWER

Did you know that you can customize folders to suit their contents? You can. Right-click the folder and click Properties on the Shortcut menu. Next, click the Customize tab in the dialog box and locate the text, What Kind of Folder Do You Want? Now from the drop-down menu, select the type of folder: Pictures, Photo Album, Videos, and more. Different folder types will provide different common tasks in a window's Task Panel.

 APPLYING FOLDER TEMPLATES

If you've customized a folder, and its subfolders pretty much contain the same types of files, then you should apply a folder template to the parent folder. This will apply your Preferences to each subfolder—perfect for categorizing digital photos. Here's what you do: Right-click the parent folder and click Properties on the Shortcut menu. Next, click the Customize tab in the dialog box and check the box below that reads Also Apply This Template to All Subfolders, then click OK.

 THAT'S BETTER THAN AN ICON

You can customize folders to make them a little more personal and easier to identify by putting a photo on the cover. First, make certain you're using Thumbnails or Filmstrip view, as you can only view pictures on your folders when you're in these views (on the Toolbar, then View>Filmstrip or Thumbnails). Right-click your folder and click Properties on the Shortcut menu. Next, click the Customize tab and click the Choose Picture button. Browse your hard drive for the photo that you want to use for your cover then click Apply.

WHAT ARE THOSE LITTLE BLACK ARROWS ON MY TASK PANES?

You can close or expand a common Task Pane using the two little black arrows located at the top right of each pane (see image). This comes in handy when viewing a file's details.

REMOVE THE TASK PANEL

If you find that Windows' common Task Panel takes up more room than it provides help, you can turn it off. Click Start then My Computer. On the Menu Bar, click Tools, then Folder Options. Next, click the General tab in the dialog box, click Use Windows Classic Folders, and then click OK.

USE FILMSTRIP VIEW TO BROWSE PICTURES

 Whenever a folder contains picture files (JPEGs, GIFs, BMPs...), a Filmstrip view is available to you. Use this view to browse your pictures; it's way cool! You'll get a large preview of the image that you can adjust (make larger or smaller) by changing the size of the window.

 THE NOT-SO-OBVIOUS POWER OF FILMSTRIP VIEW

 Now you know that Filmstrip view is great for viewing photos, but you can also do some other pretty cool things using this view. For example, you can rotate your picture, using the rotate icons directly below the preview—and this feature actually rotates the picture, not just the preview. You can also make any picture your Desktop background: Just right-click the picture and click Set as Desktop Background on the Shortcut menu.

OPEN FOLDERS IN DIFFERENT WINDOWS

By default, Windows XP opens folders in the same window, which is good because I really dislike new windows popping up all over my Desktop (I'm kind of a neat freak). If you're not like me, however, you can make folders open in different windows. Click Start>My Computer>Tools>Folder Options. Next, click the General tab in the dialog box, click Open Each Folder in Its Own Window, and then click OK.

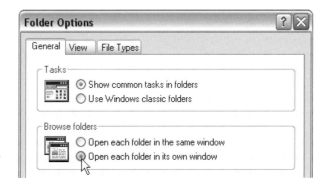

 HMMM…IT NEEDS ITS OWN WINDOW

Here's the dilemma: Windows views folders in the same window but you need a particular folder to open in its own window. Here's how to do it. From within an open window, highlight the folder that you want to open in its own window. Hold the Ctrl key and then press Enter. Your folder will open in its own window. Problem solved! This tip also works for opening multiple selected folders in their own windows.

 ## INSTANTLY VIEW A FILE'S DETAILS

A quick way to get a file's details, such as when it was created, date it was last modified, and size, is to use the Details Pane on the Tasks Panel. Click the file once or move over it with your mouse (scroll) to highlight it. When the file is highlighted, you can view its details in the Details Task Pane.

 ## DON'T LIKE TOOLBARS? DON'T USE 'EM

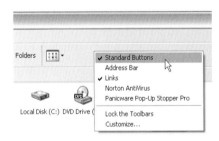

There are some of you (we won't name names, but we will name groups—DOS User group, Anywhere, USA), who actually don't feel a need to use Toolbars. Personally, I'm okay with that, but my wife...she'll let you have it. If you're not afraid of my wife, here's how to do it: Open My Computer from the Desktop, right-click the Standard Buttons Toolbar, and click each Toolbar on the Shortcut menu to uncheck it until your Toolbars are no more. Scary isn't it?

BROWSE THE WEB FROM ANY WINDOW

Windows XP is the most Web-integrated Operating System ever. And, nowhere is that more evident than the window right there in front of you. Just add an Address Toolbar and you can navigate the Web from

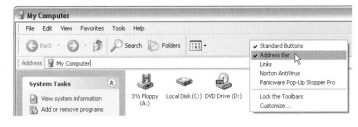

any open window on your Desktop. Open My Computer from the Desktop, right-click the Standard Buttons Toolbar, and click Address Bar on the Shortcut menu. Now just type in a URL or choose a site from Favorites and your window turns into a browser. Want to go back to your folder's window? Hit the Back button on the Toolbar.

 ## FIND FILES USING THE ADDRESS BAR

Of course you use the Address Bar to visit Web sites, but you can also use it to help locate files on your hard drive. Click the Down arrow on the Address Bar to view your hard drive. Click on a drive or directory to select it. Your selection will appear in the folder's window. Now you can browse the folders or drives until you locate your file(s).

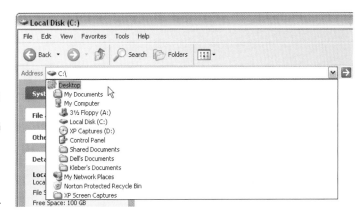

 POP-UP TASKBAR BUTTONS

  Press-and-hold the Alt key and then press the Tab key to display a pop-up dialog box that shows icons of your Taskbar items. Hit the Tab key again to move to the next icon and so on. After you've highlighted the item that you want, let go of the Alt key, and that window jumps to the foreground on your Desktop.

 VIEW STATUS BAR ON WINDOWS

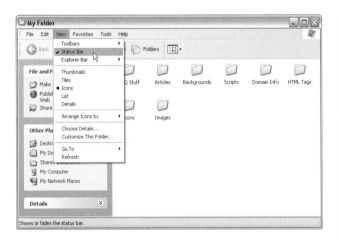

Another great way to view a file's details is by placing the Status Bar on your windows. Often the Details Pane is impossible to see because it's buried at the bottom of the Tasks Panel. But a quick glance at the Status Bar will tell you what you want to know. To enable the Status Bar on your windows, open My Computer from your Desktop, click View on the Menu Bar, and then click Status Bar.

SCREEN-SAVER SAFE

If you're the kind of person who's really freaky about your privacy, or you're working on top-secret government stuff (or maybe just doodling not-so-kind pictures of the boss in Paint), then it might be a good idea to password-protect your computer when it returns from a screen saver. (You never know, your boss might stop by when you're on a coffee break and accidentally bump your mouse.) Here's how to do it. Right-click your Desktop and click Properties on the Shortcut menu. Click the Screen Saver tab, then click On Resume, Password Protect to activate it. Click OK.

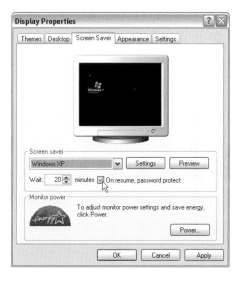

 CONTROL THE CONTROL PANEL

The new-look Control Panel takes some getting used to (the old Control Panel worked so well). If you really miss the old Control Panel, you can get it back. Click Start and open My Control Panel. In the top Task Pane (labeled Control Panel), click the Switch to Classic View link and there it is. Ah, much better!

 SIDE-BY-SIDE

You can display any two windows side-by-side on the Desktop by first clicking a window's button on the Taskbar. Next, press-and-hold the Ctrl key and right-click the second window that you want to open, then click Tile Vertically on the Shortcut menu. This works great when you want to view Word or Internet Explorer windows at the same time.

Have it Your Way

CUSTOMIZE WINDOWS XP

This is my favorite chapter. It's probably going to be yours too. XP is a fantastic operating system that's only made better

Have It Your Way

customize windows xp

by how customizable it is. You really can have it your way! It's too bad I can't have everything in life my way. That'd be great! I'd make digital cameras the size of TVs so my family and friends wouldn't have to jockey for position to stare at a screen the size of a Cheez-It® just to see my son's T-ball pictures. And every elementary-school kid would get those skinny crayons. I grew up using the fat ones and still to this day can't color inside the lines. I'd send every flight attendant to a Tony Robbins "The Customer is My Friend and I Won't Be Rude Because They Ask Me to Do My Job" seminar. The Bucs (Tampa Bay Buccaneers©) would win the Super Bowl every year! Man, I love the Bucs! And, oh yeah, I'd allow school prayer. Yep, it sure would be great to have it my way! At least we can have Windows our way.

 GROUND CONTROL…WE HAVE ICONS

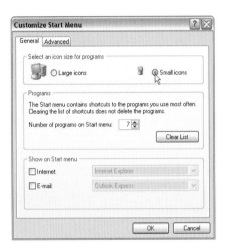

Okay, I honestly believe that astronauts on the Space Station can see my Start menu icons—they're that big. Let's change them to a size that doesn't give you vertigo every time you click Start.

Right-click Start and select Properties on the Shortcut menu. Next, click the Start Menu tab in the dialog box, and choose Customize Start menu. Now click the General tab, click Small Icons, then click OK.

 IT'S A-TO-Z FOR THE ALL PROGRAMS MENU

Being an A-to-Z kind of guy, I understand the alphabetical order, and it makes things easier to find. Apparently the All Programs menu doesn't. But here's a way to teach your All Programs menu the ABCs. Click Start and point to All Programs. Right-click the Programs menu anywhere and choose Sort by Name on the Shortcut menu. That's much better!

DON'T LIKE THE NEW START MENU? CHANGE IT BACK

If Windows XP's new Start menu just isn't doing it for you, then switch it back to Windows Classic Start menu. Right-click Start and choose Properties on the Shortcut menu. Next, click the Start Menu tab in the dialog box and click the Classic Start Menu. Click OK.

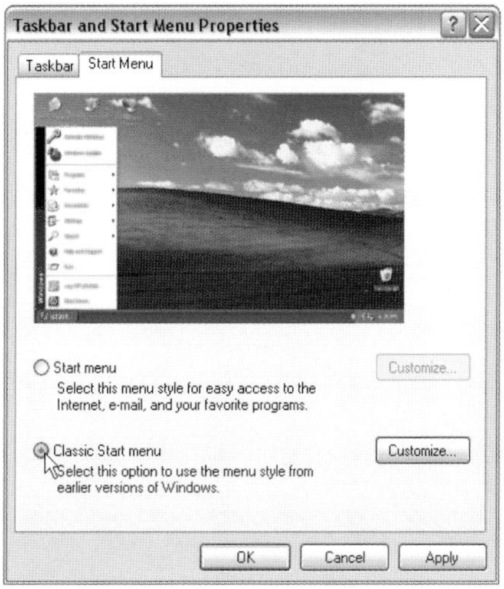

MORE PROGRAMS ON THE START MENU

By default, the Start menu will show your seven most frequently used programs, which is really convenient. In fact, it's so convenient I think I'd like to see—I don't know—how about 30 of my most frequently used programs.

Right-click Start and click Properties on the Shortcut menu. Next, click the Start Menu tab in the dialog box and click Customize. Now, just crank up the number (up to 30) of the frequently used programs that you'd like to see on the Start menu, then click OK.

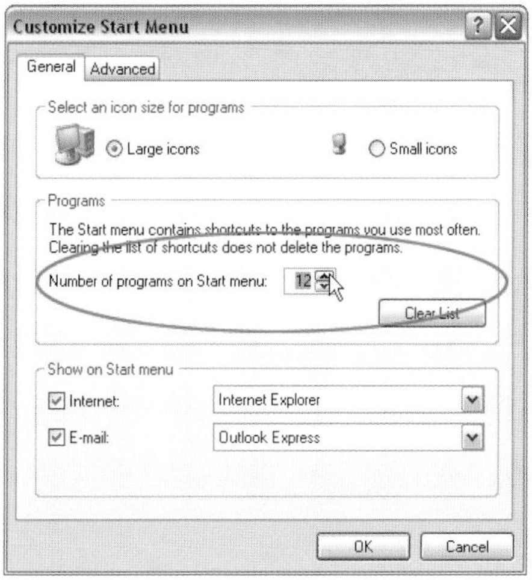

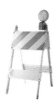

 "PIN" PROGRAMS TO THE START MENU

Want to add your favorite programs to the Start Menu? Click Start and point to All Programs. Locate a favorite program, right-click the program's icon, and select Pin to Start Menu on the Shortcut menu. That's it. You can also pin an App by dragging-and-dropping its

icon from the All Programs menu on the Start menu. The program is now "pinned" to your Start menu. To remove it, right-click the program icon on the Start menu then click Unpin from Start Menu on the Shortcut menu.

 SCROLL YOUR PROGRAMS INSTEAD

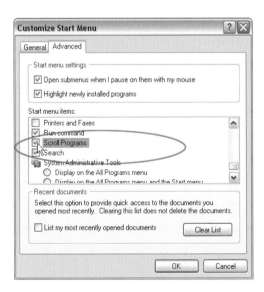

There's something annoying about opening the All Programs menu. Maybe it's the way that it covers my entire Desktop. It's almost scary the way it jumps out at you. I prefer to scroll my programs all in one nice, compact menu. If you do too, here's how: Right-click Start and choose Properties on the Shortcut menu. Next, click the Start Menu tab in the dialog box, then click the Customize button to the right of Start menu. Now, click the Advanced tab and scroll the items in Start Menu Items until you see Scroll Programs. Check this option and then click OK.

MY, MY, MY...WE GET IT

Why does Windows name all your personal folders in the Start menu with "My" as the first word? I know it's mine. "My" just seems a little rhetorical on every folder. Did you know that you can rename the "My" folders? Yes, you can! Click Start and point to any "My" folder, right-click its name, and click Rename on the Shortcut menu. Now, type in a new name for your folder—preferably something without "My" in the title.

THE INTERNET ON YOUR TASKBAR

Have you ever wanted to launch a Web page from your Taskbar? Of course you have, and here's how: Right-click the Taskbar, point to Toolbars and click Address on the Shortcut menu. Now an Internet Address Bar appears on your Taskbar. Simply type in a URL, then click Go or press Enter on your keyboard to open the page in Internet Explorer.

 TASKBAR WEB PAGES

Maybe having the Address Bar on your Taskbar isn't good enough for you? You've got to actually put a Web page on your Taskbar. Okay, right-click the Taskbar, point to Toolbars, and click New Toolbar on the Shortcut menu. In the Folder text box, type the Web page's complete URL (include http://), then click OK.

 LAUNCH APPS FROM THE ADDRESS BAR

What if you could launch an App from the Address Bar? Wouldn't that be cool? So try this: Open the Address Toolbar by right-clicking the Taskbar, point to Toolbars, and choose Address on the Shortcut menu. In the Address Bar type "notepad" (without the quotes), then click Go. You just launched Notepad from your Address Bar.

FAVORITES ALL THE TIME

Put Favorites on the Taskbar and you'll never have to launch Internet Explorer again to find a favorite site. Are you ready? Right-click the Taskbar, point to Toolbars, and click New Toolbar on the Shortcut menu. Use the dialog box to navigate to Favorites, usually located at C:\Documents and Settings\your user name\Favorites, and click the folder to select it. Click OK and you're done. Now you have the Favorites menu on the Taskbar. This also works for adding any folder to the Taskbar.

 FLOATING TOOLBARS? COOL!

The previous tip showed you how to put a folder on your Taskbar, which is cool; but it gets really wild when you start yankin' them off and floatin' them on your Desktop. To float your Toolbars, grab a Toolbar with your mouse and simply drag it onto your Desktop and let go. Floating Toolbars—Cool! You can also change the size of these windows or dock them on an edge of your Desktop.

 QUICK, LAUNCH IT!

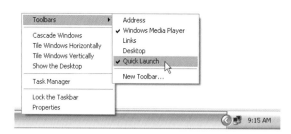

As far as Toolbars go, there's none more useful than the Quick Launch Toolbar. Quick Launch gives fast access to Internet Explorer and Outlook Express and it holds the Show Desktop icon. To open your Quick Launch Toolbar, right-click the Taskbar, point to Toolbars, and choose Quick Launch on the Shortcut menu. The Quick Launch Toolbar appears directly to the right of Start.

 QUICK LAUNCH YOUR FAVORITE APPS

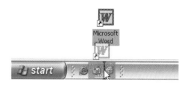

There's no need to clutter your Desktop with shortcuts to your favorite programs. Quick Launch is the perfect place to hold them. Simply, drag-and-drop your shortcuts to the Quick Launch Toolbar. Now, your favorite Apps are just one click away, always visible, and not cluttering up the Desktop.

MOVING QUICK LAUNCH ICONS

It's easy to re-order your icons after they're on the Quick Launch Toolbar. Just grab them with your mouse and move them left or right to drop them in any order you want.

 ## ONE-CLICK SEARCH

Search is also a perfect place for the Quick Launch Toolbar. I use it all the time and the more convenient it is to get to, the better. To add Search to your Toolbar, click Start then click-and-hold Search, and drag-and-drop it onto the Quick Launch Toolbar.

 TASKBAR...ON THE MOVE

The Taskbar is undoubtedly the most important tool in Windows. It's where everything happens. You'd think that something so important couldn't be fooled with, wouldn't you? Well, fool away my friend. Click-and-hold the Taskbar with your mouse and you can drag it all over the place. Dock the Taskbar on any side of the Desktop; top, left, right, it doesn't matter.

 STRETCH! AH, THAT'S BETTER

Sometimes your Taskbar gets a little tight and cramped for room. When this happens, give it a stretch. Scroll your mouse over the top edge of the Taskbar until you see the vertical resize cursor. Click-and-hold and drag it up. Isn't that better?

PEEK-A-BOO WITH THE TASKBAR

You don't have to always look at the Task-bar; you can hide it when you're not using it. Right-click Start and click Properties on the Shortcut menu. Next, click the Taskbar tab in the dialog box, check Auto-Hide the Taskbar, and then click OK. When you want the Taskbar to reappear, just move your cursor to the bottom of the Desktop and it pops back up.

 ## HIDE THE TASKBAR MANUALLY

If for any reason you need to hide the Taskbar, but don't necessarily want to use auto-hide, you can hide it manually. Scroll your mouse over the

top edge of the Taskbar until you see the vertical resize cursor. Click-and-hold and drag it down out of view. To get it back, move your cursor to the bottom of the Desktop, and when it again changes to the vertical resize cursor, click-and-drag the Taskbar back into view.

 A DESKTOP YOU CAN ALWAYS SEE

Placing your Desktop on the Taskbar gives you a quick way to access it. You'll no longer have to minimize windows to get to your Desktop folders and icons. To add the Desktop to your Taskbar, right-click the Taskbar, point to Toolbars, and click Desktop on the Shortcut menu. Your Desktop now appears as a pop-up menu on the Taskbar.

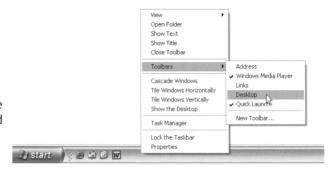

 MAKE SOME ROOM: STACK 'EM

Are too many Toolbars making the Taskbar more of a task than a bar (just couldn't resist)? Then, stack them. To do this, move your cursor to the Toolbars you want to move, scroll over the Toolbar separator on the left of the Toolbar until you see the horizontal move cursor, and then simply drag the Toolbars beneath one another to stack them in any order you want.

HUDDLE UP, GROUP YOUR BUTTONS

Know how every time you open a new
window, a new Taskbar button appears? Of
course you do. Isn't it kind of a pain digging through these buttons trying to find a
particular window? Sure it is. Well, Windows
XP helps to solve this problem. You can now
group similar buttons.

   Right-click Start and click Properties on
the Shortcut menu. Next, click the Taskbar
tab in the dialog box, check Group similar
Taskbar buttons, and then click OK. Now
when several documents of the same type
are open, they'll group together in a menu.

SPEED TIP: CLOSE A GROUP AT ONCE

Grouped buttons also allow you to handle the group as you would a single
button. Right-click the group's button to view its Shortcut menu. From
its Shortcut menu, you can choose from several actions, including closing
them all at once.

 IF I'M NOT USING 'EM, I DON'T WANT TO SEE 'EM

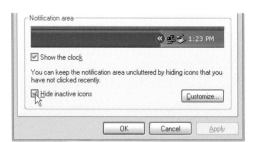

For whatever reason, software manufacturers want to put their icon in the notification area of your Taskbar. Unfortunately,
there's not an awful lot you can do about
it, but...there is a way where you won't
have to look at them.

Right-click Start and click Properties on
the Shortcut menu. Next, click the Taskbar
tab in the dialog box, check Hide Inactive
Icons, and then click OK. This will hide the
icons when they aren't being used by
Windows—which means you'll never see
most of them again.

 YOU'VE BEEN NOTIFIED...YOU'VE GOT TO GO

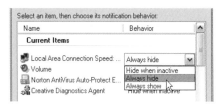

If you don't ever want to see icons in your notification area, regardless whether or not they're
in use, here's how: Right-click Start and click
Properties on the Shortcut menu. Next, click the
Taskbar tab in the dialog box then click Customize. Scroll the items listed and click its Behavior
to the right to change its status. When you're
through, click OK.

PUMP UP THE VOLUME

Turn up (or down) the volume on your computer without ever touching your speaker's volume controls. I know this isn't an earth-shattering tip, but I bet for some people this tip makes buying this book completely worthwhile (or completely worthless, I'm not sure which?). Click Start, open the Control Panel, then click the Sounds, Speech, and Audio Devices icon. Next, click the Sounds and Audio Devices icon, check Place Volume Icon in the Taskbar, and then click OK. Now, you can adjust your computer's volume right from the Taskbar.

 ## DO YOU NEED THE TIME?

If you're desperately in need of more Taskbar space and you have absolutely no need to know the time, then you can remove the clock and free up at least another whopping five-eighths of an inch. Right-click Start and click Properties on the Shortcut menu. Next, click the Taskbar tab in the dialog box, uncheck Show the Clock, and click OK.

And, how is it that you don't need a clock anyway? Never mind, I don't want to know. It's none of my business.

WORK OUT OF YOUR BRIEFCASE

I travel a lot and work out of Windows Brief-cases all the time. They're great for syn-chronizing files between my laptop and other computers, but Windows doesn't make it very easy to create them. At least you might think that, if you went searching for them. Actually they're just one click away from anywhere you'd want to create one. Right-click your Desktop (or in any folder), point to New, and click Briefcase on the Shortcut menu. It's so obvious, I bet you missed it.

 ## IT'S TIME FOR A CHANGE

There's something about sitting and staring at the same Desktop background day in and day out that just sucks time from me. Honestly, I easily forget the day of the week after a couple hours in front of my computer. Don't let this happen to you (it's too late for me). Change your Desktop background occasionally.

Right-click the Desktop and click Properties on the Shortcut menu. Next, click the Desk-top tab in the dialog box and scroll for a new background or click Browse to search your hard drive. You can preview your selections in the Desktop preview above. Click to highlight your new background then click OK.

I PREFER SOLIDS

Ok, you're a meat-and-potatoes kind of person and background pictures make you think too much. You stress over trying to find a picture that identifies you—who you are as a person. You can almost feel the anxiety, can't you? Don't put yourself through it....just pick a color for your background. Colors are easy.

Right-click the Desktop and click Properties on the Shortcut menu. Next, click the Desktop tab in the dialog box and click None for your Background. Now pick a color from the Color Picker button to the right and click OK. Are you feeling better yet?

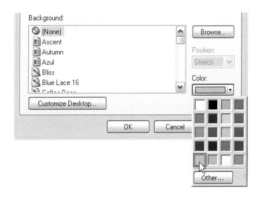

 IT'S NOT A THEME PARK, BUT IT'S CLOSE

You can easily change the entire look of your Desktop in Windows—backgrounds, pointers, colors, icons, you name it—which is great because the developers at Microsoft and I definitely don't have the same tastes.

Right-click the Desktop and click Properties on the Shortcut menu. Next, click the Themes tab in the dialog box and click the Theme Bar's Down arrow. Scroll for a new Desktop theme and when you've found that perfect one, click OK.

CREATE CUSTOM THEMES

What's the point in having a theme for your personal computer if you can't make it personal? There's no point, and Microsoft knew this. So, here's how to customize a personal theme. First, use the previous tip to select a Theme. While you're still in the Display Properties dialog box, click the Desktop, Screen Saver, and Appearance tabs to make new choices for these items. Click Apply each time you make a change. OK will close the dialog box. When you're finished, go back to the Themes tab, click Save As, give your new theme a name, and then click Save. You've just made a custom theme.

APPEARING LIVE ON YOUR DESKTOP…YOUR FAVORITE WEB PAGE

That's right! Your favorite Web page, live appearing on your Desktop, and in its own window! You can make its window bigger, smaller, move it around, or anything—just like any window—here's how: Right-click the Desktop and click Properties on the Shortcut menu. Next, click the Desktop tab in the dialog box and choose Customize Desktop. Click the Web tab in the dialog box then New. Now, just type your favorite URL in the Location text box and click OK.

A REFRESHING DESKTOP

Now that you've created a live Desktop Web page, you'll want to keep it fresh—as in refreshed. To do this manually, right-click the Desktop and click Properties on the Shortcut menu. Next, click the Desktop tab in the dialog box then click Customize Desktop. Click the Web tab in the dialog box, select the Web page you want to refresh, and click Synchronize.

You can also schedule the Web page to refresh automatically. With the Web page selected, click Properties then click the Schedule tab. Click Using the Following Schedule(s). Choose Add to create a time and click OK.

ADD COOL WEB STUFF TO YOUR DESKTOP

Is it snowing outside? Probably not for me, as I live in Florida. But if I had the weather on my Desktop, I'd know the answer without having to look outside. Well, just so I don't have to risk seeing that white stuff, I think I'll go ahead and put the weather on my Desktop. You can, too.

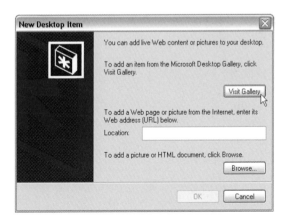

Right-click the Desktop and click Properties on the Shortcut menu. Next, click the Desktop tab in the dialog box and click Customize Desktop. Click the Web tab in the dialog box and click New. Click Visit Gallery,
which will launch your browser and take you to Microsoft's Desktop Gallery. Here you can select all kinds of cool live Web items to place on your Desktop—including the weather. Find the item you want and click Add to Active Desktop.

 ANIMATE YOUR DESKTOP

Because your Windows Desktop can display all kinds of Web stuff, it only makes sense that you can put Web animations (as in animated GIFs) on it as well. So, if you're in the mood to have bouncing balls and spinning planets doin' their thing all over your Desktop, just follow these steps: Right-click the Desktop and click Properties on the Shortcut menu. Next, click the Desktop tab in the dialog box then choose Customize Desktop. Click the Web tab in the dialog box and then New. Now, click Browse to locate any animated GIF or even an HTML document you'd like to place on your Desktop. After you've selected your file, click OK. Entertainment has never been so cheap.

 LOCK WEB ITEMS

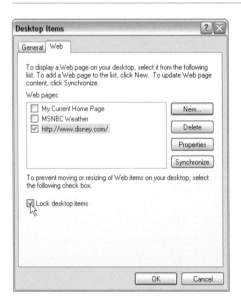

Okay, now that you've got the weather, your Internet Home Page, and bouncing balls set up on your Desktop just the way you want them, it's time to lock them in place. Again (you guessed it), right-click the Desktop and click Properties on the Shortcut menu. Next, click the Desktop tab and click Customize Desktop. Click the Web tab in the dialog box, check Lock Desktop Items, click OK, then Apply. Now, no matter what you do to your Desktop, your Web items aren't movin'.

CHANGE YOUR POINTER SCHEME

The first thing I do when I get a new computer is head straight for the cursors and
change them. It's not that the default ones
are bad; I've just been using the same ones
forever and I'm not comfortable using anything else. If you want to change your pointer
scheme, then click Start and open the Control
Panel. (*Note*: Control Panel should not be in
Category view.) Next, click on Printers and
Other Hardware, then Mouse. In the dialog
box, choose the Pointers tab and browse the
available themes. Select the one that suits
you, then click OK.

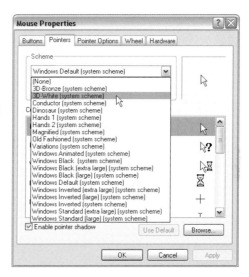

IT'S NOT EASY LOOKIN' THIS GOOD

Windows XP is a great-looking operating system;
however, there's a cost for all this beauty.
Windows' visual effects require processing speed
that can slow your system's performance—not
everyone really cares all that much about good
looks. (Not me of course. I'm very shallow;
all I care about is looks!)

If you're not like me, however, you can disable
or customize Windows' animations. Click Start
and open the Control Panel. Choose Performance
and Maintenance then click System. Next, click
the Advanced tab in the dialog box and then the
Performance Settings button. Choose the Visual
Effects tab in the dialog box and from here you
can turn off many of Windows' visual effects.

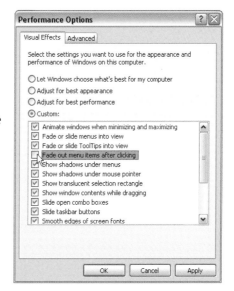

Cruisin'

NAVIGATING WINDOWS XP

I'm not sure that I know exactly how to say this, but this isn't exactly the sexiest chapter in the book. Oh, don't get me

Cruisin'

navigating windows xp

wrong. This chapter is as sexy as any chapter about navigating Windows could get. It's just that navigating Windows is plain "un-sexy." It's pretty much point-and-click and doing stuff with your mouse, although I do show some silly cool ways to do it (navigate Windows, that is). I did briefly consider using a picture of super-model Heidi Klum for my Desktop's background to liven up the screen captures, but quickly realized that was a very bad idea. (I really can't explain why it was a bad idea, it just was, and I'm very, very sorry.) So, although Heidi will not be appearing in this chapter, I'm sure you will enjoy it anyway.

 IT ALL HAPPENS HERE...GET THERE QUICKLY

Here's a great little tip that I use daily. Windows Explorer is where you go to view everything on your computer: drives, files, folders, directories, it's all here. I'm always diggin' around in Windows Explorer, and it's handy to have a really quick way to get there. Simply right-click Start and click Explore on the Shortcut menu.

 A DIFFERENT DEFAULT VIEW

It's easy to change the default startup location of Windows Explorer. Click Start, point to All Programs>Accessories. Right-click Windows Explorer and click Properties on the Shortcut menu. Next, click the Shortcut tab, and the Target text box should read something like "%SystemRoot%\explorer.exe." To change the startup location to point to, let's say, Program Files, edit the text to this: "%SystemRoot%\explorer.exe\root, C:\Program Files" (without the quotes), and click OK. Now Explorer will open to the Program Files folder at launch. Follow this example to point Explorer to open anywhere on your hard drive.

TURN ANY WINDOW INTO EXPLORER

You can turn any open window into an Explorer window by clicking the Folders button on the Standard Buttons Toolbar. When you click the Folders button, the Tasks Panel switches to the Explorer (Folders) view.

INSTANTLY EXPLORE ANY FILE

In the previous tip, we showed you how to turn any window into an Explorer window, but here's what really makes this tip useful. The next time you need to quickly explore (find the location of) a folder or file you're viewing in a window, click the Folder's button while the folder or file is highlighted. This will instantly show its location on your hard drive.

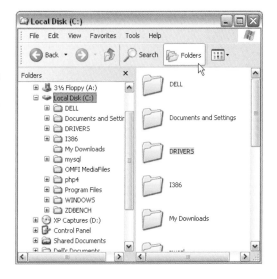

CAN'T SEE IT? DOESN'T MATTER

If you need to move a file to a subfolder that you can't see because the parent folder isn't expanded, then drag the file to the parent folder and hold it there for a second. The folder will expand, showing its contents. Now, just drag-and-drop the file onto any subfolder.

JUST TYPE ITS NAME

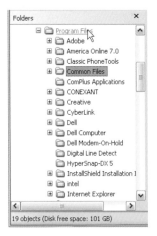

This can really come in handy when trying to locate a file in a large folder, such as My Documents. To locate a file, type the first couple of letters of the title and you'll instantly jump to documents beginning with those letters. You can even type the entire title, if necessary, to go directly to the document.

IT'S ALL ABOUT THE DETAILS

Details view is probably the best view for Windows
Explorer. Details, as the name implies, gives you details
about a file. By default, Explorer's Details view shows a
file's name, size, type, and date modified; however, you
can choose to show many other details of a file. To do
this, right-click a column heading and click an available
detail you want to display from the Shortcut menu. The
new Details column will automatically append to the
end of the existing columns.

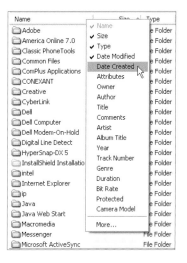

MAKING THE DETAILS FIT

Now that you've added 20 more
columns to your Details view, it
sure would be nice to actually
see a column's info—it can get
a little crowded. To see more of
your columns, move your pointer
over the separator between the
column headings. When your
pointer changes to the horizontal
cursor, click-and-hold, then drag
the separator to the left or right
to resize the column.

LET'S SORT THIS OUT

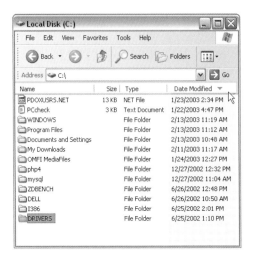

A quick way to help locate files is to sort them. Sorting lets you find a file by its alphabetical listing in the Name column, or by the date a file was created or modified from its Date Modified column. You can sort your files using any of the Details columns you have open. To sort your files, simply click a Details column, and your files sort themselves instantly.

 REARRANGE COLUMNS IN DETAILS VIEW

It never fails! You've added details to your folder but, of course, the most important detail is located at the end, and every time you want to view this detail you're forced to scroll all the way to your right to see it. That's a pain! Don't suffer; just rearrange your details. Click-and-hold the column heading that you want to move and drag-and-drop it in any order you want.

USING THE KEYBOARD TO NAVIGATE VIEWS

Try using the keyboard when you need to navigate folders quickly. You can use your Arrow keys to move up and down and to jump from column to column. When you've selected the file you want to open, press Enter.

 WINDOWS A MESS? GROUP 'EM

Organize your files by grouping them. Try this: Open a folder containing several different subfolders and file types. Right-click any empty space on the window's Contents Pane, point to Arrange Icons By, and click Show in Groups. To arrange the window's contents, right-click again in any empty space on the window's Contents Pane, point to Arrange Icons By, and click Name, Size, Type, or Modified.

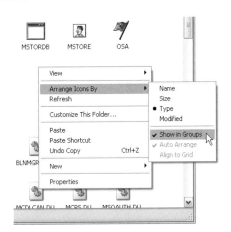

I'M FEELING A LITTLE BLUE; I'M COMPRESSED

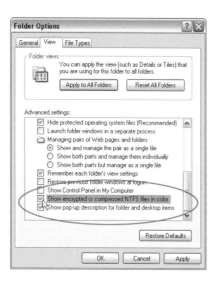

In Chapter 1, we showed you how to compress files in Windows ("You Can Make It Smaller if You Squeeze It"). You can choose to have Windows show encrypted and compressed files in color to identify them. Here's how: Click Start>My Computer>Tools>Folder Options. Next, click the View tab in the dialog box, scroll the Advanced Settings, and click Show Encrypted or Compressed NTFS Files in Color. Click OK. The text of the file's name is now blue. *Note*: Your hard drive's file system must be NTFS to use this option.

FIND YOUR HIDDEN FILES

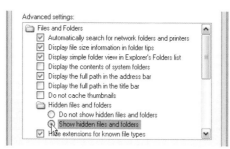

By default, Windows hides system files from your view—to prevent them from accidentally being deleted or moved. There are times, though, when it's necessary to view these files—usually by more advanced users who want to alter a System file. If you want to see your System and other hidden Windows files, you can. First, click Start>My Computer>Tools>Folder Options. Next, click the View tab in the dialog box, scroll the Advanced Settings, click Show Hidden Files and Folders, then click OK. Now you'll be able to see Windows' hidden files.

WHERE AM I?

Personally, I always like to know
where I am in any folder, and where
the files are located on my hard drive
when I'm browsing. You can always
view the path to any file by looking on the Address Bar Toolbar. First,
click Start>My Computer>Tools>Folder
Options. Next, click the View tab in
the dialog box, scroll the Advanced
settings, click Display the Full Path
in the Address Bar, then click OK. Now open
the Address Bar Toolbar by right-clicking the
Standard Buttons Toolbar and clicking Address
Bar. You can now see a file's and folder's full
path in the window's Address Bar.

 WHERE AM I? (ANOTHER WAY)

There's another way to view file paths if
you don't want the Address Bar Toolbar
on your windows. You can view paths to
your files from the Title Bar. Click Start>My
Computer>Tools>Folder Options. Next, click
the View tab in the dialog box, scroll the
Advanced settings, click Display the full path
in the Title Bar, then click OK. You can now see
a file's and folder's full path on the window's
Title Bar.

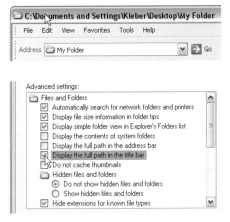

   NO GO

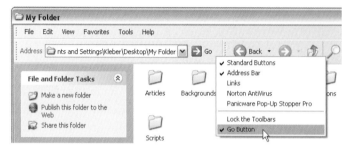

The Go button is nice, but how often do you really use it? When browsing folders—never. When browsing the Web, occasionally. I usually simply press the Enter key after typing URLs into the Address Bar Toolbar. For the most part, the Go button just takes up space, so turn it off. On the Address Bar, right-click on the Go button and click Go Button on the Shortcut menu to deselect. This removes the Go button. To get it back, right-click the Address Bar Toolbar and click the Go button again.

   DELETE THIS!

There are several ways to delete files, which is a good thing because you really can't have enough ways to delete files. Of course, you can drag-and-drop a file into the Recycle bin, or you can right-click a file and click Delete on its Shortcut menu; but there's also a couple of other ways that are quicker and more convenient. The Windows File and Folder Tasks Pane lets you delete selected files by clicking the Delete the Selected Items link. You can also put a Delete button on the Standard Buttons Toolbar.

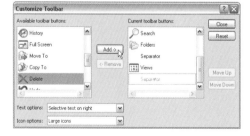

TAKING OUT THE TRASH

Now that you've deleted half your hard drive playing around with the different ways to delete a file, it's time to empty the Recycle Bin. There's no need to open the Recycle Bin to empty it, simply right-click the Recycle Bin's icon and click Empty Recycle Bin on the Shortcut menu. You'll be asked to confirm your request. Look, you just took out the trash.

 OOPS! I DIDN'T MEAN TO DELETE THAT

Okay, you've gotten careless and accidentally deleted two years' worth of family pictures taken with your digital camera. Don't panic, you can get them back. Open the Recycle Bin from the Desktop, select the accidentally deleted files, and click the Restore This Item link on the Recycle Bin

Tasks Pane. You can also restore a file(s) from the Recycle Bin by first selecting the file(s) to restore, then clicking File, and clicking Restore on the Menu Bar. Another quick way to restore a deleted file—and you do this from an open folder immediately after you've deleted the file—is to press-and-hold the Ctrl key, then press the Z key. This keyboard shortcut will undelete the file(s).

 ## NAVIGATE WINDOWS WITHOUT THE MOUSE

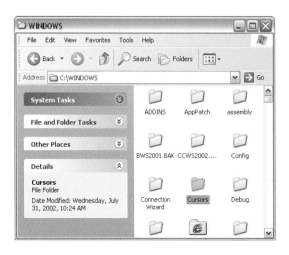

If you need (or want) to navigate the items in a window without your mouse, go right ahead and use your keyboard. Pressing the Tab key will highlight items in open windows. Just keep pressing Tab to select Toolbars, Tasks Panes, and the Content Pane. Use the Arrow keys to move to available items, then press Enter to open or choose a selected item.

 ## NAVIGATE MENUS WITHOUT THE MOUSE

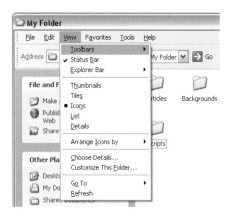

Try this keyboard tip to navigate an open window's Menu Bar: Press the Alt key and you'll notice that the first menu item on the Menu Bar (usually "File") is selected, and a small horizontal line underlining a letter of each menu item now appears. Press-and-hold the Alt key then press the menu's underlined letter on the keyboard to open the menu. Now, use the same technique to select a menu's items, then press Enter to choose the highlighted item.

 ### SAVE IT WHERE YA' WANT IT

When you save a new file or document in
Windows, the Save dialog box usually opens
in My Documents, encouraging you to save all
your files there. I don't know about you but I
rarely want to save files to the My Documents
folder. To save your files to the location of
your choice, click File on the Menu Bar then
click Save As. In the dialog box, click the down
arrow on the Save In menu to quickly view your
hard drive. Use the Save In menu to navigate to
the location of your choice and then click Save.

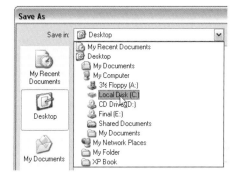

 ### QUICK SAVE

The next time you're saving files, check out the left panel
of the Save As dialog box—this panel has links to popular
destinations on your hard drive. Simply click any of these
buttons to quickly open the locations, give your file a name,
and click Save.

INSTANTLY SAVE TO A NEW FOLDER

If you're saving a file and realize that it needs to be saved to its own folder, you can do it right in the Save As dialog box. Use the Save In menu to navigate to the location on your hard drive where you want to create the new folder, then click the Create New Folder icon in the Save As dialog box. Now, a new folder appears ready to be named. Name that folder, double-click the new folder to open it, and click Save.

 SINGLE CLICK? DON'T OVERWRITE

I'm trying to save you a lot of pain with this tip. When you have Windows set up to use a single click to open an item, be cautious not to over-write files when saving. When I have similar files or documents that I'm saving to the same folder, using similar names (for example, Jarod's Birth-day Pics 1.jpg, Jarod's Birthday Pics 2.jpg, etc.), I like to select one of the names in the Save As dialog box (this makes the name appear in the File Name field), then change the 2 to 3, 3 to 4, and so on, to number the files. When saving, this is much faster than retyping the name of each file just to add a different number.

Here's where it gets sticky: If you're using single-click in Windows, make sure you do not click the file's name (doing this will overwrite the file). Point to the file name instead of clicking—this selects the name, puts it in the File Name field, and allows you to change the file's name without overwriting. Whew!

I DON'T THINK I'LL SAVE AFTER ALL

Decided that you didn't want to save after all? Don't click Exit on the File menu as this will close your window. Hit Esc(ape) on your keyboard instead, which closes the menu without taking any action. You can also click anywhere on the document, click File on the Menu Bar again, or just unplug your computer from the wall (kidding). Take your pick; they work equally well. Of course, this tip works for any Windows menu.

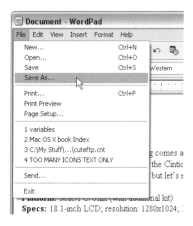

RESIZE OPEN/SAVE DIALOG BOX

Open and Save dialog boxes can get a little tricky to navigate when there are a lot of files in a folder. To make it a little easier to see a folder's contents, resize it. Click-hold and drag any side or corner of the dialog box to make it larger. That's better! Now you can see.

 YOU CAN CUT AND PASTE FROM HERE

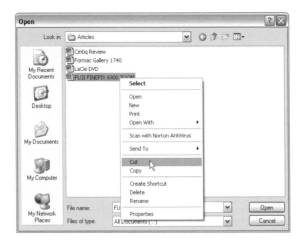

Okay, you've saved your file and realized that you put it in the wrong place. You don't have to open Windows Explorer to put it in the right spot. You can actually use the Open and Save dialog boxes to cut-and-paste the file to wherever you want. To do this, from the Open or Save dialog box, right-click the file you want to move, and click Cut on the Shortcut menu. Now, navigate to where you want to move the file on your hard drive, right-click a blank space anywhere in the folder, and click Paste from the Shortcut menu. You just moved your file!

 SHOW FILE EXTENSIONS

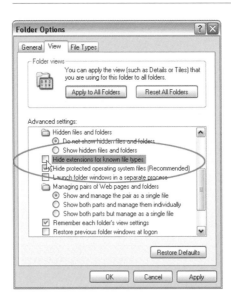

By default, Windows doesn't show the extension of known file types (.doc, .txt, .jpg, .avi, and so on). You can, however, make Windows always show a file's extension. This can be helpful when choosing a program to open a file type. Here's how to do it: Click Start>My Computer>Tools>Folder Options. Next, click the View tab in the dialog box, scroll the Advanced settings, and click on the checkbox to deselect Hide Extensions for Known File Types. Click OK. Now Windows will show a file's extension after its name.

BE CHOOSY WITH EXTENSIONS

Maybe you have no need to see all of your files' extensions all the time, but there may be an occasion when you need to view a single file's extension to help identify it. This can happen when you have more than one file type associated with a program. To see a single file's extension, click Start>My Computer>Tools>Folder Options. Next, click the File Types tab in the dialog box, scroll the Registered file types, and click the extension you always want to see. With the file selected, click Advanced, click to check Always Show Extension (at the bottom of the Edit File Type dialog box), then click OK. Now Windows will display the extension for only the selected file type.

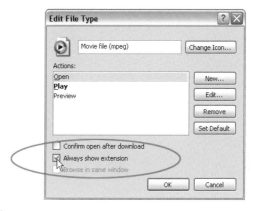

SYSTEM PROPERTIES IN A CLICK

System Properties is probably one of the most important tools in Windows and here's a quick way to open your System Properties dialog box. While holding the Alt Key, double-click the My Computer icon on your Desktop. And there it is—System Properties in a click!

YOU CAN ALWAYS GO BACK

When navigating through a folder's open window, you can always go back to where you started. There are several ways to do this. Click the Back button or Up button on the Standard Buttons Toolbar to move back one folder with each click. You can also use the Backspace key to navigate back one folder each time it's pressed. This comes in handy when a window's Toolbars aren't visible.

MOVING FILES USING THE TASKS PANE

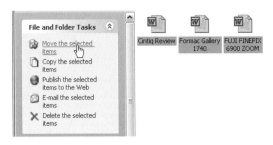

To quickly move or copy files from an open window to any location on your hard drive, simply highlight the file(s) and click the Move This File or Copy This File link in the Windows File and Folder Tasks Pane. This opens a dialog box that allows you to select a location on your hard drive. After you've navigated to the new location, click Move or Copy in the dialog box, and your file's now in its new location.

An American Icon

WORKING WITH ICONS

This chapter is named "An American Icon," not "American Idol." So, all of you out there who clearly cannot sing, please don't

An American Icon

working with icons in windows xp

send me an audition tape. What's the matter with some of those people? Really, don't they know how shockingly bad their singing is? Don't they have friends or family who would care enough to smack them on the head with a hammer rather than let them walk out the door to audition? I'd rather swallow sandspurs than be a judge for that show. Anyway, this chapter is about icons. I know, you're thinking, "Icons?" Yeah, icons. Don't dismiss them or you could miss a lot. Just about everything in XP is icon-related, and this chapter shows you what they're all about and how to do cool things with 'em. And the best thing about icons—they don't sing!

SEND SHORTCUTS TO THE DESKTOP

Don't you hate looking for frequently used programs through the All Programs menu? Me too! End the frustration and put a shortcut icon to your favorite Apps on your Desktop. Click the Start button and point to All Programs. Browse the menu and select a program. Right-click the program's icon, point to Send To, and click Desktop (Create Shortcut) on the Shortcut menu; or simply drag-and-drop the icon onto your Desktop. You now have a shortcut icon to the program on your Desktop.

MOVE FOLDERS

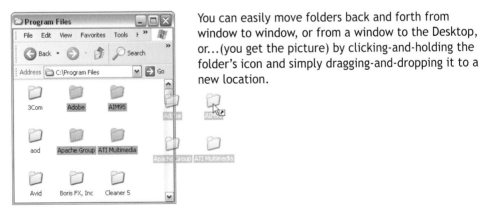

You can easily move folders back and forth from window to window, or from a window to the Desktop, or...(you get the picture) by clicking-and-holding the folder's icon and simply dragging-and-dropping it to a new location.

DRAG-AND-DROP SHORTCUTS

If you want to create a shortcut to a folder, click-and-hold the folder's icon with your mouse and drag it to a new location in the same window, Desktop, or wherever (don't let go of it), then press and hold the Alt key. You'll notice that the icon you're dragging now has a shortcut arrow on it. While still holding the Alt key, drop the icon. You just created a shortcut to your folder.

 DRAG-AND-DROP COPIES

You can also use the previous technique to create a copy of a folder, but press-and-hold the Ctrl key as you drop the icon. This creates an exact copy of your folder and all of its contents.

 CAN'T MAKE UP YOUR MIND? GIVE YOURSELF OPTIONS

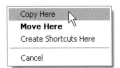

If you're not sure exactly what you want to do with a shortcut or folder, then drag-and-drop it using the right-mouse button. Press the right-mouse button, grab your icon and drag-and-drop it; when you let go, a Shortcut menu will pop up with several choices. Now you can take your time deciding whether you want to move the icon, copy it, or create a shortcut to it.

 CREATE SHORTCUTS FROM THE START MENU

The Start menu offers links to many of the most popular locations on your computer (My Documents, Control Panel, Search, and so on), and you might be tempted to put a shortcut to them on your Desktop. Well, it's easy! Click Start, then click-and-hold any menu item, and drag-and-drop it onto the Desktop.

CREATE A SHORTCUT FOR JUST ABOUT ANYTHING

There's another way to create a shortcut: Right-click the Desktop or empty space inside an open window's Contents Pane, point to New, and then click Shortcut. The Shortcut Wizard will open and ask you to browse your hard drive and locate the program or folder for which you want to create a shortcut. Once you've provided the location, click Next, name your shortcut, then click Finish.

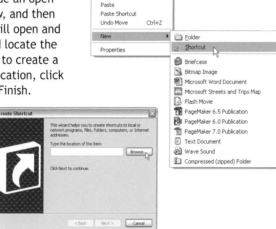

 DON'T FORGET THE SHORTCUT'S SHORTCUT MENU

You might think that you wouldn't have a Shortcut menu for a short-cut, but you do—it's just slightly different from its target. So, you still have access to many of the same timesaving links on the shortcut's Shortcut menu that you'd have on the target's Shortcut menu. (Whew, that's got to be a record for the most times the word shortcut has ever been used in a paragraph.)

I KNOW IT'S A SHORTCUT

I'm not sure why Windows automatically puts the words "Shortcut to" before the title of each shortcut. I mean, I know it's a shortcut. I just made it and it's got that annoying arrow on it. Well, you can delete those words and rename the shortcut to whatever you'd like, even the same as the target. Your computer won't crash or instantly delete files—even your computer knows it's a shortcut.

 CHANGE A SHORTCUT'S ICON

Hey, don't you just love default application icons? I think there's just one guy who makes all icons—and he doesn't have a sense of humor—so, let's change them. Right-click the shortcut and click Properties on the Shortcut menu. Next, click the Shortcut tab in the dialog box and click Change Icon. Then, browse your hard drive to select a new icon and click OK. Click Apply and you'll see your new icon.

CHANGE A FOLDER'S ICON

Did you know that when you create any new folders, they're all represented by exactly the same icon—a little boring, eh? We can change their icons, though, and here's how. Right-click a folder, click Properties on the Shortcut menu, then click the Customize tab in the dialog box. Click Change Icon, browse your hard drive to select a new icon, and then click OK. Click Apply and you'll see your new icon.

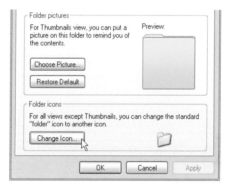

 DON'T LIKE YOUR NEW ICON? CHANGE IT BACK

If you've changed a folder's icon and realized that the new icon is just plain bad (as in not good), you can always restore the original icon. Right-click the folder's icon, click Properties on the Shortcut menu, and then the Customize tab in the dialog box. Click Change Icon, click Restore Defaults, then click Apply, and your old icon's back.

MAKE YOUR OWN ICONS

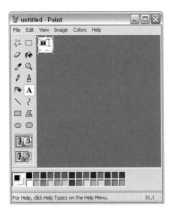

It's shockingly easy to create your own icons in XP. Let's do it: Click Start, point to All Programs, then to Accessories, and click Paint. Click Image on the Menu Bar, then click Attributes. Type 32 for both the Width and Height of the document, and make sure that Pixels is selected under Units. Click OK to create a new 32x32-pixel document: the size of an icon.

Now add type, color, or do whatever you'd like to your image. I like to shrink photos (headshots work best) to 32x32 and simply paste them into my Paint document. When you're finished, click File (on the Menu Bar), then Save As. Use the dialog box to choose where you want to save your file, then give it a name followed by ".ico" (without the quotes), and click Save. (The extension ".ico" tells Windows that it's an icon file.) You just created an icon! Now you can change any shortcut or folder to your own icon, just browse to it on your hard drive.

 ## ARRANGE YOUR ICONS

You can quickly arrange your Desktop and folder icons by right-clicking empty space on your Desktop or an open folder's Contents Pane. Now point to Arrange Icons By, and then click Name, Size, Type, or Modified on the Shortcut menu.

KEEP YOUR ICONS IN LINE

If your icons just won't stay in
line, try putting them on a grid.
To do this, right-click empty
space on your Desktop or an open
folder's Contents Pane, point to
Arrange Icons By, then click Align
to Grid on the Shortcut menu.
Now your icons will automatically
snap to an invisible grid, so no
matter where you move them,
they'll stay evenly spaced from
one another.

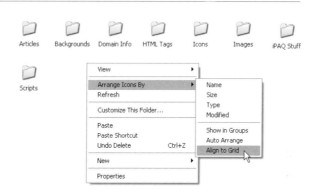

   ADJUST ICON SPACING

If the default spacing of your icons just doesn't give
you enough room for comfort, you can increase the
spacing to give your icons a bit more elbowroom and
extra space for long file names.

Right-click the Desktop and click Properties on
the Shortcut menu. Next, click the Appearance tab
then click Advanced. Select Icon Spacing (Horizontal)
on the Item drop-down menu, change the Size to
a larger number (up to 150 pixels), then click OK.
Click Apply and your Desktop will refresh, displaying
the new spacing between icons. To adjust vertical
spacing between your icons, do the same thing for
Icon Spacing (Vertical).

WHERE ARE MY DESKTOP ICONS?

By default, Windows XP now shows only the Recycle Bin's icon on the Desktop, but you can get your old familiar items like My Computer, My Documents, and other icons back. Right-click the Desktop, click Properties on the Shortcut menu, and then click the Desktop tab in the dialog box. Next, click Customize Desktop and click the General tab. Now, check the Desktop icons that you want to appear and click OK.

You can also quickly add icons back to the Desktop: Right-click My Computer or My Network Places on the Start menu and select Show on Desktop on the Shortcut menu.

 ## CHANGE DEFAULT DESKTOP ICONS

Windows' default Desktop icons (My Computer, My Documents, My Network Places, and Recycle Bin) cannot be changed using their Shortcut menus, and this might make you think that you just can't do it—but you can.

Right-click the Desktop, click Properties, then click on the Desktop tab, and then Customize Desktop. Click the General tab, select a default Desktop icon to change, and click Change Icon. Select a new icon, then click OK. Do this for any or all of the default icons. When you're finished, click OK, then Apply.

SUPER-SIZE 'EM

Want to try something really freaky? Right-click the Desktop and click Properties on the Shortcut menu. Next, click the Appearance tab in the dialog box, then click Advanced. Select Icon on the Item drop-down menu and change the Size from 32 to 72 (pixels). Click OK, then Apply. Isn't that freaky? Icons the size of your fist, weird!

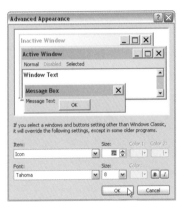

CREATE A NEW FOLDER

To create a new folder, right-click the Desktop or empty space in an open folder's Content Pane, point to New, then click Folder on the Shortcut menu. You can also click the Make a New Folder link in the File and Folder Tasks Pane.

ADD COMMENTS TO YOUR SHORTCUT ICONS

Have you ever created a shortcut some time back and now can't remember what it was to or what it was for? To help prevent this from happening in the future, you can put comments on your shortcuts. Right-click a shortcut's icon and click Properties on the Shortcut menu. Next, click the Shortcut tab in the dialog box and type any comments, descriptions, or reminders in the Comment text field, then click OK. Now, when you move your pointer over the shortcut's icon, a description pops up displaying your comments.

LOCATE A SHORTCUT'S TARGET

To locate a shortcut's target, right-click the shortcut and click Properties on the Shortcut menu. Next, click the Shortcut tab in the dialog box and look in the Target text field. This field shows the location of the shortcut's target file or folder on your hard drive.

THAT'S A LONG FILE NAME

It's pretty cool that you can give any file a name as long as a paragraph in XP, but have you noticed that as soon as you deselect the file, its 200-word title now has about three words followed by "..."? So much for the most descriptive title in history. Well, the full name is still there; XP just hides it until you need it, which is actually a pretty good thing. When you want to see your title in full again, simply scroll over or single-click the file to select it. This will once again display the file's title in full.

 ## TURN ON THE THUMBNAILS

The Thumbnails view (View>Thumbnails) is extremely useful when viewing photos, but the view also helps you to identify other file types quickly. Try opening a folder containing various file types and select View>Thumbnails. Take a look around and you can quickly see photos, movie clips, documents, and other file types—I could get used to this.

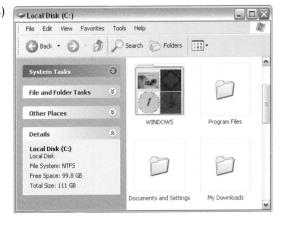

  SELECT EVERYTHING IN A FOLDER

  There are a couple of ways to select everything in a folder; for example, you can use the keyboard: Press-and-hold Ctrl-A to select every item in a folder.

 CLICK-AND-DRAG TO SELECT ICONS

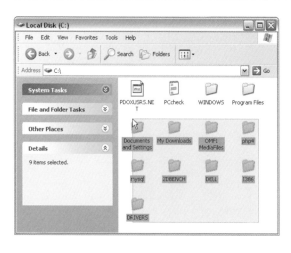 You can also click-and-drag a box around all of the items in a folder to select them. Once you've dragged your box over the items, let go of the mouse button and everything will be selected.

SELECT ALMOST EVERYTHING

If you want to select just about
everything in a folder, try this:
Use the previous techniques to select
your files, then press-and-hold the
Ctrl key and scroll over (or single-
click) to deselect each file that you
don't want.

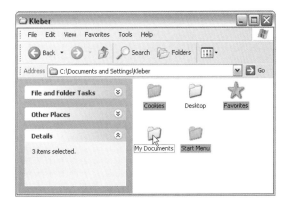

SELECT CONTINUOUS/NONCONTINUOUS FILES

To select continuous files (top image), click on the first file you want to
select, then press-and-hold the Shift key. Move your pointer to the last
file that you want to select and scroll over it (or single-click) with your
mouse, and all files in between are automatically selected. You can also
click-and-drag over the continuous files you want selected.

   To select noncontinuous files (bottom), press-and-hold the Ctrl key
and point to (or single-click) each file that you want to select.

Fast &
Furious

WINDOWS XP SPEED TIPS

This chapter isn't actually furious, but it is fast. Well, not like racecar fast—that would just be plain silly. I mean think

The Fast and The Furious

windows xp speed tips

about it: If the chapter were racecar fast, like jump-off-the-page and run-around-your-room kind of fast, it would be pretty difficult to read, and that would just completely defeat the purpose of the chapter. I mean, you do want to read the chapter, right? You probably wouldn't have bought this book if the chapters were too fast to read. But wait, we're getting completely off the subject. These are Windows tips to make you faster. Well, they don't actually make you faster. You're not going to read this chapter, then run the mile in two minutes or anything like that. Is a two-minute mile even possible? Probably not, although, wasn't there a Disney movie where a guy ran faster than a cheetah, or am I thinking of a movie about a cheetah that ran faster than a guy? I wonder what can run a two-minute mile. I bet nothing can—that's pretty fast. Oh yeah, fast. This chapter is loaded with fast Windows tips. You're gonna love it.

 DRAGGING FILES TO THE RECYCLE BIN WHEN IT'S HIDDEN

Okay, you've got folders open all over the place and your Recycle Bin is buried. And you've got files to delete. You could just select the files and hit Delete on your keyboard—but where's the fun in that? Try this drag-and-drop tip instead: Select the files you want to delete, then click-and-drag them to a blank spot on your Taskbar. Keep holding down the mouse button, hold your mouse there for a couple of seconds, and all of your open windows will minimize. Now, just drop your files in the Recycle Bin.

 A QUICKER WAY TO RENAME

iPAQ Stuff   Scripts

Renaming a file is already pretty quick and painless in Windows; however, if you want to rename your files even faster—and who doesn't—try this: Single-click or move your cursor over the file or icon to highlight it; once it's highlighted, hit F2. This keyboard shortcut selects the icon's text and quickly renames it.

 ## UNDO RENAMING MISTAKES

If you're like me, you'll never need this tip. We never make spelling mistakes, right? Actually, I make mistakes all the time; I'm just comfortable living with them. But for those who care about spelling, here ya' go. You've just begun to rename a file and, of course, completely botched the spelling. Just

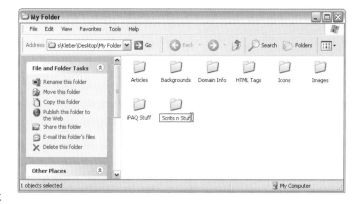

hit the Esc key while your text cursor is still active, and the file's name is restored to its original spelling; then rename it correctly.

 ## E-MAIL ATTACHMENTS FROM JUST ABOUT ANYWHERE

Here's a really handy tip. Locate a file anywhere on your hard drive that you want to e-mail, right-click the file's icon, point to Send To, and click Mail Recipient on the Shortcut menu. A new mail message will open with the file attached and ready to send. But what's really speedy about this tip is that your mail program doesn't launch. This action creates only a single new mail message. Now, to send your attachment, simply type the recipient's e-mail address in the To text field, add any accompanying message, then click the Send icon. The subject and attachment fields are already set.

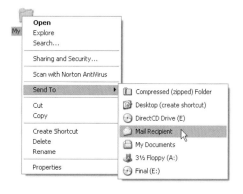

COOL! TOOLBAR DRIVES

I use this tip every day: Placing a shortcut to drives on your Links Toolbar makes copying files to CD, or any other drive, quick and convenient from any window. Here's how. Click Start>My Computer, then right-click the Standard Buttons Toolbar and click Links on the Shortcut menu. Next, click-and-drag a drive to the Links Toolbar and let go. Now, no matter which window you're in, you can drag-and-drop files to this drive or any other drive you've placed on the Toolbar.

MAKING FAVORITES A REAL FAVORITE

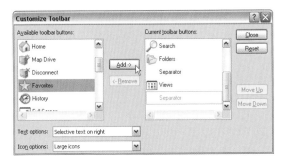

One of the really cool things about Windows is the ability to browse the Web from any open window. So, why not take full advantage of this and put Favorites on your Standard Buttons Toolbar? Click Start>My Computer, then right-click the Standard Buttons Toolbar and click Customize on the Shortcut menu. Scroll the Toolbar buttons on the left, click to highlight Favorites, click Add, and then click Close. Click the Favorites icon on the Toolbar to show the Favorites Panel. Now, you can just drag-and-drop URLs from the Address Bar to the Favorites Panel.

SPEED LAUNCH YOUR FAVORITE APPS

Of all the programs installed on my computer,
I use maybe five regularly, and it helps to be able
to access these five as quickly as possible. Creating
a keyboard shortcut is a great way to launch them
fast. Ready? Right-click an application's shortcut
icon and click Properties on the Shortcut menu.
Next, click the Shortcut tab, locate the Shortcut
Key text box, and type in a letter, number, or assign
an F key (for letters and numbers, Windows adds
Ctrl-Alt to your shortcut). Now your favorite App is
just a keystroke away.

 ## NOT JUST NO; NO TO ALL

This tip could have easily been included in
the annoying Windows stuff (Chapter 1). Have
you ever wondered why Microsoft would let
you select Yes to All when overwriting files
but not No to All? Me too—baffling isn't it?
Anyway here's how to stick it to the engineers
of this little programming blunder. Hold down
the Shift key and click No when asked. This
keyboard trick turns No into No to All.

 OPEN MULTIPLE FILES AT THE SAME TIME

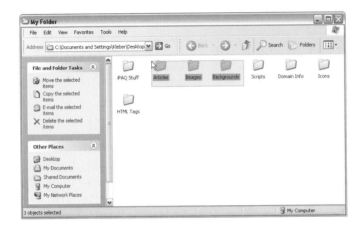

Select the files or folders you want to open and press Enter. All of the selected files open instantly. This tip will even open folders and launch applications at the same time. For example, you've selected two folders and a Word document; when you hit Enter, the two folders will open, and Word will launch to display the selected document.

 SHOW THE DESKTOP FAST; RESTORE IT EVEN FASTER

There are a couple of ways to show the Desktop. Here's my favorite with a twist. To get to your Desktop in a hurry, simply click the Show Desktop icon located in the Quick Launch Toolbar. This minimizes all open windows to display your Desktop. Now for the twist: To restore your Desktop, click the Show Desktop icon again and your windows will be restored exactly as they were.

SHORTCUT TO SHUT DOWN

Is it just me or does it require way too
many mouse clicks to shut down your
computer? By my count, it's three. If
Microsoft had really given it some thought,
I'm sure they could have added a fourth
click somewhere. Please, keep it coming!
I love carpal tunnel! Just for the fun of
it, though, let's see if we can't shut down
a little faster. Right-click your Desktop,
point to New, and click Shortcut on the
Shortcut menu. In the Type the Location
of the Item text box, type "%windir%\
System32\shutdown.exe -s -t 0" (without

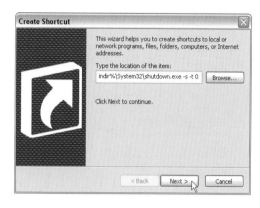

the quotes), then click Next. Give your new shortcut a name and click Finish. You now have
a Desktop icon that shuts down your computer with a single click.

SWITCH 'EM OUT AND LOCK 'EM UP

This tip falls in line with the whole three-
click shutdown controversy. Did you know
that it also takes three clicks of the mouse
to switch users? Crazy, isn't it? Anyway,
we're going to fix this wonderful bit of
thoughtful programming with another
Desktop shortcut. Right-click your Desktop, point to New, and click Shortcut on
the Shortcut menu. In the Type the Location of the Item text box, type "%windir%\
System32\rundll32.exe user32.dll,
LockWorkStation" (without the quotes),
then click Next. Give your new shortcut
a name and click Finish. You now have a
Desktop icon that allows you to quickly
switch users and a great way to instantly
lock your computer.

 A USEFUL POWER BUTTON?

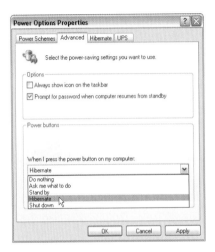

I rarely ever shut down my computer; instead, I tend to Hibernate my system. Here's a clever way to speed up this task and make your computer's Power button Hibernate for you. Click Start and open the Control Panel. Click the Performance and Maintenance icon, then click the Power Options icon. Click the Advanced tab and select Hibernate from the Power Buttons drop-down menu. Now, when you push your computer's Power button, your system will immediately Hibernate.

 QUICK QUITTING

Tired of chasing down the Close Window icon to exit active windows? Then try using the keyboard—it's faster and, well, just plain fun. Okay, it's not really fun, but it is faster. Hold down the Ctrl key and then press F4 to close active windows. Oh yeah, don't worry if a file needs to be saved, you'll be prompted to save your document before the window closes.

INSTANTLY RESIZE COLUMNS IN DETAIL VIEW

There's an easy way to instantly adjust columns in Detail view to auto-fit the columns' contents; however, it's not obvious. Put your mouse on the separator between the columns—you'll get a cross cursor with left and right arrows. Double-click when this cursor pops up and the column will automatically resize to fit the column's contents; or press Ctrl-+ (plus) to adjust all of the headers at once.

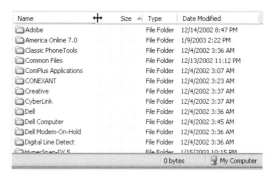

QUICKLY EXPAND FOLDERS

There are few things more tedious in Windows Explorer than clicking the little plus (+) symbol to expand or contract folders. So don't. Try this instead: Click any folder or directory in Windows Explorer, then press the asterisk (*) key on the number keypad. This instantly expands every sub-folder. Press the minus key to instantly contract the folder or directory. That's easier, isn't it?

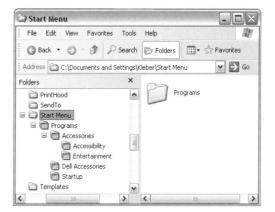

 DON'T FORGET ME, I'M SPECIAL

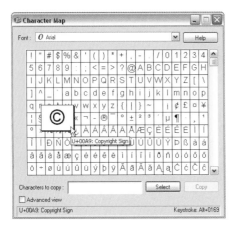

There are probably one or two special characters that you use regularly (for example, ® and ©). It can be a real time-waster to open your Character Map every time you want to insert one of these symbols. So don't! Open the Character Map by clicking Start, pointing to All Programs, and then Accessories. Point to System Tools and click Character Map. Click the © symbol. Notice that the bottom-right corner of the Character Map shows the keyboard shortcut used to insert the special character. Write it down for later use. When you want to insert that character, here's the trick: Position the cursor where you want to insert the special character, then with Num Lock on, hold down the Alt key and use the number pad keys to type the Unicode character value.

 LAUNCH FAVORITE APPS AT STARTUP

Are there programs that you open as soon as your computer boots up—like Word? Wouldn't it be nice if Windows could just open Word for you automatically at startup? You, my friend, are in luck—Windows can.

Right-click Start and click Explore on the Shortcut menu. Navigate to your Startup folder, usually located at C:\Documents and Settings\Your User Name\Start Menu\Programs\Startup. Now, just drag-and-drop an App's icon into your Startup folder to create a shortcut to it. When Windows starts up, the program will launch automatically. You can also put shortcuts to your favorite folders in Startup to have them launch instantly.

ONE-CLICK PROPERTIES

Instead of right-clicking a folder and clicking Properties
on the Shortcut menu, try this tip the next time you
need to view a folder's Properties. Hold the Alt key and
click the folder. (You can also use double-click, if that's
your style.) Now, that's faster!

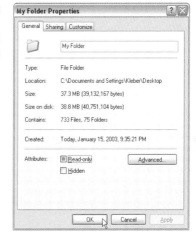

 ## TOGGLE OPEN ITEMS ON THE TASKBAR

This tip works great when
you have several documents
open at the same time. As
with Microsoft Word and most
other applications, every time
you open a new document, a
Taskbar button is created. The
Taskbar can get pretty difficult
to navigate when this happens.
A quick way to maneuver is to
hold the Alt key and press the
Esc key. This will toggle items
on the Taskbar and bring each
open document to the foreground as it's selected.

 YOU CAN BE CHOOSY WHEN OPENING FILES

You've just downloaded photos from your digital camera. By default, JPEGs are associated with Windows Picture and Fax Viewer; so, if you click a photo, it will open in Picture and Fax Viewer. But what if you don't just want to view the photos, you want to make changes to them? Well, you can quickly choose a different program to open the photo without changing the file's association. Here's how: Right-click the file's icon, point to Open With, and click the App you want to open the file. If you don't see your program listed, click Choose Program to locate it.

 DELETE AN OPEN FOLDER?

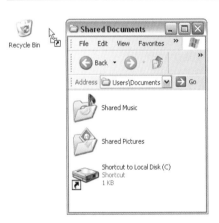

I know, you're thinking that I've lost my mind. You can't delete an open folder, right? Wrong, you sure can. In an open folder, click-and-hold the folder's icon on the folder's Title Bar, and drag it to your Recycle Bin. You just deleted an open folder. Cool!

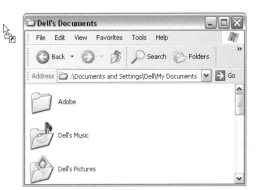

CREATE A SHORTCUT OF AN OPEN FOLDER

Many times, you don't actually realize that you need a shortcut to a folder until it's open and you're working in it. Wouldn't it be great if you could create a shortcut to it right then and there? You can! From an open folder, click-and-hold the folder's icon located on the folder's Title Bar, and just drag it to your Desktop. A shortcut from an open folder—can it get any better? I really don't think so.

OPEN AN OPEN FOLDER'S SHORTCUT MENU

Okay, I've got one more open-folder tip. Hey, if you can delete an open folder and create a shortcut from an open folder, I don't see any reason why you shouldn't be able to view an open folder's Shortcut menu. It makes perfect sense to me. Just right-click the open folder's icon located on the Title Bar, and there it is.

YOU DON'T HAVE TO SEE IT TO MOVE IT

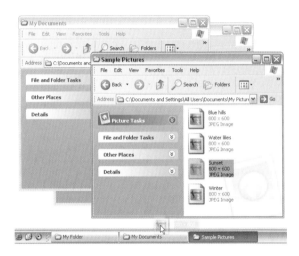

Have you ever wanted to drag-and-drop files between open windows, but you couldn't because the destination window was buried behind other open windows? Sure, we all have, but there's a way around this problem. Grab your files with your mouse, drag them to an open window's Title Bar, and let go. Problem solved!

 YOU DON'T HAVE TO SEE IT TO MOVE IT (*TAKE 2*)

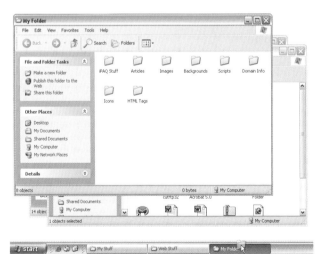

The previous tip works great if you can see the destination window's Title Bar, but what do you do if you can't see any part of the window, including its Title Bar? Using your mouse, grab the files and drag them to the destination window's Taskbar button. Hold it there for a second and the window will pop to the Desktop's foreground. Now, move your mouse to the window and drop your files.

SELECTIVELY GROUP OPEN WINDOWS ON THE TASKBAR

You've got three Internet Explorer windows open, two Word documents, and a couple of folders. Of these seven windows, you're using only three. A quick way to close the unwanted windows is to hold the Ctrl key and click the unwanted windows' Taskbar buttons to group them. Once you've selected your makeshift group, you can right-click any selected button to close, tile, minimize—you get the picture—the windows at the same time using the Shortcut menu. You can also click a button again to deselect it.

 COPY AND DELETE AT THE SAME TIME

Often, when you're moving files to a different drive (disc partition, ZIP, or CD), you're doing just that—moving them. But for some reason, Windows assumes that you actually want to copy the files instead. So, unfortunately you're forced to go back and delete the files from their original location once you've moved them. To avoid this, hold the Shift key while dragging the files to the other drives. This will move the files while deleting them at the same time from their original location.

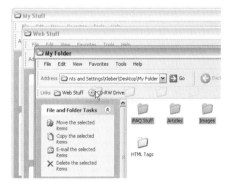

IT'S OUTTA HERE!

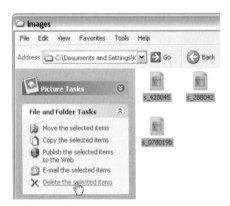

Have you ever had a file that was so repulsive, so hideous, that you just couldn't delete it fast enough? I mean a file that's so bad, even the Recycle Bin's too good for it! You have? Then try this tip the next time you need to delete an offensive file. Hold down the Shift key and press Delete, or hold down the Shift key and drag the file to the Recycle Bin. This tip deletes the file without sending it to the Recycle Bin.

 I DIDN'T WANT TO DRAG THAT

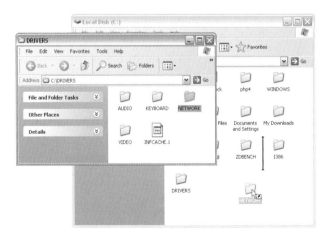

Here's a great little tip for those of us who can't seem to make up our minds. If you're dragging a file to a location and decide you really don't want to move the file after all, simply hit the Esc key on your keyboard before you let go of the mouse button and your file will magically (well, it's not really magic) return to its original location.

CLOSE A GROUP OF WINDOWS WITH ONE CLICK

If your folders open in separate windows, you know how cluttered your Desktop can get. This tip will make it a bit quicker to clean up. To close a group of windows opened from the same folder, hold the Shift key and click the Close icon on the active window's Title Bar. All windows close with a single click.

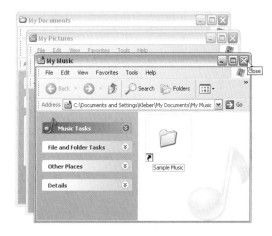

 CLOSE A GROUP OF WINDOWS WITH ONE CLICK
(BUT LEAVE THE ACTIVE WINDOW OPEN)

You're probably thinking the previous tip is great, but you're probably also thinking, "How do I leave the active window open?" After all, you had to open 10 folders to find the one you wanted. It's easy. Hold down the Shift key and click the Close icon on the folder immediately *behind* the active window. This will close all of the grouped windows except the active window.

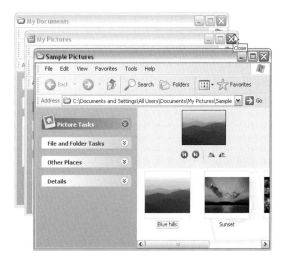

MINIMIZE ALL WINDOWS AT ONCE

If you don't use the Quick Launch Toolbar, you're not going to have an icon to click to show your Desktop; however, you don't need one. Hold down the Windows key on your keyboard and press the M key. This keyboard shortcut will minimize all open windows at once.

DIDN'T MEAN TO MOVE IT? UNDO IT

You just moved several files and suddenly you realize, "Hey, this isn't what I wanted to do at all." Well relax; we can fix this. Here's a tip to send them back to where they came from. While still in the window where you moved the misguided files, press-and-hold the Ctrl key and then press Z. This will Undo your move and return the files to their original location.

A FASTER WAY TO SEARCH FOLDERS

When I've misplaced a file, I almost always know which folder it's in, but it's usually lost in a maze of documents or buried in a subfolder. I just can't remember which subfolder. This is a great way to search a folder quickly. Locate the folder where you think the file's located, right-click the folder, and click Search on the Shortcut menu. A Search window will open, ready to search for the selected folder and only that folder. This is much quicker than launching Search and navigating your hard drive to the folder.

 DELETE THE ENTIRE WORD

I use this quick tip so often that I figured it should definitely be in this book. It doesn't happen often, but occasionally I misspell a word (actually it happens all the time!). Instead of fumbling around with the arrow keys or your mouse to move back and correct single letters, try this. Press Ctrl-Backspace, which quickly deletes the word. Now, just start over. This tip works in just about every text editor, but it doesn't work in Notepad.

We Will Rock You

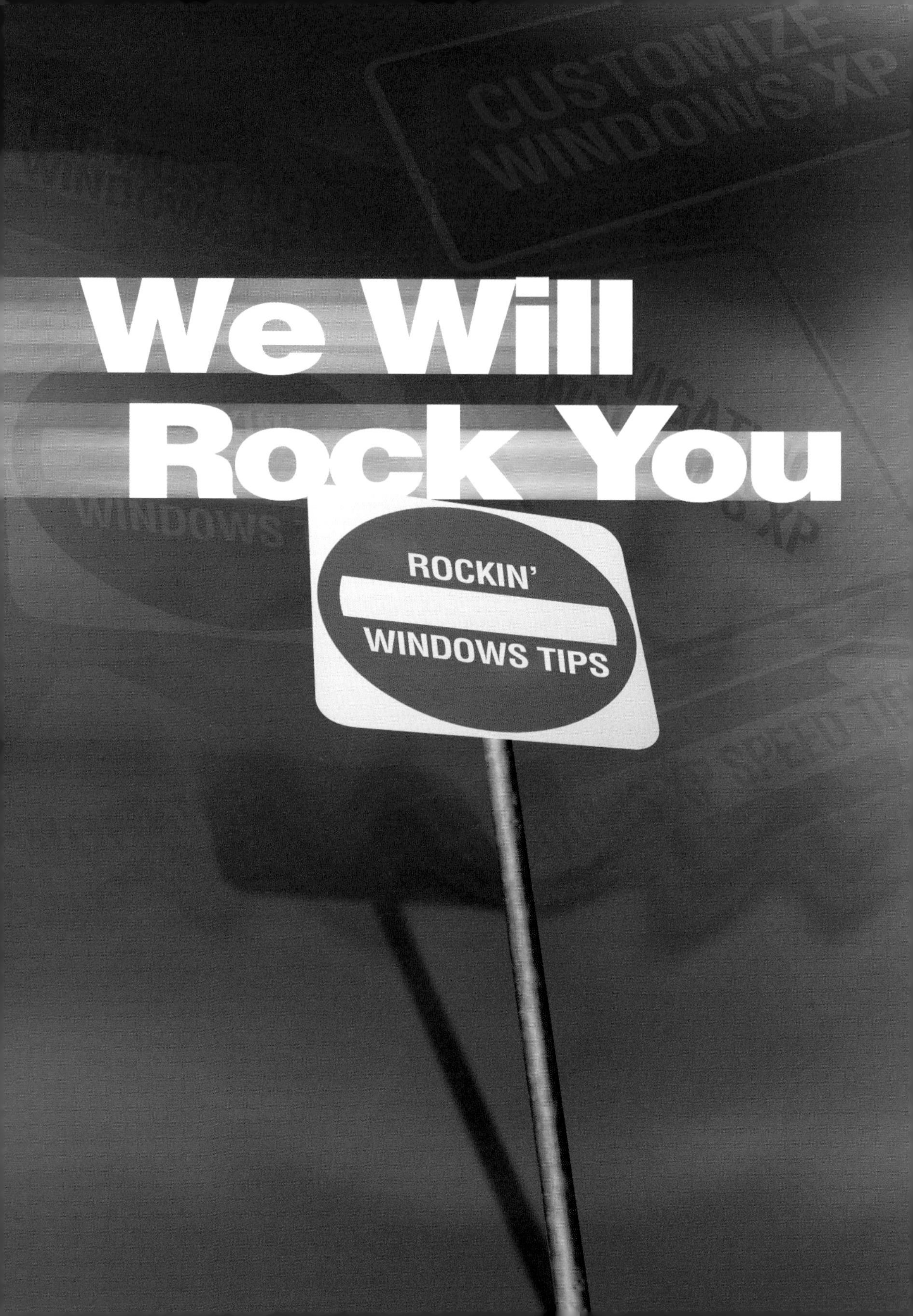

Woo Hoo! We will rock you!
With a title like that, you just
know this chapter's gonna be
good—we'll show some of XP's

We Will Rock You

rockin' windows tips

best tips, tricks, and hidden Apps. You'll
discover all kinds of things you just didn't
know you could do in XP. Or then again you
may know every single one of these tips and
find this chapter completely useless. If that's
the case, then please stop whatever you're
doing, turn off your computer, and go to
a park, Disney, the beach, or anything,
because man, you've just got to get out
more. Is your computer attached to your
chest with fanny packs and Ace bandages?
It's just a computer. The Off button is there
for a reason. Good grief, use it!

For the rest of you, it won't take fanny
packs, Ace bandages, and 20 hours a
day to learn this stuff, because you were
smart enough to buy this book. For the
other guy, please get some sun, you're not
looking very good.

 RENAME 'EM ALL AT ONCE

If you import digital photos, you're going to love this tip. Open the folder where you've saved your pictures. Select your first batch of pictures to rename. Right-click the first picture selected and click Rename on the Shortcut menu. Rename the first picture to whatever you like (for example, Boston Vacation), then click any empty space within the window to deselect the pictures. Your pictures automatically rename themselves (Boston Vacation1, Boston Vacation2, etc.). Now, that's sweet! This tip also works to rename any collection of files.

 IT'S SHOW TIME!

Boston Vacation

What's better than showing off digital pictures of your kids on the computer? Showing them as a slideshow! Here's how: Open the folder holding your photos and click the View as a Slide Show link in the Picture Tasks Pane. This creates a full-screen slide show of all the pictures in the folder.

COOL CUSTOM SCREEN SAVERS

You can also create a custom screen-saver slide show from a folder of photos. Right-click the Desktop, click Properties on the Shortcut menu, and then click the Screen Saver tab in the dialog box. Next, select My Pictures Slideshow on the Screen Saver drop-down menu. Click Settings, then click the Use Pictures in This Folder Browse button to select the location of your pictures folder, and click OK.

DON'T STAND BY, HIBERNATE

You've probably noticed that Hibernate isn't an option when you turn off your computer—actually, it is! Hold down the Shift key while the Turn Off Computer dialog box is visible, and Stand By becomes Hibernate. Why it's not a permanently visible option, I don't know (and I'm sure I never will).

Why is Hibernation cool? When your computer enters Hibernation, everything in memory is saved. The next time your computer is powered-up, programs, windows, and documents that were open at the time of Hibernation are restored exactly as they were on the Desktop.

LET WINDOWS DO THE TALKING

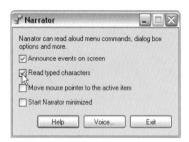

Have you ever wondered what Windows would sound like if it could talk? Well, wonder no more; turn on Windows Narrator and let Windows talk to you. Click Start, point to All Programs, point to Accessories, to Accessibility, then click Narrator. You can set up Narrator to read menus, shortcut menus, or new windows. Narrator will even read characters aloud as you type in various Windows text editors.

 ## GIVE THE SCRAPS TO YOUR DESKTOP

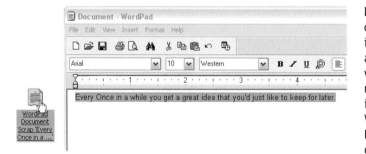

Document Scraps are one of the coolest tools in Windows. I use them all the time, especially when writing. Try this next time you're writing in a program such as Word, Notepad, or Word-Pad. Highlight a block of text and then drag-and-drop it onto your Desktop. You just created a Document Scrap. Now, you can drag-and-drop the Scrap back onto any of your documents at any time—a great way to save ideas and then drop them into documents when appropriate.

DRAG-AND-DROP DRIVES

I'm always accessing my drives, whether it's a floppy, CD/RW, or Zip drive, and it's convenient to have them where I can access them quickly from just about anywhere. Try putting a shortcut to them on your Desktop. Click Start>My Computer, then click-and-hold a drive's icon, and drag-and-drop it onto your Desktop. Now, you can quickly drag-and-drop files to your drives right on your Desktop.

 ## PERSONALIZE THE ALL PROGRAMS MENU

Here's something to keep in mind about the All Programs menu: The icons on the All Programs menu are only shortcuts. You can rename them, move them, or even delete them without harming the program. This means that it might also make sense to organize them to better suit you.

For instance, you could create a new All Programs folder named Design Apps to hold shortcuts to all of your graphic design programs, such as Photoshop, QuarkXPress, and Illustrator. Here's how to do it. Right-click Start, click Explore on the Shortcut menu, and navigate to your Programs folder (usually located at C:\Documents and Settings\All Users\Start Menu\Programs). You can create new folders and move existing program folders or shortcut icons into them to sort your programs. Now when you click Start and point to All Programs, you'll see your new customized menu, making it much easier to locate your programs.

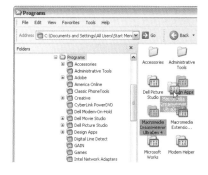

I'M REALLY GOOD AT CHECKERS

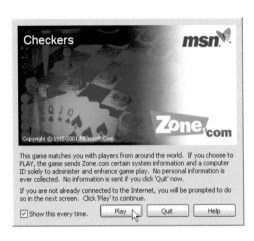

Actually I am pretty good at Checkers, but you should see me wreak havoc online. I'm tattooing people left and right. Okay, I've only played twice, but I dominated both times. XP lets you play games online against people from all over the world, and it's really easy! Click Start and point to All Programs, then point to Games and choose from five different Internet games. Checkers is my favorite—honestly, only because I'm terrible at the other ones. Anyway, make sure you're online and click the Internet game you want to play. Follow the onscreen instructions, and you're playin' Checkers against an eleven-year-old Uzbeki-stani, and you're whippin'-up on him. Heck, he's only eleven and he can't read English, but that doesn't mean that you shouldn't take him down.

RIGHT-CLICK PRINT

If you need to print a document, let's say a Word document, there's no need to launch Word first. Browse your hard drive for the file that you want to print, right-click its icon, and click Print on the Shortcut menu. This will automatically send the document to your printer without launching Word.

GRANDMA'S GETTIN' A FAX

Grandma doesn't have a computer to e-mail little Jenna's pictures to, but she's got a fax. (Why Grandma has a fax and not a computer, I don't know. This is fiction; go with it.) To fax a picture quickly, right-click the photo's icon and click Print. This will open the Photo Printing Wizard. Click Next, select the picture(s) you want to fax, and click Next, which takes you to the Printing Options. Now here's the trick: On the drop-down menu where the dialog box asks, What Printer Do You Want to Use? select Fax and click Next. Choose the layout for your photo(s) and click Next. This opens the Send Fax Wizard. The

Send Fax Wizard will walk you through setting up your fax, (recipient name, phone number, and so on). When you're done, click Finish. Grandma's gettin' a fax! This also works for any document you'd want to fax.

 ## JUST GO HOME

Put the Home button on your Standard Buttons Toolbar, and you'll always have a quick link to the Web. Just click your Home button and your Internet home page launches in the open window.

Here's how to do it: Right-click the Standard Buttons Toolbar and click Customize on the Shortcut menu. Scroll the Available Toolbar Buttons, click to highlight the Home button, then click Add and Close. Now your Internet home page is only a click away.

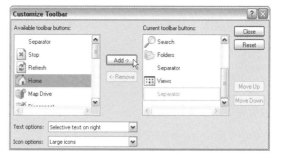

SEARCH THE WEB AT ANY TIME, FROM ANY PLACE

Any time you need to search the Web, simply type your question in the Address Bar of any open folder's window and hit Go or press Enter. Windows will search the Web and return the results in the open window. To put the Address Bar on your Toolbar, right-click the Standard Buttons Toolbar and click Address on the Shortcut menu.

INSTALL FONTS WITHOUT INSTALLING THEM

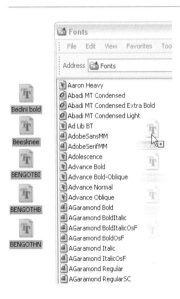

To install a new font, click Start>Control Panel, then click Appearance and Themes. Click the Fonts link on the See Also Tasks Pane, click File on the Fonts folder Menu Bar, and click Install New Font. Now, use the install dialog box to search your hard drive, select your fonts, and click install.

Whew, that seems like a lot of work, especially when you can just drag-and-drop your fonts into the Fonts folder instead. Yep, that's right, now you can just drag-and-drop fonts into the Fonts folder, and they're installed and ready to use.

NO ADOBE TYPE MANAGER? NO PROBLEM

This isn't so much a tip as it is just a great big YEAH! Previous versions of Windows couldn't install Post-Script fonts, so you had to have a program, such as ATM (Adobe Type Manager), to install these font types for you. Not any more. Now you can install PostScript fonts exactly the same as TrueType fonts using the Windows font installer, or by dragging-and-dropping them into the Fonts folder just like any TrueType font. YEAH! It's about time!

 ## PREVIEW INSTALLED FONTS

If you've owned a computer long enough, I'm sure you've done this at least once. Somehow you got your hands on a disk of 5,000 fonts and, of course, you installed every single one of them. Well, now that you have every font ever created on your computer, it'd be great to know what they actually look like. Here's how to preview your installed fonts.

Click Start>Control Panel, then click Appearance and Themes. Click the Fonts link on the See Also Tasks Pane, then click View on the Fonts folder Menu Bar, and click to check Preview. Now move your pointer over any fonts listed in the window and a quick pre-view of the font pops up. For a larger preview, you can also right-click a font's icon and click Open on the Shortcut menu.

ASSOCIATE FILES WITH MULTIPLE APPS

Here's a quick way to associate file types with different programs. Click Start>My Computer>Tools>Folder Options. Click the File Types tab in the dialog box, scroll the Regis-tered File Types, click GIF Image (for example) to highlight it, then click Advanced. Click New in the dialog box, type "Open in Explorer" (without the quotes) in the Action text field. Next, click Browse, navigate to Internet Explorer on your hard drive (usually located at C:\Program Files\Internet Explorer), click Explorer's icon to select it, then click OK. You should now see Open in Explorer listed under Actions. Click OK. Now, right-click any GIF file's icon and you'll have Open in Explorer as an option on the Shortcut menu. Click Open in Explorer to open the file in Explorer instead of its default program.

 ## "SEND TO" ANYWHERE YOU WANT

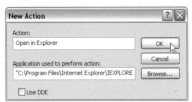

A Shortcut menu's Send To menu allows you to send files quickly to popular locations, but you can also customize the Send To menu by adding folders and drives to it—very handy when you frequently send files to the same location. For example, you have a folder named "My Favorite Pics" where you always save, well, your favorite pics. Wouldn't it be conve-nient to be able to instantly send any picture to this folder by simply using the file's Send To menu?

Here's how: First, make sure you can view hidden files and folders (the Send To folder is hidden by default). Now, right-click Start, click Explore on the Shortcut menu, then Navigate to your Send To folder (usually located at C:\Documents and Settings\Your User Name\SendTo). Simply press-and-hold the Alt key and drag-and-drop the My Favorite Pics folder into the Send To folder to create a shortcut to it. Now, right-click a picture's icon and point to Send To, and click My Favorite Pics to send your pictures instantly to the folder.

FOLDER ICONS?

Have you noticed that folders in Windows Explorer all look alike? This can make it a bit frustrating to find folders quickly. In earlier versions of Windows, there wasn't anything you could do about this; however, this is XP, and you can now change an individual folder's icon. Right-click Start and click Explore on the Shortcut menu. Locate a favorite folder, right-click its icon, and click Properties on the Shortcut menu. Next, click the Customize tab in the dialog box and click Change Icon. Browse your hard drive, select a new icon, and click OK. Then, click OK on the Customize tab. You can now see your folder's new icon. Cool! (*Note*: You may need to launch a new Explorer window to view the changes.)

 HIDDEN APPS—CHAT WITH PEOPLE ON YOUR NETWORK

There's an App named Winchat sitting on your computer right now that lets you chat with users on your network. I use it all the time on both my office and home networks. (I still can't believe it's hidden.) To launch Winchat, click Start and click Run. Type "winchat" (without the quotes) in the Open text field in the dialog box then click OK. This will launch Winchat. Now click Conversation on the Windows Menu Bar and click Dial. Select a computer (available users on the network) to call from the Dial dialog

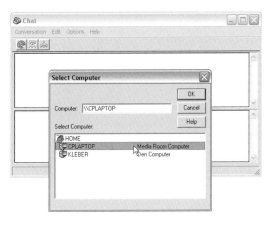

box and click OK. The user's computer will actually ring and invite the user to chat with you. Winchat can usually be located on your hard drive at C:\Windows\System32\winchat. If you have problems locating it, do a search for "winchat" (without the quotes).

CHAPTER 6 • We Will Rock You　　**119**

 HIDDEN APPS—CREATE SELF-INSTALLING PACKAGES

With Windows XP and a hidden App named IExpress 2.0, you can actually package your own Apps for installation on other computers. IExpress 2.0 lets you create your own simple self-extracting, self-installing packages of applications. You can even display your custom license agreement before allowing an installation. To launch IExpress 2.0, click Start and click Run. Type "iexpress" (without the quotes) in the Open text field in the dialog box then click OK. Follow the Wizard's step-by-step instructions to create your packages. IExpress 2.0 can usually be located on your hard drive at C:\Windows\System32\iexpress.

 HIDDEN APPS—CUSTOM CHARACTERS

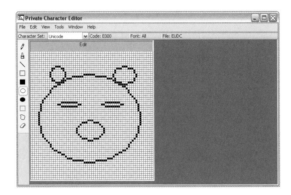

Create your own custom characters with XP's Private Character Editor. Use the Private Character Editor's Draw and Shape tools to turn your name, symbols, or logos into special characters that you can quickly place into your documents using the Windows Character Map. Click Start, then click Run and type "eudcedit" (without the quotes) in the text field in the dialog box. Click OK. This launches Windows Private Character Editor, where you can create and save your own custom characters.

HIDDEN APPS—WHAT HAPPENED TO NETMEETING?

Although NetMeeting has pretty much been
replaced by Windows Messenger, I know there
are still a lot of you out there who miss the old
conferencing program. If you really miss it, you
can still use it. NetMeeting is included with
XP and just waiting to be installed. To install
NetMeeting, click Start, then Run. Type "conf"
(without the quotes) in the Open text field in
the dialog box, then click OK.

CAPTURE ME IF YOU CAN

You're probably aware that you can take screen captures of
your Desktop by pressing the Print Screen (Prt Sc) key on your
keyboard, but what do you do if you only want to capture the
active window or dialog box? Press-and-hold the Alt key then
press the Print Screen key. This keyboard shortcut captures
only the active window.

 SAVE THAT POP-UP

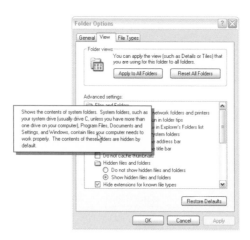

You just used the Help icon to get some info about a task in Windows, and it gave you a pop-up screen with a three-paragraph explanation. This is great, but how in the heck are you supposed to use this? As soon as you click anywhere, the pop-up disappears. The next time this happens to you, copy the explanation and paste it to a text editor, and you'll always have it for reference. To snag a pop-up, press-and-hold the Ctrl key, then press the C key—this copies the text of the Help's explanation. Next, open Notepad and press-and-hold Ctrl-V—this pastes the text into your document. You just saved a pop-up.

 OPEN SEVERAL APPS AT ONCE

It's already a little tedious to go to the All Programs menu to launch programs, but when you need to launch several programs for a project, it can be a real chore. For instance, you're creating a new Web site using Dreamweaver, Flash, and Photoshop. You could go to the All Programs menu three different times to launch the three programs, but try this instead. Click Start and point to All Programs. When the menu opens, press-and-hold the Shift key, browse the menu, and click the icons of the programs that you want to open. Each program will launch without closing the All Programs menu.

CREATE A NEW FILE WITHOUT LAUNCHING ITS PROGRAM

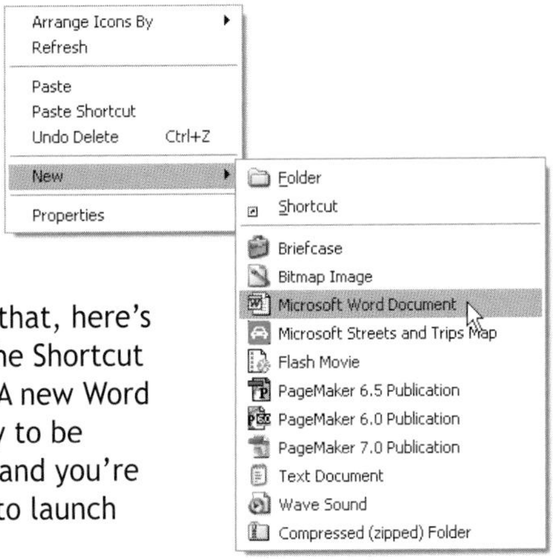

How many times have you had a great idea for the title or description of a document, only to forget it while spending what seemed like an hour trying to launch the program to type your idea and save it? Probably not as many as I have, but here's a tip that can help. For example, you can create and name a new Word Document before you even launch Word. "What?" you say. Yeah, you can do that, here's how. Right-click your Desktop, point to New on the Shortcut menu, and then click Microsoft Word Document. A new Word document icon will appear on your Desktop ready to be named. Type the document's title or description and you're finished. Now, when you're ready, click the icon to launch Word and edit the document.

TOP-SECRET, INVISIBLE FOLDERS

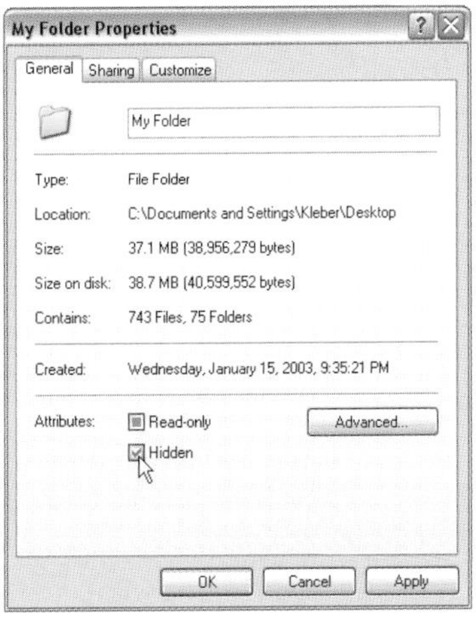

Ah, I bet this tip caught your eye! Nothing gets your attention like top-secret, invisible folders. And you can make one of those and put it anywhere, even on your Desktop. First, click Start>My Computer>Folder Options. Next, click the View tab in the dialog box, scroll the Advanced settings, click Show Hidden Files and Folders, then click Apply (keep the dialog box open). Now, right-click your Desktop, point to New, and then click Folder on the Shortcut menu. Name your new folder. Next, right-click the folder's icon and click Properties on the Shortcut menu. Click the General tab in the dialog box, check Hidden under Attributes, then click OK. Now, move into the folder the files that you want to keep secret. Go back to the View dialog box, click Do Not Show Hidden Files and Folders, then Apply. Your folder's now hidden. Just apply Show/Do Not Show Hidden Files and Folders to play "Now you see me, now you don't."

 ## DO YOU HAVE THE CORRECT TIME?

Synchronize your computer's clock with an Internet time server and you'll always have the correct time. Double-click the time in the Taskbar's notification area, and click the Internet Time tab in the dialog box, then check Automatically Synchronize with an Internet Time Server. Select a server from the drop-down menu and click OK. Now every time you connect to the Internet, your computer's clock will automatically be updated.

 ## LITTLE HELP PLEASE

You're having a problem with your computer and you have no idea how to fix it. This isn't so bad because I bet you know someone who does. Why not invite them to help? Using XP's Remote Assistance actually makes it fun to get help from friends. Before you can send an invitation, you have to enable Remote Assistance on your computer: Click Start>My Computer, then click the View System Information link in the System Tasks Pane. Next, click the Remote tab, check Allow Remote Assistance Invitations to Be Sent from This Computer, then click OK. Now you're able to send invitations for assistance from Outlook, Outlook Express, and Windows Messenger. While using Remote Assistance, your friend will be able to view your computer screen and chat with you in real time. If you allow it, your friends can even use their mouse and keyboard to work with you on your computer. Both you and your friend must be connected to the Internet and running XP to use Remote Assistance.

SEE CLEARLY WITH CLEARTYPE

Laptops should come with pop-up menus that remind you to blink every once in a while. There's just something about staring at an LCD screen for hours that feels like you rubbed your eyes with Q-Tips dipped in hot wing sauce (don't try this). You can ease this torture, however, by enabling ClearType, which can dramatically smooth screen fonts and make type easier to read.

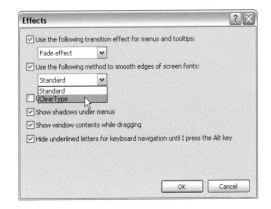

To enable ClearType, right-click the Desktop and click Properties on the Shortcut menu. Next, click the Appearance tab in the dialog box and click Effects. Now, check Use the Following Method to Smooth Edges of Screen Fonts, select ClearType from the drop-down menu, and then click OK.

SUPER-FAST MEDIA PREVIEWS

Windows Media Player is a fantastic App; however, it's a little overkill when you just want a quick preview of a media file (video or music). You can add a preview feature to your media file types so that you don't have to launch a full-blown Media Player to view them. Here's how: Click Start>My Computer>Tools>Folder Options, then click the File Types tab in the dialog box,

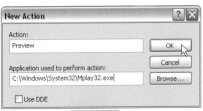

and scroll the Registered file types. Click to highlight MPEG (for example), then click Advanced in the dialog box. Click New, type "Preview" (without the quotes) in the Action text box, and type "C:\Windows\System32\Mplay32.exe" (without the quotes) in the Application Used to Perform Action text box, then click OK. You should now see Preview listed under Action. Click OK, then Close to exit the dialog box. Right-click any MPEG file's icon and you now have Preview as an option on the Shortcut menu. Click Preview to quickly launch a mini-player. Much faster!

 SAVE STREAMING MEDIA

Streaming media on the Internet is great, but you can't save it. Right? Actually you can. Once the streaming media has played completely, do a search of your hard drive for the media type played (.AVI, .MPG, .MP3, .WMV, etc.). Here's the trick, however: Make certain when you perform your search that you click the More Advanced Options Pane and check Search Hidden Files and Folders. Once you've finished your search, right-click each file, click Properties on the Shortcut menu, and look at the file's Location to see the referring URL. This helps you to identify the correct file. Now right-click the file, click Copy on the Shortcut menu, then right-click the Desktop, and click Paste. You just saved streaming media.

 KEEP 'EM OUT OF YOUR FOLDERS

There are a couple of ways to keep other users on the computer from viewing your files. First, you can make every folder under your User Profile private (My Documents and its subfolders, Desktop, Start Menu, and Favorites). This means that only you can access these folders and their contents. Other users who try to open your User folder on the hard drive will be denied access.

To do this, right-click Start and click Explore on the Shortcut menu. Right-click your User folder's icon in the Folders Pane and click Properties on the Shortcut menu. Next, click the Sharing tab in the dialog box, check Make This Folder Private, and then click OK. Now all folders and files under your User account are private. If you don't need this much privacy, you don't have to protect your entire User account. You can simply follow the same steps above to make individual folders private instead.

PRINT PHOTO SHEETS

I take a ton of digital photos and absolutely
love the picture-printing features in XP. You can
print photo sheets of any picture you'd like.
Open the folder containing your pictures and
click the Print Pictures link on the Picture Tasks
Pane. This opens the Photo Printing Wizard.

Just follow the Wizard's
instructions to select
the pictures you want to
print and the layout for
your photo sheet. Click
Finished when you're
through. Now you're
printing your own photo sheets.

ORDER PRINTS ONLINE

Don't have a photo printer? Don't sweat it;
you can use XP's online print-order feature to
send your digital pictures for printing. Here's
how. Open the folder containing your pictures
and click the Order Prints Online link on the
Picture Tasks Pane. This opens the Online Print
Ordering Wizard. Just

follow the Wizard's
instructions to select
the pictures you want
printed and the online
service to use. There
are several companies

to choose from, but they all do exactly the same thing. Next, select the pictures' print
sizes and quantities. Continue following the Wizard's setup instructions to upload your
pictures and provide billing and shipping info.

 TOGGLE DISPLAY OF FILE NAMES IN FILMSTRIP/THUMBNAILS VIEW

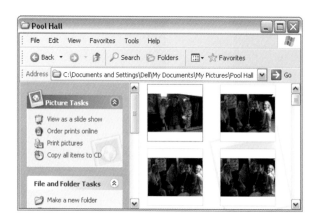

If you're viewing pictures using the Filmstrip or Thumbnails view, there's really no reason to view the file names also. You can already see the picture—the file's name is just taking up valuable space. You can turn file names on and off by pressing the Shift key when you open a folder or when you change to Filmstrip/Thumbnails view using the Views button.

 DRAG-AND-DROP PREVIEWS

If you have pictures saved on your Desktop, you can drag-and-drop them onto an open folder using Filmstrip view to quickly preview them. This doesn't move or copy the pictures; it only displays them for preview.

DISGUISE YOUR FILES

Here's something I bet you didn't know. When saving a file in Notepad or WordPad, if you enclose its name with quotes (e.g. "my file"), the file will be saved without an extension. This means that Windows can't tell what type of file it is and you won't be able to open it. Weird huh? Of course, you'll be able to select an application to try to open it.

Anyway, I'm not exactly certain why anyone would want to use this tip, unless of course you're just a devious person who wants to prevent people from reading your files. But hey, I guess if you're that kind of person, you'll really like this tip.

my file

Play That Funky Music

WINDOWS MEDIA
PLAYER 9 TIPS →

"They were dancin' and singin'
And movin' to the groovin'
And just when it hit me
Somebody turned around and

Play That Funky Music
windows media player 9 tips

shouted Play that funky music white boy
Play that funky music right . . . "

Isn't this a great song? I love it. I think I was five when it came out, but even then I knew good music. What could be better than a bunch of guys playing R&B Pop? Nothing that I'm aware of. I think Windows Media Player ranks third in the order of Microsoft "killer" Apps. You've got Internet Explorer for browsing the Web, Word for text editing, and then Media Player for pure entertainment—and it just gets better with Media Player 9. If you don't have version 9, then go to Microsoft.com and download it (free), because you'll definitely want it after reading this chapter. Hey, then you can join me and . . . .

"Play that funky music white boy
Lay down the boogie
And play that funky music till you die
Till you die, till you die, till you die . . . ."
   —"Play That Funky Music" by Wild Cherry

SKIN DEEP

Windows Media Player is shockingly large. I guess it has to be because it does practically everything; but you can change it to Skin mode, which gives you a much smaller and friendlier player. Press Ctrl-2 to switch to Skin mode. Press Ctrl-1 to switch back to Full mode.

 SHED YOUR SKIN

Let's shed some skin and change the look of Windows Media Player. Click Skin Chooser on the Taskbar and scroll through the available Skins. Select a new Skin that's just right for you and click Apply Skin. There ya go, a brand-new look!

LOVE THAT SKIN

There's not much point to spending hours looking for the perfect skin if you can't see it when other windows are open. You can keep your player handy by always leaving it on top of open windows. Click Tools>Options, then click the Player tab. Next, check Display on Top When in Skin Mode in the dialog box, and click OK.

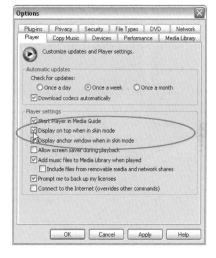

 ## ANCHORS AWAY

For some reason, Media Player leaves what it calls an Anchor open on your Desktop whenever you minimize your player and you're in Skin mode. What's an Anchor? This thing doesn't even make sense. The Anchor's about as big as the player itself and is really annoying. Here's how to get rid of it: Click Tools>Options, and then click the Player tab. Now, uncheck Display Anchor Window When in Skin Mode, and click OK.

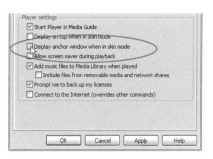

GET FUNKY

Your music just isn't music until you turn on the funk. Media Player comes with very cool visualizations. Heck, they're the best thing about Media Player. Here's how to turn 'em on. With your music playing, click Now Playing on the Taskbar, click the Now Playing Options button, point to Visualizations, and select the one for you. Feeling groovy? I know you are. To quickly change to a different effect, click the Next Visualization arrow button.

 MAXIMIZE THE FUNK

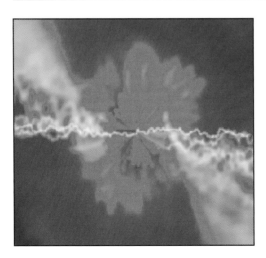

Okay, it's time to get really "trippy" and take the Visualizations full screen: Double-click anywhere on the Visualizations Pane to maximize the window. (My two-year old daughter and I could stare at it for hours.) Click again to get out of full-screen mode.

I NEED MORE

I know how you feel. You can never have too many effects that zone you out, so let's get more. Click the Now Playing Options button, point to Visualizations, and click Download Visualizations. This will launch your browser and take you to Microsoft's Media Player site, where you can download the latest and greatest.

 DRAG, DROP, PLAY

You don't have to be in Media Player to open a song. You can play any music file on your computer that's associated to Media Player by right-clicking its icon and clicking Play on its Shortcut menu. Also, you can play a song that's not listed in the Media Library: Just drag-and-drop the music file's icon onto Media Player to play it instantly.

CUSTOM COLOR

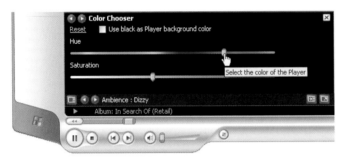

Media Player is so cus-
tomizable that it even
lets you create your
own custom colors for
it. Here's how: Click the
Now Playing Options but-
ton, point to Enhance-
ments, and click Color
Chooser. Now, just get as
weird as you want. Drag
the Hue and Saturation sliders to colorize your player. If things get a little too weird,
click the Reset link to get back the default colors. You can also choose preset colors by
clicking the Change Player Color button.

ALVIN? IS THAT ALVIN?

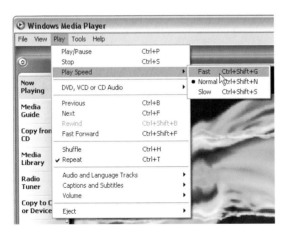

Do you remember when you were a
kid playing records and you'd speed
up the album to make it sound like
Alvin from Alvin and the Chipmunks?
Of course you do. We all did it.
Unless, of course you're twelve and
reading this book, then you have
absolutely no idea what I'm writing
about. If that's the case, please just
move on to the next tip—you're not
going to appreciate this. For everyone
else, Media Player's brought back
the fun. Press Ctrl-Shift-G on your
keyboard to fast-play your music, or
Ctrl-Shift-S to slow down your music
for that Barry White sound. To get
back to normal, press Ctrl-Shift-N.

PLAY IT EVEN FASTER

If you really want to kick it into high gear, click the Fast Play button on the Seek Bar. Keep clicking it for speeds up to five times faster than normal. I have no idea what this is good for, but for some reason I just can't leave it alone.

 WHAT'S YOUR EQ?

Media Player comes with 21 equal-izer presets, and none of them works for me. Go figure. Anyway, you can create your own custom preset by adjusting the equalizer sliders to any setting that you want. Media Player will automatically save your configuration as Custom (found under Now Playing Options>Graphic Equalizer>Custom).

 SUPER-FAST PLAYLISTS

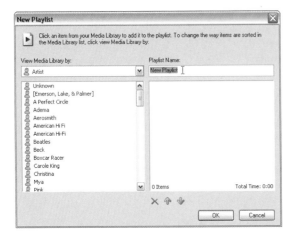

To create a new Playlist quickly, go to your Media Library and click the category heading where you want to create your new Playlist, and then press Ctrl-N. This opens the New Playlist dialog box where you can name your new Playlist and add music files.

 SHORTCUT TO PLAYLISTS

You don't have to go to the Media Library to access your Playlists, just right-click anywhere on the player's controls to get the Quick Access Panel. At the Quick Access Panel, click a Playlist to open it.

ADD FROM ANYWHERE

Here are a couple of quick ways to add media to your Playlists—as you know, you really can never have too many quick ways to add media to your Playlists. Just right-click any media file anywhere on your computer and click Add to Playlist on the Shortcut menu. This opens the My Playlists dialog box where you select a Playlist or create a new one. You can also drag-and-drop files to Playlists in Media Library.

 ADD 'EM ALL AT ONCE

If you have a folder of media files to add to a Playlist, you don't have to add each file separately. Simply right-click the folder and click Add to Playlist on the Shortcut menu. Now, select a Playlist or create a new one using the dialog box, then click OK and all of the files in the folder will be added instantly.

IT'S AUTOMATIC

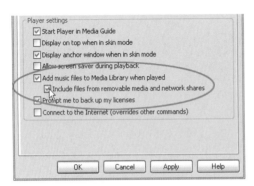

Here's a tip that can make your life a little easier. You can add music automatically to Media Library when it's played: Click Tools>Options, then click the Player tab. Now, check the box to Add Music Files to Media Library When Played. Check Include Files from Removable Media and Network Shares to add files played from these locations as well.

 GIVE IT ONE STAR

If you've ever accidentally downloaded a really bad song—you know, you thought you were downloading Blink 182 but what you got was A Flock of Seagulls—don't just delete the fraudulent file, humiliate it. Give it a one-star rating. Media Player lets you rate your media files from one to five stars.

To rate your music, right-click the file's name, point to Rate Selected Items on the Shortcut menu, and then click a rating. Now, give the Flock a shameful one-star rating. Go ahead, it'll make you feel better. I figure that one-star rating's got to be used for something.

BUILT-IN POWER SORTING

If you're not using Media
Player's Auto Playlists, you
should be. All music located in
the Media Library is automatically sorted by Auto Playlists.
Let's say you want to listen to
all of the music that you've
rated 4 or 5 stars. Well, click Go
to the Media Library, then Auto
Playlist, and there's a 4- and
5-star-rated Playlist already set
up and ready to play or copy
to disk.

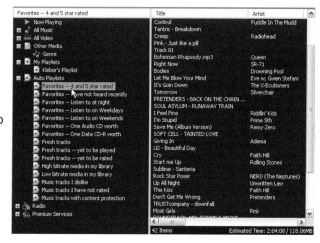

 LET'S SORT IT OUT

Another way to sort your music is by clicking
the column headers of a Playlist. You can add
more columns by right-clicking any header in
the Media Library and selecting new columns
on the menu. When you're finished adding
columns, rearrange them by dragging-and-
dropping them in any order you want in the
Media Library.

SURPRISE ME

Want to mix things up a bit? Click the Shuffle button to, well, shuffle the play order of your Playlist. Click the button again to return the Playlist to its original order. You can also press Ctrl-H to shuffle your Playlist quickly.

  QUEUE-IT-UP

If you want to just listen to a music file without adding it to your Media Library, you can "Queue-It-Up." Right-click a media file anywhere on your computer and click Queue-It-Up on the Shortcut menu or drag-and-drop the file onto the Playlist Pane in Now Playing.

IT'S MINI-PLAYER!

Yeah! I love mini-player! A new feature of Media Player 9 is the mini-player. I use it constantly: It's got everything and it's always visible on the Windows Task-bar for easy access. To use mini-player, right-click the Windows Taskbar, point to Toolbars on the Shortcut menu, then click Windows Media Player. You must have Media Player 9 installed to see this option. Now, when you minimize Media Player, it becomes mini-player on the Taskbar.

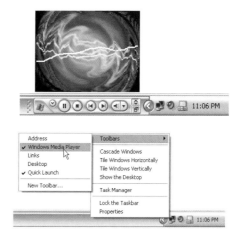

 MINI-PLAYER'S MINI INFO

Want to know what song is playing when you're using mini-player? You don't have to restore Media Player: Just scroll over the Windows logo on the mini-player and the Info Pane pops up showing the file's info.

MINI-FUNK

Mini-player's cool: It's not just Media Player without the funk—and Microsoft knew this. So, mini-player comes complete with Mini-Visualizations. Click the Show Video and Visualization Window button to display the effects. You can quickly change effects by clicking the window. Click the button again to turn off the window.

PLAY IT AGAIN

Just can't get enough of that song? Well, the fun never has to stop. Press Ctrl-T when a song or Playlist is playing and it will continuously repeat.

IT'S A CONTROL THING

The one thing you'll probably find yourself doing more than anything else in Media Player is adjusting the volume—up, down, or off. The quickest way to do this is to use the keyboard. Here are a few keyboard shortcuts to help you out: Press F10 to pump up the volume, F9 to turn it down, and F8 to mute it.

 IT'S WORTH WAITING FOR

If you're using a standard modem (56 Kb) to connect to the Internet, then you're probably used to streaming media pausing, stopping, and then restarting. This kind of defeats the purpose of streaming media, doesn't it? Well, maybe you can't do anything about your connection, but you can do something about the poor streaming media.

Increase the amount of time your player spends buffering the stream and you'll get a much better stream, free of breaks and pauses. Click Tools>Options, then click the Performance tab, and increase your Network Buffering. By default, buffering is set to 5 seconds. You can increase the Buffer up to 60 seconds of content. Increase it as much as necessary to get media to stream properly.

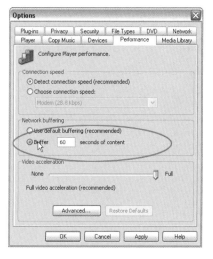

MAKE IT RIGHT

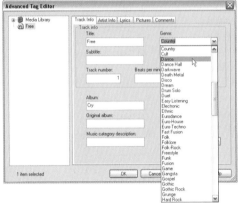

Often when you download music from the Web, the song or group's name will be misspelled or it might list the wrong genre. Well, you can quickly change a song's info using the Advanced Tag Editor. Right-click a song title and click Advanced Tag Editor on the Shortcut menu. On the Track Info tab, you can change whatever info needs correcting, or you can add new info to help you to identify and sort the file.

 GETTIN' GEEKY

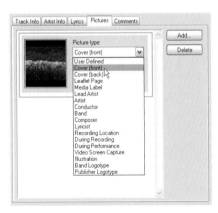

Okay, it's time to get really geeky with Media Player. If you don't like an album's cover art, you can change it to anything you'd like. Here's how: Right-click any song title and click Advanced Tag Editor on the Shortcut menu. Next, click the Pictures tab in the dialog box and click Add to browse your hard drive to locate the image you want to use. Now, select a Picture Type—this is what you'd like your photo to represent, which can be anything from the album's cover to the band picture. Click Apply, and you're done.

I'LL TELL YOU WHERE TO LOOK

Media Player automatically monitors your My Music folder for changes and updates the Media Library whenever new files are added to it. Which is fine, but you're a rebel. You save your music to a different folder on your hard drive. So, how can you make Media Player monitor this folder also? Please send $5.00 and a stamped return address envelope to... just kidding.

Click Tools>Options, then click the Media Library tab in the dialog box, and click Monitor Folders. Now, click Add to select the folder(s) on your hard drive that you want Media Player to monitor. You can also remove locations from here, including the default My Music folder.

CAN'T TAKE THE HIGHS AND LOWS

Okay, I've done my fair share of downloading music from the Web, and I'm sure you probably have too. You've probably noticed that there can be a huge difference in the quality of music you download. The biggest problem is with the volume level from song to song, and it can

be a real pain to constantly adjust the player's volume. Well, there's a way to fix this problem: Turn on Auto Volume Leveling.

From Now Playing, click the Now Playing Options button, point to Enhancements, and click Crossfading and Auto Volume Leveling. Next, click the Turn on Auto Volume Leveling link. Now all the music in the Playlist will sound the same.

LEVEL THE PLAYING FIELD

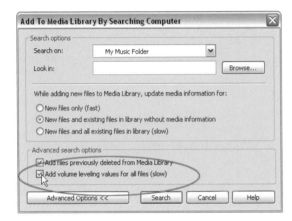

Save yourself the hassle of turning on Volume Leveling for each Playlist; instead, level your tracks when they're first imported into the Media Library. Here's how: Click File on the Menu Bar, point to Add to Media Library, and then click By Searching Computer. Next, click Browse to select the folder containing the Windows Media or MP3 files to which you want to add Volume Leveling. Now, click Advanced Options and check Add Volume Leveling Values for All Files (Slow). Media Player will now automatically add Volume Leveling to the files as they're added to the Media Library.

CAN YOU RELATE?

Has this ever happened to you? You come across a song that you love. It's perfect for the moment, event, whatever, and you'd love to find similar music but don't know where to start looking. This actually happens to me a lot. Kind of sad isn't it? Well, Media Player can help.

When you have a song playing and the Info Center view is open, click the Related Music link. Wasn't so obvious until I pointed it out, was it? Anyway, clicking this link will automatically search the Web and return a list of similar (related) music. Very cool! If you don't see the Info Center view, you can open it by going to Now Playing and clicking View on the Menu Bar, then clicking Info Center View>Always Show.

SING ALONG

Did you know that you could add your own lyrics to your favorite songs? You can. Click the Lyrics button in the Info Center view and then click Add Lyrics. Now you can type or paste in the lyrics for the song. Click Save Lyrics when you're finished.

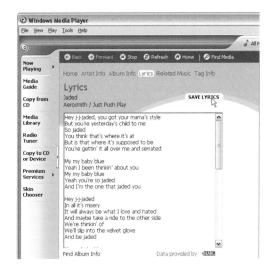

 WOW!

The SRS WOW Effect is the best new enhancement in Media Player 9—it blew me away. The WOW effect simulates Surround Sound for small or large speakers, or even headphones. It works wonders on my laptop speakers. To WOW your computer speakers, click the Now Playing Options button on the Info Center view, point to Enhancements, and click SRS WOW Effects. Next, click the Turn On link. Now, throw in your favorite DVD or play a music file and check out the difference!

YOU CAN FIND IT FROM HERE

Media Player is not only a great tool for playing music, it's also fantastic for searching for media. From the Info Center view, click Find Media. Type the name of a band, song, or album, and click Search. The results page displays all media found—music and video. Pretty cool!

[icons] **IT'S ALL IN THE NAME**

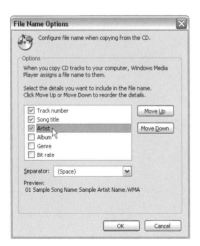

Follow this one closely. It can get a little confusing. By default, when you copy music from a CD, Media Player names your tracks using the track number and song title, which is good. It's nice to know the name of your music, but you can automatically add details to the song's name when it's saved. You can add the artist's name, album, genre, and bit rate. So, a title that would usually look like "01_Jaded" could look like "01_Jaded_Aerosmith_Rock." This is really handy for identifying and sorting your music. Here's how to do it.

Click Tools>Options, then click the Copy Music tab in the dialog box, and click File Name. Now, check the details that you want to add to the file name. You can also change the order of the details and add different types of separators.

THIS ISN'T GOING ANYWHERE

I have no idea why Media Player automatically starts up in Media Guide. This is a real pain if you're not connected to the Internet, because Media Player will spend several seconds looking for a connection. This is a good five seconds of torture. I know it's not going anywhere. Well, you can spare yourself this torment and turn off Media Guide at startup. Click Tools>Options, then click the Player tab in the dialog box. Next, uncheck Start Player in Media Guide, then click OK. Now when you launch Media Player, it opens to Now Playing.

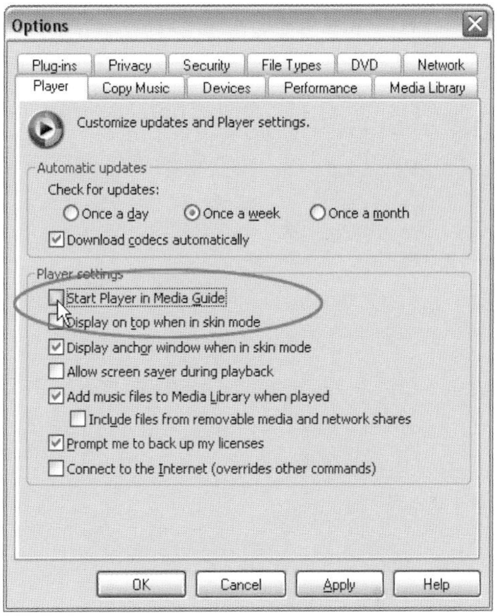

It's a
Small World

INTERNET EXPLORER TIPS

There's no doubt that the Internet is the greatest technology of my generation, that and the Xbox© of course,

It's a Small World

explore your world with internet explorer

and it's now the number one reason for owning a personal computer, though some would say it's not all good. The Net's made us gleefully lazy. It's true; I have no reason ever to leave my house. I bet there's someone sitting in a burning house right now just waiting for his computer to save him (or her). I wonder what Lewis and Clark would think of this new tool of exploration—probably not much. They'd probably whack all of us in the head. Chill out Lewis and Clark—that's exactly what makes the Internet great. We don't have to be Lewis or Clark to examine the buffalo-hunting tribes that lived along the Missouri. We can just fire up our computers. Lazy? Sure. Putting the world literally at our fingertips? Absolutely—explore away!

DON'T TYPE YOUR URLS

Let's see—http://www. That's not right; let's try again: http://www.disnee.com. No,
that's not right either. Why can't I do this? Why is this so hard? It's not our fault. Typing
http://www.yada-yada-yada.blah just isn't natural. It just feels wrong, so don't do it.
In Internet Explorer's Address Bar simply type the site's domain name (e.g. Disney),
then press-and-hold Ctrl and hit Enter. This keyboard shortcut wraps "http://www." and
".com" stuff around the domain name you typed and launches the URL. And, if your site
doesn't use .com, don't sweat it. Internet Explorer keeps searching for the site using
various extensions.

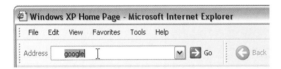

BACK AND FORTH IN A FLASH

You probably know that you can use the back and forward buttons to go backward or forward exactly one page; however if you want to jump several pages at once, click the Down
Arrow beside the buttons to view recently visited pages. Click on any page title to jump to
it immediately.

BACK AND FORTH USING THE KEYBOARD

Another quick way to move back and forth is to use your keyboard. Press the Alt key then the Left and Right Arrow keys to jump backward and forward, respectively, through recently visited pages.

YOU SHOULD KNOW YOUR HISTORY

Okay, you're browsing the Web and you come across the coolest site you've ever seen, and right at that moment your browser crashes. You didn't have time to Bookmark the site and you can't remember how you got there. Well, you're just out of luck; you'll never find that site again—just kidding. You can actually view every site you've visited in the last couple of weeks. Yeah, isn't that great? Internet Explorer automatically saves where you've been on the Web. To check out where you've been surfin', click the History button to open the History Pane. Now, you can search for sites you visited today, yesterday, or two weeks ago.

QUICK FAVORITES

Here's a handy Favorites tip. Press Ctrl-D on your keyboard to quickly add the current Web page to your Favorites folder.

DRAG-AND-DROP FAVORITES

The previous tip works great for quickly adding Web pages to Favorites, but it doesn't let you specify a folder within Favorites—which makes it fast, but not friendly. And using the Add to Favorites dialog box is, well, clunky. There's a better way. Click the Favorites button to display the Favorites Pane. Now, you can simply drag-and-drop URLs from the Address Bar to any folder within Favorites.

THAT MAKES NO SENSE

You know, I think there's a conspiracy out there to name Web pages as vaguely as possible. Half the time a page's title has nothing to do with the actual content of the page. This can make it almost impossible to locate the page in Favorites later. You can prevent this by renaming saved Favorites to something more descriptive that will help you to remember what the page is all about. Right-click the title of a Favorite and click Rename on the Shortcut menu. Now, simply type any name you want.

 FOLDERS FOR FAVORITES

Eventually you're going to need to add new folders to Favorites to help keep things organized. Here's how to do it fast: Right-click anywhere in the Folders Pane and click Create New Folder on the Shortcut menu. A new folder appears ready to be named. You just created a new Favorites folder.

 NEVER ORGANIZE FAVORITES

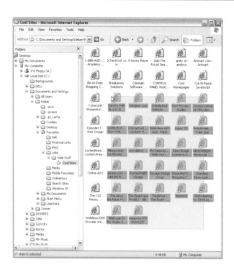

Never—I repeat never—use the Organize Favorites dialog box to organize Favorites. It hates you. Well, it probably doesn't actually hate you, but the way it works, you definitely wouldn't call it your friend. There's a much better way to organize Favorites. Click Favorites on the Menu Bar, then press-and-hold the Shift key and click Organize Favorites. This opens Favorites in its own window; now you can select any number of pages and move them anywhere you'd like. Grab multiple folders and drag them to other folders. Select multiple pages and delete them. Just go nuts. By the way, for whatever tortuous reason, you can't do this using the Organize Favorites dialog box. There, you can only move or delete a single page or folder at a time.

 HOME'S A DRAG

To set Internet Explorer's home page quickly, click the page's icon in the Address Bar and drag-and-drop it onto the Home button. This shortcut instantly sets the page you're viewing as your browser's home page.

SPEED SEARCH

You don't have to open the Search Pane to search the Web in Explorer. Instead, try typing your keywords or question directly in the Address Bar, and then click Go. Explorer will search the Web and display the results.

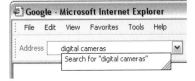

 I WANT A NEW WINDOW

Don't we all? You can never have too many new Explorer windows. In fact, I know exactly how many new Explorer windows I can open before my computer runs out of memory and crashes. It's a lot, but that's not the point. Often, you want to leave your Web page visible, but you also want to continue browsing the Web. What to do? Hmm, let's try pressing Ctrl-N. Hey, that worked: a brand new Explorer window.

 ## LIKE IT? SEND IT TO A FRIEND

If you come across a Web page that you've just got to tell your friends about, why not do it right then and there? Click the Mail button and click Send Page on the menu. This will automatically open Outlook Express with the page attached. Now, simply type your friend's e-mail address in the To box and click Send.

 ## DON'T JUST SEND IT; ARCHIVE IT

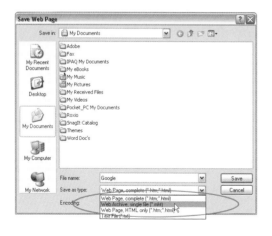

Using the previous tip, your friend can only view the page you sent them if they're online, which is probably fine, after all they had to be online to receive your e-mail, right? True, but you can create a Web archive and save all of the information needed to display the page in a single MIME-encoded file. They won't have to be online to actually open and view the page.

To create an archive of a Web page, click File on the Menu Bar, then click Save As. Choose a location, perhaps your Desktop, to save the file, then in the Save As Type box, select Web Archive, Single File, and click Save. Now attach the file to your e-mail and send it. When your friend opens the file, it will launch her browser and display the page exactly as it appears on the Web.

ERASE YOUR HISTORY

There's gonna come a time when you need to erase your browser's history. Maybe your anniversary is coming up and you've been checking out jewelry Web sites for that perfect gift for your wife. Or, you're planning a romantic getaway with your husband and don't want him to know that you've spent the last two days browsing Travelocity® for the best airfares to the Bahamas. I understand, and I'm here to help you keep your secret. Click Tools>Internet Options. Next, click the General tab in the dialog box and click Clear History. Now you can relax, your secret is safe.

 COVER YOUR TRACKS

This tip falls in line with the whole cover-your-tracks idea. Internet Explorer caches the Web sites that you visit to a folder named Temporary Internet Files. Caching helps to make Web sites load faster the next time you visit them. Assuming that you visit the same sites frequently, this is pretty useful. It can also show where you've been surfing—not always a good thing. You can quickly delete these files at any time. Click Tools>Internet Options, then click the General tab in the dialog box. Next, click Delete Files (under Temporary Internet Files), and all cached files are now gone.

KillerTips

COVER YOUR TRACKS AUTOMATICALLY

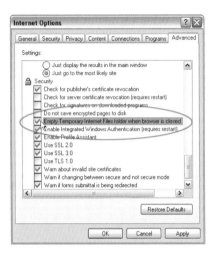

If you're really serious about keeping people out of your browsing business, you can automatically delete your cached files every time you close your browser. To do this, click Tools>Internet Options, and click the Advanced tab in the dialog box. Next, scroll to Security, check Empty Temporary Internet Files Folder When Browser Is Closed, and then click Apply. Now, every time you close your browser, your cached files will automatically be deleted.

MASTER OF DISGUISE

Let's say for whatever reason, you really don't won't to delete your cached Internet files but you still don't want anyone to know where you've been browsing. Well, you can get really clever and move your Temporary Internet Files folder, and here's how: Click Tools>Internet Options, and click Settings on the General tab. Next, click Move Folder, select a new location on your hard drive to save your cached Internet files, and click OK.

Now, if you want to get really freaky about covering your tracks, you can make the folder hidden. Right-click the folder and click Properties on the Shortcut menu. Next, check Hidden on the General tab of the dialog box and then click OK—but, good grief, what in the world are you doing on the Web? Never mind, it's none of my business.

I DON'T NEED THAT MUCH SPACE

For some reason, Internet Explorer reserves enough of your hard drive to cache probably about one-third of the entire Internet. Personally, I'd much rather use my disk space for more important things. You can reduce the amount of disk space reserved for Internet Explorer by clicking Tools>Internet Options. Next, click the General tab in the dialog box and, under Temporary Internet Files, click Settings. Now, grab the slider and pull it to the left to decrease the amount of disk space used by Explorer. Once you've changed it to a more reasonable amount, click OK.

 POWER SEARCH

By default, when Explorer searches the Web, it takes you to the most likely site. But you can make it take you to the most likely site *and* display the search results at the same time. This gives you tons more options and ultimately speeds up your searches. Here's how: Click Tools>Internet Options, and click the Advanced tab in the dialog box. Next, scroll the Settings, and under Search from the Address Bar, check Display Results, and Go to the Most Likely Site, then click Apply. Now perform a search and look at the difference. Much better!

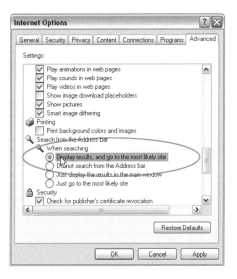

 SUPER-FAST BROWSING

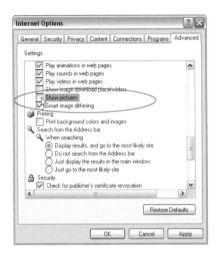

This tip is for people with low-bandwidth connections to the Web. If you're browsing a news site where what's important is the text and not the graphics, then turn 'em off. This can dramatically increase your browsing speed. To turn off graphics, just click Tools>Internet Options, and click the Advanced tab in the dialog box. Next, scroll the Settings, and under Multimedia, uncheck Show Pictures, then click Apply. No more graphics means super-fast browsing.

 VIEW IT OFFLINE

I use this tip all the time. I travel quite a bit, and if you do too, you already know that you can't use wireless devices while in flight. So, browsing the Web just isn't going to happen while you're 30,000 feet in the air. But this doesn't mean that you can't actually view Web pages; you just need to save them for offline viewing.

Navigate to the page you want to be able to view offline, add the page to Favorites, check Make Available Offline, and then click OK. Next right-click the title of the page in Favorites and click Synchronize on the Shortcut menu. Now, just select the page from Favorites when you're working offline to view it.

TAKE IT A STEP FURTHER

The previous tip showed you how to view a Web page offline, but what if you want more than just the one page? Well, you can do that too. Right-click the Web page in Favorites (that you just made available offline) and click Properties on the Shortcut menu. Next, click the Download tab in the dialog box, type in how many links deep (up to 3) from this page that you'd like to make available offline, and check whether or not to follow links outside of the page's Web site. When finished, click OK. Now, right-click the title of the page in Favorites and click Synchronize on the Shortcut menu.

QUICK SAVE WEB GRAPHICS

You can quickly save just about any graphic (pictures, photos, animations) you see while browsing the Web. Simply right-click the image and click Save Picture As on the Shortcut menu. Now, choose a location on your hard drive where you want to save it and click Save. You can do this even faster by simply dragging-and-dropping an image from Explorer onto your Desktop.

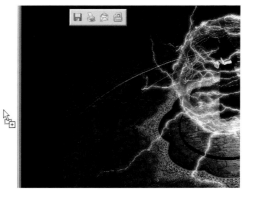

MAKE IT YOUR BACKGROUND

Maybe simply saving that Web graphic isn't good enough? You love it so much you've just got to see it all the time. That's okay, it's happened to me too. Well, you can set any image displayed in your browser as your Desktop's background: Just right-click the image and click Set as Background on the Shortcut menu. Now you can see it all the time, any time.

 ### CLEARING PASSWORDS

When you're looking for files in either List view or Column view, it's almost certain that by default, Internet Explorer's AutoComplete feature will save passwords, addresses, and other information entered into forms. This means you don't have to re-enter the information each time you visit a site. That's good, but—it also means that someone using your computer can access your password-protected accounts. That's not good. So, there may be times when it's necessary to clear your passwords, and here's how: Click Tools>Internet Options, then click the Content tab in the dialog box. Next, click AutoComplete Settings, uncheck Usernames and Passwords on Forms, and then click OK.

WHO'S RELATED?

There's a button available on the Standard Buttons Toolbar labeled Related that should really be on the Toolbar by default—but it's not. It's my favorite button. Well, that and the Refresh button. I just can't get enough of Refresh, can you? Anyway, Related (Powered by Alexa) will find sites similar to the one you're currently viewing. This can make hunting down info on the Web much easier. To add the Related button, right-click the Standard Buttons Toolbar and click Customize on the Shortcut menu. Scroll the Available Toolbar buttons, click Related, and then click Add. Now, browse to a favorite site and click Related.
Note: If Related isn't listed on your Available Toolbar button menu, then visit Alexa.com to get it.

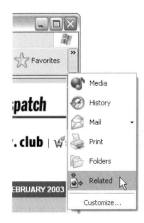

SMART PRINTING

I have to admit it—I'm a sports nut. I practically live on ESPN's Web site. When I find a topic of interest, such as the Tampa Bay Buccaneers (they rule!), I'll read the article and just about every related link on the page. I'll even print articles to take with me to read later. Well, I discovered a way to get really geeky and print not only the page I'm viewing, but all of the associated pages that are linked to it as well. If you want to get geeky like me, try this: First, put a ream of paper in your printer, click File>Print, then click the Options tab in the dialog box. Next, check Print All Linked Documents, and click Print.

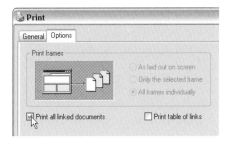

 YOU DON'T HAVE TO SEE IT TO SAVE IT

This tip works best for saving media. More often than not when you click a video or audio link, the media will stream in your browser, and it doesn't give you the option to save it to your hard drive. Well, if you decide you want to save the media, right-click the referring link and click Save Target As on the Shortcut menu. This allows you to download the file and save it to wherever you'd like.

 SEND IT TO YOUR DESKTOP

If you want to save a Web page displayed in your browser, you can right-click anywhere on the page and click Create Shortcut to send it to your Desktop. Or you can simply click the URL's icon in the Address Bar and drag-and-drop it onto your Desktop.

TAB YOUR WAY THROUGH FORMS

Online forms are a pain. They're necessary and useful but
not a whole lot of fun to navigate. Clicking your mouse in
each text box to type in them just seems, I don't know,
painful. Let's stop the insanity and use the Tab key on the
keyboard to navigate forms. Press the Tab key to jump
from field to field. Press Shift-Tab to jump back to
previous fields.

 ## ONE-CLICK FAVORITES

In earlier chapters, I wrote about the power of
the Links Toolbar, and since the Links Toolbar
was actually intended for Internet Explorer,
I guess it would be appropriate to mention it in
this chapter as well. You probably know where
this is going.

   The Links Toolbar is the perfect place to hold
your most important and frequently visited
sites. To place a Web page on the Links Toolbar,
simply click the URL's icon in the Address Bar
and drag-and-drop it onto the Links Toolbar. Now
your favorite links are always visible—just one
click away. To show your Links Toolbar, right-
click the Standard Buttons Toolbar and click Links
on the Shortcut menu.

Come Together

**E-MAIL
MADE EASY**

You know, e-mail is exactly what I needed in my life. I'm a maniac! I need to do everything faster and better. It's just the way I am.

Come Together

e-mail made easy

And, being able to communicate faster and better is right up my alley. Honestly, I can't even remember my professional life without e-mail. How did you old guys get along without it? Geez, I bet you actually owned a typewriter. You must be so old, your memory is in black and white. Yep, you're so old, you walked into an antique store and they kept you. I'm sorry. I have no excuse. I just had another birthday and it makes me feel better to berate anyone older. I'm not handling it well. With that said, the key on Benjamin Franklin's kite was to your house. I'm sorry. I can't stop. Please, just turn the page.

 I JUST WANT TO START UP

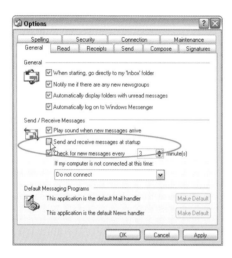

I'm not sure why Send and Receive Messages at Startup is set up as the default. I personally think this is the most annoying thing since "The Thong Song." I mean, sometimes I just want to open Outlook Express and type an e-mail, read an e-mail, or just look at my e-mail. Unfortunately, there's not a kill option for this feature, only Off. Here's how to do it. Click Tools>Options, then click the General tab, and uncheck Send and Receive Messages at Startup. Click OK. Whew, that's better!

 YOU'VE GOT A NEW MAIL SOUND

By default Outlook Express uses the Windows XP Notification, which sounds kind of like every other XP sound. So, if you'd actually like to know that you've received new e-mail, you can make the notification sound a little more distinguishable. Click Start>Control Panel>Sound, Speech, and Audio Devices>Sounds and Audio Devices, then click the Sounds tab in the dialog box, scroll to find then select New Mail Notification in Program Events. Now, choose a new sound from the Sounds drop-down menu or browse your hard drive to choose a new sound. If you have AOL installed on your computer, you may want to use AOL's "You've Got Mail" sound. When you're finished, click OK.

GO DIRECTLY TO YOUR INBOX

When launching Outlook Express, I always go to my Inbox first, typically because I'm opening the program to check for new e-mail and it just saves time to start there. To take the fast track to your Inbox, click Tools>Options, then click the General tab in the dialog box. Next, check When Starting, Go Directly to My 'Inbox' Folder, then click OK. Now Outlook Express will open in your Inbox.

 ## READ IT, BUT LEAVE IT

It's pretty convenient to be able to check your e-mail on the road using your laptop, PDA, or from another computer, but what's not convenient is that the mail is then removed from your server: By default, incoming messages are automatically deleted from your server when received. So, what do you do to be able to read the received mail from other computers? Leave copies of your e-mail on the server, which allows you to download it again later from another location.

Here's how: Click Tools>Accounts and click the Mail tab in the dialog box. Next, click to highlight the e-mail account that you're checking for new messages and then click Properties. Now, click the Advanced tab and check Leave a Copy of Messages on Server, and click OK. You'll now be able to download the same messages from different computers.

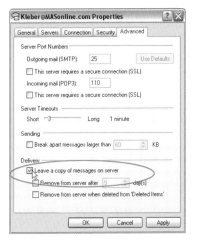

 GROUP 'EM

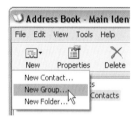

If you often e-mail the same message to several people—for instance, family, friends, or co-workers—you should create a group. Groups make it much easier to send multiple contacts the same message at the same time. To create a group, click the Address Book button, then click New in your Address Book, and select New Group. This opens the New Group Properties dialog box where you can name the group and select members from your existing contacts. When finished, click OK. Your new group's name now appears in your Contacts. To send e-mail to the group, simply type or select the group's name in the To field. Now everyone in the group will be sent the message.

 ADD NEW MEMBERS

This isn't as obvious as you might think. To add contacts to an existing group, click the Address Book button on the Toolbar to open your Address Book. Next, scroll your Contacts, locate the group where you want to add new members, and double-click the group's name to open it. Now, use the dialog box to add new members, remove existing members, or create new contacts for the group. Click OK once you're finished.

BCC IS BETTER

Something to keep in mind when sending
e-mail to groups is that everyone receiving
the message will see the e-mail address
for each member on the list—some people
in the group may not be crazy about this.
There's a clever way around this problem,
however. On a new message window, click
To to select the recipients, but instead of
adding your group to the To field, add it
to the Bcc (Blind Carbon Copy) field. Now
when you send messages to the group,
members will only see who sent the message, not who the recipients were.

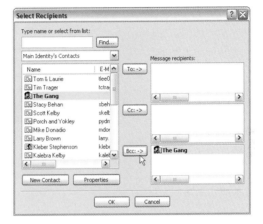

 RIGHT-CLICK TO E-MAIL

To quickly send e-mail to contacts, try right-clicking
their names in Contacts and clicking Send E-Mail on
the Shortcut menu. If you don't see Contacts, click
View>Layout, check Contacts, and then click OK. You'll
now see Contacts beneath the Folder List.

 MANAGE YOUR MAIL

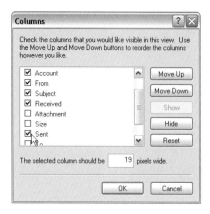

You can organize Outlook Express' Messages Pane the same way as Details in folder views. You can add columns by right-clicking any column header, clicking Columns on the Shortcut menu, and then checking the columns that you want to appear. You can also arrange columns by grabbing any column header and dragging-and-dropping it in any order you'd like.

 WHAT'S THE SUBJECT?

Click on any column header to sort your messages quickly; for example, click Received to list your messages by the date and time they were received or click Subject to sort messages by their subject line. If you have multiple accounts, you might want to sort by using the Accounts column. This will tell you which accounts received messages.

FLAG IT

I receive a ridiculous amount of e-mail throughout the day, and if I'm expecting an important e-mail, I'll set up a message rule to automatically flag it to notify me that it has arrived. To flag incoming messages, click Tools>Message Rules>Mail and create a new mail rule using the dialog box. In the first menu, check Where the From Line Contains People; in the second menu, check Flag It; and in the third menu, click on the Contains link and add the person's name and e-mail address. Next, name your new rule and click OK. Now, when a message arrives from this person, it will be flagged immediately for easy recognition.

 YEP, WE RECEIVED IT

This works best for accounts that receive lots of e-mails with similar requests; for instance, your Web site's Info account. This e-mail account might receive tens or even hundreds of e-mails each day requesting information and it might take you days to respond. To create an auto-reply that lets senders know that you've received their messages, open Notepad by clicking Start>All Programs>Accessories>Notepad, type a generic reply, and save it wherever you'd like using the ".eml" extension (e.g. reply.eml). This saves your reply as an e-mail message.

Now open Outlook Express, click Tools>Message Rules>Mail, and create a new mail rule using the dialog box. In the first menu, check Where the Message Is from the Specified Account; in the second menu, check Reply with Message; and in the third menu, click the Specified link and add the account that receives the messages. Click the Message link, navigate to the reply that you created earlier in Notepad, and select it. Next, name your new rule and click OK. Now, when a message is received by this account, your reply will be sent automatically.

 ## SHORTCUT TO YOUR BEST FRIEND

Do you have someone who you e-mail a lot—a friend, family member, or co-worker? Of course you do, so this tip will make your life a bit easier. Right-click your Desktop, point to New, and click Shortcut on the Shortcut menu. In the Type the Location of the Item field, type mailto:*your friend's e-mail address*—for example, mailto: kleber@masonline.com—then click Next. Give your shortcut a name and click Finish. Now, when you click your friend's e-mail shortcut on your Desktop, a new mail message window will open with your friend's e-mail address already in the To field. Just type your message and click Send.

 ## PERSONAL PHONE BOOK

Here's a quick way to have your Contacts' phone numbers available: Just click the Address Book button and click Print on the Address Book Toolbar. Now, select All for the Print Range, Phone List for the Print Style, and then click Print. This will print a complete list of your Contacts' phone numbers. You can also select Business Card for the Print Style to print each Contact's business card.

SIGN IT AND FORGET IT

For most accounts, especially business accounts, you'll almost always have the same Signature—meaning that you'll usually end your messages with the same name and any contact information. You don't have to type this information each time you send an e-mail (unless you just really like to type). You can create a Signature just once and add it to your messages whenever you want.

Here's how: Click Tools>Options, then click the Signatures tab in the dialog box. Next, click New and give your Signature a name. In the Edit Signature dialog box, select Text, then type your Signature, and click OK. You can also select a text file on your hard drive to use for your signature. To use your new Signature, open a New Message window and place your cursor in the message where you want your signature to appear. Now, click Insert>Signature to place the Signature into your message.

 ## DID YOU GET MY MESSAGE?

Don't you hate not knowing whether someone received your e-mail? I mean, you asked for a reply but, of course, they never sent one. So, you're just left hanging. Did they get it? Did my server eat it? You don't know and because they won't reply, you never will. Stressful, isn't it? Well, there's a way that you can encourage the recipient to acknowledge that they received your e-mail. From a New Message window (before you send your message), click

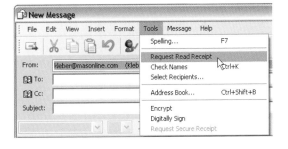

Tools>Request Read Receipt. Now, when they receive your message, they'll be prompted to acknowledge that they received it. If they do, you'll receive notification that it was received. If they don't, then subscribe their e-mail address to every spammer on the Web. That'll teach 'em!

 SNAG THAT STATIONERY

Someone just sent you an e-mail and it has the coolest stationery attached that you've ever seen. Wouldn't it be great if you could snag it for yourself? You're in luck, you can.

With the e-mail message open, displaying the stationery in the Preview Pane, click File>Save as Stationery. Next, name the stationery and click Save. Now, when you apply stationery to messages, you'll see your new stationery listed. Oh, and by the way, be sure to send your friend a thank-you note for using their stationery—they'll appreciate that.

 I CAN'T GET ENOUGH

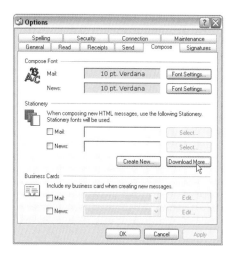

Yeah, this stationery stuff is great, isn't it? Just can't get enough? Me too, so let's keep the fun rollin' and go nuts downloading all we can get our hands on. Click Tools>Options, then click the Compose tab in the dialog box. Next, click Download More. This opens your browser and takes you to a download page at Microsoft's Web site. Now, select new Stationery and follow the online instructions for installing the downloads.

DO-IT-YOURSELF STATIONERY

If you're familiar with basic HTML, you can create you own custom Stationery. This is great for branding corporate e-mail. Using FrontPage, Dreamweaver, GoLive, or any HTML editor, create an HTML page using your own graphics and background colors and save it to your Stationery folder with the extensions ".html" or ".htm." (The Stationery folder should be located at C:\Program Files\Common Files\ Microsoft Shared\Stationery. If you have trouble locating it, do a search for "Stationery.") Next, simply copy your saved Stationery and any graphics to the Stationery folder. Now, your new Stationery is available for e-mail messages.

You can also create a simpler version of custom Stationery using the Stationery Setup Wizard. Click Tools>Options, then click the Compose tab in the dialog box. Next, click Create New and follow the Wizard's directions for creating custom Stationery.

 THINGS TO DO

It's a good thing that you can add folders to Outlook Express, because I get way too many e-mails for the default folders to handle. When I open Outlook Express for the first time, I always create a Things To Do folder where I can store e-mail to be worked on later. You can create folders to help keep your e-mail organized—it's easy. Right-click Local Folders and click New Folder on the Shortcut menu. Next, give your new folder a name and click OK. Now you'll see your new folder listed under Local Folders.

MOVE MESSAGES QUICKLY

Now that you've added folders to organize your e-mail, it's time to start using them. To move e-mail, simply drag-and-drop your messages to any folder listed under Local Folders.

 DRAG-AND-DROP TO EDIT

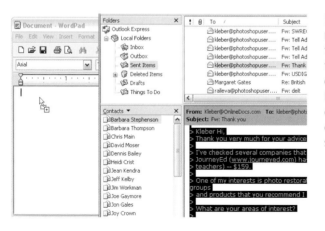

If you want to save an e-mail message as a text file, try this: Open WordPad or Word, then highlight the text of your e-mail in Outlook Express' Preview Pane and drag-and-drop the text into your text editor. Now you can edit and save the message.

CAN'T SPELL?

Let's face it, most of us can't spell. (I can, but then I can do everything—it's a burden.) Well, Outlook Express can help. You can set up Outlook Express to check your spelling automatically before you send messages. To do this, click Tools>Options, then click the Spelling tab. Next, check Always Check Spelling Before Sending, and click OK. You're feeling smarter already, aren't you?

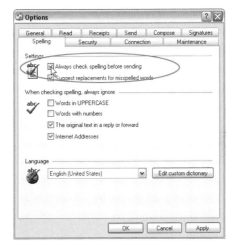

 TEACH IT TO SPELL

You can teach Outlook Express to spell. This really comes in handy for frequently used personal and corporate names. Add these names to your Dictionary and Outlook Express won't continually ask you to check their spelling before sending messages. To add words to your Dictionary, click Tools>Options, then click the Spelling tab. Next, click Edit Custom Dictionary and type each word on its own line. Then click File>Save and close the text document.

 JUST SHOW ME NEW MESSAGES

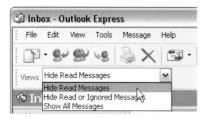

Is your Inbox getting a little crowded? Well if it is, you can hide messages that you've already read to help identify new incoming e-mail. Here's how: Right-click the Toolbar and click Views Bar on the Shortcut menu. Now, select Hide Read Messages in Views and you'll no longer see messages that you've already read.

 THAT'S THE FONT FOR ME

It's a good thing that you can customize the text of incoming e-mail, because I have to tell you that some people have a twisted sense of which fonts look good. You can receive e-mail with so many different typefaces and sizes that you're not even sure if they're written in English. Well, you can customize your incoming e-mail so that it displays the same typeface and font size.

To do this, click Tools>Options and click the Read tab in the dialog box. Next, click Fonts, scroll the Proportional Font box to choose your font, then select a Font Size. Click Set as Default, then click OK. Now, all of your incoming messages will have the same look.

NO MAIL FROM YOU

Are you getting annoying e-mail from someone? If you are, you can block the sender's e-mail address, so you won't see their messages. (I do it to all the time just for fun, but that's me; I'm just mean.) Anyway, when you block an e-mail address, any mail received from that address is automatically placed in your Deleted Items folder. You don't ever have to see it.

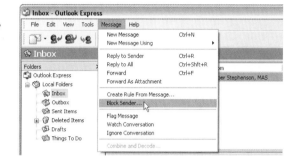

Here's how: Select their e-mail message and click Message>Block Sender. This instantly adds the sender's e-mail address to your Blocked Senders List. To remove someone from the list, click Tools>Message Rules>Blocked Senders List, select the e-mail address, and click Remove. You can also manually add an address to your list using the Blocked Senders List dialog box.

 ## CHECK E-MAIL CONTINUOUSLY

If you check your e-mail throughout the day and have a constant connection to the Internet, then there's no need for you to check manually for new messages. Let Outlook Express automatically check for you. First, click Tools>Options and click the General tab in the dialog box. Now, check Check for New Messages Every __ Minutes and type a number for how often Outlook Express should check for new messages, then click OK. Now, minimize Outlook Express and it will automatically check for new messages.

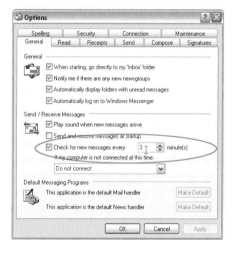

GOT MAIL? YOUR NOTIFICATION AREA KNOWS

Now that you've minimized Outlook Express, how do you know if you've received new messages? The Taskbar's Notification area knows. When new messages arrive at your Inbox, the You Have New E-Mail icon will appear informing you that you've received new e-mail.

QUICK ADD CONTACTS

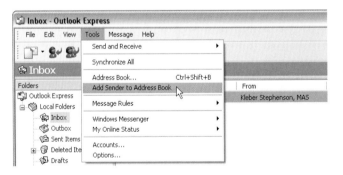

Here's a quick way to add someone who has sent you e-mail to your Contacts. With their message selected, click Tools>Add Sender to Address Book. That person now appears in your Contacts.

WHO'S ONLINE?

You can quickly make anyone listed in Contacts an Online
Contact by right-clicking their name and clicking Set as
Online Contact on the Shortcut menu. The contact needs
to have a Microsoft .NET Passport to be added as an Online
Contact; if they don't, Outlook Express will prompt you to
send them an e-mail requesting that they get one. Anyway,
once they're set up, you can use Contacts to monitor their
online status.

SAY "HEY" INSTANTLY

If you notice that a Contact is currently online, you can
quickly say "Hey." Just right-click the person's name and click
Send Instant Message on the Shortcut menu. This will launch
Instant Messenger, letting you type and send your message.

 TOO RACY? TURN IT OFF

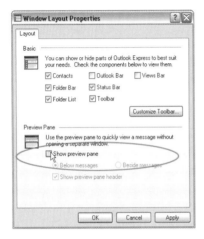

Okay, you're in the den playing with the kids, having a great time (as usual), and in between giggles, you figure it would be a good time to check your e-mail. Unfortunately, you received e-mail from a spammer who's sent you a message containing adult images—that's great! This is a conversation I could have put off for the next decade.

Well, you can avoid this by turning off the Preview Pane. Click View>Layout, uncheck Show Preview Pane, then click OK. Now, received messages won't display their contents, only that the e-mail was received; however, you can quickly view any e-mail by right-clicking the message and clicking Open on the Shortcut menu.

 DRAG-AND-DROP ATTACHMENTS

If you're attaching files to an e-mail, you can simply drag-and-drop them onto the New Message window. This will instantly attach your files.

CREATE A VCARD

A vCard in Outlook Express is the same as a business card. Once you create a vCard, you can attach it to your e-mail by clicking Insert>My Business Card from a New Message window. When customers receive your e-mail, they can save your vCard, giving them a digital copy of your contact info. Here's how to create yours. First create an entry for yourself in the Address Book, and then select your name from the Address Book list. Now, click File>Export and click Business Card (vCard). Choose a location to save your vCard, then click Save.

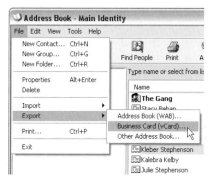

 GIVE ME DIRECTIONS

Do you need directions to a contact's street address? You can get them right in Outlook Express. Right-click anyone's name in Contacts and click Properties on the Shortcut menu. Click the Home or Business tab and make certain that you've listed their street address. Now, click View Map. This will launch your Web browser, taking you to Microsoft's Expedia Web site and displaying a map to the address.

 ## MESSENGER—ARE YOU THERE?

You start a conversation with someone and type and send your message. You wait...nothin'. So, you send an "Are you there?" message. You wait a little longer then send another "Are you there?" message. You're not being ignored; your friend's probably just typing slowly. I have quite a few friends who type slowly—you know who you are. Anyway, wouldn't it be great if you were able to see in real time that they were responding instead of just ignoring you? Now, you can. Just look at the bottom of your Conversation window and you'll see the typing status of your friend. When your friend is responding (typing on the keyboard), you'll see it in real time. So, now you'll know when they're responding and you won't have to send annoying "Are you there?" messages.

 ## MESSENGER—GIVE ME A BREAK

When you press Enter while typing in Messenger, you don't get a line break as you might expect. This actually sends your message. Frustrating, isn't it? Well, next time you need a line break, press Shift-Enter or Ctrl-Enter. This shortcut lets you place line breaks wherever you need 'em.

MESSENGER—DRAG-AND-DROP TO SEND

To quickly send files to someone using Messenger, simply drag-and-drop a file onto the Conversation window. This instantly sends the file to whomever you're chatting with. This action is similar to sending attachments using Outlook Express, only better, because the recipient receives the file instantly and you obtain immediate confirmation of receipt. Messenger will notify you once they've accepted the file.

 MESSENGER—.NET ALERTS

.NET Alerts are great! There's just no other way to describe them. You can subscribe to all kinds of alerts: news, sports, travel, finance, and more. To subscribe to new .NET Alerts, first turn on Tabs by clicking Tools>Show Tabs, and select Microsoft .NET Alerts on the Menu Bar. Next, click the .NET tab, click the Go To link, and click Add an Alert. This launches Microsoft's .NET Alerts in your Web browser, where you can subscribe to various content providers. To view Alerts you've subscribed to, click the Provider button.

 MESSENGER—YOU'RE BLOCKED

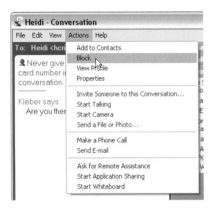

Eventually, you may find it necessary to block someone from sending you messages. There are many reasons for this, but we're not going to discuss any of them. I'm just going to tell you how to do it.

When you receive a message from someone that you want to block, click Actions>Block on the Menu Bar and that person will no longer be able to send you messages. Unfortunately, there's no way to remove yourself from their Messenger contacts; however, you'll always appear offline to them, making it impossible for them to send you messages. Now, if you decide to forgive this person for whatever they did to you, you can remove them by clicking Tools>Options on the Menu Bar and selecting the Privacy tab in the dialog box. Now, select that person's name in the My Block List and click Allow. This puts them back in the My Allow List.

 MESSENGER—SUPER-FAST GROUPS

Groups are essential for organizing your Messenger contacts, and you can quickly create new groups by right-clicking any existing group and clicking Create New Group on the Shortcut menu. Now, name your new group and you're ready to start adding contacts to it. To view groups, click Tools>Sort Contacts By and select Groups on the Menu Bar.

MESSENGER—QUICKLY ADD CONTACTS TO GROUPS

If there are several contacts that you want to appear in multiple groups, don't just drag-and-drop them. That just moves them. Instead, hold the Ctrl key as you drag-and-drop your contacts. This shortcut creates copies of your contacts rather than moving them.

 ## MESSENGER—WHAT DID THEY SAY?

This happens all the time. As soon as you've closed the Conversation window, you wish you hadn't because you can't remember your friend's directions, recipe, joke, or whatever. You should have saved your conversation. Oh, you didn't know you could do that? Well, you can. Here's how: Before you close your Conversation window, click File>Save As. Next, name your conversation, then click Save. This saves your entire conversation. Now to view your conversation, simply navigate to the saved file and open it.

 MESSENGER—SEND MESSAGES FROM THE TASKBAR

When signed-in, Windows Messenger always appears in the Notification area of your Taskbar. So, even if Messenger is closed, you can still send an instant message: Just right-click the Messenger icon in the Notification area and, on the Shortcut menu, click Send an Instant Message. This opens a dialog box listing contacts that are currently online. Select the names of the contacts to whom you want to send a message, then click OK. This opens the Conversation window. Now, type your message and click Send to start chatting.

 MESSENGER—MAKE IT A PARTY

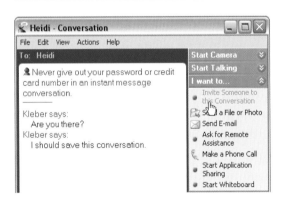

A great feature of Windows Messenger is the ability to invite other contacts to your conversations. This really comes in handy when conferencing. To invite other contacts to your current conversation, simply click the Invite Someone to This Conversation link on the sidebar, select additional contacts, and click OK. This will send an invitation for them to join you. You can have up to five people participating in a conversation.

MESSENGER—GET RID OF POP-UPS IN A HURRY

There are annoying pop-ups that, well, pop up from time to time from the Messenger icon in the Notification area. These can be Alerts or advertisements, but they're always annoying, and there's no obvious way to get rid of them. Although eventually they do go away on their own, there is a way to get rid of them on your terms and in a hurry. The next time a pop-up window appears, right-click it. This will instantly close the window.

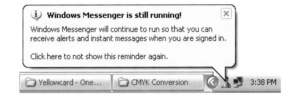

It's a Wrap

WINDOWS MOVIE MAKER 2 TIPS

Windows Movie Maker 2 causes me to get on my soapbox. This is exactly the kind of thing that drives me nuts about

It's a Wrap!

movie making with movie maker 2

Microsoft. They create this killer App that blows away similar programs offered on other platforms, but what good does it do? Nobody even knows that it's on their computer. Other platforms out there sell computers just because of this type of software and theirs isn't as good as Movie Maker. I've actually had friends call and ask me to recommend a movie-making program. Good grief! You've got one of the best I've ever used (at any price) sitting right there in front of you. Microsoft will spend tens of millions of dollars marketing a guy in a butterfly costume—which is fine; I don't have a problem with butterflies—but you'd think they could at least drop a couple of million dollars to advertise one of the best things about XP. It's not like they don't have the cash. Windows XP really does let you do amazing things. Wouldn't it be great if Microsoft would actually tell people about it? Okay, thanks for letting me vent, I feel much better. By the way, if you don't have Movie Maker 2, you can download the free upgrade at microsoft.com.

SUPER-SIZE THE STORYBOARD

Movie Maker's Storyboard view is great. It makes creating movies ridiculously easy; however, the default view is really small—too small. Well, you can actually super-size the Storyboard. Grab the Storyboard's separator bar and drag it up to increase the size of your clips. That's much better!

TRIMMING MADE EASY

Trimming your clips can be a little tricky if you try doing it in the default Timeline view. To be more accurate when trimming your clips, zoom in on the Timeline. Click the Zoom In button or press the Page Down key to see a more detailed view of the Timeline, then click a clip to select it, and pull either end to trim it. You can also watch Movie Maker's monitor (Preview window) as a visual indicator while trimming a clip. The monitor will display exactly where you are on the clip as you trim it. To zoom back out on the Timeline, click the Zoom Out button or the Page Up key.

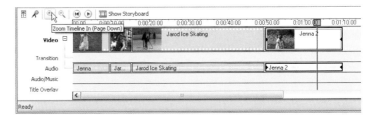

UN-TRIM YOUR CLIPS

Did you get a little carried away trimming your clips? If you did, don't worry, the entire clip is still there. Simply click the clip to select it, drag the trim marker back out, and there's the rest of your clip. Movie Maker doesn't remove the trimmed video from your clips; it only hides it. So, you can always get your original clips back. You can also quickly restore all of your trimmed clips at once by pressing Crtl-Shift-Delete. This shortcut clears all trim marks instantly.

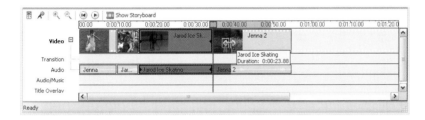

TRIM A PICTURE

By default, Movie Maker will display an inserted still picture for five seconds. Well, this might not work for your movie. Fortunately, you can trim still pictures exactly the same way as video clips. Click the picture and trim it so that it displays for the appropriate amount of time. You can increase or decrease the display time.

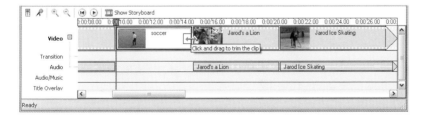

QUICKLY REARRANGE CLIPS

You can rearrange your clips on the Storyboard by simply dragging-and-dropping them in any order you'd like. So, if you decide that the clip on the end of your movie will work better at the beginning, simply drag-and-drop it into place.

 ## CREATE TITLE EFFECTS

Did you know that you could add effects to your titles? You can. Pretty cool, huh? Create a title for your movie by clicking Tasks on the Toolbar then, on the Movie Tasks Pane under Edit Movie, click Make titles or credits.

Next, select the type of title or credit you want to create, and then type your text, but when you're finished, don't click Done. Instead, click the Choose the Title Animations link under More options. Now, select an animation for your title—you have a ton to choose from. After you've selected an animation, click the Done, Add Title to Movie link and your animated title is inserted into your movie.

QUICK CHANGE TITLE TEXT

If you realize you misspelled one or even several words in your title, you don't have to trash it and start all over again. Simply double-click the title in the Storyboard or Timeline view and the Title Pane opens with the title's text displayed and ready to be edited. When you're finished making your corrections, click Done.

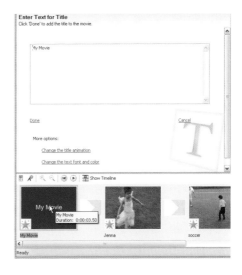

SNAG A STILL SHOT

If you want to capture a still shot from a video clip, you can. Here's how: Use the Timeline or the monitor's (Preview window) Seek Bar to locate the image that you want to capture from your clip, then click the Take Picture icon (see image). Movie Maker will ask you where you'd like to save the picture on your hard drive. Choose a location and click Save in the dialog box. Movie Maker will save the capture as a JPEG and automatically import it into the source clip's Collection. The picture will appear in the Collection's Contents Pane. Now, simply drag-and-drop the picture anywhere on the Storyboard.

FREEZE FRAME

The previous tip is great for snagging still images, but here's a way to put the tip to good use: Create a freeze frame effect for your movie. Split the clip at the same point on the Timeline where you captured the still image by clicking Split Clip on the monitor (Preview window). This splits the clip into two clips on the Timeline. Next, insert the picture that you captured earlier in between the two clips. Now, preview your video. Isn't that a great effect?

 AUDIO ONLY

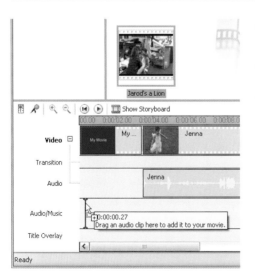

Movie Maker makes it a breeze to use only the audio portion of a video clip. Drag-and-drop the video clip onto the Audio/Music Track of the Timeline. Now, you can see the clip's audio on the Timeline, but there's no video. Very quick and very cool!

GET RID OF THE AUDIO

Well, if you can get rid of the video portion of a clip, it's only fair that you should be able to get rid of a clip's audio and just keep the video, right? Right! Here's how: On the Timeline, right-click the audio portion of your video clip on the Audio Track of the Timeline and click Mute on the Shortcut menu. Now, when you preview your movie, the video clip's sound is removed.

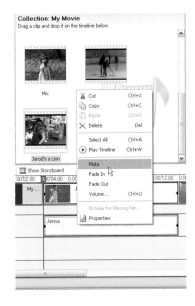

 AUTOMOVIE

Movie Maker is such a great App that you don't have to know how to create a movie. If you're in a hurry, or just don't feel like using the Timeline, then let Movie Maker do it for you. Import your clips into a new or existing Collection. Next, open the Collection so that you can view the Collection's clips in the Contents Pane. Then, click Tools>AutoMovie on the Menu Bar. This opens the AutoMovie Pane, which allows you to select from several different styles for your movie. Select a style, then click Done, Edit Movie. Movie Maker actually creates your movie for you, complete with splits, transitions, titles, and credits. When AutoMovie's finished, the layout of your new movie appears on the Timeline. This allows you to edit any part of the movie quickly, then save it.

ADD BACKGROUND MUSIC

You can add background music to your movie by dragging a music file from the Contents Pane anywhere onto the Audio/Music Track on the Timeline. Then, simply drag the file into position and trim it to match a video clip or your entire movie. Keep in mind that when you add background music to your movie, it plays at a 50/50 volume level with the existing clip or movie's Audio Track. You can, however, adjust the background's audio to play louder or softer than 50/50 by right-clicking the Audio Track on the Timeline and clicking Volume on the Shortcut menu. Now, slide the Volume control in the dialog box to adjust the background's music to play louder or softer, and then click OK.

To add a nice touch to your background music, right-click the background Audio Track and click Fade Out on the Shortcut menu. This will automatically fade out instead of abruptly ending the music at the end of the audio file's Timeline. This technique can also be used to control the volume of any sound effect or narration.

NARRATE YOUR MOVIES

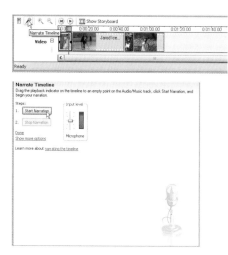

Do you need to explain to your audience what they're seeing? You can by adding narrations to your movie. Here's how: Drag the Timeline slider to the location on your movie where you want to begin the narration. Next, click Narrate Timeline. Then, on the Narrate Timeline Pane, click Start Narration and speak into your computer's microphone. Click Stop Narration when finished. Your narration now appears on the Audio/Music Track on the Timeline.

GETTIN' GEEKY WITH TRANSITIONS

Okay, we all know that you create transitions by simply dragging-and-dropping them into the transition window between clips on the Storyboard. And, you've probably always stopped there, not realizing that you can add some pretty cool effects to transitions. Try this: Highlight a transition on the Storyboard, click Tasks on the Toolbar, then click Make Titles or Credits on the Movie Tasks Pane. Next, click Add Title on the Selected Clip in the Timeline, then type your text, and add a title animation. When you're finished, click Done, Add Title to Movie, and you've just applied text and text animations to a transition.

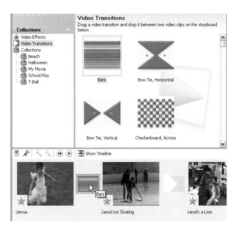

 ## CROSS-FADE CLIPS

This is my favorite hidden-effects trick in Movie Maker. You can cross-fade any two clips to add a truly professional transition between them, and it's really easy. Here's how to do it: Grab a clip on

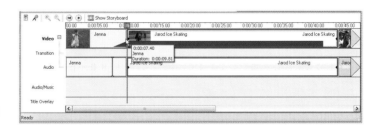

the Timeline and drag it onto the clip directly to the left. You'll see a blue transition bar that indicates the length of the cross-fade. When you have the clip where you want it, drop it. Now, preview your movie. Check out that transition. Very nice!

 DOUBLE TIME

Smudge Stick   Speed Up, Double

Here's a nice way to speed things up. You can double the playback speed of any clip on the Storyboard by applying the Speed Up, Double effect to a clip. To add the effect, click Tasks on the Toolbar and click View Video Effects on the Movie Tasks Pane. Then, drag-and-drop the Speed Up, Double effect onto a clip on the Storyboard. Now preview your movie. That's fast, isn't it?

Want to make it play even faster? Apply the effect again. You reapply effects to clips (up to six times) by repeatedly dragging-and-dropping them onto a clip.

This technique is actually useful and works especially well when lightening a clip by using the Brightness, Increase effect. Keep applying the effect to increase the brightness of a dark clip.

 GETTING PRECISE WITH THE TIMELINE

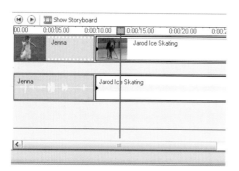

Press-and-hold the Alt key and then press the left or right arrow key to move the Timeline forward or backward exactly one frame at a time. This allows you to trim your clips to precise locations on the Timeline and helps to identify the best frame of a video clip for still-shot captures.

BACK TO THE BEGINNING

You'll find when creating movies that you're constantly stopping and then restarting previews, and it can only help to do this quickly. So, to jump back to the beginning of your movies, press Ctrl-Q or the Home key. Both of these shortcuts will quickly return the Timeline to the beginning of your movie.

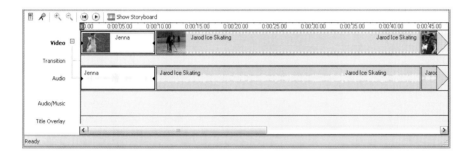

 ## QUICK FADES

Fade In and Fade Out are a couple of my favorite effects and apparently they're also favorites of the Movie-Maker programmers, because they gave us a quick shortcut to them. To add a fade-in or fade-out effect to your clips quickly, simply right-click any clip on the Storyboard or Timeline and click Fade In, Fade Out, or both on the Shortcut menu. Preview your movie to see the effect.

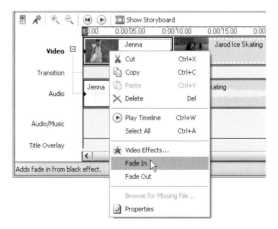

 DON'T SPLIT MY CLIP

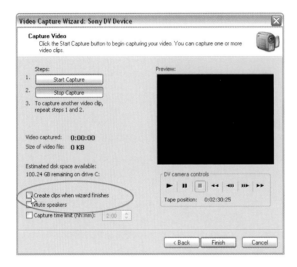

By default, Movie Maker automatically separates your video into multiple clips as they're imported into a Collection. You can avoid this by clearing the Create Clips When Wizard Finishes checkbox on the Video Capture Wizard. Now, your video will be imported as a single video clip.

 DO-IT-YOURSELF CLIPS

Okay, you used the previous tip to import your video into Movie Maker as a single clip; but now you've realized that there are several places throughout the movie where you'd like to create transitions and apply special effects. What are you going to do? Don't worry, try this: Simply drag the Timeline to the location on your movie where you'd like to insert a transition or special effect and click Split Clip on the monitor (Preview window). This splits the movie into two clips on the Timeline. Repeat this as many times as necessary to create as many clips as you want.

SHARE YOUR CLIPS

Movie Maker lets you share clips between your Collections. For example, let's say you have five Collections of imported video clips and you want to use a few clips from each Collection to make a movie. Well, you can and here's how: Click Collections on the Toolbar, then right-click the Collections folder on the Collections Pane and click New Collection on the Shortcut menu. Next, name your new folder and just start dragging-and-dropping clips from other Collections into your new Collections folder. Now your clips are sorted and ready to be made into a movie. *Note*: You can drag-and-drop copies of a clip by holding the Ctrl key when moving them into the new folder. This keyboard tip copies the clip to the new folder instead of just moving it.

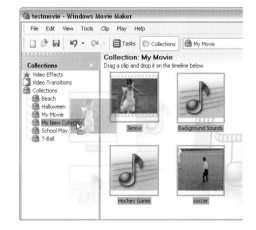

Hacked Off

Those Annoying Things You Do →

There's not a lot about XP that really annoys me, but the things that do, really do. It's amazing what sets me

Hacked Off

those annoying things you do

off. I can just be doing my thing in XP and open a search and BAM! There's that dog, just sittin' there waggin' his tail. What does this puppy have to do with searching my computer? Once again, those engineers over at Microsoft are "cute-ing" me to death. If you want to impress me, stick a Tomahawk Cruise missile on there. Now, that's my kind of search. Come on guys, show a little attitude for cryin' out loud.

In this chapter, I've also thrown in a few tips on how to really tweak your friends. I have to admit I started to get a little carried away here and had to scale it back. I realized that I could do some really mean things to someone's computer and had nightmares for a week. I mean really, how could anyone do those kinds of things, and to a computer? It was awful. I'm not proud of myself.

 ## YES, I REALLY WANT TO DELETE

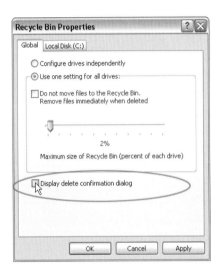

Oh, I appreciate the fact that Windows thinks I may have been kidding when I tried deleting that file, but it's just gotta stop asking me. Once and for all—Yes, Yes, Yes, I really want to delete that! Here's how to show Windows that you're serious too. Right-click the Recycle Bin's icon and click Properties on the Shortcut menu. Next, click the Global tab in the dialog box, uncheck Display Delete Confirmation Dialog, and then click Apply.

 ## I KNOW, I INSTALLED IT

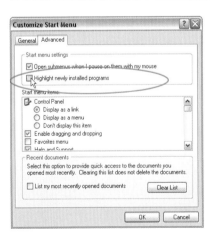

Have you noticed that XP highlights newly installed programs on the All Programs menu? Isn't that nervy? This one really gets me; I know I've installed a program. I did it, and I even know where it's located. Yep, believe it or not, I've used Windows before. I really wish Microsoft would stop assuming that we've never used Windows before. Honestly, how many people out there are brand-new to Windows, maybe 20 or so? Well, let's turn this off and maybe I won't feel like my OS thinks I'm an idiot.

Right-click Start and click Properties on the Shortcut menu. Click the Start Menu tab in the dialog box and click Customize. Next, click the Advanced tab, uncheck Highlight Newly Installed Programs, then click OK.

STOP PRINTING

Don't ever try to get to your
Printer's folder to stop a print job.
You'll never make it in time. It's
buried somewhere in the Control
Panel. By the time you get there,
your printer will have already
finished printing, sorting, stapling,

and stacking your documents. Fortunately, there's a much faster way.

When you send files to your printer you'll notice a Printer icon appears in the Taskbar's
Notification Area. Double-click this icon, which will open your Printer folder. Now right-
click the print job that you want to stop and click Cancel on the Shortcut menu.

 ## DON'T REPORT ME

By default, XP will request that you send an error
report to Microsoft whenever you experience a
problem. Yikes, why in the world would anyone
want to do this? I don't know how to explain exactly
why I think this is a bad idea and be kind, so I
won't. Let me just say that I really don't know how
an error with my computer's OS and software is
going to help Microsoft produce a better product.
So, I'm going to politely decline and turn this feature off so that I don't have a mini-meltdown every
time I see it.

If you'd like to avoid mini-meltdowns too, do the
following: Click Start then the Control Panel. Next,
click Performance and Maintenance>System, then
click the Advanced tab in the dialog box, and click
Error Reporting. Now, select Disable Error Reporting
and click OK.

 ## A LESS-FRIENDLY SEARCH

As discussed in this chapter's introduction, the Search puppy has to go. Here's how: Click Start then Search. Next, click the Change Preferences link under What Do You Want to Search For? and then click Without an Animated Search Character. See ya, pooch.

 ## I'LL UPDATE MYSELF

I kind of resent being interrupted by my computer, especially to inform me about updates. I mean, if my computer's going to interrupt me, make it good and tell me it's time for lunch, not that there may be some nondescript update available for my OS. I'd rather have my computer scanned for needed updates when I choose. There's just something freaky about my OS doing this in the background. I prefer to check for updates manually. If you do too, click Start then Control Panel. Next, click Performance and Maintenance>System. Now, click the Automatic Updates tab in the dialog box, uncheck Keep My Computer Up to Date..., then click OK.

NO MORE POP-UPS

XP is a power-user's OS, but I really don't think
the developers at Microsoft get this. All the little
"helpful" extras, such as pop-up descriptions in XP,
just seem unnecessary. They're more in the way
and a distraction than helpful, but at least you can
turn 'em off. Click Start then Control Panel. Next,
click Appearance and Themes, and then Folder
Options. Click the View tab in the dialog box,
scroll the Advanced settings and uncheck Show
Pop-Up Description for Folder and Desktop Items,
then click OK.

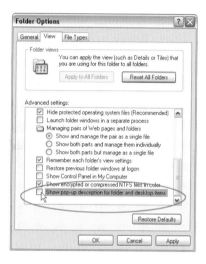

 ## BIGGER, SMALLER—THEY'RE THE SAME

Double-click the volume icon in the Taskbar's
Notification Area. You see your Volume Control,
right? Now, press Ctrl-S and you see a much
smaller Volume Control, right? What's up with
that? It's exactly the same volume control only
smaller. Why is this even an option?

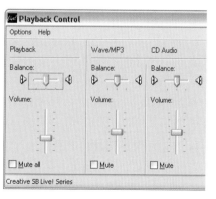

I'M DISTRACTED

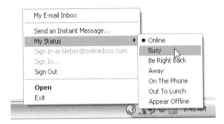

Windows Messenger is a killer App! I use it constantly. There's only one problem though. Everyone I know also uses it constantly, and if I'm online, everyone knows it. Now, I'm easily distracted—I don't know why, but it's a problem. So, if people start sending me instant messages, before you know it, I'm chatting away completely forgetting about whatever I was working on.

Well, you can change your online status to help prevent this type of distraction by right-clicking the Windows Messenger icon in the Taskbar's Notification Area. Next, point to My Status and click Busy on the Shortcut menu. Now, Messenger is still available to you, but you won't be distracted by incoming messages.

 WHY WOULD I WANT TO RESTART?

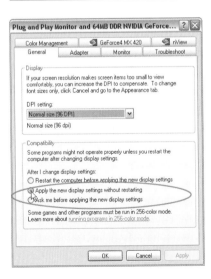

Have you ever changed your Display settings and been asked to restart your computer before applying the new settings? Yeah, me too. Of course I don't want to restart my computer. I'd rather lick the sidewalk than restart my computer. Do you know how long that takes? Way too long. That's how long. As a matter of fact, Windows should never do anything to my computer that forces me to restart. I cringe every time I even consider turning off my computer. In fact, I usually don't turn it off, just to avoid having to turn it back on. If you get this should-be-error message when you change your Display settings, do this: Right-click the Desktop and click Properties on the Shortcut menu. Next, click the Settings tab in the dialog box and click Advanced. Click the General tab, select Apply the New Display Settings Without Restarting, then click OK.

BEAT YOUR CD PLAYER TO THE PUNCH

Here's a new annoying feature, courtesy of XP. When you insert a CD, you get an AutoPlay dialog box that pops up asking what you'd like to do with the CD and listing several options, depending on the CD's contents. Well, thanks for holding my hand through this whole inserting-the-CD thing, but I think I'd rather go it alone. But that's just me. I'm a rebel. If you're a rebel too and prefer to go it alone, then you can beat XP to the punch and tell it what to do with your CDs before you insert them. Click Start then My Computer. Right-click your CD drive's icon and click Properties on the Shortcut menu. Now, click the AutoPlay tab in the dialog box and click Select an action to perform. Use the drop-down menu to select different CD types and then assign an action to them. Now, when you insert a CD you won't see the AutoPlay pop-up.

 WHY CAN'T I DRAG-AND-DROP IT? YOU CAN, BUT IT'S WEIRD

A friend called me with a problem he was having and I have to admit, it baffled me for a couple of minutes. He opened the Desktop Toolbar on the Taskbar and tried to drag-and-drop files to it, but couldn't. I thought,

"Rookie," until I tried it and it didn't work for me either. But, how could this be? Sure it's a Toolbar, but it's still a folder (Desktop or not). I shouldn't have any trouble dragging files to it. Well, I discovered that you can, it's just a little weird. Start by opening the Desktop Toolbar—right-click the Taskbar, point to Toolbars, and click Desktop. Now, open a folder and try dragging any file onto the Toolbar. You can't, but here's the trick: Move the file to the right of the word "Desktop," now you can drop it. Why can't you just drop it on the folder's name? I have no idea. Annoying isn't it?

 SCIENTIFIC CALCULATOR?

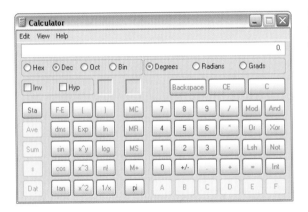

Have you ever used a Scientific Calculator? Do you know anyone who has ever used a Scientific Calculator? What the heck is a Scientific Calculator? Did you even know that you have a Scientific Calculator? Yes, you do. You can see it by opening the Calculator and clicking View>Scientific. Now, hurry, close it. If you look at it long enough it'll make you feel stupid. That's just annoying.

 ANNOY OTHERS—FREAKY DESKTOP

This is mild but very freaky. Right-click the Desktop, point to Arrange Icons By, and click (uncheck) Show Desktop Icons. Now, they're gone! Freaky, isn't it? This should keep 'em guessing for a while. If they figure it out, you can keep the fun going; just reapply it every time they leave the room.

ANNOY OTHERS—MY DOCUMENTS ARE GONE!

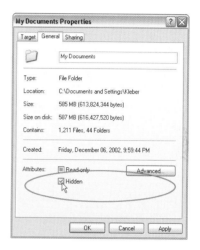

Have you ever seen your friend or co-worker completely dazed and confused? If not, it's probably about time that you did. This look can easily be achieved by hiding My Documents. Click Start, then right-click My Documents, and click Properties on the Shortcut menu. Next, click the General tab in the dialog box, check Hidden, then click OK. When the confirmation dialog pops up, select Apply changes to this folder, subfolders, and files, and click OK.

Now, here's what gets 'em every time. Even though you told Windows to hide the My Documents folder, it won't. (I don't know why.) So, because he can see the folder, your friend will never think that it could simply be that the folder "somehow" became hidden. But every folder and file in My Documents is hidden. In other words, gone! Yep, he's starting to get that dazed and confused look. Can you see it?

 ### ANNOY OTHERS—NOTHING BUT SHORTCUT MENUS

Want to get a co-worker on the bad side of your IT person? Switch her mouse buttons. Now every time, she clicks the left-mouse button, all she'll get is a Shortcut menu. She'll think that her mouse has gone bad, for sure. After the IT person tries two or three mice without fixing the problem and figures out what's really happening, it'll be too late for your friend. The tech won't think it's funny. Yep, it'll be a cold day in you-know-where before she gets assistance again. In fact, she might just be working on a 386 (very old and crappy) machine by the end of the week.

To switch the mouse buttons, click Start then Control Panel. Next, click Printers and Other Hardware>Mouse. Now, depending on the mouse driver, click the Buttons tab in the dialog box, click Switch the Primary and Secondary Buttons, and then click OK.

ANNOY OTHERS—CAN YOU SEE ME NOW?

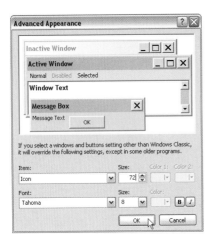

You know, I think the icons on my friend's Desktop are just too small. Yeah, way too small, let's amp 'em up and see what happens. Will he buy a new video card, a new monitor, re-install Windows, or see an eye doctor? Let's try it and find out. Right-click the Desktop and click Properties on the Shortcut menu. Next, click the Appearance tab in the dialog box and click Advanced. Select Icon on the Item menu, crank-up the size (up to 72 pixels), then click OK. Wow, those are pretty big icons. I'm guessing a re-install is in order.

 ANNOY OTHERS—SHUT DOWN AT STARTUP

Here's an annoying tip that could actually give someone an ulcer. In Chapter 5, I showed you how to create a shutdown shortcut for your Desktop ("Shortcut to Shut Down"). Well, let's have some fun with a co-worker. *Important: Make absolutely certain that you can start their computer in Safe Mode before attempting this, or it won't be funny at all.*

Copy the Shutdown Shortcut and paste it into his Start-up folder, usually located at C:\Documents and Settings\ User Name\Start Menu\Programs\Startup. Now, every time he starts up his computer, it will immediately shut down as soon as Windows tries to launch. He'll never be able to launch Windows. Pretty funny, huh? Actually, this isn't really that funny. At least not to your victim, so please make sure that you're close by when he starts pounding on his computer and cussing the Internet for giving him a virus.

To undo this, you'll have to launch Windows in Safe Mode (usually by pressing F8 as the computer starts up). After Windows has launched in Safe Mode, delete the file from Startup and restart the computer.

ANNOY OTHERS—LAUNCH EVERYTHING AT ONCE

This isn't damaging but it is annoying. She'll be pushing keys left and right trying to stop this deluge of Apps. It cracks me up every time. Similar to the previous tip, copy shortcuts of as many Apps as possible and put them in your friend's Startup folder. The more you put in there, the funnier it is—trust me on this. You just can't launch too many Apps at the same time—on your friend's computer that is. It's not funny at all on your computer.

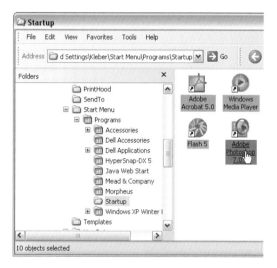

Doh!

TROUBLESHOOTING

TIPS

Okay, I'm sure Windows has never crashed on you or caused you any problems; but when (I mean if) you ever do have a

Doh!

troubleshooting . . . smash forehead on keyboard to continue

problem, it's your fault. Please step away from the computer. You clearly have no idea what you're doing. Just kidding! You can sit back down. There's just nothing good about troubleshooting. We don't want to do it and feel that we shouldn't have to anyway. My computer's supposed to work perfectly—all the time! It's not as if I did anything to cause this. (Keyboards are supposed to be waterproof, right?) Well, I have only two pieces of advice when it comes to troubleshooting. First, be patient; whatever the problem, you can fix it. Secondly, don't actually smash your forehead on the keyboard. It doesn't work. I've tried it. I just got a nasty bump and it didn't fix a thing.

THREE-FINGER SALUTE

Folks, if you remember only one keyboard shortcut in XP, this is the one, because eventually you're gonna need it. This tip is truly for those of you who are new to Windows. Everyone else who's been using Windows for at least six months has already learned the Windows Ctrl-Alt-Delete three-finger salute. This is not what I'd consider a killer tip; however I just wouldn't feel that I was doing my job if I didn't include it. It's been too much a part of my life to leave out. So, here we go.

Believe it or not, eventually a program might freeze on you or Windows will just inexplicably stop responding. When this happens, press Ctrl-Alt-Delete on your keyboard. This opens the Windows Task Manager. Now, click the Applications tab in the dialog box and select the program that's not responding, then click End Task. If this still doesn't do the trick, you can shut down by clicking Shut Down>Restart on the Task Manager's Menu Bar.

WHERE'S MY SCANDISK?

I was probably using Windows XP for about two weeks before I went looking for the comfort of my trusted ScanDisk. I thought I was going to be sick—I couldn't find it. ScanDisk wasn't there. Well, I'm here to save you from going through this trauma. ScanDisk isn't included in Windows XP; instead you get the improved Check Disk tool. You can use the Error-Checking tool to check for system file errors and bad sectors on your hard drives. To use Check Disk, click Start>My Computer, then right-click the hard drive you want to check, and click Properties on the Shortcut menu. Next, click the Tools tab in the dialog box and click Check Now (under Error Checking).

KNOWLEDGE CAN MAKE YOU SMARTER

Without a doubt, the best feature in the Help and Support Center is its online access to Microsoft's Knowledge Base. The Knowledge Base is Help on steroids—its über-Help. Just about any kind of problem you're having with Windows has probably been addressed here. Which is great, but what's really useful is its hidden power. You can use the Knowledge Base to find help for practically any software title that Microsoft develops. Here's how: Click Start>Help and Support and click the Set Search Options link directly under the Search text box. Next, click to expand the menu for Microsoft Knowledge Base and select the program that you need help with. Now, uncheck Suggested Topics and Full-Text Search Matches to search only the Knowledge Base, then type a search term, and click the Start Searching arrow button. There ya go, instant help for all of your favorite software. Just keep in mind that you must be online to search Microsoft's Knowledge Base.

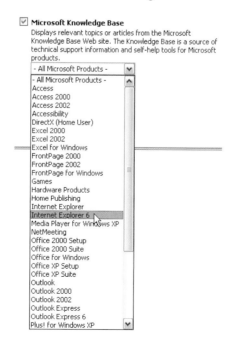

AM I CONNECTED?

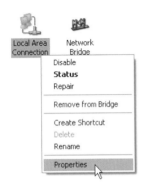

There's a really quick way to tell whether your connection to the Internet or network is active: View its status in the Taskbar's Notification area. Click Start>My Network Places and click View Network Connections under Network Tasks. Next, right-click the Local Area Connection or any network icon and click Properties on the Shortcut menu. Check Show Icon in Notification Area When Connected, and then click OK. Now, you can view your network connections on the Taskbar. You'll never be left hanging again. If your Web page isn't loading or if you're not able to access files on the server, you'll know whether it's your computer melting down, or it's simply a bad connection. And you'll know it instantly, as both monitors on the Connections icon light up when the connection is active. You won't have to stare at a blank Web page or watch your hourglass spin for five minutes before figuring out that you may not be connected.

GIVE IT A BOOST

Remember when Mom would remind you to clean your room? You hated it, didn't you? Well, I'm here to bring back the good ol' days because I'm definitely gonna get after you to clean your computer. Over time, your computer can get cluttered with all kinds of junk, much like toys under the bed and dirty clothes in the closet—you can't necessarily see the mess, but it's there. Disk Cleanup can free up a ton of space by searching your hard drive for files, such as unnecessary program files, temporary files, and cached Internet files, and deleting them. To run Disk Cleanup, click Start>All Programs>Accessories>System Tools>Disk Cleanup For, then select the drive you want to clean, and click OK. The search will return a list of files that can be deleted safely. Click OK to delete the files.

FEELING SLUGGISH?

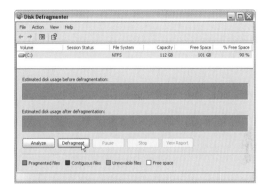

If Windows begins to get sluggish, you probably need to defrag your hard drive. As you install and remove programs, add files and delete files, your hard drive can become a little fragmented—this means that parts of your files and Apps become a little scattered on your drive. This makes your hard drive take longer to locate files and respond more slowly. You can get Windows back up to speed by running Disk Defragmenter and getting your files back together. Here's how: Click Start>All Programs>Accessories>SystemTools>Disk Defragmenter. Now, select the drive you want to defrag and click Defragment. Oh, by the way, it's a good idea to plan your vacation around this—it might actually be finished when you get back. In other words, it takes a long time.

 WE'RE COMPATIBLE

You love XP, but you're simply devastated that you can no longer run your favorite game—*Invasion of the Mutant Space Bats of Doom*, an actual game made for Windows 95. Well, bring back the Bats! They can invade once again. You've just got to make your old game compatible. You can get older games and programs to run on XP by using the Program Compatibility Wizard. The Wizard lets you test your older programs in different Windows environments; in other words, if you have a program designed to run in Windows 95, then you can set its compatibility mode to Windows 95 so that it runs in XP.

To set a program's compatibility, click Start>All Programs>Accessories>Program Compatibility Wizard. When the Wizard opens, simply follow the instructions to select your program and set its compatibility.

 IT COULD BE HUNG UP

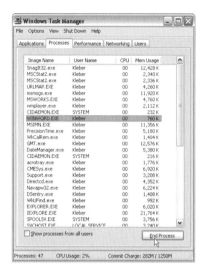

Have you ever tried to launch a program and nothing happened. Tried it again—nothin'! Again—nothin'! Well, don't start reinstalling the program just yet. It might simply be hung up. The next time this happens, press Ctrl-Alt-Delete to open Task Manager. Click the Processes tab in the dialog box, select the App that you were trying to launch, and click End Process. Now, try to launch the program again.

 SAVE SEARCHES

You go through a lot of trouble to search for something on your computer. You may have to perform several different searches using various keywords to find what you're looking for. Of course, just as soon as you close the search window, you wish you hadn't, because you can't remember where the file was, and you can't remember how you found it to begin with. Well, that bites! Fortunately, this will never happen to you again, because you're going to save your search results. Here's how: Click Start>Search and perform a search (for whatever). Once you've found the desired results, click File>Save Search on the Menu Bar. Now, pick a location on your hard drive to save your search results and click Save.

HELP AND SUPPORT FAVORITES

You already know how
frustrating and time-
consuming locating files
using Search can be, but
have you ever searched
for info using XP's Help
and Support Center? Oh
yeah, this is user friendly!
You could be digging for
hours before you find what you're looking for. Apparently the developers at Microsoft knew
this, because they were kind enough to give Help and Support its own Favorite—I bet you
never noticed it. Try this: Once you've finally finished a search, don't close the window;
you'll never find it again. Instead, click Add to Favorites, which will save your search
results to Help and Support's Favorites. Now, to get back to your search results, simply
open the Help and Support Center, click Favorites on the Toolbar, and there it is.

I CAN'T MOVE MY TOOLBARS

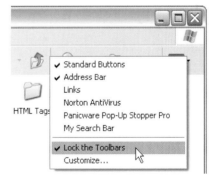

Can't move your Toolbars? There's a simple
explanation for this: You're using a pirated copy
of XP and Microsoft's been notified. Yep, you're a
criminal—just kidding. (I bet that made a couple
of you sweat.) Actually, your Toolbars are locked,
so right-click the Windows Taskbar or the Toolbar
that's giving you trouble and uncheck Lock the
Toolbars on the Shortcut menu. Now, you should
be able to move them wherever you'd like. If you
still can't move 'em, then you really are using a
pirated copy of XP and you're a bad person.

I WISH I COULD GO BACK

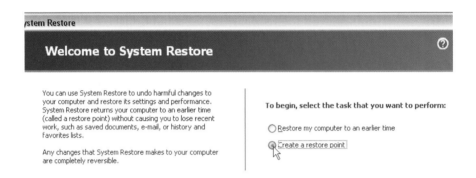

This is a simple task that can save you tons of frustration and make you look like a genius. Before installing or removing programs, or making significant changes to your Operating System (OS), you should consider creating a Restore Point. A Restore Point saves the state of your computer at the time you create it. So, when you download and install that must-have beta game from the Internet on your office server and it brings down the entire network, you can quickly restore the computer to the way it was before you installed the game. You can go back. Your boss will think you're a complete idiot for installing it in the first place, but she'll think you're a genius for covering your you-know-what by creating a Restore Point first.

Here's how to do it: Click Start>Help and Support and click System Restore (under Additional Resources), which launches the System Restore Wizard. Now, select Create a Restore Point, click Next, then give your Restore Point a name, and click Create. Now, if the changes you made to your computer cause problems, simply come back to the same Wizard and select Restore My Computer to an Earlier Time, and select your Restore Point to get back to normal.

PROTECT FILES FROM SYSTEM RESTORE

When is using System Restore to restore your computer a bad thing? When it removes files and folders that you wanted to keep. Any new files or folders that were added to your computer after the Restore date you select are subject to removal. This is not the point of System Restore. You can protect files from System Restore, however, by moving any files that you feel

may be affected by a System Restore to your My Documents folder. System Restore doesn't affect the My Documents folder; that is, whatever's in My Documents before a system restore will still be there afterward.

DON'T JUST CLICK OK

I bet you've received an error message in Windows and tried to remember what it read (which never works), or quickly looked for a pen to write down the error. We all have. I also bet that the entire time you were writing, you were thinking, "There's got to be a better way to do this." Well you were right. There is a better way to do this; you just didn't know about it until now.

The next time an error dialog box pops up, press Ctrl-C. This keyboard shortcut copies the text of the error message. Open Notepad, WordPad, or any text editor, and paste the error's message (Ctrl-V). Now you can save the message for reference. This really comes in handy when contacting technical support or when using Microsoft's Knowledge Base for help, because you can use keywords, specific error numbers, or codes from the error message to help identify the problem.

SAVE THE BLUE SCREEN OF DEATH

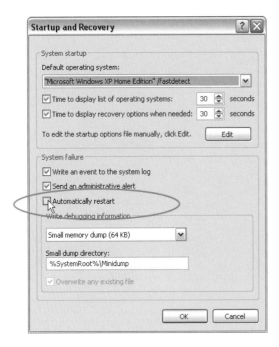

When things really go bad in Windows, you're going to get the worst of all errors: the Stop error—also known as the Blue Screen of Death. This is usually caused by a bad device driver and can be frightening the first time you see it. But don't be afraid; it tells you exactly what the problem is. Depending on your setup, the Stop error will quickly disappear and your computer will automatically restart. Well, that's just great! Not only is the error in geek-speak, but it also disappeared as you were writing it down.

Let's stop the insanity and make the Blue Screen of Death work for us. First, turn off Automatic Restart under System Failure by clicking Start>Control Panel>Performance and Maintenance>System, then clicking the Advanced tab in the dialog box. Next, click Settings under Startup and Recovery, uncheck Automatically Restart, then click OK. Now, the Stop error will appear indefinitely. The next time you receive a Stop error, make special note of the error's name, code, and driver details. Use this information when contacting technical support or when searching Microsoft's Knowledge Base.

HOW MUCH SPACE DO I NEED?

Here's a simple tip that will save you a lot of time and aggravation. A standard CD will hold 650 MB of data, so before you begin copying files to your CD/RW drive, calculate how much disk space you're going to need. If your files are all contained in a single folder, right-click the folder, click Properties on the Shortcut menu, then click the General tab in the dialog box, and look at the folder's size. This will tell you exactly how large the combined files in the folder are. If your files exceed 650 MB, you'll know it beforehand and can make adjustments before you start copying to your CD.

 TRASH THE GARBAGE

You know, I've never really understood the purpose of the Windows Temp folder. I mean, I get why it's there and what it does; I just don't understand why it holds onto files like grim death. Basically, just about any time you install new software, Windows shuts down improperly, or a program or Windows crashes, files will be created in the Windows Temp folder. These files are useless. You can safely delete them without damaging Windows. There's my point: Why in the world doesn't Windows do a better job of eliminating this garbage? If Windows ever begins giving you trouble, check your Windows Temp folders. I've actually seen thousands of files in Temp folders consuming Gigs of drive space. That's just crazy!

Your Temp folders are in two locations, C:\Windows\Temp and C:\Documents and Settings\Username\Local Settings\Temp. Local Settings, under Documents and Settings, is hidden by default, so you'll have to enable Show Hidden Files and Folders in Folder Options to see this folder. Anyway, navigate to these Temp folders and delete the files inside them. If you've never visited your Temp folders before, you'll probably be shocked at what you find.

PREFETCH?

Windows is at it again. The Temp folders just weren't eating up enough of your hard drive space, so Microsoft's developers thought it would be a good idea to create more folders that do basically the same thing. Hey, thanks! No, really, thanks. We can't possibly have enough disk-eating folders. And to make it worse, they're giving them new names. Yeah, they know that we're onto the whole Temp folder thing, so this new one's called Prefetch.

Prefetch functions differently from the Windows Temp folder; however, like the Temp folders, it will hang on to your Trash forever—if you let it. Prefetch tends to get pretty cluttered with Application files no longer being used, so you should occasionally empty this folder. (You should find Prefetch at C:Windows\Prefetch.) And, don't worry; you can't damage Windows by removing these files. Any deleted files that Windows needs will be re-created automatically.

 10% IS TOO MUCH

Do you need more disk space? I do too. We all do. Well, believe it or not, your Recycle Bin does more than eat your Trash; it steals your disk space too. By default, Windows reserves a whopping 10% of your hard drive for your Recycle Bin. Yeah, 10%! My hard drive is a little larger than 100 GB. Now, I'm not Stephen Hawking, but I can quickly calculate—even without breaking out the scientific calculator—that my Recycle Bin has reserved more than 10 GB of my hard drive to hold my Trash. My first network of computers didn't have that much disk space. And if you don't routinely empty your Recycle Bin, you could very quickly be using Gigs of disk space without even realizing it.

I just want a Trash can, not an entire landfill. So, let's see if we can't reclaim a little (or a lot) of this disk space. Right-click the Recycle Bin and click Properties on the Shortcut menu. Next, click the Global tab in the dialog box and move the slider to a more reasonable percentage, say 1% or 2%, then click OK.

STAY UP TO DATE WITH UPDATE

Windows Update is the single best tool for maintaining your computer's performance. Windows Update will automatically scan your system and inform you of OS, driver, and critical updates available for your computer. Once Windows Update scans your system, it returns a list of recommended updates that you can select to install. This really is a great feature that will leave you wishing everything in Windows worked this well. You can check for updates by clicking Start>Control Panel>Windows Update—located under See Also on the Tasks Panel. Once Windows Update launches, click the Scan for Updates link to begin. You must be online to use Windows Update.

 ## I FORGOT MY PASSWORD, NOW WHAT?

Okay, this is always pure torture. You've forgotten your password, and now you can't get into Windows—nice. Well, you can either reinstall Windows or insert your password disk to create a new password and get back into Windows. Oh, you didn't create a password-reset disk, did you? That's really too bad because if you had, you'd be in Windows by now. Instead, you're hunting for your Windows install disk, because you're probably going to have to reinstall your OS to get out of this one.

Sounds kind of bad, doesn't it? Let's go ahead and prevent this agony and create a password-reset disk. Click Start>Control Panel>User Accounts, then click your user account name. Next, click the Prevent a Forgotten Password link under Related Tasks on the Tasks Panel. This launches the Forgotten Password Wizard. Follow the directions for creating your reset disk. Now, if you forget your password, you'll only be hunting down your reset disk not the Windows install disk.

 WHAT'S THE PROCESS?

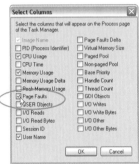

When an error occurs in Windows, the first place you should look for answers is in the Windows Task Manager. When you have a problem, check your Processes. Press Ctrl-Alt-Delete to launch the Task Manager, then click the Processes tab. The info listed here is fairly useful—you can check your CPU and memory usage for running programs—but what you may not be aware of is that you can get additional statistics on the Processes page. Click View>Select Columns on the Menu Bar, now check whatever additional details you want to add, then click OK. My personal favorites are Page Faults and Peak Memory Usage. These details can offer an enormous amount of info to help you identify problems.

 SPECIAL EVENTS

Every time an error occurs in Windows, it's saved. These error records are extremely valuable when troubleshooting problems—they actually make sense. You can view these records by clicking Start>Control Panel>Performance and Maintenance> Administrative Tools>Event Viewer. Windows saves errors in three Log Files: Application, Security, and System. Click any of the three Log Files to view saved errors in the appropriate pane. Now when you have a problem, make note of the date and time the error occurred, then check the Event Viewer for errors that were saved at the same time. Most recorded events are informational, but pay close attention to "Error" and "Warning" entries. Once you identify the correct error entry, use its information to search Microsoft's Knowledge Base for help.

I'M A NETWORK GURU

Have you ever had a problem with your computer's network connections? Did you feel completely helpless? Of course you did. You have no idea where to begin to figure out a networking problem. We're not supposed to understand this stuff—networking problems are for engineers and IT personnel. Well, actually there's a little-known tool in Windows that can help you discover exactly what your network problem is.

The next time you lose connectivity to the Internet or your network, click Start> All Programs>Accessories>System Tools> System Information, then click Tools>Net Diagnostics on the Menu Bar. Next, click the Scan Your System link. The scan pings your DNS servers, SMTP and POP3 mail servers, and gateways; checks your modems and network adapters; and provides a ton of other network info.

So next time you have a network problem, you can go to your IT person and say, "I'm not receiving a reply from the DHCP server or my Inbound Mail server when I ping them. It's probably a problem with my network adapter. Could you get on that as soon as you get a chance?" Then just turn and walk away, knowing that the guy's jaw just hit the floor. It's always fun stickin' to the IT guy!

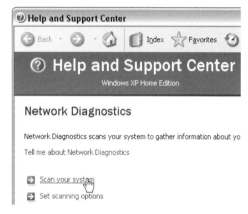

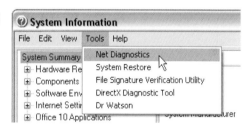

Feeling Fearless?

WINDOWS XP
REGISTRY HACKS

WARNING! CAUTION! 911! Got your attention? Good! This chapter is for what I would consider advanced users of

Feeling Fearless?

windows xp registry hacks

Windows XP. Do not attempt any of these tips unless you know and completely understand what you're doing. Just like I would never dip myself in honey and run naked through a killer bee farm, I would never joke around about Windows Registry. It's mean, it's nasty, and it will make you cry. There's nothing worse than booting up to a blank, gray screen. I've seen it happen, and, yes, they cried. So, if you're not familiar with Windows Registry, if you've never seen, much less used, Registry Editor, or if you feel uncomfortable in any way editing your Registry, then close the book...you're finished. I hope you enjoyed it.

Okay, the warning's over. Are you still with me? Alright! Let's get to it. This chapter has some of my favorite and most popular Registry hacks. So, enjoy! And, oh yeah, be careful! I'm not kidding—they actually cried!

 BACK UP YOUR REGISTRY

This is your official warning: Back up your Windows Registry before making any changes to it. There are several ways to back up your Registry; however, the best is to use Backup. By default, the Windows Backup utility is not preinstalled on XP Home Edition, so you're going to have to install it. You can find it on your Windows XP Home Edition CD-ROM in the ValueAdd folder. Also, you should create a Restore Point. Again, do not make any changes to your Registry before backing it up. So, in case you're not quite getting it...back up your Registry. Okay? Okay!

 REGISTRY FAVORITES

Right off the bat, this is gonna save you a ton of time. Navigating Registry keys to find just the right attribute can take time and more than a few steps, but fortunately your Registry has its own Favorites. So, once you've finally arrived at your destination, click Favorites on the Menu Bar, and then click Add to Favorites. Next, give your location a name and click OK. Now, any time you want to get back to that attribute, it's just one click away instead of 20.

I PREFER TRASH

By default, you can't rename the Recycle Bin. That stinks (no pun intended)! I really want to rename my Recycle Bin to Trash. It just makes more sense to me. Well, we've gotta do something about this.

To rename your Recycle Bin, click Start>Run, then type "regedit" (without quotes) in the dialog box, and click OK. This launches Windows Registry Editor. Navigate to "HKEY_CLASSES_ROOT\CLSID\{645FF040-5081-101B-9F08-00AA002F954E}\ShellFolder." Next, double-click Attributes in the right pane to open the Attributes dialog box. You'll see a data value of "0000 40 01 00 20." Highlight the 40, then change the 40 to 50 so that the Value Data looks like "0000 50 01 00 20," then click OK. Also, make certain that the Call for Attributes data value is

set to 0x00000000 (0), by double-clicking it and typing 0 (zero) as its Value Data if necessary. Now, right-click your Desktop and click Refresh on the Shortcut menu. Now right-click the Recycle Bin and you now have Rename as an option on the Shortcut menu. If you want to get rid of Rename on your Shortcut menu, change back the Attributes Value Data from 50 to 40.

IT'S ALL IN THE NAME

Are you selling your computer or did your company just change names? Whatever the reason, you may actually need to update the registered owner of your system's OS eventually. Here's how: Open Registry Editor and navigate to HKEY_LOCAL_MACHINE\SOFTWARE\Microsoft\Windows NT\CurrentVersion. In the right

pane, double-click RegisteredOrganization. Now, type your new name in the Value Data text field in the dialog box then click OK. Repeat the process for RegisteredOwner.

SPEEDIER MENUS

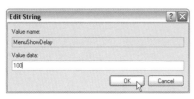

This is a hack I always use. Have you ever noticed the delay before the Start and All Programs menus expand. If you haven't, try it. See how it takes a second or two for the menu to expand once you've pointed to it? Well, you can speed this up. Open Registry Editor and navigate to HKEY_CURRENT_USER\Control Panel\Desktop. Next, double-click MenuShowDelay in the right pane, and then change the Value Data to something like 100. Now, restart Windows and check out how much faster your menus are.

I DON'T NEED THE ARROWS

I extremely dislike (I can't say hate) shortcut arrows on my icons. It's just bad design, and they really annoy me. So, here's one of my personal favorites. Let's get rid of the arrows. Open Registry Editor and navigate to HKEY_CLASSES_ROOT\lnkfile, and rename the existing IsShortcut string value to IsShortcutOld. Now, restart Windows and the arrows are gone! If, for whatever crazy reason, you ever want them back, simply change the string value back to the original.

START WITHOUT ME

Do you know that it's you using your computer? If you don't, you can just look at the top of your Start menu and there you are. It's a good thing that Windows tells me that it's me using my computer, because sometimes I'm just not sure. In case you can't tell I'm being sarcastic, I actually think that it's annoying that my user name appears on my Start Menu, so I'm going to remove it.

Open Registry Editor and navigate to HKEY_CURRENT_USER\Software\Microsoft\Windows\CurrentVersion\Policies\Explorer, and create a new DWORD Value in the Attributes Pane. To do this, right-click in the Attributes Pane, point to New, and click DWORD Value on the Shortcut menu, and then name it "NoUser-NameInStartMenu." Next, double-click your new attribute and give it a Value Data of 1 (0 = display user name, 1 = hide user name), then click OK. If the NoNameInStartMenu value already exists, simply change the Value Data to 1. Restart Windows to view the change.

I'VE GOT A TIP FOR YOU

This is actually pretty cool and a lot of fun. You can change Windows default tips to whatever you'd like. At my office, we change them to motivational remarks and cruel jokes about the hygiene of co-workers, but that's just us. I'm sure you can find your own uses for 'em.

Open Registry Editor and navigate to HKEY_LOCAL_MACHINE\SOFTWARE\Microsoft\Windows\CurrentVersion\Explorer\Tips. Now, simply double-click an existing String Value, replace the existing tip with one of your own in the Value Data text field, and then click OK. If you want to add new tips, just right-click in the Attributes Pane, point to New, and click String Value on the Shortcut menu. Number your new values in numerical order to the existing values, double-click the new value, type your tip into the Value Data text field, and then click OK. You now have new Windows tips.

MY MEDIA PLAYER

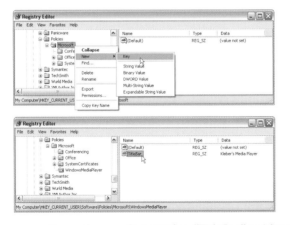

I think I'm going to name Windows Media Player after me. Why not? I use it enough. Open Registry Editor and navigate to HKEY_CURRENT_USER\Software\Policies\Microsoft. Now, create a new Registry key: Right-click the Microsoft folder, Point to New, and click Key on the Shortcut menu. Now, name your new Key "Windows-MediaPlayer" (without quotes). Next, with the WindowsMediaPlayer key selected, right-click in the Attributes Pane (at right), point to New, and click String Value on the Shortcut menu. Name the new String Value "TitleBar" (without quotes). Now, double-click the TitleBar attribute, type any name you'd like in the Value Data text field, and click OK. Then, restart Windows and launch Media Player. Media Player has a new name. Your new text follows "Windows Media Player provided by" on the Title Bar.

OUTLOOK EXPRESS SHOULD START HERE

This is a cool hack—I don't know why it's cool, it just is. There's just something about being able to change programs in ways that you didn't know you could that's, well, just cool.

Open Outlook Express and click the Outlook Express icon in the Folders List. You see the default start page, right? Now, open Registry Editor or navigate to HKEY_CURRENT_USER\ Identities\"Your Identity"\Software\Microsoft\Outlook Express\5.0. Next, right-click in the Attributes Pane, point to New, and click String Value on the Shortcut menu. Name the new String Value "FrontPagePath"

(without the quotes). Now, double-click the FrontPagePath attribute, type any URL you'd like in the Value Data text field, and click OK. Restart Windows and launch Outlook Express. Now, click the Outlook Express icon in the Folders List and your Web page will be displayed instead of the default start page.

 CONTROL THE CONTROL PANEL

Do you want to keep users from changing settings in the Control Panel? Heck, do you want to keep users from even being able to access the Control Panel? You can do that. Here's how: Open Registry Editor and navigate to HKEY_LOCAL_ MACHINE\SOFTWARE\Microsoft\Windows\

CurrentVersion\policies\Explorer. If you don't see the Explorer Key (folder), then create it under policies. Here's how: Right-click "policies," then click New>Key on the Shortcut menu, and name the new key "Explorer." Next, create a new DWORD Value by right-clicking on the Attributes Pane on the right, point to New, and click DWORD Value on the Shortcut menu. Then name it "NoControlPanel." Next, double-click the new DWORD Value,

type 1 in the Value Data text field, then click OK. Now, try to access tools in your Control Panel. You can't, can you? Cool! To get your Control Panel back, simply change the Value Data to 0 (zero). *Note:* You may have to restart Windows for the changes to take effect.

 HACK IE'S TITLE BAR

Did you know that you can customize Internet Explorer's Title Bar with your company name, slogan, or whatever? Well, you can—if you hack it. This actually offers a nice touch when giving browser-based presentations to clients. It's also great for simply personalizing your browser.

Open Registry Editor and navigate to HKEY_CURRENT_USER\Software\Microsoft\Internet Explorer\Main. Next, right-click in the Attributes Pane, point to New, then click String Value on The Shortcut menu. Name the new String Value "WindowTitle" (without quotes). Now, double-click the new WindowTitle attribute, type any name you'd like in the Value Data text field, and click OK. Launch Internet Explorer, and your text will appear in IE's Title Bar (you may have to restart Windows). To get back the default IE Title Bar, simply delete the WindowTitle attribute.

 HOW ABOUT OUTLOOK EXPRESS' TITLE BAR?

I just love branding my programs with my company name, so let's keep the fun going and hack Outlook Express' Title Bar as well. Open Registry Editor and navigate to HKEY_CURRENT_USER\Identities\"Your Identity"\Software\Microsoft\Outlook Express\5.0. Next, right-click in the Attributes Pane, point to New, then click String Value on the Shortcut menu. Name the new String Value "WindowTitle" (without quotes). Now, double-click the new WindowTitle attribute, type any name you'd like in the Value Data text field, and click OK. Then, launch Outlook Express to view your new Title Bar (you may have to restart Windows). To get back the default Outlook Express Title Bar, simply delete the WindowTitle attribute.

FRIENDLY TREES AREN'T FRIENDLY AT ALL

Windows Explorer does something
that I find to be very annoying. It
uses Friendly Trees (auto-expanding
folders). Sounds harmless, doesn't it?
But, here's the problem with Friendly
Trees. Basically, the term Friendly
Trees refers to the way that an entire

folder or directory expands when you click on them in
Explorer's Folders Panel. Doesn't the folder already open in
the right pane of Explorer? Yeah, it does. Well, maybe it's
just me, but this just makes everything look unnecessarily
cluttered. Let's make Windows Explorer truly friendly.

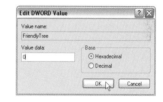

 Open Registry Editor and navigate to HKEY_CURRENT_
USER\Software\Microsoft\Windows\CurrentVersion\Explorer\
Advanced. Next double-click the FriendlyTree binary string, change the Value Data to 0 (zero),
then click OK. Now, launch Windows Explorer and click any folder. It didn't expand, did it? To
get your Friendly Trees back, simply change the Value Data back to 1.

YOU'VE BEEN INFECTED

Want to really freak somebody out? Display a message when Windows starts up.
This could be any message; for example,
"Your computer has been infected with a
virus. Your Hard Drive will automatically
be reformatted in 10 seconds!" Now,
when they fire up Windows, just sit back
and watch the best 10-second display of

panic you've ever seen. Or instead, you could just remind
that special someone that you're thinking of them. They're
both good.

 Anyway, open your Registry Editor and navigate to
HKEY_LOCAL_MACHINE\SOFTWARE\Microsoft\Windows
NT\CurrentVersion\Winlogon. Next, double-click
LegalNoticeCaption in the right pane, type a caption name in the Value Data text field for the
Message dialog box, then click OK. Now, double-click LegalNoticeText, type the message you
want to appear, and then click OK. Restart Windows.

YOU CAN'T NOTIFY ME

This is for people who truly can't stand icons in their Taskbar Notification area. And I know you're out there. This hack will remove every single icon, not just hide them. They're gone! They're outta here!

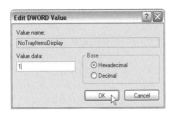

You'll never be notified of another single thing.

Open Registry Editor and navigate to HKEY_ LOCAL_MACHINE/SOFTWARE/Microsoft/Windows/ CurrentVersion/policies/Explorer. If you don't see the Explorer Key (folder), then create it under policies. Here's how: Right-click "policies," then click New> Key on the Shortcut menu, and name the new key "Explorer." Next, create a new DWORD Value: Right-click on the Attributes Pane on the right, point to New, and click DWORD Value on the Shortcut menu. Next, name the value "NoTrayItemsDisplay" (without quotes), double-click the new attribute, type 1 in the Value Data text field, and then click OK. Now, restart Windows. To get your Notification icons back, simply change the Value Data to 0 (zero). *Note:* You may have to restart Windows for the changes to take effect.

GROUPING, MY WAY

The new Taskbar Grouping feature in XP is great for keeping things from getting out of hand on the Taskbar; only you can't change how many similar windows should be allowed to be open

before the Taskbar groups 'em. Grouping happens dynamically depending on your display's resolution, which is nice, but I want to be able to tell Windows when to group buttons. I'm a control freak—it's a problem. So, let's get pushy.

Open Registry Editor and navigate to HKEY_LOCAL_ MACHINE\SOFTWARE\Microsoft\Windows\CurrentVersion\ Explorer\Advanced. Next, create a new DWORD Value by right-clicking on the Attributes Pane, point to New, and click DWORD Value on the Shortcut menu. Name the value "TaskbarGroupSize" (without quotes), double-click the new attribute, type a number, and then click OK. (I like five, but that's just me.) Restart Windows. Now, your similar windows will automatically group when five are opened.

Simply delete this attribute to return to the Windows default setting.

 "SHORTCUT TO" NOWHERE

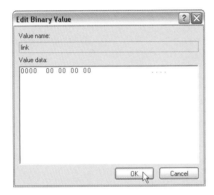

This is one of my all-time favorite Registry hacks. When you create a shortcut in Windows, not only does it come complete with the shortcut arrow, but its name also automatically begins with "Shortcut to." I think we all get that it's a shortcut. We just made it. Anyway, the first thing I do is delete the "Shortcut to" from the file's name, which automatically removes the "Shortcut to" text from your shortcuts when they're created.

Open Registry Editor and navigate to HKEY_CURRENT_USER\Software\Microsoft\Windows\CurrentVersion\Explorer. Next, double-click Link

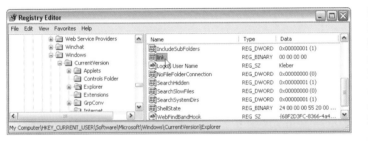

in the Attributes Pane (on the right). If you don't see the Link attribute, then create it. Here's how: Right-click in the right Attributes Pane and click New>Binary String on the Shortcut menu, then name the new value "link."

If the Link Attribute is already present, you'll see a Value Data of "0000 1E 00 00 00." Highlight the 1E, change the 1E to 00 so that the Value Data looks like "0000 00 00 00 00," then click OK. Now, restart Windows and create a shortcut. The "Shortcut to" text isn't there. That's much better! To get your shortcut text back, simply modify the Value Data back to "1E 00 00 00."

NOT-SO-RECENT DOCUMENTS

Use this hack to
automatically clear
your Recent Docu-
ments folder each
time that Windows is
shut down. This will
keep any unwanted
users from knowing
what you've been
up to. Maybe you're

working with sensitive documents or maybe you're just
really paranoid. Either way, open Registry Editor and
navigate to HKEY_LOCAL_MACHINE\SOFTWARE\Microsoft\
Windows\CurrentVersion\policies\Explorer. If you don't see
the Explorer Key (folder), then create it under policies.
Here's how: Right-click "policies," then click New>Key
on the Shortcut menu, and name the new key "Explorer."

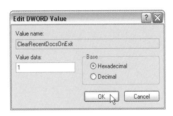

Next, create a new DWORD Value by right-clicking on the Attributes Pane, pointing to New,
and clicking DWORD Value on the Shortcut menu. Name the value "ClearRecentDocsOnExit"
(without quotes). Now, double-click the new attribute, type the number 1 for the Value
Data, then click OK. Now, restart Windows. When Windows launches, your Recent Documents folder is empty. To keep your recent documents, simply change the Attribute Value
Data to 0 (zero). *Note:* You may have to restart Windows for the changes to take effect.

 WHO ARE YOU?

Do you want to rename My Computer to your user name and computer name? Sure you do. Actually this is helpful, especially if you work from different workstations and need to quickly identify which computer you're working at and the user who's currently logged on.

Open Registry Editor and navigate to HKEY_CLASSES_ROOT\CLSID\{20D04FE0-3AEA-1069-A2D8-08002B30309D}. Double-click the "LocalizedString" Attribute in the right pane, highlight and copy the existing Value Data, and save this string in case you want to reset the attribute to its default setting. Next, replace the existing Value Data text

Kleber on
KLEBER

with "%USERNAME% on %COMPUTERNAME%" (without quotes) and then click OK. Now, right-click your Desktop and click Refresh on the Shortcut menu. When you restart, your user name and computer name will now be displayed under the My Computer icon.

NO ACCESS

With this hack, you can prevent users from opening specific programs. Maybe you want to keep Solitaire all to yourself, or you don't want the kids to use Internet Explorer. Well, here's how to keep 'em out. There are two parts to this hack, so follow along carefully.

First, open Registry Editor and navigate to HKEY_CURRENT_USER\Software\Microsoft\Windows\CurrentVersion\Policies\Explorer. Then, create a new DWORD Value by right-clicking on the Attributes Pane (on the right), point to New, and click DWORD Value on the Short-cut menu. Name the value "DisallowRun" (without quotes). Now,

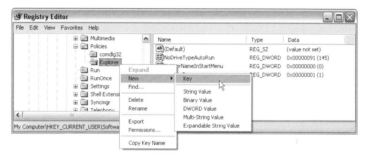

double-click the new attribute, type the number 1 for the Value Data, and then click OK. This enables application restrictions.

Next, right-click the Explorer key (folder) on the left, point to New, and click Key on the Shortcut menu. Name the new Key (folder) "DisallowRun" (without quotes). Then, click the new DisallowRun Key to open it. Right-click on the Attributes Pane, point to New, and click String Value. Name the new String Value using the number 1. Now, double-click the new String Value, type the applications name (e.g. notepad.exe), then click OK.

To add additional programs, simply number them consecutively, along with the Apps name as the Value Data. Restart Windows and try to launch Notepad. You can't.

 HYPER-TRASH

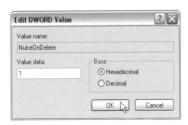

It's time to get serious about the Trash. This hack will delete files *immediately*, bypassing the Recycle Bin. If you use the Shift-Delete shortcut to bypass the Recycle Bin to delete files quickly and permanently, then this is the perfect timesaving tip.

Open Registry Editor and navigate to HKEY_LOCAL_MACHINE\SOFTWARE\Microsoft\Windows\CurrentVersion\Explorer\BitBucket. Next, double-click the Attribute NukeOnDelete, change the Value Data to 1, and then click OK. Now, when you delete a file it's really gone. Restart Windows to start using your new hyper-trash.

You can get back your default delete by changing back the NukeOnDelete Value Data to 0 (zero).

INDEX

A

Adobe Type Manager (ATM), 117
Address Bar. *(See Internet)*
Address Toolbar. *(See Toolbars)*
Advanced Tag Editor.
(See Media Player 9)
All Programs, 32, 74, 113, 122, 212
animations. *(See also Desktop)*
archive Web page, 160
AutoMovie. *(See under MovieMaker 2)*

B

background. *(See Desktop)*
Blue Screen of Death, 232
Briefcase, 46

C

CD
  file size, 233
CD Player, 217
Character Map, 98
ClearType, 125
clock, 45, 124
compatibility.
  (See Help and Support Center)
compressed files, 10, 60
contacts. *(See e-mail)*
Control Panel, 5, 245
cursors, 51
custom characters, 120

D

delete, *(See also Recycle Bin)*
  62, 90, 100, 104, 212
Desktop, 42
  animations, 50-51
  background, 46-47, 166
  icons, 218
  themes, 48
  Quick Launch, 94
  Web pages on Desktop, 48-50

Details Pane, 24
Details view. *(See views)*
Disk Cleanup, 226
Disk Defragmenter, 227
Document Scrap, 112

E

e-mail, 171-195
  attachments, 91, 188
  Bcc, 175
  Block Sender, 185
  contacts, 175, 178, 186-189
  Inbox, 173
  fonts, 184
  group, 174
  Hide Read Messages, 184
  Message Pane, 176
  Messenger, 190-195, 216
  new mail rules, 177, 185
  notification, 172, 186
  Preview Pane, 188
  Read Receipt, 179
  save, 182
  Signature, 179
  Spell options, 183
  startup, 172
  status, 216
  stationery, 180-181
  subject, 176
  To Do, 181
  vCard, 189
equalizer. *(See Media Player 9)*
error
  copy dialog box, 231
  Log Files, 236
  Processes, 236
  reporting, disable, 213
Escape, 104
Explorer.
  (See Internet and Windows Explorer)

F

Favorites, 37, 92-93
fax, 115

file(s),
  create 123
  compressed 10, 60
  delete, 62, 104
  explore, 55-56
  extensions, 68-69, 129
  full name, 85
  group, 59
  hide, 60, 219
  move, 56, 70, 102-103
  open multiple, 94
  open with, 100
  rename, 90-91
  save, 65-68, 233
  search, 107
  Send To, 118
  sort, 58
Filmstrip. *(See views)*
folders
  create, 83
  delete, 100
  hide, 123, 219
  icons, 79, 119
  move, 74
  Properties, 99
  private,126
  rename, 110
  search, 107
  select, 86-87
  templates, 20
fonts, 116-117, 184
Friendly Trees. *(See Registry Editor)*

G

Games, 114
Go, 62
group, 59, 174

H

hack. *(See Registry Editor)*
Help. *(See also Remote Assistance)*
  save pop-ups, 122
Help and Support Center
  Favorites, 229
  Microsoft Knowledge Base, 225
  Program Compatibility Wizard, 227

Hibernate, 96, 111
History, 155, 161
Home, 115, 158

I

icons, 26, 32, 74-87
  add comments, 84
  arrange, 80-82
  change default, 82
  create, 80
  folder, 79, 119
  shortcut, 74, 78
  restore, 79
  resize, 220
  select, 86
  Toolbar, 12-13, 16-17
Inbox. *(See e-mail)*
Internet, 154-169
  Address Bar, 159
  archive Web page, 160
  AutoComplete, 166
  browse/search the Web, 24, 116,
    159, 163-164
  connection, 226
  Explorer (IE), 118
  Favorites, 156-158
  History, 155, 161
  Home, 115, 158
  Links Toolbar, 169
  offline viewing, 164-165
  password, 166
  related, 167
  print, 167
  save, 165, 168
  send Web page, 160
  temporary Internet files, 161-163

L

levels. *(See Media Player 9)*
links. *(See also under*
  Toolbars), **15-17**
  drives shortcut, 92
lock, 95

M

maximize, 6, 8
media
  find, 150
  preview, 125
  streaming, 126
Media Player 9, 132-151
  Add Lyrics, 149
  Add Music, 140
  Advanced Tag Editor, 146
  anchor, 133
  Auto Volume Leveling, 147
  custom color, 136
  equalizer, 137
  File Name Options, 150
  Find Media, 150
  Media Guide, 151
  mini-player, 143-144
  monitor folders, 147
  Playlists, 138-139, 141, 144
  play speed, 136-137
  Queue-It-Up, 142
  rating, 140
  Skin mode, 132-133
  sort, 141
  SRS WOW Effects, 149
  visualizations, 134-135
  volume, 145
  Volume Leveling, 148
Message Pane. *(See e-mail)*
Messenger, 190-195
  block, 192
  conversation, 191-194
  groups, 192-193
  Instant Message, 194
  .NET Alerts, 191
  Pop-ups, 195
Microsoft Knowledge Base, 225
minimize, 7, 106
mini-player. *(See Media Player 9)*
mouse buttons, 219
move
  undo move, 106
MovieMaker 2, 198-209
  audio, 202-203
  AutoMovie, 203
  clips, 198-200, 205, 208-209
  fade, 205-207
  freeze frame, 202
  music, 204
  narration, 204
  still shot, 201
  Storyboard, 198
  Timeline, 206-207
  title, 200-201
  transitions, 204
  trim, 198-199

N

Narrator, 112
navigating, 54-70
  menus, 64
  windows, 64
Net Diagnostics, 237
.NET Alerts. *(See Messenger)*
NetMeeting ,121
network problems.
  (See Net Diagnostics)
Notification icons.
  (See Registry Editor)

O

Outlook Express. *(See e-mail)*

P

password, 166, 235
photo sheets, 127
Pictures Task Pane, 110
Playlists. *(See Media Player 9)*
pop-ups, 122, 195, 215
Prefetch, 234
print, 114
  photo sheets, 127
  prints online, 127
  stop, 213
  Web pages, 167

Private Character Editor, 120
Processes, 236
program
compatibility, 227
hung up, 228

Q

Queue-It-Up. *(See Media Player 9)*
Quick Launch, 38-39, 94

R

Recycle Bin, 62-63, 90
deleting files, 62, 90
Hyper-Trash, 254
Properties, 234
rename, 241
restoring files, 63
Registry Editor, 239-254
Backup, 240
Control Panel, 245
Favorites, 240
Friendly Trees, 247
Hyper-Trash, 254
Outlook Express, 245-246
prevent access, 253
Recent Documents, clear, 251
rename, 241-244, 252
Remote Assistance, 124
rename, 110
restart, 216
Restore Point. *(See System Restore)*
Restore Down button, 9

S

save, 65-67, 165-168, 182
ScanDisk, 224
Scientific Calculator, 218
screen captures, 121
screen-saver, 111
scroll, 18-19
search, 107, 159, 163, 214, 228
shortcuts, 74-77, 84, 92, 113
icon, 74, 78, 84
open folder, 101

Shortcut menu, 77
shutdown, 95, 220
switch users, 95
skin. *(See Media Player 9)*
slide show, 110
sort, 32, 58
startup
change default, 54
e-mail, 172
launch favorite Apps, 98
launch all Apps, 221
Start menu, 33-34
stationery, 180-181
Status Bar, 27
Storyboard. *(See MovieMaker 2)*
System Restore, 230-231, 240

T

temporary folders
Prefetch, 234
Internet, 161-163
windows, 233
Three-Finger Salute, 224
Timeline. *(See MovieMaker 2)*
Toolbars, 12-16, 24, 37
Address Toolbar, 12, 25, 36, 61
black arrows, 15
Links Toolbar, 15-16, 169
trash. *(See Recycle Bin)*
troubleshooting, 224-237

U

Undo move, 106
updates, 214, 235
URLs. *(See Internet)*
User Account, 4-5

V

vCard, 189
Views, 11
Details view, 57, 97
Filmstrip view, 22, 128
Thumbnail view, 85
toggle, 128

visualizations. *(See Media Player 9)*
volume
computer sounds and audio, 45
Media Player, 145
Volume Control, 215

W

Web. *(See Internet)*
windows, 64
group, 103-105
minimize, 106
quick quit, 96
temporary files, 233
Windows Explorer, 54-55, 97
hidden Apps, 120-121

Z

Zip. *(See compressed files)*

Microsoft Office 2003   Killer Tips

Microsoft Office 2003 Killer Tips Team

TECHNICAL EDITOR
Polly Reincheld

EDITOR
Barbara Thompson

PRODUCTION EDITOR
Kim Gabriel

PRODUCTION
Dave Damstra
Dave Korman
Mary Maibauer

COVER DESIGN AND CREATIVE CONCEPTS
Felix Nelson

SITE DESIGN
Stacy Behan

PUBLISHED BY
New Riders / Peachpit Press

Copyright © 2005 by Kelby Corporate Management, Inc.

FIRST EDITION: July 2004

All rights reserved. No part of this book may be reproduced or transmitted in any form, by any means, electronic or mechanical, including photocopying, recording, or by any information storage and retrieval system, without written permission from the publisher, except for inclusion of brief quotations in a review.

Composed in Myriad and Helvetica by NAPP Publishing

Trademarks
All terms mentioned in this book that are known to be trademarks or service marks have been appropriately capitalized. New Riders / Peachpit Press cannot attest to the accuracy of this information. Use of a term in the book should not be regarded as affecting the validity of any trademark or service mark.

Microsoft and Windows are either registered trademarks or trademarks of Microsoft Corporation in the United States and/or other countries.

Warning and Disclaimer
This book is designed to provide information about Microsoft Office 2003 tips. Every effort has been made to make this book as complete and as accurate as possible, but no warranty of fitness is implied.

The information is provided on an as-is basis. The author and New Riders / Peachpit Press shall have neither liability nor responsibility to any person or entity with respect to any loss or damages arising from the information contained in this book or from the use of the discs or programs that may accompany it.

ISBN 0-7357-1437-1

9 8 7 6 5 4 3 2 1

Printed and bound in the United States of America

www.peachpit.com
www.scottkelbybooks.com

For my Lord,

Jesus Christ.

As with all things

in my life, I give

you the Honor,

the Praise, and

the Glory.

ACKNOWLEDGMENTS

Debbie Stephenson—You've made my life wonderful. You're the best part of every day. Your wonderful sweetness and kindness just makes people want to be around you. Thank you for being my best friend, a loving wife, and an extraordinary mother. You'll always take my breath away. I love you!

Jarod Stephenson—I know that anyone can be a father but Jarod, you make me want to be a spectacular father. One of my favorite things in the world is just going outside and throwing a baseball with you. You've got a heck of an arm for a six-year-old. I'm amazed at who you are and who you're becoming. I'm very, very proud of you!

Jenna Stephenson—If boys make men fathers, then girls make men daddies. Jenna, I absolutely couldn't get through a day without you—you're my little princess. I honestly didn't think that God was capable of making anything so unique, beautiful, sweet, and wonderful as you.

Kleber and Barbara Stephenson—Mom and Dad, as always, I can never thank you enough for everything you do. You're the most extraordinary people anyone could ever know. You're truly a blessing and I only hope that I do as good a job raising my children as you did with me.

My sisters—I'm getting a little tired of always singing your praises. It's exhausting because there are so many to be sung. Cheryl, Kalebra, Julie, Heidi, you're simply the coolest sisters a guy could have. You're all so special to me. Thanks for your love, encouragement, and support. I deserve it. ;-)

Scott Kelby—Bro! You're one of the most creative and talented people I know, as well as being an inspiration and good friend. Thanks for your support, vision, and for creating the most creative environment on the planet.

Dave Moser—The way you do anything is the way you do everything. You have a great talent for doing it right. Thanks for your endless encouragement and constant flow of great ideas.

KW Media Group—A special thanks to Polly Reincheld, Barbara Thompson, Felix Nelson, Kim Gabriel, Dave Damstra, Dave Korman, Margie Rosenstein, Christine Edwards, and Mary Maibauer. All of you are insanely talented. It amazes me how you accomplish what you do. Thanks for your dedication and very hard work.

The Lord, Jesus Christ—God has always blessed me more than I deserve. I can't make it through a day without speaking to Him. Thanks for always listening, allowing me to do what I love, and for blessing me with such a wonderful life.

ABOUT THE AUTHOR

Kleber Stephenson

Kleber Stephenson is Director of Seminars and Director of Windows Technologies for KW Media Group, Inc., a Florida-based software education and publishing firm. He's also the author of the best-selling *Windows XP Killer Tips* and co-author of *The iTunes for Windows Book*, both from New Riders Publishing/Peachpit Press.

A contributing technology reviewer for *Mac Design Magazine* and *Photoshop User,* Kleber has more than a decade of experience analyzing and implementing business computing infrastructures based on the Windows platform. In addition, he has designed and developed real-world network and administrative solutions based on Microsoft technologies and the Windows OS architecture.

Kleber lives in the Tampa Bay area of Florida with his wife, Debbie, his son, Jarod, and his daughter, Jenna.

As Editor for the Killer Tips series, I'm excited not only to bring you another Killer Tips book, but I'm particularly excited to introduce you to an author who is going to take you to a whole new level of speed, efficiency, productivity, and sheer unadulterated out-and-out fun using Microsoft Office 2003. (I just realized that when you put the words "sheer" and "unadulterated" together, it sounds kind of dirty, but it's not meant to be. That comes later.) But first, a little background on this book.

The idea for this type of book came to me one day when I was at the bookstore, browsing in the computer section, when I thought to myself, "Man, these authors must be making a ton of money!" No wait, that wasn't what I was thinking (it's close, mind you, but not exactly). Actually, I was standing there flipping through the different books on Adobe Photoshop (I'm a Photoshop guy at heart). Basically what I would do is look for pages that had a tip on them. They're usually pretty easy to find, because these "rich book authors" usually separate their tips from the regular text of the book. Most of the time, they'll put a box around the tips, or add a tint behind them, or maybe have a tips icon—something to make them stand out and get the readers' attention.

Anyway, that's what I would do—find a tip, read it, and then start flipping until I found another tip. The good news—the tips were usually pretty cool. You have to figure that if an author has some really slick trick, maybe a hidden keyboard shortcut or a cool workaround, he probably wouldn't bury it in blocks of boring copy. No way! He'd find some way to get your attention (with those boxes, tints, a little icon, or simply the word "Tip!"). So, that's the cool news—if it said tip, it was usually worth checking out. The bad news—there are never enough tips. Sometimes there were five or six tips in a chapter, but other times, just one or two. But no matter how many there were, I always got to the last chapter and still wanted more tips.

Standing right there in the bookstore, I thought to myself, "I wish there was a book with nothing but tips: hundreds of tips, cover to cover, and nothing else." Now, that's a book I'd go crazy for. I kept looking and looking, but the book I wanted just wasn't available. That's when I got the idea to write one myself. The next day I called my editor to pitch him with the idea. I told him it would be a book that would be wall-to-wall with nothing but cool tips, hidden shortcuts, and inside tricks designed to make Photoshop users faster, more productive, and best of all, make using Photoshop even more fun. Well, he loved the idea. Okay, that's stretching it a bit. He liked the idea, but most importantly, he "green-lighted it" (that's Hollywood talk—I'm not quite sure what it means), and soon I had created my first all-tips book, *Photoshop 6 Killer Tips* (along with my co-author and good friend, *Photoshop User* magazine Creative Director Felix Nelson).

As it turned out, *Photoshop 6 Killer Tips* was an instant hit (fortunately for me and my chance-taking editor), and we followed it up with (are you ready for this?) *Photoshop 7 Killer Tips*, and then *Photoshop CS Killer Tips*, which were even bigger hits. These books really struck a chord with readers, and I like to think it was because Felix and I were so deeply committed to creating something special—a book where every page included yet another tip that would make you nod your head, smile, and think, "Ahhh, so that's how they do it." However, it pretty much came down to this: People just love cool tips. That's why now there's an entire series of Killer Tips books covering cool applications such as DreamWeaver, QuarkXPress, InDesign, Illustrator, and many more.

So how did we wind up here, with a Killer Tips book for Microsoft Office 2003? Well, there was an intermediate step: I wrote *Mac OS X Killer Tips* for Macintosh users switching over to Apple's UNIX-based operating system. It turned out to be such a big hit, it actually became "biggety-big" (a purely technical term, only used during secret book-publishing rituals).

That naturally led to a *Windows XP Killer Tips* book. The only problem was that I'm really a Photoshop guy and I wanted the Windows XP book to surpass the Mac book's "biggety-bigness," so it needed a pretty special author. That person was Kleber Stephenson. I chose him for one simple reason: The similarity of his first name to my last name. Heck, it's almost the same name (Kleber Kelby. See what I mean?). That was enough for me. Okay, that's actually not the reason at all (just a lucky coincidence). I chose Kleber because he fit every criterion I had set for the ideal Killer Tips author. First, he totally "gets" the Killer Tips concept because, just like me, he's a tip hound—a tip junkie (if you will). Second, I've always enjoyed his writing style, humor, and the completeness of his research and attention to detail, and how he really immerses himself in a project. Third, like me, he's a die-hard Tampa Bay Bucs fan. Fourth (and perhaps most important), he knows more Windows tips and has a better understanding of the Windows operating system than anyone I know. Period.

That's why, when we decided to do this book on Microsoft Office 2003, I called Kleber first. Honestly, if he had decided to pass on the project, you wouldn't be reading this book now, because he was *so* the right person to do this book that I didn't have another person in mind as a backup plan. I wanted Kleber, and if I couldn't get him, I'd shelve the idea and move on to another project. That's how strongly I felt that he was the right person for the job, and I'm absolutely delighted that you're holding his book right now. Kleber has really captured the spirit and flavor of what a "Killer Tips" book is all about, and he proved that with his *Windows XP Killer Tips* book. And I can tell you this—you're gonna love this book, as well!

Kleber has a great sense of humor and a casual, conversational writing style. He has a keen sense for uncovering those inside tips that the pros use to get twice the work done in half the time. He's one of those people who doesn't do anything the "hard way," and he knows every timesaving shortcut, every workaround, and every speed tip to make something different, something special, and to make this the only book of its kind in a very crowded Microsoft Office 2003 book market.

I can't wait for you to "get into it," so I'll step aside and let him take the wheel, because you're about to get faster, more efficient, and have more fun using Microsoft Office 2003 than you ever thought possible.

All my best,

Scott Kelby
Series Editor

CHAPTER 1   1
A Day at the Office
Get the Most Out of Office 2003

Turn Off the Task Panes   2
They're Expandable   2
Task Panes on the Move   3
Quick Menu Expand   3
Customize Your Menus   4
Keep the Fun Rollin'—Customize your Toolbars   4
Split the Toolbars   5
Open and Close Toolbars the Easy Way   5
Toolbars Getting Crazy…Reset 'Em   6
Linking Your Buttons   6
Getting Geeky with Toolbar Buttons   7
The Move Button Trick   7
Side by Side…So Cool   8
Add Places   8
Show Small Icons in My Places Bar   9
Save It Here Instead   9
No Access…I'm Protected   10
Copy and Paste on Steroids   10
The Assistant's Got to Go   11
Help Me Made Easy   11
I'm Hung Up, But I'll Recover   12
Get Faster with Shortcut Keys   12
Research This!   13
Do-It-Yourself Repairs   13
Link Your Docs   14
You Can Cut, Paste, and Delete from Here   15

CHAPTER 2   17
Spread the Word
Working with Word

Print Word's Shortcuts   18
Repeat That Search   18
Instantly Open Your Last-Used Document   19
Customize Your Dictionary   19
Shortcut to Your Text   20
Word's Rising in the Charts   20
Flirting with Disaster   21
I've Only Got One Sheet of Paper   21
Keeping Up to Date with Fields   22
Super-Fast Time and Date   22
Turn Fields into Text   23
Stop Control-Clicking (It's Bad for You)   23
Find and Replace Using the Clipboard   24

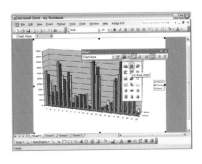

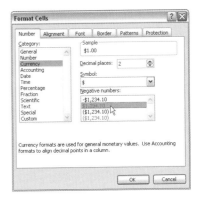

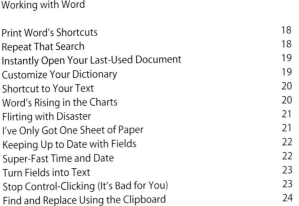

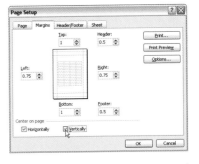

TABLE OF CONTENTS

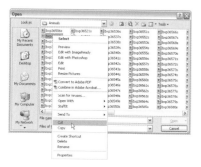

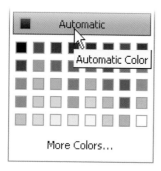

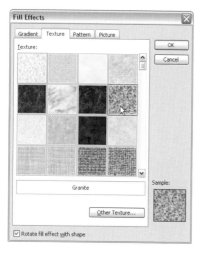

Word's Super-Secret Work Menu	24
I Can Actually Select That Table	25
Oui, Oui—I Can Translate	25
Don't Just Paste It, Spike It	26
Smart Tags Really Are Smart	26
Print Like the Post Office	27
I Don't Use Avery Labels	27
Print a Portion	28
Backward Is Better	28
Give Me a Hundredth of an Inch	29
Groovy Menus	29
Send, Share, Compare	30
You're Restricted	30
Split and Edit	31
You Can Use Your Toolbars in Full Screen Mode	32
Word Hopping	32
Edit Multiple Pages	33
Save 'Em All, Close 'Em All	33
Navigating the Easy Way	34
Yay, Previews!	34
There's a Comparison to Be Made	35
Bookmarks Are Better	35
Need a Table of Contents?	36
Reading Layout's Got to Go	36
Lacking Creativity? Make It Work for You	37
Quick Print Preview	37
Autocorrect My Abbreviations? Cool!	38
Lots O' Lines	38
I Knew There Had to Be a Better Way	39
Tab Your Cells	39
Preserve Your Formatting	40
Excel's Got Nothin' on Word	40
It's All About the Plus (and Minus) Signs	41
A Template of Your Very Own	41
Splitting Up Isn't Hard to Do	42
Shrink Your Document	42
I've Made a Mistake	43
Undo It All	43
Pick the Pilcrow	44
Customize Your Bullets	44
I Need a Little Room	45
Type It Again	45
That's Not Page One	46
Save That Table Size	46
Control Your Column Widths	47
AutoFit Just One Column	47
Find All the Same	48
Quick Synonyms	48

It's All in the Line Number 49
In Summary… 49
Give the Scraps to Your Desktop 50
Resume or Résumé 50
Remembering Shortcuts 51
Want Control Over Your Text? Then Shift 51
Editable Print Previews 52
Quick Case 52
Picky Selections 53
Fake It, Dummy 53
The Easy Way to Get Text Above Your Table 54
Voice Your Comments 54
Drag, Hover, Drop 55
Now You See Me, Now You Don't 55
The Key to Tests 56
AutoColor 56
Edit Cycling in Word 57
F8 to Extend 57
Click It, Then Type It 58
Personalize Your Envelopes 59
Super-Charge Word's Performance with Placeholders 59
Quick Graphic Resize Trick 60
Resizing the Right Way 60
Be Exact 61
Getting Precise with Word's Grid 61
Not Your Ordinary Text Box 62
Adding Captions 62
I Need More AutoShapes 63
Getting Precise with AutoShapes 63

CHAPTER 3 65
Bright Outlook
Working with Outlook

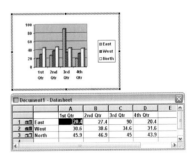

Protect Your Personal Folders 66
Just Start Up 66
Same Email…Different Computers 67
Be Choosy with Field Chooser 68
Sort Your Mail 68
Email Shortcut 69
I've Got Things to Do 69
Fast Track to the Inbox 70
Organize Your Messages Quickly 71
Easy Edit 71
Keep Email Consistent 72
Drag-and-Drop Your Attachments 72
Control-Click Hyperlinks 73
Email Your Notes 73

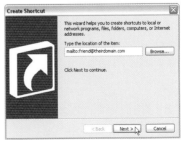

TABLE OF CONTENTS

Sticky Notes…Really!	74
Choose an Account	74
Track Down the Personal Folders	75
Personalize Personal Folders	75
Un-Junk Email	76
Can't Spell?	76
Save Your Searches	77
Collapsible Groups	77
Even a Folder Needs a Home (Page)	78
Maximum View	78
Start Up Where You Want	79
Launch Outlook at Startup	79
Don't Dump It, Archive It Instead	80
Snag Stationery	80
Compare Folders	81
Get Rid of the Junk	82
Outlook's Hidden Help	82
Auto-Sort Email	83
Web Browsing with Outlook	84
Single Task, Multiple Categories	84
A Reading Pane You Can Actually Read	85
A Reminder to Turn Off Reminders	85
Using Shortcuts in Outlook	86
Get Rid of J	87
You've Got Mail…Sounds	87
Back Up the Bad	88
Sign It	88
Flag It	89
Follow-Up Flags	89
Color-Code Messages	90
Bcc Groups	90
Don't Reply There	91
Request a Receipt	91
Show Only the Unread	92
Oops, I Didn't Mean to Send That	92
Zip It!	93
Quick, Send Webpages	93
You've Always Got Mail	94
You've Been Notified, You've Got Mail	94
No Office? No problem!	95
Right-Click Contacts	96
Right-Click Attachments	96
You're Annoying	97
You're Safe	97
Quick Junk Button	98
Turn Off the Reading Pane	98
Sort the Junk with AutoPreview	99
Stop Desktop Alerts	99

Let 'Em Vote on It   100
Print Your Contacts   100
I Prefer Nicknames   101
Check a Contact's Activities   101
Find a Group of Contacts   102
Get Directions   102
You Can Picture It   103
Quickly Add to Contacts   103
Categories Can Remind You   104
Don't Just Reply, Send an Instant Message   104
Forward a vCard   105
Snail Mail Your Contacts   105
Quickly Create Appointments   106
Print Blank Calendars   107
Share Your Calendars   108
I Need My Weekends   109
Master Time Zones   109

CHAPTER 4   111
Power(ful)Point Of View
Working with PowerPoint

Changing Colors   112
Snag Slides   112
Deliver the Package   113
Begin or End in a Flash   113
Tab a Bullet   114
Shift to Slide Master   114
Master Your Presentation   115
Don't Print, You're Hidden   116
Quick Copy   116
Web It   117
Don't Forget to Embed   117
That's Perfect!   118
Global Font Replacement   119
Super-Fast Shapes   119
More and More Shapes Made Easy   120
Perfectly Spaced Shapes   121
Give Me More Guides   122
Picture This!   123
Options Are Great!   123
Word Presentations?   124
Link 'Em   124
Size Down   125
Take a Picture   126
Control the Shadows   127
Super-Fast Symbols   128
Kiosk Cool   128

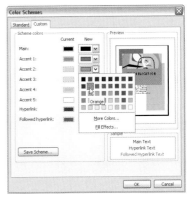

TABLE OF CONTENTS

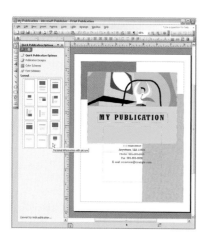

Mix It Up	129
Can't Miss That Logo	129
It's Good to Take Notes	130
Giddyap	130
Don't Just Flip, Transition	131
Pixel Pushing	132
Power Albums	132
Summary Slide	133
Blackout	134
Objects Too Small?	134
Give Credit	135
Can You Spell Business?	136
Become a Template Designer	137
Don't Cut, Crop Instead	138
We're Connected	139
I'd Like to Comment	140
Quickly Animate Objects	141
More Templates	142
I'm Compressed!	142
Preview and Edit	143
Quick Notes	144
Customize Your Customers	145
Don't Have Transitions for the Web?	145
Quick Defaults	146

CHAPTER 5 — 149
Time To Excel
Working with Excel

Stop Flinching	150
Gettin' Crazy with Backgrounds	151
Whoa, That's a Different Worksheet	152
Centering Text	153
A Quicker Calculator	154
It's Picture Time	155
Take a (Real) Picture	156
My Favorite Workbook, Right Away	157
ABC's to 123's	158
Better Prints	159
Control Your Prints	160
It's Time to Break Up	161
A Familiar Print	162
Print a Workbook Range	163
Am I Rich Yet?	164
You Could Save a Pence	165
It's a Random Thing	166
.2989345?	167
Share Your Formatting	168

The Title's the Same	169
How Long Til My Birthday?	170
Quick Calculations	171
Total Your Worksheets	172
Another Quick Calculation	173
Quick Lists	174
More Quick Lists	175
My Own Quick Lists	176
I Want More	176
Movable Data	177
Protect Your Worksheets	178
Be Impatient	179
Freeze!	180
In the Red	181
Wrap Text	182
It Looks Cool, So It Must Be Done	183
Share (Kind Of)	184
Do You Validate?	185
Give Me Fractions	186
Check All of My Spelling	187
The Formula to Comments	188
Wingdingin' It	189
Excel Can Be Lonely	190
Let's Hook Up	191
Quick Graphs	192
Jumpin' Here, Jumpin' There	193
Smart Navigation	193
Power Sharing	194
Hide Worksheets	195
Don't Forget the Pixels	196
Case-Sensitive Sorts	196
Select Large Ranges	197
Show Off Your Formulas	198
Remember to Color Code	199
"Watch" Your Window	200
Don't Save the Geek-Speak	201
Paint Columns and Rows	202
CHAPTER 6	205
Easy Access	
Working with Access	
Your Very Own Tooltips	206
It's Your Default	207
I'm Important!	207
Say No to Snap to Grid	208
Instant Fit	208
Can You Picture It?	209

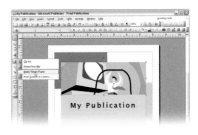

T A B L E O F CONTENTS

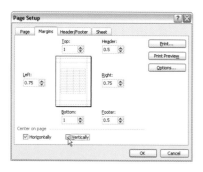

The Object of Shortcuts	210
Access Specifications	211
All I See Are Asterisks	211
Don't Import—Link	212
Take It to the Web	213
Menu Bar Objects	214
Don't Double-Click	214
Zoom Zoom	215
Instantly Launch a Form	215
Instantly Launch a Record	216
Get Your Tabs in Order	217
Hidin' Out	217
A Better View	218
How's Your Relationship?	219
Line 'Em Up	220
Quick Calendar	221
A Better Preview	222
Shift Size	223
Title Pages Made Easy	224
Can't Close	225
Can't Add	225
Set the Timer	226
What's This?	227
Gettin' Around	227
Super-Fast Append	228
Report Snapshot	229
Analyze This!	230
Quick Dates	230
One-Click Excel	231
CHAPTER 7	233
Get Published	
Working with Publisher	
Edit in Word	234
Delete the Whole Thing	234
Navigate Web Publications	235
Customize Color Schemes	235
Get Personal	236
Control Groups	237
That Should Be a Picture	237
The Key to the Web	238
Headin' to the Printers	238
Publisher-Friendly Printers	239
I've Been Framed	239
Flowing Text	240
Transparent Shapes	241
Paint Your Formatting	241

Don't Stress Over Fonts   242
What Are Your Measurements?   243
Drag, Drop, Move   244
Drag-and-Drop Duplicates   245
Faux Frame   246
Line Up   247
Exact Rotation   247
Find the Right Words   248
Rulers Anywhere   248
Wrap Text   249
Recolor Pictures   250

Index   255

A Day at the Office

GET THE MOST OUT

OF OFFICE 2003

I almost failed kindergarten when I was a child (not as an adult, of course). I couldn't color. I mean, I could color; I just couldn't do it very well. My parents would only

A Day at the Office

get the most out of office 2003

buy me the fat crayons—you know the ones I'm talking about—so I wasn't able to stay within the lines. Who could with those fat crayons? Everybody else had the skinny crayons. They breezed through coloring, but not me. I didn't have the best tools. I had crayons, but not the crayons to get the job done. I still can't color to this day. Every time my children break out the crayons, I get preschool flashbacks, and that's kind of how it must be for anyone anywhere using any other office suite. Microsoft Office is simply the best tool for the job, much like skinny crayons. So I can only assume, since you're reading this book, that you use Microsoft Office. Count yourself blessed and fortunate, because bad tools can really mess you up.

 ## TURN OFF THE TASK PANES

The first thing I do in just about every Office application once it's launched is click the Close button on the Startup task pane. The task panes are helpful if you've never used an Office application, but for everyone else, they can be annoying (and they take up an enormous amount of workspace). I don't know about you, but I try to keep from being annoyed as much as possible, so I turn off the Startup task pane, and it never appears when an Office application is launched. You too can do this by clicking Tools>Options in the menu bar of most applications. Next, click the View tab in the Options dialog and deselect the Startup Task Pane checkbox located under the Show category, then click OK. Now the Startup task panes will never annoy you again.

 ## THEY'RE EXPANDABLE

Here's a tip to keep in mind when working with task panes: They're expandable. So, when you're forced to scroll through a task pane, don't. Instead, simply place your cursor over the left border until your mouse pointer turns into a two-sided arrow, then click-and-drag the border of the task pane to the left to expand the pane to fit the content. Task panes are already taking up way too much space, so what's a little more space to make them readable?

TASK PANES ON THE MOVE

By default, task panes open on the right side of an Office program window. Well, maybe you don't like the task pane on the right. Maybe you'd like the task pane on top of the document window, at the bottom, or on the left side of the window. Well, you're in luck; you can move it to any side you'd like. To do this, move your mouse pointer over the upper-left corner of the task pane until your pointer turns into a four-sided arrow. Next, drag-and-drop the task pane to any side of the program window to dock it, or drag-and-drop it anywhere else on the program window to float the task pane. To move the task pane back, simply drag-and-drop it onto the far right side of the program window.

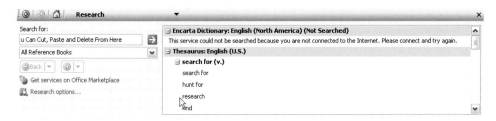

 ## QUICK MENU EXPAND

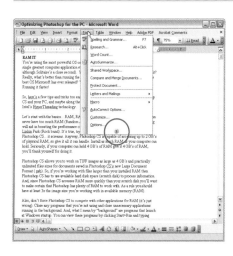

It never fails: The task that you're looking for is always somewhere at the bottom of the menu that you open, which means that you can't see it because Office applications don't fully expand menus automatically. Well, you could click the arrow button at the bottom of the menu to expand it (shown circled), but that's just crazy… there's a better way. To expand menus quickly, simply double-click the menu title. Now you can actually see the tasks you're looking for. However, if you really detest this personalized menu feature, you can get really smart and permanently turn it off. Click Tools>Customize, then click the Options tab in the Customize dialog. Next, select the Always Show Full Menus checkbox under the Personalized Menus and Toolbars category, then click Close.

 ## CUSTOMIZE YOUR MENUS

One of the most useful features of Office 2003 is the ability to create your own custom menus—very handy for grouping tasks that you use most frequently. To create a new menu, click Tools>Customize in the menu bar. Next, click the Commands tab in the Customize dialog, scroll to the bottom of the Categories list, and click New Menu. Drag-and-drop the words "New Menu" from the Commands window onto the menu bar at the top of your screen. Now, give your menu a new name by right-clicking the words "New Menu" and typing a new name in the Name field. To add commands to your menu, drag-and-drop them onto the open menu (not on the menu title). You'll notice a black line indicating where the command will be positioned when you release your mouse button. When you're finished, click OK in the Customize dialog, and all of your favorite commands are now located in one convenient menu. (*Note:* You can only rename and add commands to your new menu when the Customize dialog is open.)

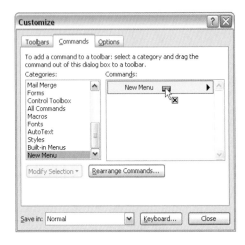

 ## KEEP THE FUN ROLLIN'—CUSTOMIZE YOUR TOOLBARS

I showed you how to create a customized menu above; well, let's keep the fun rollin' along and create a customized toolbar. It's another great way to increase your productivity in Office. To create a customized toolbar, click Tools>Customize in the menu bar. Next, click the Toolbars tab in the Customize dialog, then click the New button. Type a name in the Toolbar Name field, then, with the Customize dialog still open, drag-and-drop buttons from other open toolbars onto your new toolbar. When finished, click OK in the Customize dialog, and you've just created your very own custom toolbar.

SPLIT THE TOOLBARS

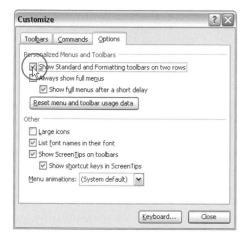

By default, Word, Excel, PowerPoint, and Publisher display the Standard and Formatting toolbars on the same row. This can make things a bit cluttered and, depending on the size of the application's window, makes tasks difficult to access. To show the Standard and Formatting toolbars stacked as two rows instead, right-click anywhere on any toolbar, and click Customize in the shortcut menu. Next, click the Options tab and check Show Standard and Formatting Toolbars on Two Rows, then click Close. You now have the toolbars on two separate rows.

OPEN AND CLOSE TOOLBARS THE EASY WAY

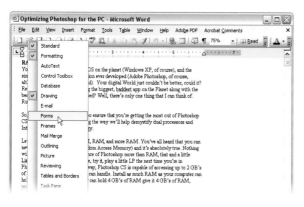

If you need to add new toolbars to your Office applications, you don't have to use the Customize dialog. I mean, you can if you like wasting time and doing things the hard way, but if you don't, try right-clicking any toolbar to view other available toolbars. Next, click a toolbar in the shortcut menu that you'd like to display. If the toolbar is floating when you open it, you can dock the toolbar by dragging-and-dropping it next to other docked toolbars. To close a toolbar, simply right-click any menu or toolbar and deselect that toolbar in the shortcut menu.

 TOOLBARS GETTING CRAZY…RESET 'EM

I'm the kind of person who likes to mix things up and, because I'm a rebel, I may not always think that the button layout in the default toolbars works best for me. I find myself changing the position of buttons on my toolbars pretty frequently depending on the project that I'm working on. It just makes sense to have the most frequently used buttons grouped for easier access. This can get confusing at times, however, and will probably make it just about impossible for anyone else to find tasks on these customized toolbars. So…to reset your toolbars to their default state, click Tools>Customize in the menu bar, then click the Toolbars tab in the Customize dialog. Select the toolbar that

you want to reset by clicking on its name in the Toolbars window, click the Reset button (to the right), then click Close. Your scrambled buttons are now back to normal.

 LINKING YOUR BUTTONS

Did you know that you could assign hyperlinks to any button or menu command? Okay, I haven't found a good use for this feature, but it has to be there for a reason, and you may just have one. So, if you want to attach a hyperlink to one of your buttons or commands, here's how. Click Tools>Customize in the menu bar. Then, with the dialog open, right-click a button or open a menu and right-click a command. Next, go to Assign Hyperlink at the bottom of the shortcut menu and click Open. In the dialog, browse to link to a file from your hard drive or type a URL in the Address field to link to a document located on the Internet or office Intranet, then click OK. Click the Close button in the Customize dialog. Now, when you select the button or command, the linked file will open or your Web browser will launch to display the webpage.

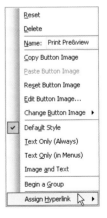

GETTIN' GEEKY WITH TOOLBAR BUTTONS

If you really want to get geeky with your toolbar buttons, try this: Click Tools>Customize to open the Customize dialog, then right-click any toolbar button to view its shortcut menu. Using the shortcut menu, you can perform any number of changes to it; you can rename the button (as I did here) or change or edit its image. When finished, click Close in the Customize dialog.

 ## THE MOVE BUTTON TRICK

This trick is for those of you who know how tedious it is to move a toolbar button within Windows (as you know, there's no simple way). Try this to move a toolbar button quickly within any Office application: Press the Alt key on your keyboard, then click any button, and drag-and-drop it to any location on any toolbar. Isn't that great? If you want to delete a button from a toolbar, just press the Alt key and click-and-drag the button off the toolbar. When an "x" appears under the mouse pointer, release the mouse button, and the toolbar button is gone. I really think the Office developers should get together with the Windows developers and share the wealth. This kind of stuff just kills me.

SIDE BY SIDE…SO COOL

New in Office 2003 for Word and Excel is the
Compare Side by Side With option that allows
you to, well, compare two open documents side
by side. I use this feature all the time, and you
probably will too once you know where it is.
To compare documents side by side, open at

least two documents, then select Window>Compare Side by Side With. If you have more
than two documents open, this command will open the Compare Side by Side dialog. Select
the document that you want to compare with the document that you're currently working
on, then click OK. Your documents will automatically tile vertically.

 ADD PLACES

The My Places bar, which appears along
the left-hand side of the Open or Save
As dialogs, gives you quick access to
frequently used locations on your hard
drive, but what makes the bar really
useful is when you add locations. To add
your favorite locations to the My Places
bar, go to the File menu and choose
Open or Save As to open one of those
dialogs, navigate to the folder or drive
that you want to add, then click the
Tools drop-down menu (at top right of

the dialog), and select Add to "My Places." The new location now appears on the My Places
bar along the left side of the dialog. To remove a location from the My Places bar, right-click a
location icon and click Remove in the shortcut menu.

SHOW SMALL ICONS IN THE MY PLACES BAR

Now that you've added 20 new locations to the My Places bar, you have a new problem: You have to spend more time scrolling to locate your locations than it would take to navigate your hard drive. That's not good. Well, to make the My Places bar a bit more user-friendly, shrink the My Places bar icons. To do this, right-click on any icon in the bar and select Small Icons in the shortcut menu. That's better!

 ## SAVE IT HERE INSTEAD

When saving new documents, Office will attempt to save them in your My Documents folder. I guess there should be a default location in which to save all of your documents; however, the My Documents folder may not be the most convenient for you. If this is the case, you can change the default location for saved documents. Click Tools>Options in the menu bar, then click the File Locations tab in the Options dialog. Next, under File Types, click Documents, then click the Modify button. Use the Modify Location dialog to browse your hard drive to select a new location to store your saved documents. When finished, click OK. Now when you click File>Save As, your new location will appear in the Save As dialog.

NO ACCESS…I'M PROTECTED

Here's one for all of you secret-service agents or seriously paranoid people out there. I'm seriously paranoid, so I password protect just about all of my documents. Actually, there are all kinds of great reasons that any perfectly sane person would want to password protect his or her documents. For instance, I travel a lot, and it's possible that my laptop could be stolen or left behind at any of America's airports, so I always password protect sensitive documents. To password protect your Word, Excel, or PowerPoint documents, click Tools>Options in the menu bar, then click the Security tab in the Options dialog. Type a password in the Password to Open field and click OK, then you'll be prompted to type your password again to verify it. Enter your password again and click OK. Now when you attempt to open the document,

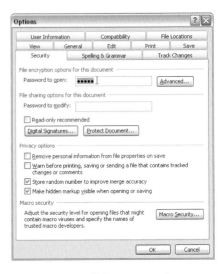

you'll be prompted for your password before you can open it. To turn off the password protection, simply delete the password from the Password to Open field in the Options dialog and click OK.

 ## COPY AND PASTE ON STEROIDS

If you're like me, you're usually all over the place when working in Office; I'll be working on related documents in just about all Office applications at the same time. Well, the Office Clipboard can make your life (if not your productivity) much better. For example, you can quickly assemble a presentation in PowerPoint by copying multiple blocks of text in Word (or Excel) and then using the Office Clipboard task pane to paste the contents into PowerPoint. To view the Office Clipboard, click Edit>Office Clipboard in the menu bar. This opens the Office Clipboard, where you can view all of your copied items. Now simply click to insert the item that you want to paste into your document, or click the Paste All button in the top left of the task pane to paste everything from the Clipboard at once.

THE ASSISTANT'S GOT TO GO

There are few things that I dislike (I can't say hate) more in life than the Office Assistant. I don't know why I hate, I mean dislike, the Office Assistant, I just do. There's no logic behind it. I guess application animations just freak me out. Well, if you're like me, or if you have your own reason for disliking the Office Assistant, you can easily get rid of it: Just right-click the Assistant when it appears, select Options in the shortcut menu; then in the Office Assistant dialog, click the Options tab, uncheck Use the Office Assistant, and click OK. The Office Assistant will never bother you again—sweet!

 ## HELP ME MADE EASY

There are probably hundreds of keyboard shortcuts available to Office applications (I haven't actually counted all of the keyboard shortcuts, but hundreds sound about right to me—well, at least tens and tens anyway), but the most important keyboard shortcut to remember in Office is for the Help task pane. Press F1 on your keyboard while working in any Office application to open the Help task pane. Now help is just a keystroke away.

 I'M HUNG UP, BUT I'LL RECOVER

I'm sure that your programs never crash or hang up on you. Mine never do either, but I've heard of it happening. If it ever happens to you, click Start>All Programs>Microsoft Office>Microsoft Office Tools>Microsoft Office Application Recovery, which launches the Office Application Recovery dialog, where you can recover or end an Office application. If your Office program is hung up, then select the program in the

dialog window and click the Recover Application button. Office will attempt to recover your documents and help prevent you from losing any of your work.

 GET FASTER WITH SHORTCUT KEYS

I live by shortcut keys; they make everything faster. Shortcut keys are the quickest way to increase your speed and productivity in just about any program, and Office provides a great way to help you learn shortcut keys. Click Tools>Customize, then click the Options tab. Next, check the Show Shortcut Keys in ScreenTips, then click Close. Now, move your mouse pointer over a button or icon, and you'll see a pop-up screen tip showing that command's shortcut key.

RESEARCH THIS!

The Research task pane is one of the best enhancements to Office 2003. The Research task pane provides an extensive collection of reference books and online services to help you. For example, you can find the definition of a word, look up a word in the *Encarta Encyclopedia* online, view a word's synonym, or translate words and phrases into different languages. And that's just for starters. To open the Research task pane, right-click any word in your document and click Look Up in the shortcut menu. To set your research options, click the Research Options link at the bottom of the task pane or click the Get Services on Office Marketplace link to add additional services to the Research task pane.

 ## DO-IT-YOURSELF REPAIRS

If Office starts acting up or you believe an Office document may be corrupt, you can perform a quick diagnostic to try to repair any problems. Select the Help menu and click Detect and Repair to open the Detect and Repair dialog. Next, choose your options and click Start. Detect and Repair automatically finds and fixes errors in your Office files.

LINK YOUR DOCS

Using hyperlinks in your documents is a great way to include information from other programs or even webpages. For instance, include hyperlinks in a Word document to link to an Excel spreadsheet or to webpages that provide additional information about the subject matter, or even include a link to

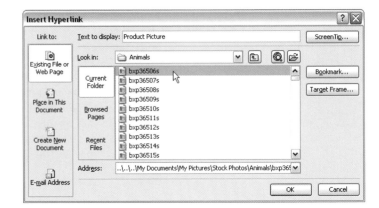

launch PowerPoint to begin a presentation. To include a hyperlink in your Office documents, press Control-K on your keyboard to open the Insert Hyperlink dialog. Next, click the Existing File or Web Page button in the Link To bar on the left, browse your hard drive to select a document or type a URL in the Address field, then click OK. A new link will appear where your pointer was positioned in your document. Control-click the URL to view the document. If you linked to a webpage or a document in another application, Control-clicking the URL will automatically launch your Web browser or the program that the link refers to.

YOU CAN CUT, PASTE, AND DELETE FROM HERE

You don't have to open Windows Explorer to move or delete files. You can actually use either the Open or Save As dialog for this task. To do this, go to the File menu, choose Open or Save As to open a dialog, then right-click the file you want to move, and click Cut in the shortcut menu (or click Delete to send the file to the Recycle Bin). Now, navigate to where you want to move the file on your hard drive, right-click any blank space in that folder, click Paste in the shortcut menu, then click the Cancel button to close the dialog. You just moved your file!

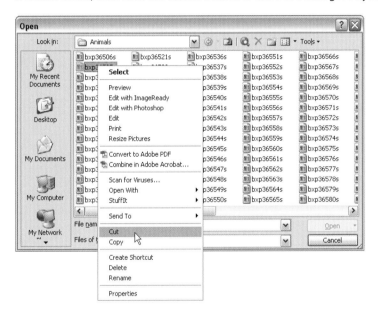

Spread the Word

WORKING WITH WORD

What would the world be like without Microsoft Word? You've probably never given it much thought. Well, I have (I have way too much free time), and it would be

Spread the Word
working with word

awful! It would be an awful, awful world full of typewriters and Wite Out™. People would have to actually learn how to spell and check their own grammar! I don't know about you, but this isn't a world that I'd want to live in. I'm the kind of person who gives credit where credit's due, and I pretty much give credit to Microsoft Word for our civilization as we know it today. Oh, computers played their part, but Microsoft Word gave us something to do with 'em. Grammar! Can you just imagine it? Wait, don't! It's just too painful. Imagine the look on the faces of the typewriter manufacturer executives the first time they saw Word. I bet it was awful!

PRINT WORD'S SHORTCUTS

This is probably the best tip in this chapter. I'm sure you've noticed by now that I'm a keyboard-shortcut junkie. I use them as much as possible. They just make everything faster, and when I'm working, faster is always better. Problem is, there's no single place to go within Word to view all of the available shortcuts…or so you might think if you went looking. Actually, there is, and here's how to get to it: Click Tools>Macro>Macros, then choose Word Commands from the Macros In drop-down menu. Next, select ListCommands under the Macro

Name field and click the Run button. Check All Word Commands in the resulting dialog, then click OK. Word opens a new document displaying every imaginable keyboard shortcut. Now print the list for future reference, and you'll be flying through Word in no time.

 REPEAT THAT SEARCH

There aren't many occasions where you're going to need this, but when you do, you'll be thankful that you know how to do it because it's really quick—I personally live for tips just like this (sad, isn't it?). Say you've just finished searching for a word or phrase using the Edit>Find command

and need to search for the word again; don't open the Find and Replace dialog in the Edit menu and retype the word, just press Shift-F4 on your keyboard. This keyboard shortcut will automatically search your document for the last-searched word or phrase. Faster, better. I bet you'll be using this tip even when you don't need to…just 'cause you can.

INSTANTLY OPEN YOUR LAST-USED DOCUMENT

Oh yeah—shortcuts to shortcuts, can it get any better? Nope! How often do you launch Word by opening the last document you were working on? A lot? Me too! I promise this tip will make your life better (at least your Office life). Locate Word (WINWORD.exe) by doing a search on your hard drive (Start>Search). Then right-click the icon and click Send To>Desktop (create short-cut) in the shortcut menu. Next, right-click the shortcut on your desktop and click Properties in the shortcut menu. Click the Shortcut tab in the Properties dialog and in the Target field type a space, then type "/mfile1" (without the quotes) at the end of the existing target (e.g., "C:\Program Files\Microsoft Office\OFFICE11\ WINWORD.EXE" /mfile1). (*Note:* Be sure to enter a space before the forward slash.) Click OK. Now when you click the shortcut icon, Word will automatically launch the last document used in Word.

 CUSTOMIZE YOUR DICTIONARY

In almost every document that you write, there will be words that Word thinks are misspelled but aren't—especially in documents that include names of people and companies—and adding each word one at a time to the Word dictionary can be almost painful. Well, there's a faster way. Click Tools>Options in the menu bar, then click the Spelling & Grammar tab in the Options dialog. Next, click the Custom Dictionaries button, select the New button, then right-click the CUSTOM file, and click Open With in the shortcut menu. Choose Notepad from the Programs list in the dialog and click OK. Word's dictionary will open in Notepad. Now add as many new words as you'd like to the CUSTOM file, placing each word on its own line. When you're finished, choose File>Save in Notepad to save your changes, and then close Notepad. Click Cancel in the Create Custom Dictionary dialog, then click OK in both the Custom Dictionaries and Options dialogs. Your new words will be added, and Word will no longer ask if those words are spelled correctly.

SHORTCUT TO YOUR TEXT

Here's a really slick way to open a document at the exact text passage you want. Select a block of text, a paragraph, sentence, phrase, or whatever, then right-click the highlighted text and drag-and-drop it to your desktop. Once you drop the text, select Create Document Shortcut Here in the shortcut menu that appears. Now when you double-click the shortcut's

icon on your desktop, Word will launch, opening your document at that text passage, word, or whatever. This is a great way to quickly begin a document where you left off, or to jump to the section of your document that you were editing. This shortcut can also be shared with users to provide quick access to important text within a document.

 ## WORD'S RISING IN THE CHARTS

Charts are one of Word's coolest tools. I use them all the time for no reason at all, and it amazes me how few users even know about them. Word allows you to add many types of customizable charts to your documents. Here's how: Place your cursor where you want to create a chart in your document, then select Insert>Picture>Chart from Word's menu bar. A chart will appear with an open datasheet. Take note of the menu bar—it's changed. You're now using Microsoft Graph, which has its own menus and tools. Now,

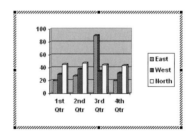

update the chart's datasheet with your own numerical values, headings, etc., and your chart is instantly updated. When finished, simply close the datasheet. You can get really geeky by using Microsoft Graph's menu bar to change the type, style, colors, and more in your chart. In addition, you can import existing data into your chart from Excel by choosing Edit>Import File. Go nuts!

FLIRTING WITH DISASTER

When you're creating a new document, how long does it take before you realize that you haven't saved it? With a distinct feeling of impending doom, you very carefully aim for the Save button in the Standard toolbar and click. Whew, that was close. We've all known the agony of

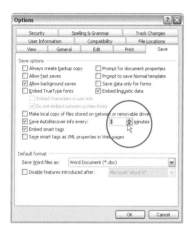

losing documents because our computer decided to crash, freeze, or freak out just prior to saving our work. Good news…you don't have to live in fear any longer because Word 2003 uses AutoRecovery. By default, this feature is enabled and set to save your work automatically every 10 minutes, but I can do a lot of work in 10 minutes. Instead, I like to have Word automatically save my work every minute. I don't mind redoing 1 minute of work, but 10 is just crazy. To access Auto-Recovery, click Tools>Options in the menu bar, then click the Save tab in the Options dialog. Next, under Save Options, change the Save AutoRecover Info Every field from 10 minutes to 1 minute, then click OK.

 ## I'VE ONLY GOT ONE SHEET OF PAPER

Have you ever had several pages to print but only one sheet of paper? It's absolutely pathetic, but this happens to me all the time. I'm always running out of paper. Well, you can use Word's Print dialog to print several pages on one piece of paper. You may have to break out the mag-

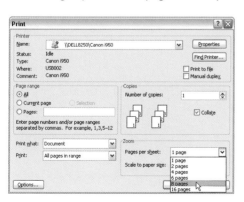

nifying glass to read it, but you can at least get it on paper (which is usually good enough for me). Here's how: Press Control-P on your keyboard to open the Print dialog. Next, open the Pages Per Sheet drop-down menu in the Zoom category, select how many pages of your document should be printed to a single piece of paper, then click OK. There you go…a book printed on one sheet of paper.

 KEEPING UP TO DATE WITH FIELDS

If you use the same document frequently and are continuously changing its date, then make the date a "field" instead. This is very handy for fax cover sheets and form letters. Select Insert>Field from the menu bar, then select Date in the Field Names list on the left. Choose your format in the Date Formats list on the right and click OK. You'll now see the current date appear…this is a field. The cool thing about this field is that from now on, whenever you open the document, the date will automatically update. While you're in the Field dialog, be sure to look around at the different fields that are available—there are a ton.

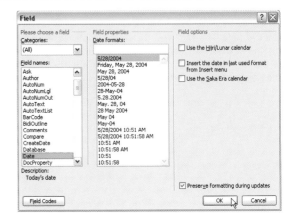

 SUPER-FAST TIME AND DATE

Because the current date and current time are the two most frequently used fields, wouldn't it be great if there were a quick way to insert them? Well, there is (otherwise this wouldn't be a tip). Place your cursor where you want to insert a date or time field and press Alt-Shift-D to insert the current date or press Alt-Shift-T to add the current time.

TURN FIELDS INTO TEXT

In a previous tip, I showed you how to insert a field into your documents, which as you now know is very cool, but if you're going to email the document or share it over a network, then you'll probably want to turn the field into regular text, otherwise the field will continue to update anytime anyone opens the document. To quickly convert your field to text, click within the field and press Control-Shift-F9.

STOP CONTROL-CLICKING (IT'S BAD FOR YOU)

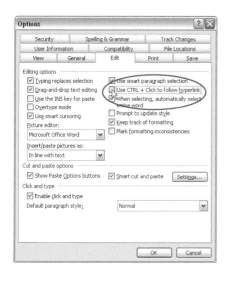

By default, anytime you type a hyperlink into your document, you can only open it by pressing-and-holding the Control key and clicking the link with your mouse pointer. (It's crazy, I know.) This can be somewhat ineffective at times, especially when you want readers to be able to follow your links. You can turn the Control-click feature off by selecting Tools>Options, then clicking the Edit tab in the Options dialog. Uncheck Use CTRL + Click to Follow Hyperlink, and click OK. Now all you have to do is click any hyperlink in your document to immediately open the linked file or URL.

CHAPTER 2 • Working with Word   **23**

FIND AND REPLACE USING THE CLIPBOARD

Find and Replace works great for finding and replacing words in your documents, but you can get really geeky with it and replace words with the contents on the Office Clipboard (told ya…geeky). For example, you may want to replace all instances of a word (such as the word "Search") in your document with a picture (of binoculars, for instance). To do this, press Control-F to open the Find and Replace dialog. Next, click the Replace tab and in the Find What field, type the word to be replaced (in our example, "Search"). Then in the Replace With field, type "^c" (press Shift-6 then type a lowercase c), and click Replace All. All of the words are quickly replaced with the Office Clipboard contents. *Note:* Before doing the Find and Replace, make sure to copy a picture of binoculars to the Office Clipboard (by choosing Insert>Picture>Clip Art, choosing your image, and clicking Edit>Copy to copy the image to the Clipboard) or this tip won't work at all.

 ## WORD'S SUPER-SECRET WORK MENU

I love secret stuff! So, I love the fact that Word's most useful menu is completely hidden and undocumented (just kidding!). Word's Work menu is ridiculously useful and allows you to group your most frequently used documents for quick access. Here's how to add the Work menu: Right-click any menu or toolbar and click Customize in the shortcut menu. Next, click the Commands tab and select Built-in Menus in the Categories list. Now drag-and-drop the Work menu from the Commands pane onto the menu bar or onto any toolbar. To add the document that you're working on to the menu, click Work>Add to Work Menu. Your document now appears on the Work menu, ready to be opened at any time with a click of your mouse. To remove items from the Work menu, press Control-Alt–- (hyphen), then click any item in the menu.

I CAN ACTUALLY SELECT THAT TABLE

I'm all about speed, and anytime I find a quicker way to do something, I'll do it. So, in my quest to do everything faster, I discovered this little shortcut for selecting a table. Click anywhere inside a table and press Alt-5 on the numeric keypad (making certain that the Number Lock key isn't active), and just like magic (it's not really magic), your table is selected. To deselect the table, simply click anywhere inside or outside your table.

 ## *OUI, OUI*—I CAN TRANSLATE

Have you ever wondered how to spell "bottled water" in Spanish? If you've been to Central America, then you probably have, and fortunately, as long as you have Word and an Internet connection, you can quickly get the help you need to translate just about any word or phrase for numerous languages. To do this in Word, select a word or phrase, right-click the selected text, and click Translate in the shortcut menu. This opens the Research task pane. Now, select the language that you'd like to translate your text into from the To drop-down menu, and the translation will appear at the bottom of the Translation window. Depending on how you've set up Word on your computer, you may have to be online to translate into various languages.

DON'T JUST PASTE IT, SPIKE IT

Anything called Spike in a computer program just has to be good—and Word's Spike is. The Spike allows you to move multiple objects (text, graphics, etc.) and paste them all at the same time into a document. To "spike" your documents, first select the text and graphics that you want to move, then press Control-F3 on your keyboard. Do this as many times as necessary for as many objects as you want to move (there's no limit to how much you can save to the Spike—actually I'm sure there is, but I've never been able to max it out). When you're ready to paste the objects into your document, place your cursor where you want to insert the content, then press Control-Shift-F3. If you don't want to empty your Spike, click Insert>AutoText>AutoText in the menu bar, then select Spike from the Enter AutoText Entries Here field, and click the Insert button. *Note:* If you don't see Spike listed in the AutoText entries, add it by typing "Spike" (without the quotes) in the Enter AutoText Entries Here text field, then click Add. Spike will now appear as a selection.

 SMART TAGS REALLY ARE SMART

To quickly add an email address for someone in your Outlook Contacts list, simply type his or her name, and the name will appear underlined with a purple dotted line. The dotted line indicates that there are Smart Tags available for the text. Move your cursor over the name and click the down-facing arrow on the Smart Tag's information button. Next, click Insert Address in the Smart Tag menu and Word will automatically add the contact's address to your document. *Note:* If Smart Tags don't appear, go to Tools>AutoCorrect and click the Smart Tags tab in the dialog. Turn on the Show Smart Tag Actions Button checkbox and be sure to select the Person Name (Outlook E-mail Recipients) checkbox in the Recognizers category.

PRINT LIKE THE POST OFFICE

Want to make certain that your mail gets to where it's supposed to? Of course you do, that's kind of the entire point of mailing a letter. Well, you can actually print U.S. delivery point bar codes (postal ZIP codes) on your envelopes (we all know the post office needs the help). To do this, click Tools>Letters and Mailings>Envelopes and Labels. Click the Envelopes tab in the Envelopes and Labels dialog. Now, click the Options button, then check the Delivery Point Bar Code checkbox in the Envelope Options tab, and click OK. Now anytime you print an envelope and include the recipient's ZIP code, Word will automatically print the destination's bar code. The U.S. Postal Service appreciates the help.

 I DON'T USE AVERY LABELS

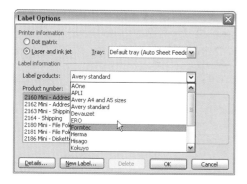

If you print labels, you probably use Avery labels (it's nice to be Avery). Avery labels are so popular that Word uses its label styles by default. Believe it or not, there are other label manufacturers out there, and you just might be using them. Well, Word can actually help you print to labels made by other companies. To select your labels in Word, click Tools>Letters and Mailings>Envelopes and Labels. Click the Labels tab in the Envelopes and Labels dialog, then click the Options button. Click the Label Products drop-down menu in the Label Information category and select your label manufacturer. Now you can locate and print your labels by selecting them from the Product Number list. Click OK when finished.

▬ ▣ ☒ PRINT A PORTION

Printing a portion of a document is shockingly difficult, so follow along carefully. First, select the text block or blocks that you want to print, then press Control-P on your keyboard to open the Print dialog. Now, check Selection under the Page Range category and click OK. Only the selected text will be printed (unless you're trying to print text that appears within a text box, as part of a table, etc.). I know this is a tough one, so read it a few times if you're not quite getting it. ;-)

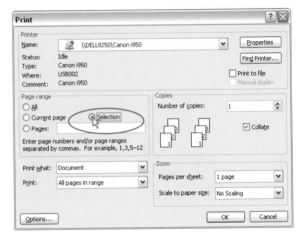

▬ ▣ ☒ BACKWARD IS BETTER

If you own a printer that prints your documents face up, it just makes sense to change your default print setup. To prevent yourself from having to reorder your printed documents every time you print, change the print order so that the last page prints first, and your pages fall into order (page 1 through whatever). To do this, click Tools>Options in the menu bar, click the Print tab, check Reverse Print Order under the Printing Options category, and click OK. Now when you print your documents, they'll print in reverse order, which is actually the right order.

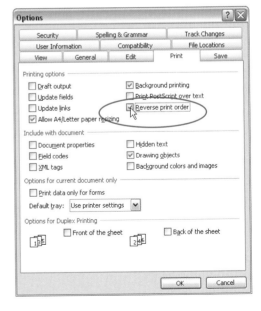

⊟ ☐ ☒ GIVE ME A HUNDREDTH OF AN INCH

I've never had a reason to use this, but I still think it's pretty cool. If you ever need to use the rulers to measure hundredths of an inch instead of the default tenths of an inch, press the Alt key while clicking on the rulers. You can now move tab stops to measure within a hundredth of an inch.

⊟ ☐ ☒ GROOVY MENUS

Want to spice up Word's menus? Try animating them. Click Tools>Customize in the menu bar, then click the Options tab in the Customize dialog. Next, click the Menu Animations drop-down menu in the Other category. Here you can select from four different animations for Word's menus (there really should be at least five, but I'll take what I can get). Once you've selected an animation, click Close and then click any menu to see your animations in action. Exciting, isn't it?

SEND, SHARE, COMPARE

You can easily share your documents
with friends and colleagues so they
can review and edit them. Not me, of
course; I hate sharing. But if you want
to do this, click File>Send To>Mail
Recipient (for Review) in the menu bar.
Outlook 2003 will open, and you can
add a recipient's email address. When
finished, click the Send button to send
your document. When you receive the
document back, Word will prompt you
to merge the two documents to show
the changes that were made.

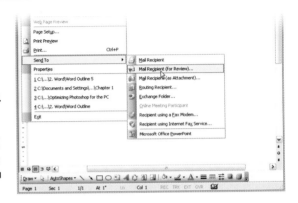

 YOU'RE RESTRICTED

If you want to share a document, but you don't want anyone to
actually make changes to it, then you should protect your document before sending (this is more my style). Here's how: Click
Tools>Protect Document in the menu bar. Now, check Allow Only
This Type of Editing in the Document under the Editing Restrictions
category in the Protect Document task pane. Next, click the Editing
Restrictions drop-down menu and select an option. For this purpose,
I'd recommend selecting Comments, which allows recipients to place
comments throughout your document but doesn't allow them to
edit it. To finish, click the Yes, Start Enforcing Protection button,
and Word will prompt you for a password for the document. Type
a password and then click OK. Now when you share your document,
users can only post comments.

SPLIT AND EDIT

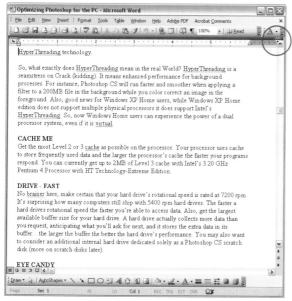

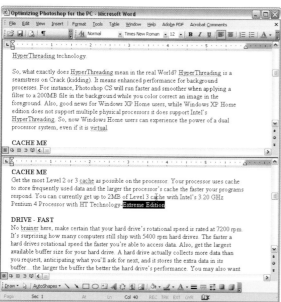

Microsoft is master of the obvious—here's a perfect example: Have you ever noticed the little handle above the right scroll bar? No? Hmm, how did you miss it? Well, even if you had noticed it, you probably never thought to grab and slide it down to split your page. If you had, you'd have found that this little bar does a pretty slick trick: It splits your current document so you can edit two parts of it at the same time, in the same window. Go ahead, grab it, and slide it downward to any position in your document to split the page. Now you can scroll and edit two sections of the same document at the same time. To get back to normal, simply drag-and-drop the divider bar back to the top of the window.

YOU CAN USE YOUR TOOLBARS IN FULL SCREEN MODE

I have to admit it: I really like working in Full Screen mode in Word and I'm man enough to admit it. I just have more room for everything. Not everyone likes it as much as I do, however, and I found out why: People think you lose your toolbars. Well you do, but you can get them back and dock or float them anywhere on your screen. Here's how: Click View>Full Screen in the menu bar. Now, click the down-facing arrow on the floating Full Screen menu and point to Add or Remove Buttons>Customize. Next, check the Toolbars tab in the Customize dialog, check the toolbars that you'd like to view in Full Screen mode, and then click Close…there's your toolbars! You can now dock or float them anywhere on your screen.

WORD HOPPING

To quickly jump from word to word in a sentence, press the Control-Left Arrow keys to jump to the start of the previous word; press the Control-Right Arrow keys to jump to the start of the next word. These keyboard shortcuts are a great way to navigate sentences quickly to make changes to individual words.

EDIT MULTIPLE PAGES

To edit multiple pages in Word, click the Print Preview button on the Standard toolbar, then right-click anywhere within the Print Preview toolbar, and click Standard to open the Standard toolbar. Next, put your mouse pointer on the Multiple Pages button in the Print Preview toolbar and when it highlights, press the Alt key and start to drag. Now, hold the Control key while dragging-and-dropping the Multiple Pages button onto the Standard toolbar. When you click the Close Print Preview window, the Multiple Pages button will still appear on your Standard toolbar. Now you can view and edit multiple pages. Isn't that great?

SAVE 'EM ALL, CLOSE 'EM ALL

Wouldn't it be nice if we could save all of our open documents at once? But when we click File in the menu bar, we only have the option to save the current document. Well, there's a way around this: Press-and-hold the Shift key on your keyboard, then click File in the menu bar. You now have options to Save All and Close All.

NAVIGATING THE EASY WAY

Navigating your documents doesn't have to be difficult, unless you like to do things the hard way. If that's the case, then don't read this tip—it's only helpful and you'll resent it. If you like doing things the easy way, however, try clicking the Select Browse Object button located near the bottom of the right scroll bar. You can quickly browse by field, comment, heading, graphic, and many other objects. Click an object and Word will automatically begin to browse your document for that object. Also, notice the arrows above and below the Select Browse Object button—they turn blue when any option other than Browse by Page is selected, allowing you to search above or below your insertion point.

 YAY, PREVIEWS!

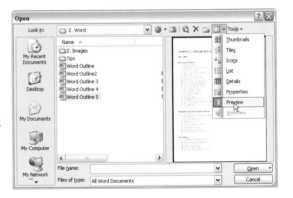

Do you have trouble trying to locate the correct file to open? I always do. I guess I'm just not very good at giving my files very descriptive names. I can't even find a document that I was working on literally five minutes ago…it's bad. Well, I found a way to end my distress. I open my documents with preview images. Now I can see a thumbnail of my document before I open it. To do this, click File>Open in the menu bar. Next, click the down-facing arrow next to the Views button near the top right of the dialog and select Preview. Now, select a document in the Name window, and you'll see a preview of your file in the Open dialog (File>Open) before you open it. If you want to see a thumbnail image of your entire document in the Open dialog, click File>Properties while working in a document that you want to preview later as a thumbnail, and click the Summary tab in the Properties dialog. Click the Save Preview Picture checkbox, then click OK.

THERE'S A COMPARISON TO BE MADE

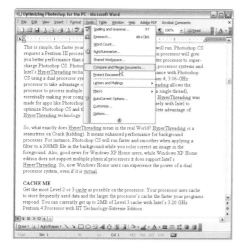

To compare two versions of the same document, click Tools>Compare and Merge Documents in the menu bar. Choose which document to compare with the original or current document, click the Legal Blackline checkbox, and click Compare in the dialog. Word will show you all of the changes made to your document. You can also merge the document into the current document or merge both documents into a new document by clicking Tools>Compare and Merge Documents, selecting the document to merge into your current document, and then clicking the down-facing arrow within the Merge button. Select either Merge into Current Document or Merge into New Document. This is a great way to track changes you've made and be selective about which changes to keep for your final draft.

BOOKMARKS ARE BETTER

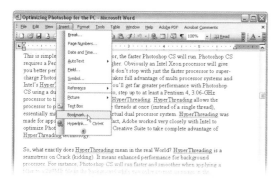

To find your place in a document quickly, just create a bookmark. Highlight text or place your cursor in the document where you'd like to create the bookmark, then click Insert>Bookmark from the menu bar. Type an appropriate name in the Bookmark Name field, click the Add button, and you've created a bookmark. To jump to a bookmark in your document, click Insert>Bookmark in the menu bar, then select the bookmark name in the list and click the Go To button to jump instantly to that location in your document.

NEED A TABLE OF CONTENTS?

If you've created a long document that includes several headings, you can create a table of contents (it only makes sense). To do this, place your cursor where you want to insert your table of contents, choose Insert>Reference>Index and Tables from the menu bar, then click the Table of Contents tab in the Index and Tables dialog, make any changes you'd like, and click OK. Word will create a table of contents from the headings in your document. Now you can quickly navigate your document using its very own table of contents.

READING LAYOUT'S GOT TO GO

I find it just a little annoying that DOC files open in Reading Layout mode anytime I open an attached Word (.doc) file from an email. I typically receive Word files to edit or comment on; very seldom do I get them just to read. Anyway, I find this annoying enough to do something about it, and you can too. To turn off Reading Layout mode for email attachments, select Tools>Options from the menu bar, click the General tab in the Options dialog, uncheck Allow Starting in Reading Layout (near the top-right corner of the tab), then click OK. Now your attached Word files will launch in an editing mode instead of Reading Layout mode.

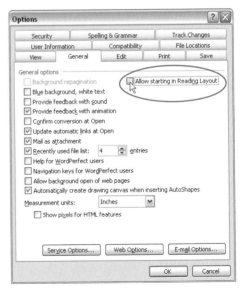

LACKING CREATIVITY? MAKE IT WORK FOR YOU

I'm not very creative—most of my documents tend to follow a similar look and feel. I'm working on the problem (without much luck) but I've found a way to make this work for me. I can quickly create a new document that has the look and feel of an existing document (I'm an enabler) by simply clicking File>New in the menu bar and clicking the From Existing Document link in the New Document task pane. This opens the New From Existing Document dialog, where you can select your file, which Word will open as a new document. When you're finished making changes, simply save it with a new file name by choosing File>Save As.

 QUICK PRINT PREVIEW

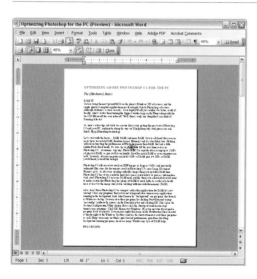

Try this undocumented keyboard shortcut the next time you need to quickly view a document in Print Preview mode. Press Control-Alt-I to switch to Print Preview. Press the shortcut again to switch back to Normal viewing mode.

AUTOCORRECT MY ABBREVIATIONS? COOL!

AutoCorrect is more powerful than you might think; for example, it has the ability to interpret custom abbreviations of text passages, which is perfect for repetitive text such as your name, address, or for the closing of a letter (name, address, phone, email, etc.). Try this: Type your name and address, select the text, and click Tools>AutoCorrect Options in the menu bar. The AutoCorrect dialog will open, displaying the Auto-Correct tab, which shows your name and address in the With field. Now, type an abbreviation in the Replace field, such as "mna" (without the quotes), short for "My Name and Address," then click OK. Now, type "mna" and hit Enter or the Spacebar, and Word will instantly replace "mna" with your name and address. Very cool!

 LOTS O' LINES

You're probably familiar with the trick to create a solid line in Word: Type three hyphens (---) then press Enter on your keyboard. But did you know that you could use similar tricks to create all kinds of lines? For example:

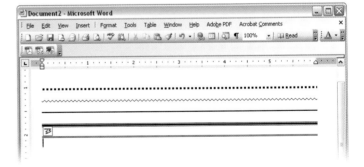

• Type three asterisks (***) then press Enter to create a dotted line.
• Type three tilde symbols (~~~) then press Enter to create a wavy line.
• Type three underscores (___) then press Enter to create a bold line.
• Type three pound symbols (###) then press Enter to create a triple line.
• Type three equal signs (===) then press Enter to create a double line.

I KNEW THERE HAD TO BE A BETTER WAY

How many of you go to the menu bar to add a row at the end of a table? Yep, we all do, but there's a faster way. Click the last cell in the bottom row of your table, then press the Tab key on your keyboard. This automatically adds a new row to the bottom of the table—now that's faster!

TAB YOUR CELLS

If you've ever had to add a Tab character to a table cell, you probably found yourself scratching your head because you can't add a Tab character to a cell! Pressing the Tab key only jumps you from cell to cell. There's a way around this, though. Press Control-Tab, which will place a Tab character in your cell. Now you can stop scratching your head…problem solved.

PRESERVE YOUR FORMATTING

If you want to maintain your text's formatting when copying-and-pasting it to a new document, be sure to include the text's last paragraph mark. To view paragraph marks, click the Show/Hide button in the Standard toolbar, then copy (Edit>Copy) your text, including all the formatting marks and paste it (Edit>Paste) to its new location. Click the Show/Hide button again to hide the document's formatting marks. *Note:* This will only work if the Use Smart Paragraph Selection checkbox is selected in the Edit tab of the Options dialog (Tools>Options).

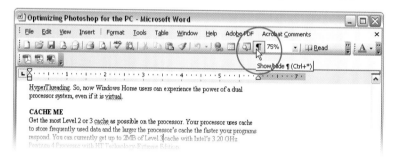

 EXCEL'S GOT NOTHIN' ON WORD

Excel isn't the only Office program capable of calculating numbers. Word can perform calculations in tables, too. To calculate numbers in a table's row, place your numbers in the row's cells, leaving the last cell empty. Next, click the last cell in the row and click Table>Formula in the menu bar. Use the default formula of "=SUM(LEFT)" and click OK. Word will calculate the previous cells and place the added results in the last cell. Repeat the same procedure for calculating columns, using the default formula "=SUM(ABOVE)."

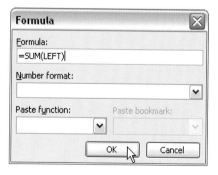

IT'S ALL ABOUT THE PLUS (AND MINUS) SIGNS

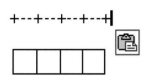

Did you know that tables are made up of plus and minus signs? It's true, try this: Using the number keypad, type a plus sign (+) followed by two minus signs (––) followed by a plus sign (+), then press Enter. You just created a single-cell table. Repeat this pattern (e.g., +––+––+––+––+) for each cell that you'd like to create.

 ### A TEMPLATE OF YOUR VERY OWN

If you've designed your letterhead or other frequently used documents in Word, you may want to save them as templates. To save a document as a template, first apply your formatting and any graphics, then click File>Save As in the menu bar. In the Save As dialog, type a descriptive name

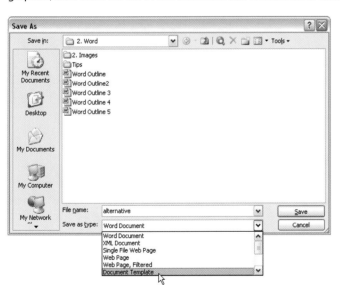

for your document in the File Name field, then select Document Template in the Save As Type field, and click Save. To open your new template, click File>New, which opens the New Document task pane. Click the On My Computer link under the Templates category, then click the General tab in the Templates dialog. Now, select your template and click OK.

 SPLITTING UP ISN'T HARD TO DO

You've just finished typing a ten-page article and suddenly realize that the editor wanted your story in two columns. Well, too bad; it's too late. You're a loser, and they're gonna fire you (kidding). We can fix it, here's how: First, place your cursor where you want the columns to begin, then click Format>Columns in the menu bar. Next, click the Two icon under the Presets category and click OK. All the text following your cursor is instantly formatted into two columns.

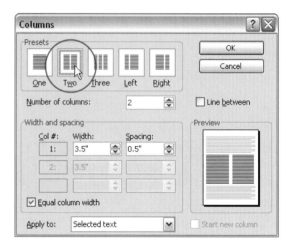

 SHRINK YOUR DOCUMENT

It can be a pain trying to get the last couple of sentences to fit onto a page. Most documents fit on a single page (they just do, I'm not making this stuff up), and if

they don't, we'll stop at practically nothing to get the last couple of sentences to fit so that we don't have to print a second page. We'll try experimenting with font sizes, deleting every other word—you name it—but there's an easier way. Press Control-Alt-I to view your document in Print Preview and then click the Shrink to Fit button in the Print Preview toolbar. This will shrink your document by adjusting the font size to include the extra text. Now you can print your document on only one sheet of paper.

I'VE MADE A MISTAKE

We can do some pretty awful things to text—too many words underlined, bolded, itali-cized—it can get crazy. When your formatting gets out of hand, you can get things back to normal by selecting the offending text and pressing Control-Spacebar. This will reset your text style in the Formatting toolbar to Normal. You can do the same to a paragraph's style by selecting it and pressing Control-Q to return it to normal paragraph style.

 ## UNDO IT ALL

You probably already know that you can perform multiple undos in Word by pressing Control-Z repeatedly, but what if you want to undo tens or even hundreds of changes? That's a lot of Control-Zs. Try this instead: Click the down-facing arrow next to the Undo button in the Standard toolbar, and you'll see a list of literally hundreds of changes that you've made to your document (that is, if you've made hundreds of changes). Now, you can simply scroll through the list until you find the point where you'd like to undo all previous changes. Simply click the item on the list and Word will instantly perform all of the undos that you've selected.

 PICK THE PILCROW

When pasting together a document from
several different sources, you're going to
get several differently formatted paragraphs,
but you can quickly give your paragraphs
the same formatting. To do this, click the
Show/Hide button (it looks like a backward
"P") in the Standard toolbar to show your
formatting markers. Next, double-click
to select the paragraph marker (called a
"pilcrow") that you'd like to copy, then
right-click the marker, and click Copy in
the shortcut menu. Now, double-click the
marker at the end of the paragraph to which
you'd like to apply the copied paragraph
formatting, right-click the marker, and
select Paste in the shortcut menu. Your
paragraph's formatting will change to reflect
the look of the copied pilcrow. Repeat this as
many times as you'd like to apply consistent
formatting to your paragraphs.

 CUSTOMIZE YOUR BULLETS

Do you use bullets? Sure you do, we all do. You don't have to be
like everyone else, though. You can customize your bullets for
a personal touch. Click Format>Bullets and Numbering in the
menu bar, then click the Bulleted tab, click on any style icon, and
click the Customize button. Next, click the Character button in
the Customized Bulleted List dialog to use one of the Windows
character symbols or click Cancel to go back to the Customize
Bulleted List dialog and click the Picture button to use a picture
or to import your own graphics. When finished, click OK. Now go
back to Format>Bullets and Numbering, select your customized
bullet, and begin inserting your new bullets.

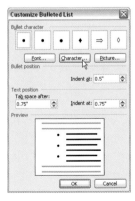

I NEED A LITTLE ROOM

1. Line 1
2. Line 2
3. Line 3
4. Line 4
5. Line 5
6. Line 6
7. Line 7
8. Line 8
9. Line 9
10. Line 10

Have you noticed how tight the line spacing can appear when using automatic numbering? Personally, I need some room. So, if you need a little more spacing between your numbered lines, try this: Select your numbered text and press Control-Zero on your keyboard. That's better! Press Control-Zero again to return your numbering to its regular line spacing.

TYPE IT AGAIN

Word has a secret key that will repeat the last several words you've typed. I've used this to type repeating words and for adding filler text, and I'm sure you'll find your own uses for it. Try this: Type your name, then press the F4 key on your keyboard. Word inserts your name again. Press the F4 key as many times as you'd like to continue adding the text. Personally, I love seeing my name typed over and over again. It's very soothing.

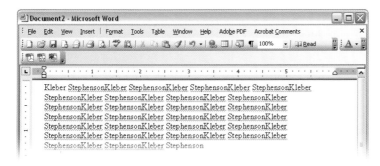

THAT'S NOT PAGE ONE

Even Word needs a little help once in a while. Here's an example: You've written a multipage document and numbered the pages (Insert>Page Numbers), but your first page is your title page. Word doesn't know this and will number your title page as page 1, even though the second page is actually page 1. See, Word needs help. To fix this, go to Insert>Page Numbers in the menu bar, select your page number positioning (i.e., the bottom of the page, top, etc.), and uncheck Show Number on First Page. Wait, you're not finished. Next, click the Format button and check Start At in the Page Numbering category and type "0" (zero without the quotes), click OK, and then click OK to close the Page Numbers dialog. Now, check out your page numbering. Page 1 begins on the second page.

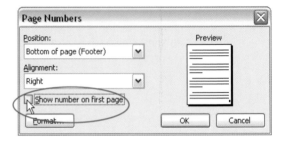

 ## SAVE THAT TABLE SIZE

If you find yourself using the same table size over and over again, and it's not Word's default table dimensions, then you should save your custom table size. You can easily do this the next time that you insert a table by clicking Table>Insert>Table. This opens the Insert Table dialog. Now, change the number of columns and rows to whatever you'd like, but before you close the dialog, check Remember Dimensions for New Tables, then click OK. Now, your preferences are saved, so every time you open the Insert Table dialog, your custom table dimensions are displayed by default.

CONTROL YOUR COLUMN WIDTHS

If you want to change only the size of the left or right column in a table, while keeping your other columns evenly spaced, hold the Control key while dragging the column border to the left or right (your mouse pointer will turn into a double-sided arrow). When you release your mouse, the column will be resized, while keeping all of your other columns evenly spaced.

 AUTOFIT JUST ONE COLUMN

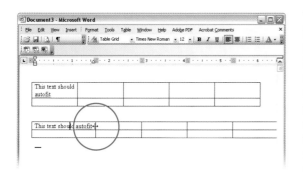

To automatically fit a single column, first select the column by clicking above it, then right-click anywhere in the column, and click AutoFit> AutoFit to Contents. But doing it this way affects every cell in the table. Try this instead: Select the cell that you want to autofit, then double-click the right border of the column (your mouse pointer will turn into a double-sided arrow, as shown) until your text fits…instant autofit. Unlike the AutoFit to Contents command, this technique only affects the cell you're double-clicking; it doesn't affect other cells.

FIND ALL THE SAME

Here's a great shortcut for finding similarly formatted text, whether it's headings, bold or italic text, or any other type of text formatting. Simply select the formatted text, then right-click the text and click Select Text with Similar Formatting in the shortcut menu. Word will automatically select all text in your document that's formatted in the same way. Once your text is selected throughout your document, add any new formatting you'd like and it's applied to all of the selected text. This tip is perfect for quickly changing the format of headings throughout your document.

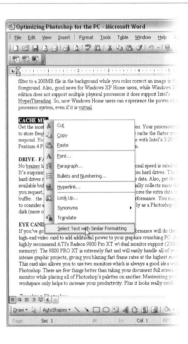

QUICK SYNONYMS

Most of us (especially me) need all the help we can get, and fortunately Word can be very helpful. Here's a good example: If you need a quick list of alternative words (synonyms) for terms in your document, simply right-click the word and point to Synonyms in the shortcut menu for a quick list of alternatives.

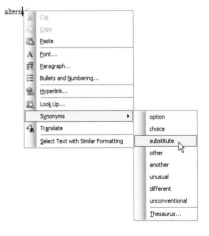

IT'S ALL IN THE LINE NUMBER

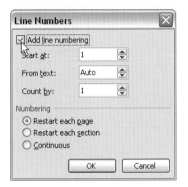

I use line numbers all the time—for referencing important text, debugging code, or as a reminder of edits that need to be made. To turn on line numbers for your document, click File>Page Setup, then click the Layout tab in the Page Setup dialog. Next, click the Line Numbers button and check Add Line Numbering in the Line Numbers dialog. Now, tell Word how to number your pages and click OK. Your new line numbers will appear in the left margin of your pages.

 ## IN SUMMARY…

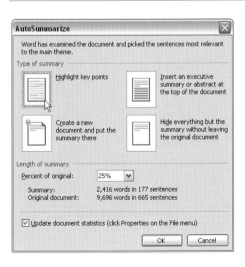

An extremely useful (or useless, I'm not sure which) feature of Word is AutoSummarize. Using AutoSummarize, you can quickly get important info about your document that would otherwise take a considerable amount of time to figure out. You can ask Word to create a quick summary of your document by clicking Tools>AutoSummarize. You'll have several options for creating your document's summary. When finished, click OK in the AutoSummarize dialog.

GIVE THE SCRAPS TO YOUR DESKTOP

Document Scraps are extremely cool, useful, and one of my favorite features in Word. I use them all the time, especially when writing. Try this next time you're writing: Select a block of text in Word, right-click on it, and then drag-and-drop it onto your desktop. In the shortcut menu that appears, select Create Scrap Here. You just created a Document Scrap. This is a great way to save your ideas and then drag-and-drop them from Scrap into your documents whenever you'd like.

 RESUME OR RÉSUMÉ

What's more fun than accented characters? I can't think of a thing (just kidding, accented characters really aren't fun). Follow the keyboard shortcuts below, and you'll actually be able to finally type résumé and other un-American words in no time. Actually, accented characters are a little fun, but be careful: You may find yourself underlining text and creating new documents if you don't type these commands correctly.

(é)	Press Control-'-E (apostrophe)
(Ü)	Press Control-Shift-;-U (semicolon)
(ç)	Press Control-,-C (comma)
(Ñ)	Press Control-Shift-`-N (tilde)

Resume or Résumé

REMEMBERING SHORTCUTS

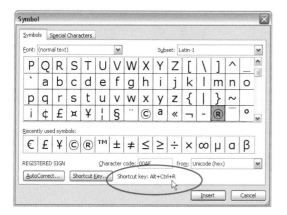

In the previous tip, I showed you how to insert accented characters using keyboard shortcuts. Where can you find these keyboard shortcuts? In Word's Symbol dialog. Using the Symbol dialog is a super-fast way to learn keyboard shortcuts for all of your favorite symbols (such as ©, ®, ™, etc.). Click Insert>Symbol to open Word's Symbol dialog and click a symbol that you'd like to insert into your document. Notice the text just to the right of the Shortcut Key button at the bottom of the dialog; it shows the symbol's keyboard shortcut. Use the shortcut to quickly insert your most frequently used symbols in the future—saves a ton of time.

 WANT CONTROL OVER YOUR TEXT? THEN SHIFT

To increase the size of selected text, press Control-Shift-> (period key) or quickly decrease the size of selected text by pressing Control-Shift-< (comma key). You can also select blocks of text above or below the cursor by repeatedly pressing Control-Shift-Up Arrow or Control-Shift-Down Arrow.

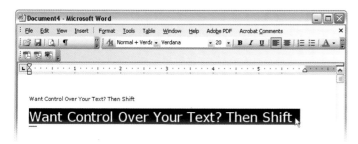

☐☐☒ EDITABLE PRINT PREVIEWS

Print Preview is often the perfect view—it allows you to see exactly what your document will look like when printed, but wouldn't it be great if we could edit our documents in Print Preview? Nobody wants to go back and forth between editing documents and previewing them. Well, you don't have to—you can edit in Print Preview. Here's how: First, press Control-Alt-I to show Print Preview. Next, click the Magnifier button in the Print Preview toolbar and zoom in on your text. You won't see your cursor, but all of the other keyboard commands will work. Type and your text will appear, press Enter

to create line breaks, or use the Up and Down Arrow keys to navigate in your document. When you're finished making your changes, click the Magnifier button to zoom back out to preview your document again.

☐☐☒ QUICK CASE

You can quickly change the case of any word or words by first selecting your text, then pressing Shift-F3 on the keyboard. Continue pressing the F3 key while holding the Shift key to change the case of your text from title case to uppercase to lowercase (as shown).

The Quick Brown Fox Jumps
THE QUICK BROWN FOX JUMPS
the quick brown fox jumps

PICKY SELECTIONS

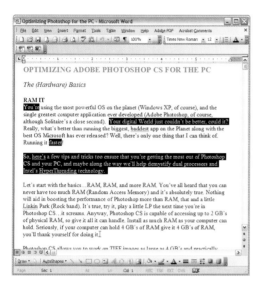

If you ever need to select different text blocks, sentences, or individual words throughout a document to change formatting or text, color, or whatever, press-and-hold the Control key, then make your selections. As long as you're holding the Control key, you'll be able to make multiple selections throughout your document. When finished, make any changes and then deselect your text.

 ## FAKE IT, DUMMY

There comes a time in everyone's writing career when we just have to fake it—with our text, that is. You can easily place fake text (dummy text) in your document: Just place the cursor where you want to insert the dummy text, type "=rand(5,7)" (without the quotes), then press Enter on your keyboard. This command will place five paragraphs of fake text, each containing seven sentences. Of course, you can change the (5,7) to any number you'd like—the first number represents the number of paragraphs (5); and the second represents the number of sentences per paragraph (7).

THE EASY WAY TO GET TEXT ABOVE YOUR TABLE

This has happened to everyone—don't deny it. You need to place text above a table at the top of your document and there's only one workaround. You have to cut the table, insert your text, then paste the table back into your document, right? Well, that works, but there's a better way. Click inside the first cell in the top row of the table, then press Control-Shift-Enter on your keyboard to insert a paragraph above the table. I bet you knew there had to be a better way.

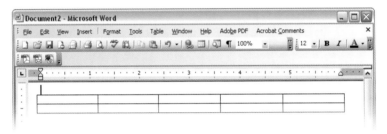

 VOICE YOUR COMMENTS

From time to time you're going to want to place text comments into your document—to remind you of edits, check word definitions, or suggest ideas—but did you know that you could also record voice comments? Here's how: Right-click any toolbar and select Reviewing in the shortcut menu. The Insert Voice button isn't on the Reviewing toolbar by default, so if you don't see the Insert Voice button, click the down-facing arrow at the end of the toolbar and go to Add or Remove Buttons>Reviewing and click Insert Voice. The button now appears on the Reviewing toolbar. To insert a voice comment, select the text that you want to comment on, click the Insert Voice button, and then click the Record button.

DRAG, HOVER, DROP

To move selected text objects quickly between Word documents (or any open Office applications), click-and-hold the object with your mouse, then drag it to the Windows Taskbar and hover over the document's button where you want to place the object. After hovering for a moment, the document becomes active and appears in the foreground, where you just drop the object into place.

 ## NOW YOU SEE ME, NOW YOU DON'T

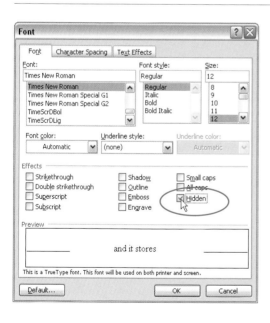

If you have sensitive information in a document that you don't want others to see (or if you're just really paranoid —I'm sure you have your reasons), you can hide your text. Just select the text that you want to hide, click Format>Font in the menu bar, then click Hidden under the Effects category, and click OK. Your text is gone. Actually, it's still there, but you can't see it anymore. To once again display your text, click Tools>Options in the menu bar, click the View tab in the Options dialog, then check Hidden Text under the Formatting Marks category, and click OK. You can once again see your hidden text. It now has a dotted line underneath it, indicating that it's hidden text.

⊟ ▣ ☒ THE KEY TO TESTS

There's actually a great use for hiding your text; for example, educators hide their text all the time (they're very sneaky). Hiding text was made for exams. Teachers (or just about anybody who has to test people) can create one master document with both the questions and the answers, then hide the answers and print the test, and also print an answer key showing only the answers. Brilliant, isn't it? To do this, follow the same steps as mentioned in the previous tip to create hidden text. Once you've hidden the answers, simply print a copy to use for testing by clicking File>Print. To print a copy to use for grading (to create an answer key), go to File>Print, click the Options button in the dialog, and select Hidden Text under the Include With Document category. Click OK to print a test with the answers.

⊟ ▣ ☒ AUTOCOLOR

If you plan to use a background color rather than white, or want to use multiple background colors in your document, be sure to select Automatic Color. This feature automatically chooses a text color that contrasts with the background color, ensuring that you can read your text regardless of the document's background color (which you can change by choosing Format>Background). To use Automatic Color, click the down-facing arrow next to the Font Color button in the Formatting toolbar and click the Automatic Color icon. Now you'll automatically type black text on a white background, white text on a black background, and so on.

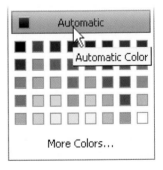

EDIT CYCLING IN WORD

A super-fast way to find your last three edits is to press Shift-F5. This keyboard shortcut will cycle your cursor through your last three edits, but the really cool thing about the Shift-F5 shortcut is that it's persistent, meaning that even when you close a document, Word will remember the last three edits. When opening a document, this provides a pretty slick way to find where you last left off.

 ### F8 TO EXTEND

You may know that the F8 key is extremely useful for selecting text in Word. Press the F8 key once and Word goes into extend mode; press it twice to select the current word; a third time will select the current sentence; four times selects the current paragraph; and five or six times selects the current section and entire document, respectively. But you can also make the F8 key select text from the insertion point to a specific letter. Try it: Press F8 and then press any letter. All of the text between the insertion point to that letter is instantly selected (as shown). To escape Word's extend mode, press Escape (Esc) on your keyboard, then click anywhere on the document.

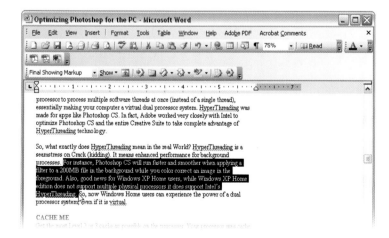

CLICK IT, THEN TYPE IT

A newer feature in Word—Click and Type—allows you to double-click in any blank space in your document to instantly create an insertion point, which gives you a lot more formatting flexibility. There's a catch to using it, however. If you're not able to click and type, then you're using Word's Normal view. For whatever reason, you can only click and type in Print Layout view or Web Layout view. So, to use the Click and Type feature, select View>Print Layout or View>Web Layout in the menu bar. If you still can't use Click and Type, select Tools>Options in the menu bar, then click the Edit tab in the Options dialog. Next, check Enable Click and Type (it's near the bottom of the dialog), then click OK.

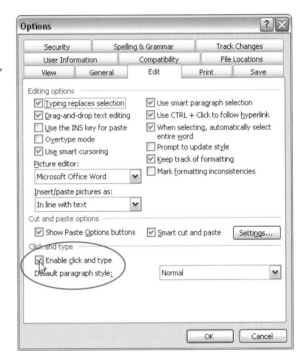

▢▢▢ PERSONALIZE YOUR ENVELOPES

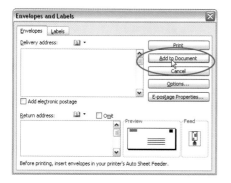

I'm about to share a tip with you that will forever change the way you print envelopes. Keep reading and you'll see what I mean. People love to personalize things—heck, I'd trim my hedges into a big "S" (for Stephenson) if my wife would let me, but if you're not as gung-ho about personalizing your stuff, then start small…start with your envelopes. When you're ready to print an envelope, click Tools>Letters and Mailings>Envelopes and Labels in the menu bar, then click the Envelopes tab in the Envelopes and Labels dialog. Next, add your delivery and return addresses in the appropriate fields, then click the Add to Document button. Your envelope will now appear at the top of your document (as the first page in a multipage document). Now you can edit the envelope as you would any document in Word. Add clip art, text boxes, company logos, and so on.

▢▢▢ SUPER-CHARGE WORD'S PERFORMANCE WITH PLACEHOLDERS

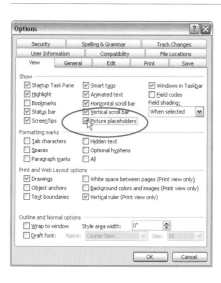

Okay, you've placed about 30 or 40 pictures into your document, which looks great, but now it takes you half an hour to scroll your document (rendering graphics is a tedious business). Well, you could just throw your underpowered PC into the trash, but if this seems a little harsh, you might want to consider replacing your pictures with picture placeholders to improve performance. To do this, click Tools>Options, then click the View tab in the Options dialog. Check Picture Placeholders under the Show category, then click OK. Your pictures are now displayed as empty frames (aka picture placeholders). To show your pictures again, simply uncheck Picture Place-holders in the Options dialog, then click OK.

CHAPTER 2 · Working with Word   **59**

QUICK GRAPHIC RESIZE TRICK

Okay, you've imported a graphic and resized it so many times that you have no idea what its original size was. You're probably feeling like a loser right about now, and you should be (kidding), but I can help. That's what I'm here for. Simply press-and-hold the Control key on your keyboard, then double-click inside your graphic to get it back to its original size (as I did here for the second image). You're feelin' better already, aren't you?

RESIZING THE RIGHT WAY

You probably know that you can simply drag any image's corner handles to resize it as large or as small as you like, while maintaining the image's proportions. However, if you notice, your graphic resizes itself by increments of about a tenth of an inch. I don't pretend to understand Microsoft math, but limiting me to resizing my images by increments of a tenth of an inch is just bad math no matter who's writing it. Try this: Hold the Alt key on your keyboard, then click-and-drag corner handles to resize your image. You can now resize it within a hundredth of an inch. Hmm, shouldn't resizing work this way by default?

 **BE EXACT**

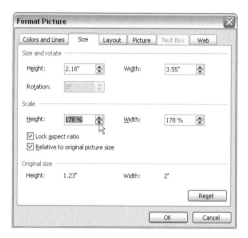

Let's say you have a mildly psychotic client who insists that you resize all of his images to an exact dimension. (Hey, they're out there.) Well, there's a way to be exact: Select an image, click Format>Picture in the menu bar, then click the Size tab in the Format Picture dialog. Look at the Height and Width fields in the Scale category. These numbers tell you what percentage your image has been scaled from its original size. Now, you can use the Height and Width fields to input exact dimensions for your other graphics. When finished, click OK.

 **GETTING PRECISE WITH WORD'S GRID**

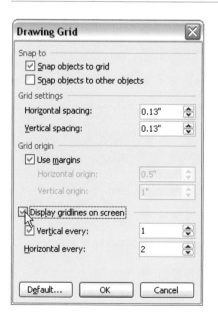

When you need to bring a little order to your layouts and precisely arrange graphic elements, turn on Word's grid. First, display the Drawing toolbar by right-clicking any toolbar or menu and click Drawing in the shortcut menu. Next, click Draw>Grid in the Drawing toolbar. Adjust your grid's dimensions in the Grid Settings category, check Display Gridlines on Screen in the Grid Origin category, then click OK. Now you can lay out your page's graphic elements with precision.

NOT YOUR ORDINARY TEXT BOX

You may think that text boxes are pretty boring, but you can get really geeky with text boxes and add a ton of very cool effects. Try this: Create a new text box by clicking Insert>Text Box in the menu bar, then click-and-drag inside the drawing canvas to create your text box. Next, click Format>Text Box in the menu bar, then click the Colors and Lines tab in the Format Text Box dialog. Click the Color down-facing arrow under the Fill category and choose Fill Effects. From the Fill Effects dialog, you can choose to fill your text box using a Gradient, Texture, Pattern, or Picture. When finished, click OK.

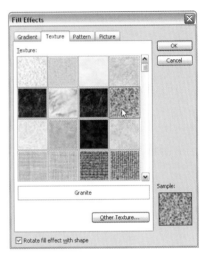

ADDING CAPTIONS

Graphics are great visualizations, but they become even more effective when you add captions to 'em. Here's how: Select your graphic, then click Insert>Reference>Caption in the menu bar. Next, type any additional description in the Caption field in the dialog, then click OK.

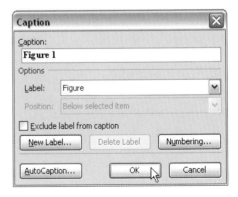

I NEED MORE AUTOSHAPES

There are many things that you can never have too much of, and you can add AutoShapes to that list. I could play around with them for hours. Actually, I have—I honestly have nothing better to do. Anyway, when you do finally get sucked into AutoShapes (if you're not already), be sure not to overlook More AutoShapes (just when you thought it couldn't get any better…). Click the AutoShapes button in the Drawing toolbar, then click More AutoShapes. This opens the Clip Art task pane, with even more AutoShapes to keep the fun going.

 GETTING PRECISE WITH AUTOSHAPES

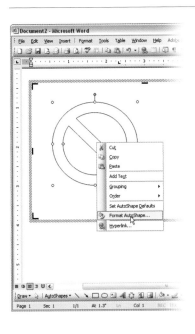

If you need to assign a precise size for your AutoShapes, right-click a shape that you've placed (see previous tip) and click Format AutoShape in the shortcut menu, then click the Size tab in the Format AutoShape dialog. Now, simply enter your required dimensions and click OK. Word will instantly adjust the size of your AutoShape.

Bright
Outlook

WORKING
WITH
OUTLOOK

Does Outlook make you feel powerful? I don't mean take-over-a-country powerful, or bench-press 400 lbs powerful, but in-control powerful. It does? Good, I thought it

Bright Outlook
working with outlook

was just me. There's something about being in constant communication with friends, family, and business colleagues that just makes me feel powerful. Okay, maybe I'm getting a little carried away, but I'm literally sitting here, right now, receiving email, sending email, Instant Messaging, and video conferencing with my sister Julie (hey Julie!)—all at the same time. Man, I've really got it going on. I'm the master of information, the Great Communicator —a powerful, powerful man. I should be stopped. I might be getting a little carried away, but it's not my fault. It's Outlook's. It's like a drug. It's the first application I open and the last I close. Hmm…maybe I'm not powerful, maybe Outlook's powerful and it's just using me to do its dirty work…hmm.

PROTECT YOUR PERSONAL FOLDERS

I love password protection and use it for just about everything. I even use it for my refrigerator's ice dispenser (seriously—it's sad). So, password protecting my email folders is a given. To password protect your email folders, right-click Personal Folders in the Navigation pane and click Properties for "Personal Folders" in the shortcut menu. Next,

click the Advanced button in the dialog, then click the Change Password button. Type a password in the New Password field, then type it again in the Verify Password field. Make sure that "Save this password in your password list" is unchecked so that you're always required to supply a password when Outlook is launched. Click OK when finished. The next time you launch Outlook, you'll be prompted for a password before you can access Outlook's mail folders.

JUST START UP

I'm not sure why "Send and receive at startup" is set up as the default. I personally think this is the most annoying thing ever. I mean, sometimes I just want to open Outlook and type an email or read an email or just look at my email. Unfortunately, there's not a kill option for this feature—only off. Here's how to do it: Click Tools>Options in the menu bar, then click the Mail Setup tab in the Options dialog. Next, uncheck Send Immediately When Connected, then click OK.

SAME EMAIL…DIFFERENT COMPUTERS

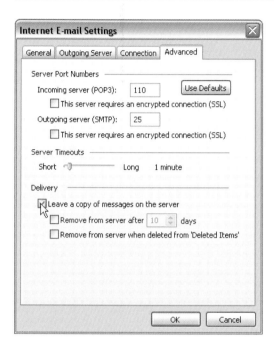

It's pretty convenient to be able to check your email on the road using your laptop, PDA, or another computer, but what's not convenient is that the mail is removed from your server. By default, incoming messages are automatically deleted from your server when received. So, what can you do to be able to read the received messages from other computers and not delete them? Just leave copies of your email on the server, which allows you to download them again later from another location. Here's how: Click Tools>Options in the menu bar, then click the Mail Setup tab in the Options dialog. Next, click the E-mail Accounts button, select "View or change existing e-mail accounts," and click Next. Now, double-click your POP account to open its email account settings. In the E-mail Accounts dialog, click the More Settings button, click the Advanced tab in the Internet E-mail Settings dialog, check "Leave a copy of messages on the server" under the Delivery category, and then click OK. You'll now be able to download your POP account's email messages from different computers.

▣◻▣ BE CHOOSY WITH FIELD CHOOSER

You can organize Outlook's Inbox folder's details (headers) the same as in other folders. You can add columns by right-clicking any column header in the Inbox window and clicking Field Chooser in the shortcut menu. Next, simply drag-and-drop any available field onto the column header in any order you like.

▣◻▣ SORT YOUR MAIL

Click on any column header to quickly sort your messages in the Inbox folder. For example, click the Received header to list your messages by the date and time they were received or click Subject to sort messages by their subject lines. If you have multiple accounts set up, you might want to sort by using the Accounts column. This will quickly tell you which accounts received messages.

EMAIL SHORTCUT

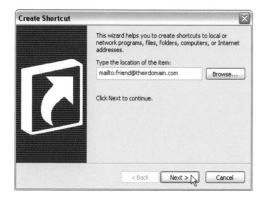

Do you have someone that you email a lot—a friend, family member, or co-worker? If you do, this tip will make your life a bit easier. Right-click on your desktop and point to New and click Shortcut in the shortcut menu. In the "Type the location of the item" field, type "mailto:" (without the quotes) followed by your friend's email address (for example, mailto:friend@mydomain.com), then click Next. Give your shortcut a name and click Finish. Now, when you double-click your Outlook email shortcut icon on your desktop, a new mail message window will open with your friend's email address already in the To field—just type your message and click the Send button.

 I'VE GOT THINGS TO DO

It's a good thing that you can add folders to Outlook because I get way too much email for the default folders to handle. When I opened Outlook for the first time, I created a Things To Do folder, where I can store email to work on later. You can also create folders to keep your email organized—it's easy. Here's how: Click the Mail button in the Navigation pane, right-click Personal Folders in the Mail pane, and click New Folder in the shortcut menu. Give your new folder a name, then click OK. Now you'll see your new folder listed under Personal Folders in the Navigation pane.

FAST TRACK TO THE INBOX

I always go to my Inbox when launching Outlook because I'm usually opening the program to check for new email, and it just saves time to start there. To take the fast track to your Inbox, click the Shortcuts button at the bottom of the Navigation pane, then click Outlook Today under the Shortcuts link near the top of the pane. Next, click the Customize Outlook Today button at the top-right corner of the Outlook Today window. Now uncheck "When starting, go directly to Outlook Today" and click the Save Changes button at the top right of the pane. Now Outlook will automatically open your Inbox upon launch.

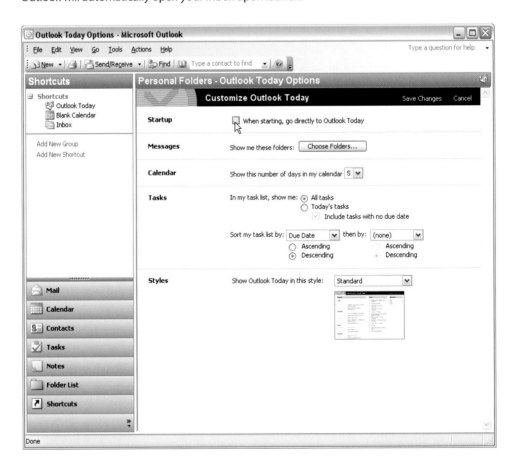

ORGANIZE YOUR MESSAGES QUICKLY

Now that you've added folders to organize your email, it's time to start using them. To move email, simply drag-and-drop your messages to any folder listed under Personal Folders.

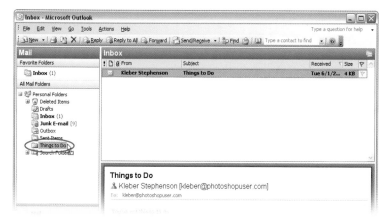

 **EASY EDIT**

If you want to save an email message as a text file, try this: Open WordPad or Word, highlight the text of your email in the Reading pane in Outlook, then drag-and-drop the text into your text editor using your mouse. Now you can edit and save the message.

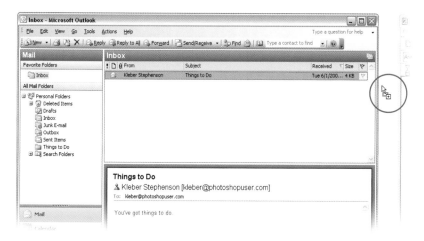

KEEP EMAIL CONSISTENT

It's good that you can customize the text of incoming email, because I have to tell you, some people have a real twisted sense of which fonts look good. You can receive email with so many different typefaces and sizes that you're not even sure if they're written in English. Well, you can customize your incoming email so that it displays the same typeface and font size. To do this, click Tools>Options, click the Mail Format tab in the dialog, and click the Fonts button. Then, individually click the three Choose Font buttons to select your default font options for composing and replying to email, and click OK. Now all of your incoming and outgoing messages will have the same look.

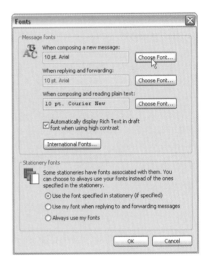

DRAG-AND-DROP YOUR ATTACHMENTS

If you're attaching files to an email, you can simply drag-and-drop them onto the email's Message window. This will instantly attach your files.

CONTROL-CLICK HYPERLINKS

By default, when inserting hyperlinks into a new email message or a reply, you can't simply click on a hyperlink to test it; however, you can get around this and test your hyperlinks by pressing-and-holding the Control key while clicking on the hyperlink. This will launch your Web browser, which will bring up the site.

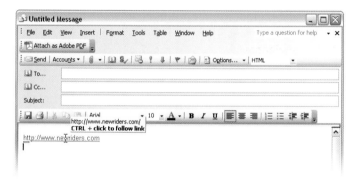

 EMAIL YOUR NOTES

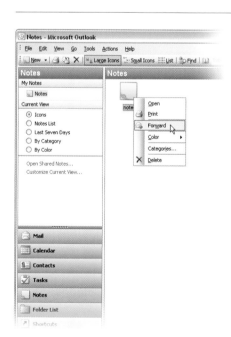

I use Outlook Notes all the time, and I often email my notes to people. You can quickly email your Outlook Notes by clicking on the Notes icon at the bottom of the Navigation pane. In the Note window, right-click any note and click Forward in the shortcut menu. This will open a new email message with your note attached. Simply provide a recipient in the To field, along with any comments, then click the Send button. You just emailed a Note document.

STICKY NOTES…REALLY!

When using Notes, keep in mind that they're sticky. You can use them just about anywhere. Drag-and-drop a note on your desktop or add them to Outlook's Shortcuts link for quick access (click the Shortcuts button at the bottom of the Navigation pane, right-click the Shortcuts link at the top of the pane, and select Notes in the resulting dialog). Just keep in mind that if you edit a note, changes may alter the name of the note, possibly making its shortcut unusable. You can also quickly change the color of your notes by right-clicking any note, pointing to Color in the shortcut menu, and picking a new color.

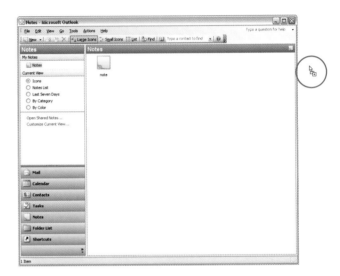

CHOOSE AN ACCOUNT

If you've set up Outlook to use multiple email accounts, then you'll need to select the account from which to send email messages. To do this, click File>New>Mail Message and simply click the Accounts button on the Email toolbar, then select the account that you want to use. The email account's server address will appear above the To field.

TRACK DOWN THE PERSONAL FOLDERS

To view the location on your hard drive of your Personal Folders, with the Mail pane open, right-click Personal Folders and click Properties for "Personal Folders" in the shortcut menu. Next, click the Advanced button in the dialog. The location is displayed in the Filename field.

 PERSONALIZE PERSONAL FOLDERS

If you don't necessarily care for the name that Outlook has given your folders (Personal Folders), then change it to something a little more personal. To do this, right-click Personal Folders in the All Mail Folders pane, then click Properties for "Personal Folders" in the shortcut menu. Next, click the Advanced button in the dialog, type a new name in the Name field, and click OK. Your Personal Folders folder is now renamed.

UN-JUNK EMAIL

I get hundreds of junk emails a day and occasionally, as I'm blasting junk email left and right, I'll
unintentionally drag-and-drop good email from
my Inbox into my Junk E-mail folder. Well, you can
quickly fix this by finding the email that you want
to recover in your Junk E-mail folder, then right-
clicking the email and clicking Junk E-mail>Add

Sender to Safe Senders List in the shortcut menu. Now you'll be able to once again receive
email from the sender (but you'll still have to drag-and-drop the email back into your Inbox
or another folder for safekeeping).

 CAN'T SPELL?

Let's face it, most of us can't spell
(I can, but I can do everything…it's
a burden). Well, Outlook can help. You
can set up Outlook to automatically check
your spelling before you send messages.
To do this, click Tools>Options, then
click the Spelling tab. Next, check "Always check spelling before sending" and
click OK. You're feeling smarter already,
aren't you?

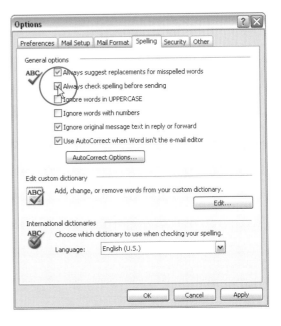

SAVE YOUR SEARCHES

If you find yourself performing repeated searches for a particular word or term, you should save your search results by creating a search folder; that way you don't have to repeat the search in the future. To open Find in Outlook, press Control-E or click the Find button in Outlook's Standard toolbar. Next, type your search term in the Look For field, select your search location using the Search In drop-down menu, and click Find Now. When your search is finished, click the Options drop-down menu in the right corner of the window and select Save Search as Search Folder. Type a name for your search folder in the resulting dialog, then click OK. The folder will appear under Search Folders in the All Mail Folders pane. Now, the next time you need to view the results of the search, simply double-click the Search Folder to access your saved search folder.

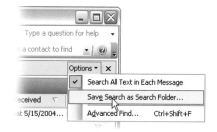

 COLLAPSIBLE GROUPS

Outlook automatically groups your messages in your mail folders by when they were received (today, yesterday, last week, last month). To make groups easier to navigate, you can collapse them to view only the group's heading by clicking any group heading, then press the Left Arrow key on your keyboard (or press the Right Arrow key to expand the group).

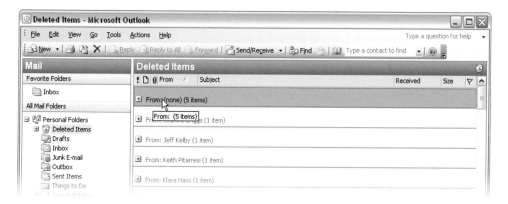

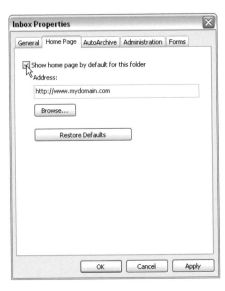 EVEN A FOLDER NEEDS A HOME (PAGE)

Here's a pretty cool little trick you can do with your mail folders: Add a home page to them. This is useful for reminding you of a folder's contents or to quickly view a frequently visited webpage. You can add a home page to some folders by right-clicking the folder in the All Mail Folders pane and clicking Properties in the shortcut menu. Next, click the Home Page tab in the dialog and type a URL in the Address field or click the Browse button to browse your hard drive. If you want the webpage to appear by default each time you open the folder, check "Show home page by default for this folder." When you're finished, click OK. If you've selected to show a webpage by default, then you should see your folder's home page displayed when you go to that folder.

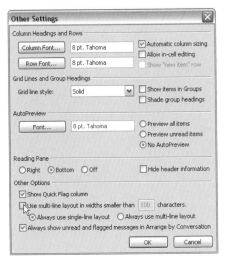 MAXIMUM VIEW

I honestly get about 900 emails a day (of course 875 of them are spam), but I still like to see as many messages as possible in my Inbox. A bigger view just makes sorting the good email from the bad quicker. To view more messages in your Inbox, be sure the Mail pane is active, then click View>Arrange By>Custom in the menu bar, click the Other Settings button, and uncheck "Use multi-line layout in widths smaller than [100] characters" listed under the Other Options category (near the bottom of the dialog), then click OK.

START UP WHERE YOU WANT

I always go to my Inbox when opening Outlook; however, you may not. You can set up Outlook to open automatically in any folder. Here's how: Click Tools>Options in the menu bar, then click the Other tab in the dialog. Next, click the Advanced Options button and click the Browse button in the top-right corner of the dialog. Now, select a folder to start up in, click OK, and close Outlook. When you reopen Outlook, it will now automatically open the folder you selected.

LAUNCH OUTLOOK AT STARTUP

Wouldn't it be nice if Windows could just open Outlook for you automatically at startup? You, my friend, are in luck because Windows can. Right-click Start in the Windows Taskbar and click Explore in the shortcut menu. Navigate to your Startup folder (usually located in C:\Documents and Settings\<user>\ Start Menu\Programs\Startup). Now, just press-and-hold the Control key as you drag-and-drop Outlook's application icon from your desktop into your Startup folder to create a shortcut to it. When Windows starts up, the program will launch automatically. You can also put shortcuts to your favorite folders in Startup to have them launch instantly as well.

DON'T DUMP IT, ARCHIVE IT INSTEAD

If you're the kind of person who never throws anything away, including your email, then do yourself a favor and archive your old email messages. This will boost the performance of Outlook when opening and searching folders. To archive a folder, right-click it and click Properties in the shortcut menu. Next, click the AutoArchive tab in the dialog, select "Archive items in this folder using the default settings," then click OK. Once you've created archive folders, you can add to them by simply dragging-and-dropping messages into them. *Note:* Items stashed in saved search folders can't be archived.

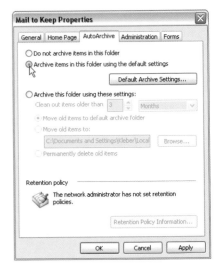

SNAG STATIONERY

Someone just sent you an email, and it has the coolest stationery attached that you've ever seen. Wouldn't it be great if you could snag it for yourself? You're in luck—you can. Here's how: Double-click the message containing the stationery to open it in its own preview window. Next, click File>Save Stationery in the menu bar, name the stationery, and then click OK. Now, when you apply stationery to new messages (by choosing Actions>New Mail Message Using>More Stationery), you'll see your new stationery listed in the Select a Stationery dialog. By the way, when you save stationery in Outlook, it's also saved to Word's stationery. *Note:* If you're not able to save stationery that you've received, it's probably because it's actually a Microsoft Word theme and not stationery. Outlook can't save Word themes.

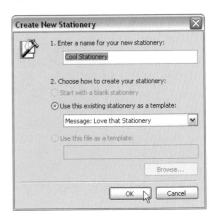

COMPARE FOLDERS

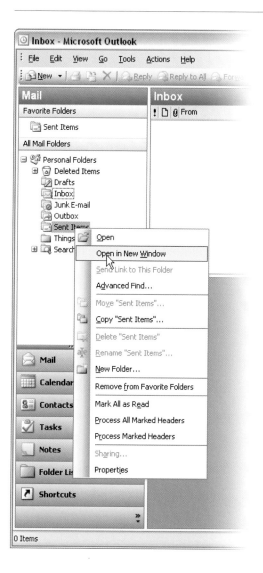

If you need to compare the contents of folders in Outlook, you can. Simply open the folders in their own windows. To do this, right-click any folder other than the one that's currently open, then click Open in New Window in the shortcut menu. This opens the folder in its own window.

GET RID OF THE JUNK

If you're plagued by spam (who isn't?), you can let Outlook get rid of most of it for you. Click Tools>Options in the menu bar, then click the Preferences tab in the Options dialog. Next, click the Junk E-mail button, select "High: Most junk e-mail is caught, but some regular mail may be caught as well. Check your Junk E-mail folder often," and click OK. Outlook does a fantastic job of detecting and removing junk email. You'll be surprised how well it works. Also, as recommended, be sure to check the Junk E-mail folder occasionally to ensure that good mail isn't being placed there accidentally.

OUTLOOK'S HIDDEN HELP

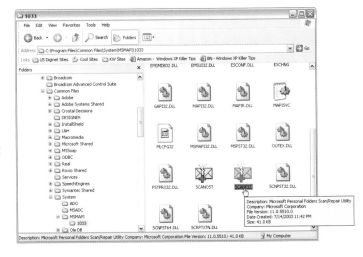

I get all giddy over hidden apps, and Outlook has one of the best-hidden apps out there. If Outlook's Personal Folders ever start causing you grief, and you begin receiving error messages while using your Personal Folders, then there's a hidden app that can probably help. Right-click Start on the Windows Taskbar, then click Explore in the shortcut menu. Now, use Windows Explorer to navigate to C:\ Program Files\Common Files\ System\MSMAPI\1033. Next, double-click the SCANPST file to open the Inbox Repair Tool dialog. Now, browse your hard drive to locate the PST file you want to scan, then click Start. (*Tip:* If you're not sure where your PST files are stored on your hard drive, do a search by choosing Start>Search in the Windows Taskbar.) Follow the prompts in the dialog to complete your scan.

AUTO-SORT EMAIL

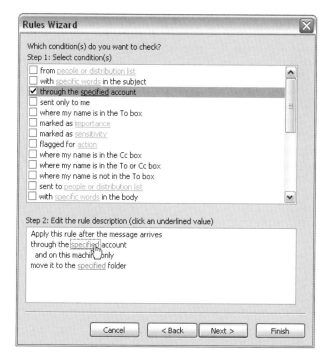

A super-fast way to keep your email organized is to move it to the correct folder when receiving it. For example, you may want to move all email sent to your office email address to a "Things To Do" folder when they're received. This can help keep messages organized and speed up archiving. To do this, click the down-facing arrow next to New in the menu bar and select Folder. Name your folder and click OK. Now click Tools>Rules and Alerts in the menu bar, then click the E-mail Rules tab in the Rules and Alerts dialog. (*Note:* Outlook can't filter HTTP email accounts, so you may get a warning dialog. Just click OK.) Next, click New Rule at the top left of the dialog, then select "Move messages from someone to a folder" under the Stay Organized category, and click Next. Now under Step 1, uncheck "from people or distribution list" and check "through the specified account." Under Step 2, click the word "specified" in the "through the specified account" and choose the email account in the Account drop-down menu. Then, click the word "specified" in the "move it to the specified folder" description under Step 2, and choose the folder to move the email to. Click Finish when you're done.

WEB BROWSING WITH OUTLOOK

To browse the Web using Outlook, right-click the Standard toolbar and click Web in the shortcut menu to display the Web toolbar. Next, click the Start Page button (it looks like a tiny house) to open your home page in Outlook's Reading pane. Use the Web toolbar to browse, navigate, or search the Web.

SINGLE TASK, MULTIPLE CATEGORIES

If you've created a task and would like to associate it with several categories, there's no need to re-create the same task for each category. There's a faster way: Click Tasks in the Navigation pane and select By Category in the Current View category of the Tasks pane, then simply drag-and-drop the task into any new category.

A READING PANE YOU CAN ACTUALLY READ

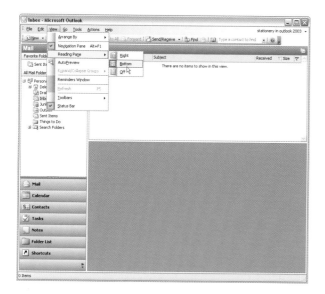

Outlook's Reading pane is displayed by default to the right of the Inbox pane, which makes total sense…I don't actually want to be able to read my messages. Yeah, that works well (kidding, that doesn't work well at all). Fortunately, we can move the Reading pane just in case you actually do want to read your email. Here's how: Click View>Reading Pane>Bottom in the menu bar. Now your Reading pane appears below the Inbox window, actually giving you enough room to read your messages.

 ## A REMINDER TO TURN OFF REMINDERS

By default, Outlook will set a reminder automatically for every new task, which is just annoying, and because we don't like anything annoying, we're gonna turn this off. Click Tools>Options in the menu bar and in the Preferences tab, click the Task Options button. Uncheck "Set reminders on tasks with due dates," then click OK. I'm feelin' much less annoyed!

▢▢▢ USING SHORTCUTS IN OUTLOOK

Outlook 2003 is the most user-friendly and customizable Outlook yet—a good example of this is Outlook's shortcuts. You can add URLs, application shortcuts, or even links to documents, putting all of your most-used tools just a click away. First, click Shortcuts in the Navigation pane. Now simply drag-and-drop any webpage icon, application shortcut, or document shortcut into the Shortcuts link at the top of the Shortcuts pane. Click any shortcut to use it.

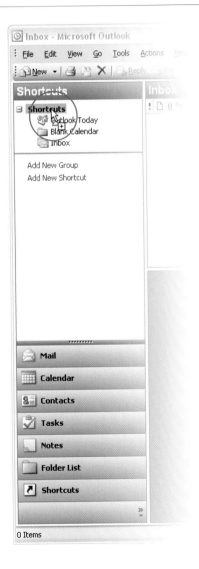

GET RID OF J

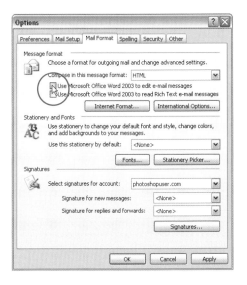

If you type a smiley :-) emoticon and Outlook replaces it with a "J" symbol, then Outlook is using Word to edit your email messages. Well, you can get your smileys back by using Outlook's editor instead. To use Outlook's text editor, click Tools>Options in the menu bar, then click the Mail Format tab in the Options dialog. Next, uncheck "Use Microsoft Office Word 2003 to edit e-mail messages" and click OK. Now, create a new message and type a smiley. There ya go.

YOU'VE GOT MAIL…SOUNDS

By default, Outlook uses the Windows XP System Notification sound, which sounds kind of like every other XP sound. You can, however, make the notification sound a little more distinguishable if you'd like to know that you've received new email. Here's how: In the Windows Taskbar, click Start>Control Panel>Sound, Speech, and Audio Devices>Sounds and Audio Devices. Next, click the Sounds tab in the dialog and scroll in the Program Events category to select New Mail Notification. Now, select a new sound from the Sounds drop-down menu at the bottom of the dialog or browse your hard drive to choose a new sound that you've saved. When finished, click OK.

CHAPTER 3 • Working with Outlook   **87**

 **BACK UP THE BAD**

Okay, you've gone to a lot of trouble blocking spammers (or people you're just trying to avoid), and this is a list that you want to keep backed up. If anything ever happens to Outlook, you'll want to be able to replace your blocked senders list, or you may even want to share the list between computers. To back up your list, click Tools>Options in the menu bar, then click the Junk E-mail button. Next, click the Blocked Senders tab in the Junk E-mail Options dialog

and click the Export to File button. Now, choose a location to save the file to, give your backup file a name, and click Save. Click OK to close out of the open dialogs. If you want to import your backed-up blocked senders list, click the Import from File button in the Junk E-mail Options dialog.

 **SIGN IT**

For most accounts, especially business accounts, you'll almost always have the same signature—ending your messages with the same name and any contact information. You don't have to type this information each time you send an email (unless you really like typing). Instead, you can create a signature just once for each email address (POP account) and Outlook will automatically add it to your messages. Here's how: Click Tools>Options in the Standard toolbar, then click the Mail Format tab in the Options dialog. Next, click the Signatures button at the bottom of the dialog and click New in the Create Signature dialog. Follow the Create New Signature dialog to name and create your signature. When you're

done, click Finish, and then click OK to close the Create Signature dialog. In the Options dialog, select the POP account (for which you just created the signature) from the Select Signatures for Account drop-down menu. Then, in the Signatures category, choose to use your signature for new messages, replies, and forwards, and then click OK.

 FLAG IT

I receive a ridiculous amount of email throughout the day, and if I'm expecting an important email from someone, I'll set up a message rule to automatically flag it to notify me when it arrives. To automatically flag incoming messages, click Tools>Rules and Alerts in the menu bar and in the E-mail Rules tab, click the New Rule button and select "Flag messages from someone with a colored flag" under Step 1, then click Next. Now check "from people or distribution list" under Step 1, then click the "people or distribution list" link under Step 2, specify a contact, and click the From button or type an email address in the From field. Click OK to close the dialog. Next, click the words "a colored flag" in the "flag message with a colored flag" description under Step 2 and select a flag color in the resulting dialog. Click Finish when you're done. Now, when a message arrives from this person, it will immediately be flagged for easy recognition.

 FOLLOW-UP FLAGS

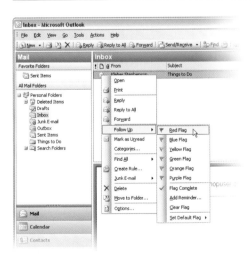

A quick way to add reminders to your email is to flag 'em; for example, you can flag important emails that require extra attention. To do this, right-click any email message, point to Follow Up, and click a flag color in the shortcut menu to identify your email. Your message will be flagged immediately. To remove a flag, right-click the message, point to Follow Up, and click Clear Flag. Another way to quickly flag an email is to select the message and press the Insert key on your keyboard. This shortcut instantly flags your message with a red-colored flag.

CHAPTER 3 • Working with Outlook   **89**

 COLOR-CODE MESSAGES

Another way (and probably my favorite) to highlight email from individuals is to color-code entire messages. To color code a message from individual addresses, click Tools>Organize and click the Using Colors link under Ways to Organize Inbox. Choose "from" in the

Color Messages drop-down menu, type an email address in the field, and choose a color in the drop-down menu. When finished, click Apply Color. Now any message received from the email address you specified will be colored, making it very easy to recognize.

 BCC GROUPS

Something to keep in mind when sending email to groups is that everyone receiving the message will see the email address for each member on the list. Members of your group might not be crazy about this. There's a clever way around this problem, however. On a new message window, click the To button to select the recipients, but instead of adding your group to the To field, add it to the Bcc (Blind Carbon Copy) field near the bottom of the Select Names dialog. Just click a name or group in the window and click the Bcc button. Now when you send messages to the group, members will only know who sent the message, not who all of the recipients were.

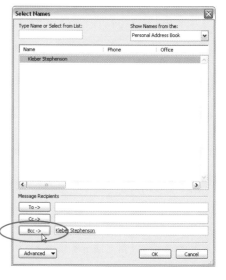

DON'T REPLY THERE

If you send email from someone else's computer, using his or her email address, then you probably don't want any replies sent back to your friend's account (it doesn't belong to you). Well, there's a way around this. Outlook can actually forward replies to a different email account than the one you sent the email from. To do this, create a new message, click the Options button on the Message toolbar, and check "Have replies sent to" under the Delivery Options category. Type an email address in the "Have replies sent to" field, then click Close. Now any replies to your message will be sent to the email account you specified.

 ## REQUEST A RECEIPT

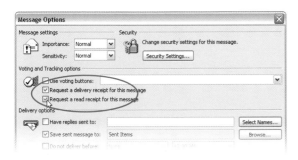

Don't you hate not knowing if someone received your email? I mean, you asked for a reply but of course one was never sent. So, you're just left hanging. Did the person get it? Did your server eat it? You don't know and because the person won't reply, you may never know. Stressful, isn't it? Well, there's a way that you can encourage the recipient to acknowledge that your email was received. Here's how: Create and compose a new message, then click the Options button in the Message toolbar. Next, check "Request a delivery receipt for this message" and/or "Request a read receipt for this message" under the Voting and Tracking Options category. Click Close when finished. Now, when recipients receive your message, they'll be prompted to acknowledge that they received it. If they do, you'll receive notification that it was received. If they don't, then subscribe their email address to every spammer on the Web. That'll teach 'em.

 SHOW ONLY THE UNREAD

Is your Inbox getting a little crowded? Well, if it is, you can hide messages that you've read to help you quickly identify incoming (unread) email. Here's how: Click the Inbox in the All Mail Folders pane, click View>Arrange By>Custom in the menu bar, then click the Filter button in the dialog. Next, click the More Choices tab in the Filter dialog and check "Only items that are" and select "unread" from the drop-down menu. Click OK when finished, and you'll no longer see messages that you've already read.

 OOPS, I DIDN'T MEAN TO SEND THAT

Don't you wish there was an Undo button for sent email? Well, actually, there is. You can recall email sent from Outlook by first double-clicking the sent email in the Sent Items folder to open it in its own preview window, then clicking Actions>Recall This Message in the menu bar. You'll then see a pop-up dialog asking whether to delete the email or to replace the email with a new message. Choose which works best for you, then click OK. Now, before you start firing off an email to your employer

telling him exactly what you think, there's a catch. The recipient has to be logged on to the Internet and the message must be received but not read. Yeah, pretty big catch, huh? Well, if you're able to successfully retrieve a message, Outlook will notify you and let you know that you just avoided a very close call.

 ## ZIP IT!

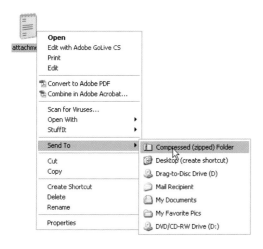

By default, Outlook doesn't allow you to view attachments that it determines may be harmful—containing viruses, for example. This is helpful until Outlook starts removing your attachments sent to others or removing attachments received from contacts that you know are perfectly fine. To prevent Outlook from removing your attachments, Zip them first by right-clicking the file and selecting Send To>Compressed (zipped) Folder. Now attach your file to your email message. Outlook doesn't filter zipped files, so you can send and receive zipped files without Outlook taking any action.

QUICK, SEND WEBPAGES

You can quickly email a webpage to someone using Outlook. First, open the webpage in Outlook by entering a website in the Address field of the Web toolbar (which you can access by right-clicking any toolbar and selecting Web in the shortcut menu). Now click Actions>Send Web Page by E-mail. A new message window will open with the webpage and URL attached. Simply type a recipient in the To field, enter a message if you'd like, and then click the Send button.

⬜◻❎ YOU'VE ALWAYS GOT MAIL

If you check your email throughout the day and have a constant connection to the Internet, there's no need for you to check manually for new messages. Let Outlook automatically check for you. First, click Tools>Options in the menu bar, then click the Mail Setup tab in the Options dialog. Next click the Send/Receive button, check "Schedule an automatic send/receive every [ ] minutes," and type a number in the field for how often Outlook should check for new messages, then click Close. Now, minimize Outlook by clicking on the Minimize button in the top-right corner of Outlook's window, and it will automatically check for new messages while it's docked in the Windows Taskbar.

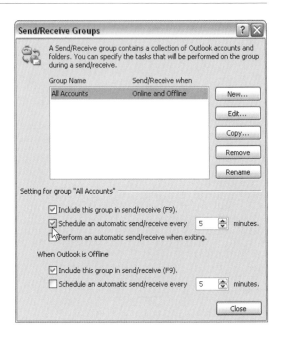

⬜◻❎ YOU'VE BEEN NOTIFIED, YOU'VE GOT MAIL

Now that you've minimized Outlook (see previous tip), how do you know if you've received new messages? The Window's Taskbar knows. When new messages arrive at your Inbox, the "You have new unopened items" icon will appear, informing you that you've received new email.

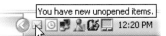

NO OFFICE? NO PROBLEM!

Believe it or not, there are people out there who don't use Office…shocking, isn't it? Well, just because they don't use Office, it doesn't mean that you can't share your documents. Outlook lets you send Office documents, such as Access, Excel, Publisher, and Word files, via email without the recipients having those programs installed on their computers. For example, to share a Word file, go to the Standard toolbar and click Actions>New Mail Message Using>Microsoft Office>Microsoft Word Document in the menu bar. A Word document opens that is ready to be created and emailed. Now, create your document (or copy-and-paste text from an Office file), type an email address in the To field, then click Send a Copy. Your Word document will be emailed, and you'll then be prompted to save the Word document that you just created.

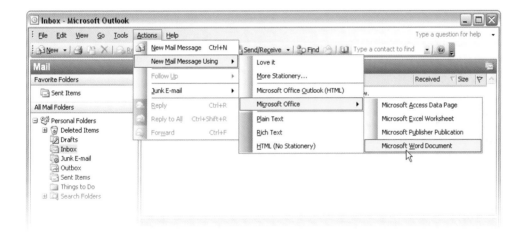

RIGHT-CLICK CONTACTS

Here's a quick way to send email to contacts. Click the Contacts button in the Navigation pane. With your contacts visible in the Contacts window, right-click a contact header (name) and click New Message to Contact in the shortcut menu.

 RIGHT-CLICK ATTACHMENTS

This whole right-clicking thing is really catching on—you can even use it to send files (attachments) via email. Try this tip the next time you need to send a file to someone. Locate the file you want to email, then right-click it and click Sent To>Mail Recipient in the shortcut menu. This will open a new Outlook message window with your file attached and ready to be sent. Now, just type the recipient's email address in the To field, type a message if you'd like, and then click Send.

YOU'RE ANNOYING

Are you getting email from someone who's really annoying? If you are, you can block that person's email address so that you won't see messages received from him or her. I do it all the time just for fun, but that's me. I'm just mean. Anyway, when you block an email address, any mail received from the address is automatically placed in your Deleted Items folder. You don't ever have to see it. To block a sender, right-click the email message and click Junk E-mail>Add Sender to Blocked Senders List in the shortcut menu. To remove someone from the list, click Tools>Options in the menu bar, and in the Preferences tab, click the Junk E-mail button under the E-mail category. Next, click the Blocked Senders tab and locate the person's email address, then select it and click Remove. Click OK when finished.

 YOU'RE SAFE

If you've set up Outlook to filter your email for spam, and you're worried that important email might get removed by mistake, you should add your contacts to your Safe Senders list. This gives your contacts a free pass with Outlook. No matter what they send you, it'll breeze right through untouched by Outlook. To add a contact to your Safe Senders list, simply right-click any message that person has sent you and click Junk E-mail>Add Sender to Safe Senders List in the shortcut menu. To remove this person from the list, click Tools>Options, click the Junk E-mail button, and in the resulting dialog, click the Safe Senders tab. Choose your sender from the list, click Remove, and then click OK.

QUICK JUNK BUTTON

The quickest way to whack spam the second it appears in your Inbox is to add the Junk E-mail button to Outlook's Standard toolbar, then you can get rid of spam in just one click. To do this, click Tools>Customize in the menu bar, then click the Commands tab. Select Actions listed under Categories, then click-and-drag Add Sender to Blocked Senders List from the Commands category to any location on Outlook's toolbar. Now anytime you get spam, you're only a click away from blocking that sender's address from ever sending you email again. To remove the button, click Tools>Customize in the menu bar, then simply drag the button off the toolbar until an "x" appears below your mouse pointer, then release your mouse button.

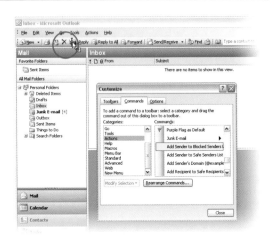

TURN OFF THE READING PANE

We all get spam—some worse than others—for example, junk mail containing adult images. And, if you work around children or co-workers who can see your monitor, then you need to be careful when checking your email. Well, fortunately, you can avoid displaying images by turning off the Reading pane. To do this, click View>Reading Pane>Off in the menu bar. Now received messages won't display their contents. You can quickly view any email, however, by right-clicking the message and clicking Open in the shortcut menu.

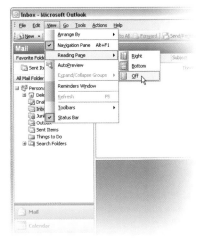

SORT THE JUNK WITH AUTOPREVIEW

Another great way to censor your email is to use Outlook's AutoPreview. Try this: Close the Reading pane by clicking View>Reading Pane>Off in the menu bar. Now, click View>AutoPreview in the menu bar. Messages in Outlook will now display the first few lines of an email's message. This helps you to quickly separate the valid email from the spam.

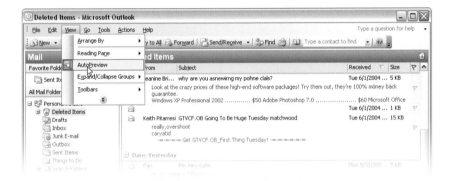

STOP DESKTOP ALERTS

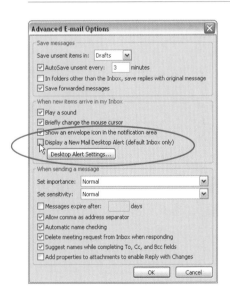

The first thing I do when I fire up my computer is open Outlook, check my email, then minimize Outlook, which I've set up to check my email continuously. Now, I'm receiving email just about every minute of the day, and Outlook's new email desktop alerts start to get really annoying by the 16th or 17th one. This is supposed to be helpful, but it's not—it's just annoying. Fortunately, we can stop Outlook from being so helpful by clicking Tools>Options in the menu bar. In the Preferences tab, click E-mail Options under the E-mail category, and then click Advanced E-mail Options in the dialog. Now, uncheck Display a New Mail Desktop Alert (default Inbox only) under the "When new items arrive in my Inbox" category, then click OK.

LET 'EM VOTE ON IT

A great way to get instant feedback about an email is to poll the recipient. You can request that the recipients use voting buttons to provide quick answers to questions or proposals. For instance, if you're sending a proposal that requires someone's approval or rejection, you can send an email to request that the recipient replies with a response of, well, approval or rejection. Here's how: On a new message window, click Options in the Standard toolbar, then check Use Voting Buttons under the Voting and Tracking Options category. Next, choose the

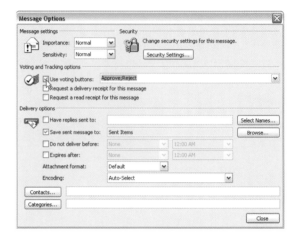

type of available responses from the drop-down menu (Approve;Reject, Yes;No, etc.), then click Close when finished. Now the recipient will be requested to respond using the voting dialog. Once the recipient responds, you'll receive a confirmation email displaying the results of your poll.

 ## PRINT YOUR CONTACTS

Now that you've gone to all the trouble of putting every person you've ever known into Outlook's Contacts list, you should print a directory to keep handy around your office or home. To print a copy of your contacts, click the Contacts button in the Navigation pane and click File>Print in the menu bar. Next, select Phone Directory Style under the Print Style category and click OK. You now have a printed copy of your contacts.

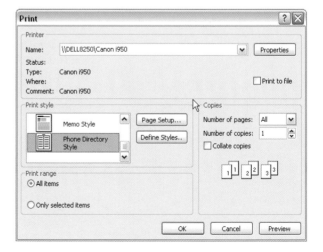

I PREFER NICKNAMES

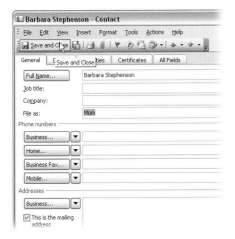

When looking up contacts, you may find it better to use nicknames or initials; for example, I like to find my mother by looking up "Mom." To look up contacts using nicknames or initials, double-click any contact in your Contacts list, then in the General tab, type a nickname or initials in the File As field, and click the Save and Close button. Now type the nickname or initials into the "Type a contact to find" search field in the toolbar to display the contact's info.

 CHECK A CONTACT'S ACTIVITIES

To view all messages sent to you by a contact, click Contacts in the Navigation pane and double-click a name in the Contacts list to open a contact. Next, click the Activities tab on the contact's window and select All Items from the Show drop-down list. Now all messages from this contact in every Outlook folder will appear in the window. You can simply scroll the list to locate a particular message.

 FIND A GROUP OF CONTACTS

The "Type a contact to find" field in the
Standard toolbar of the Contacts pane is
another great way to locate a group of
contacts. If you need to locate all contacts
from the same domain to send email to the
group or to change the group's domain, type
the domain name (e.g., msn) and press Enter
on your keyboard. You'll be shown a list of
everyone in your Contacts list who has that
domain in his or her email address.

 GET DIRECTIONS

Do you need directions to a contact's street address? You can get it right in Outlook. With the
Contacts list open, double-click any contact for which you've saved an address and click the
Display Map of Address button (it looks like a yellow street sign) in the toolbar. This will launch
your Web browser, taking you to Microsoft's MapPoint website. Click the Get Map button on
the webpage to display a map of the address.

YOU CAN PICTURE IT

Your contacts just aren't complete until you give 'em a picture. This could be a picture of the actual person or any graphic that reminds you of that person (use your imagination). To add a picture to a contact, open any contact by double-clicking the name in the Contact list, then click the Add Contact Picture icon (it looks like a generic person in the dialog). Now, browse your hard drive using the Add Contact Picture dialog and click OK once you've selected your picture. The picture is now displayed in place of the Add Contact Picture icon. To remove a contact's picture, double-click the name in the Contacts list and then click Actions>Remove Picture in the Contact window's menu bar.

QUICKLY ADD TO CONTACTS

Here's a quick way to add an email sender's name to your Contact list. Drag-and-drop the message onto the Contacts button in the Navigation pane, which will open a new Contact window, including all of the contact's info. Now, make any changes or additions to the contact's info, then click the Save and Close button.

⬛🔲❎ CATEGORIES CAN REMIND YOU

I have about 80 contacts listed in my Outlook's
Contacts list at any given time, and sometimes it's difficult for me to remember why they're there. A quick
way to remind yourself of who these contacts are is
to categorize them. To do this, click Contacts in the
Navigation pane and double-click a contact's name.
Next, click the Categories button at the bottom of the
Contact window. Now, simply check all the categories
that describe the contact, click OK in the dialog when
finished, and then click the Save and Close button
in the Contact window. Now, you can just check the
Categories field in the contact's info the next time you
forget exactly who a contact is.

⬛🔲❎ DON'T JUST REPLY, SEND AN INSTANT MESSAGE

If you receive an email from a contact and
you want to respond so urgently that only
an instant message will do, then click the
contact's Personal Names Smart Tag. When
you receive an email from someone that
you've set up as a Microsoft Messenger
contact (i.e., you've entered the person's
IM name in the IM Address field in the
General tab of the Contact window for that
contact), you'll see a Smart Tag next to the
person's name in the From field, as long as
his or her online status is anything other
than offline. To reply with an instant message, click the Smart Tag and click Send
Instant Message in the shortcut menu. This
will open the Messenger Conversation
window, where you can type your message
and click Send.

FORWARD A VCARD

To share a contact's complete information with others or between computers, just attach a contact's vCard to an email. To do this, click Contacts in the Navigation pane, open a contact from your Contacts list, and click Actions>Forward as vCard in the Contacts menu bar. Next, type the recipient's email address in the To field, include any message, and then click the Send button.

 SNAIL MAIL YOUR CONTACTS

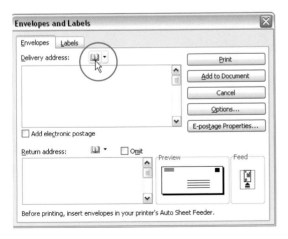

You can use Word's Envelopes and Labels dialog if you need to print a contact's address onto an envelope or label. Here's how: Launch Word and click Tools>Letters and Mailings>Envelopes and Labels in the menu bar. With the Envelopes tab open, click the Insert Address button (it looks like a book) next to the Delivery Address field to open Outlook's Contacts list. Now, simply select a contact from the list and click OK. The contact's name and mailing address will appear in the Delivery Address field. Click the Print button when finished.

 QUICKLY CREATE APPOINTMENTS

You can easily turn any message into an appointment by dragging-and-dropping it from a folder or your Inbox onto the Calendar button in the Navigation pane. This will open a new Appointment window. Now make any changes, set the appointment's start and end times, then click the Save and Close button when you're finished. To turn your appointment into a meeting, click the Scheduling tab in the Appointment window, add anyone who's invited to the meeting in the All Attendees list on the left-hand side of the window, then click File>Save. Now click the Send button to email meeting invitations to those attendees who are saved in your Contacts list.

⊟ ⊡ ☒ PRINT BLANK CALENDARS

My Outlook calendar fills up pretty quickly, making it impossible for me to print a blank calendar for other purposes. Well, there is a way in Outlook to print a blank calendar: Click the Calendar button in the Navigation pane, click the Month button in the toolbar to display your calendar in Month view, select the month that you want to print by clicking on the top month's name in the Calendar pane, then choose your month from the shortcut menu. (*Tip*: Click-and-drag in the pane to highlight any extra dates that you want to add to your calendar.) Next, click File>New>Folder and type a name for your new folder (e.g., My Blank Folder), then click OK. Now click the checkbox to the left of your new folder under My Calendars in the Calendar pane to open your calendar (be sure to uncheck any other calendars). Next, click File>Page Setup>Monthly Style in the menu bar, click the Print button in the dialog, and click OK in the Print dialog.

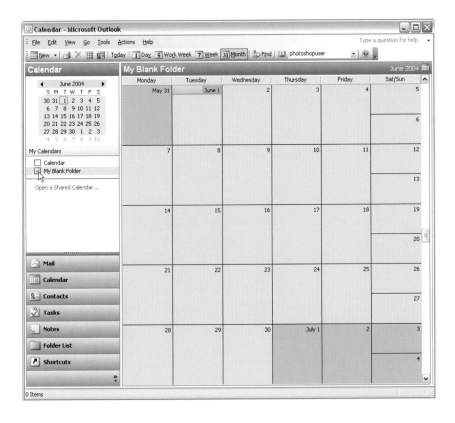

SHARE YOUR CALENDARS

The easiest way to share your Outlook calendars with others is to save them as webpages. To do this, click Calendar in the Navigation pane, then click File>Save as Web Page in the menu bar. Next, choose a start and end date for your calendar on the Save As Web Page dialog. You can also choose to include a background graphic and include appointment details. Click the Browse button to the right of the File Name field to give your calendar webpage a name and to choose where you want the file saved on your hard drive, then click Select. Now click Save in the Save As Web Page dialog.

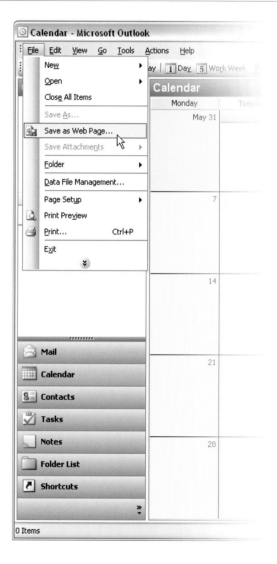

I NEED MY WEEKENDS

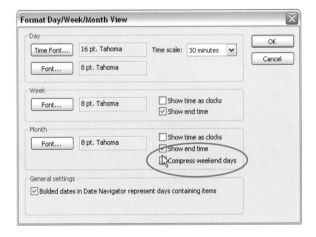

For some reason, Outlook calendars just don't think weekends are important; they're not even represented with their own boxes. They're lumped together (Sat/Sun). Well, I work all the time and my weekends are just as busy as my weekdays, so I need a full-sized box for my weekend days. To make an Outlook calendar show weekend days in their own fields, right-click your calendar while in Month view (View>Month), then click Other Settings in the shortcut menu. Next, uncheck Compress Weekend Days and click OK. Saturday and Sunday now appear in separate fields on the calendar.

 MASTER TIME ZONES

If you're traveling overseas or even to different time zones, you can always keep your time differences straight by adding two time zones to your calendars. To display two time zones while you're in Day or Work Week views (which you can select in the Calendar toolbar), click Tools>Options in the menu bar. In the Preferences tab in the Options dialog, click Calendar Options, then click the Time Zone button near the bottom of the dialog. In the Time Zone dialog, check Show an Additional Time Zone and choose the time zone to be displayed from the Time Zone drop-down menu. You can also give a name to your time zones using the Label fields. Click OK when finished, and you're now the master of two time zones.

Power(ful)
Point of View

WORKING
WITH
POWERPOINT

I apologize for the fact that I'm a little distracted as I'm writing this. The Tampa Bay Lightning, the "Bolts," are ten minutes and twel...eleven seconds from winning the Stanley

Power(ful)Point of View
working with powerpoint

Cup! Is Tampa the mecca of the sports world or what? If we could only get the Devil Rays (MLB) going, there would be no doubt. The Calgary Flames just scored a point off a power play that should have never happened...BAD CALL! The ref called a bad penalty that set up the point. We're still up with a score of 2 to 1, though. Anyway, PowerPoint is a great application that everybody who creates presentations should use. This chapter will show you how to do all kinds of cool things in PowerPlay, I mean PowerPoint. "Habi" (Nikolai Khabibulin, the goalie) is playing lights-out hockey—we should take this. I'll let you know how it turns out...WE WON! WE WON THE STANLEY CUP! STANLEY'S GETTING A TAN!

▬ ▣ ☒ CHANGING COLORS

Have you ever found the perfect
clip art picture, but couldn't use
it because it didn't match the
color theme of your presentation?
If you have, then you're gonna
love this. Insert a clip art image
by clicking Insert>Picture>Clip
Art, then search for an image that
you like, and drag-and-drop the
image from the Clip Art task pane
onto a slide. Next, double-click the
image to open the Format Picture
dialog, and in the Picture tab, click

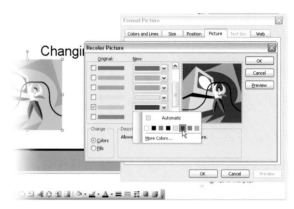

the Recolor button, and there it is…the coolest tool in PowerPoint. Using the Recolor Picture
dialog, you can change any color in the clip art image. Just look for the image color you want
to replace by selecting that color's checkbox under the Original category to the left, then
select a new color to replace it using the corresponding color's New drop-down menu. Click
OK when finished.

▬ ▣ ☒ SNAG SLIDES

If you've ever thought it would be great to
insert slides from an existing presentation
into your current presentation, then you're
not alone. This is a great idea and you can
have PowerPoint do it for you. Here's how:
Navigate in your existing presentation using
the Slides tab to where you'd like to insert
the new slide, then click Insert>Slides from
Files in the menu bar. (*Note:* PowerPoint will
insert the slides underneath the slide you're
working on.) Under the Find Presentation
tab in the Slide Finder dialog, click Browse
to locate the presentation that you want to
snag a slide from. When you find the presen-

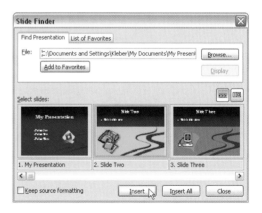

tation and click Open, check out the Select Slide window in the dialog. There are all of your
slides. Now simply click the slide(s) to insert, and click Insert. The slide(s) now appears in your
current presentation…sweet!

DELIVER THE PACKAGE

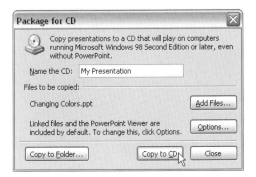

PowerPoint's new Package for CD feature is great for distributing corporate presentations to customers; sending animated holiday greetings to family, friends, and associates; and even for storing (backing up) your presentations. To package your presentation to CD, click File>Package for CD in the menu bar. Follow the Package for CD dialog to give your presentation a name, add files to the CD, and choose additional options to save with your presentation. Click the Add Files button to add any media files included in your presentation. Click the Options button to include the PowerPoint Viewer (which allows the viewer who doesn't have PowerPoint to play a presentation), play the presentations automatically when the CD is inserted, and to embed TrueType fonts. In the Options dialog, you can even password protect the presentation if it contains sensitive information. When you're finished packaging your presentation, click Copy to CD, and PowerPoint will prompt you to insert a blank CD (if you haven't already done so) and will begin copying your presentation to a CD.

BEGIN OR END IN A FLASH

While in Slide Show view (View>Slide Show or press F5), you can quickly jump to the end (last slide) of your presentation by pressing the End key on your keyboard. You can also jump back to the beginning (first slide) of your presentation by pressing the Home key on your keyboard.

TAB A BULLET

If you need to insert a Tab character into a bulleted list, don't press the Tab key—it won't work. Instead press Control-Tab on your keyboard. This will insert the Tab character without messing with your bulleted list.

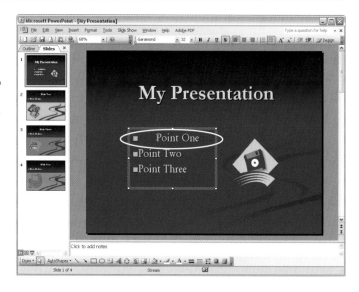

SHIFT TO SLIDE MASTER

The only thing that could make the Slide Master better is if we could access it more quickly. Fortunately, we can by using this little trick: To quickly change to PowerPoint's Slide Master view, Shift-click the Normal View button beneath the Slides pane. This changes Normal view to Slide Master View. Use the same technique for the other views' buttons for additional view options. Hey, and keep the fun going by also pressing Shift-Control and clicking the view buttons for even more options.

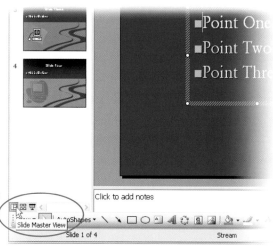

MASTER YOUR PRESENTATION

When designing a presentation that has several repeating objects, such as your company logo, located in the same positions, use the Slide Master to insert them. This ensures that the look of your presentation is consistent and objects are always placed in the same spot on each slide. Besides, if you need to move your logo, moving it on the Slide Master will move it to the exact same spot on each slide simultaneously. To do this, click View>Master>Slide Master. Next, click Insert>Picture>From File (or click Insert>Picture>Clip Art, as I did here). Use the Insert Picture dialog to browse for your logo on your hard drive, clicking Insert to place the logo (or just drag-and-drop a clip art image onto your document). Position the image wherever you'd like. Now click the Close Master View button in the Slide Master View toolbar, and you can see that your logo appears in the same location on each slide.

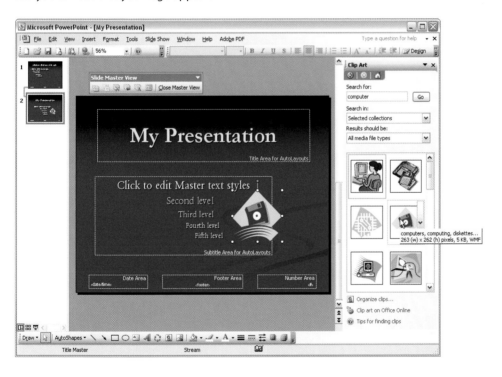

DON'T PRINT, YOU'RE HIDDEN

I often print my presentation, usually just for a different visual perspective, but I don't always need to print all of the slides to accomplish this. So, I hide the slides that I don't want to print. To hide slides, right-click any slide in the Slides tab and click Hide Slide in the shortcut menu. Now before you print the presentation (File>Print), be sure to uncheck Print Hidden Slides in the bottom right-hand corner of the Print dialog, then click OK.

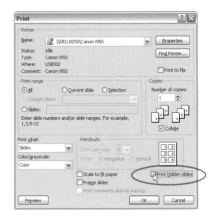

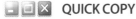 **QUICK COPY**

To quickly copy a slide in PowerPoint, drag-and-drop any slide within the Slides pane using your right mouse button. When you drop the slide where you want to place the copy, choose Copy from the shortcut menu. You've just copied a slide.

 **WEB IT**

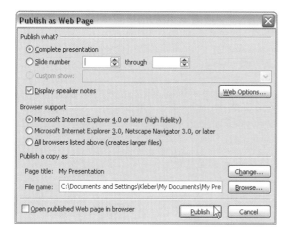

If you need to share your PowerPoint presentation on the Web, then you're in luck—PowerPoint makes it easy. When you're ready to share your presentation, click File>Save as Web Page in the menu bar, then click the Publish button on the Save As dialog. Next, choose whether to publish the entire presentation or only certain slides, whether to display speaker notes (if any), which browser to support, and where to save your file. When finished, click Publish and your presentation is packaged and ready to post to the Web.

 DON'T FORGET TO EMBED

Don't assume when you share your presentations that others will have the same fonts installed on their computers that you've used in your presentation. To ensure that others view your presentation as you've intended and with the fonts you've used, you'll want to embed your fonts when you save. To do this, click File>Save As in the menu bar, then click Tools>Save Options on the Save As dialog. Next, check Embed TrueType Fonts in the Save Options dialog and click OK. Now your fonts will be included with your presentation.

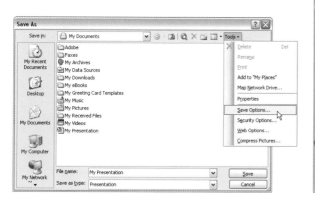

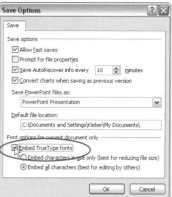

⊟ ⊡ ☒ THAT'S PERFECT!

The two most common shapes drawn in PowerPoint are an oval and a rectangle. The Power-Point developers knew this—that's why each shape has its own shape button on the Drawing toolbar. Now, ovals and rectangles are great, but what I really need are perfect circle and square buttons. If you went looking, you might think PowerPoint doesn't have them, but they're there: You just have to know how to access them. Make sure the Drawing toolbar is open by right-clicking any toolbar or menu and clicking Drawing. Press-and-hold the Shift key on your keyboard while drawing with the Oval tool to create a perfect circle (as I did here). Press-and-hold the Shift key while drawing with the Rectangle tool to create a perfect square. You can also use the Shift-key trick to create perfectly straight lines in PowerPoint using the Line tool.

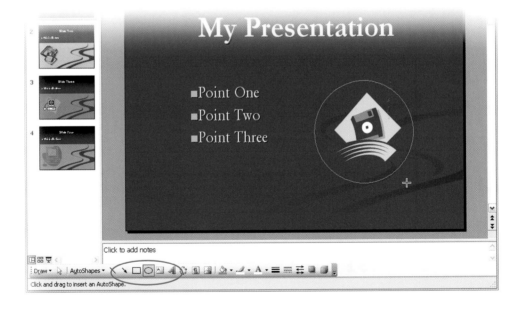

GLOBAL FONT REPLACEMENT

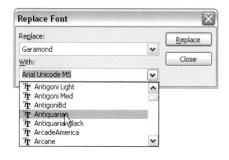

We all make bad judgment calls when it comes to fonts, and realizing that Comic Sans just won't cut it for your corporate presentation can be a painful experience, especially when faced with the prospect of manually changing the font through-out your entire presentation. This is just bad. To quickly fix your font disaster, click Format>Replace Fonts in the menu bar. This opens the Replace Font dialog. Use the Replace drop-down menu to select the font you want to change in your document, then choose the replacement font using the With drop-down menu. Click Replace when finished and all of the selected fonts are instantly changed, then click Close.

 SUPER-FAST SHAPES

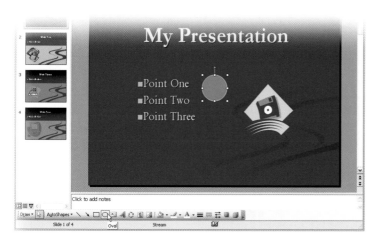

When creating shapes, most PowerPoint users draw a shape man-ually (using their mouse) and then use the shape's resize handles to adjust its size and positioning. Well, there's a faster way to create shapes: Press-and-hold the Control key on your keyboard, then simply click the shape tool's button in the Drawing toolbar (I Control-clicked the Oval button). This will instantly create the shape and place it in the center of your slide. Now, go ahead and resize and reposition your shape.

MORE AND MORE SHAPES MADE EASY

If you need to draw the same shape multiple times, first double-click any shape's button on the Drawing toolbar before you begin (I chose the Rectangle tool in this example). Double-clicking the button will leave it active, meaning that you can continue to draw using that shape until your hand cramps up and you black out from exhaustion. When you come to, click the shape button once more to deactivate it.

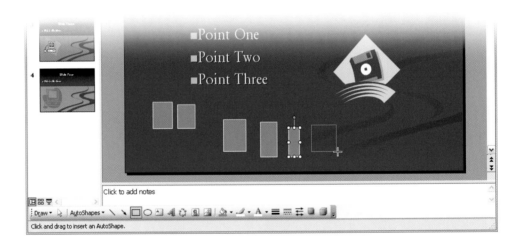

PERFECTLY SPACED SHAPES

Spacing shapes evenly can be a pretty tricky proposition. I once had 15 objects to line up—it took me three hours and a shot of Demerol and they still weren't quite right. So, I took some more Demerol, shut down my computer, and became a pharmaceutical salesman (kidding). Actually, I found a better way to line up my shapes. Click any shape tool and draw your shape, then press Control-D on your keyboard to duplicate the shape. Drag the duplicated shape to the exact spacing for your additional shapes, then press Control-D again and again to space them exactly the same distance apart.

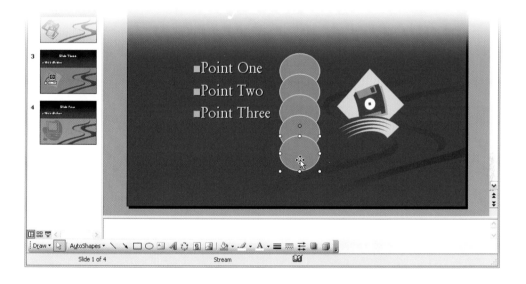

GIVE ME MORE GUIDES

When creating presentations, I use several guides to help lay out my slide's objects. You can view guides by pressing Control-G on your keyboard while you're in Normal view (View>Normal). Next, check "Display drawing guides on screen" in the Grid and Guides dialog, and uncheck any Snap To or Grid Settings options if you don't want to display a grid, then click OK. This will display two intersecting guides on your slides, which is great, but I need more. To create additional guides, press-and-hold the Control key on your keyboard while dragging an existing guide. Release your mouse button to drop the new guide into place. Repeat this to create as many guides as you want. To delete a guide, drag-and-drop it off any edge of your slide.

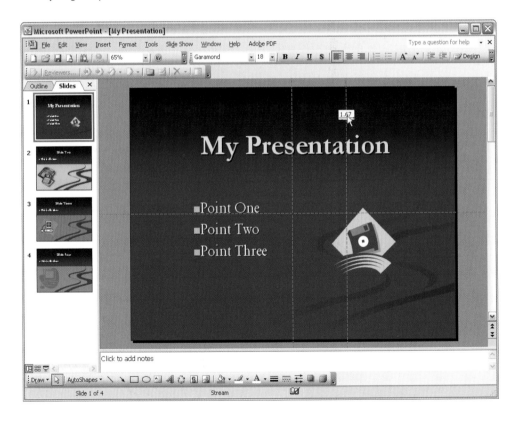

⊟▢✕ PICTURE THIS!

Pictures say a lot, and if you want to say a whole lot, then use one as the background for your entire presentation or individual slides. Here's how: Right-click any blank space on a slide and click Background in the shortcut menu. Next, click the drop-down menu under Background Fill and click Fill Effects. Then click the Picture tab in the Fill Effects dialog and click the Select Picture button. Browse your hard drive to locate your picture, click Insert, and then click OK in the Fill Effects dialog. Now, in the Background dialog, click Apply to All to apply the picture to every slide in your presentation or click Apply to affect only the slide you're currently working on.

⊟▢✕ OPTIONS ARE GREAT!

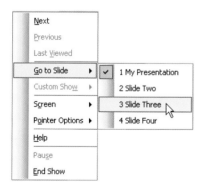

I'm an options kind of guy…I need 'em and lots of 'em, because I'm never completely sure what I'm doing. I found a great option in PowerPoint that adds real flexibility when designing presentations. Try this: View your presentation in Slide Show view by clicking View>Slide Show in the menu bar or simply press F5 on your keyboard. Next, right-click anywhere on the current slide and check out all of the great options available in the shortcut menu. You can navigate your presentation, change the appearance of your screen, jump to different slides (as shown here), and change your mouse pointer to draw or highlight objects. I love options!

CHAPTER 4 · Working with PowerPoint   **123**

WORD PRESENTATIONS?

The truly great thing about Office is how everything works so amazingly well together. For example, did you know that you could convert a Word outline into a PowerPoint presentation? Yep, you sure can. To do this, you first must have created an outline in Word using Word's headings in the Styles and Formatting task pane (see Word Help for formatting a document if you need assistance). PowerPoint interprets Word's Heading 1 paragraph style

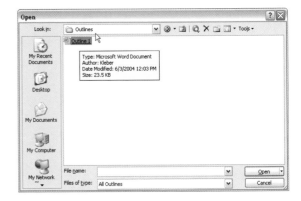

as an individual slide, Heading 2 as a top-level bullet point, and Heading 3 as a second-level bullet point. So, once you've set up your outline in Word, launch PowerPoint, click File>Open in the menu bar, and then choose All Outlines in the Files of Type drop-down menu in the Open dialog. Next, browse your hard drive for the outline you created in Word, click Open, and PowerPoint opens the outline and converts it into a presentation.

LINK 'EM

PowerPoint has the capability to create hyperlinks from just about any object to just about anything, and one great use for this is to launch a webpage during your presentation. Here's an example: You're giving a presentation and at a certain point you'd like to open your Web browser (this requires an active Internet connection) to visit your corporate website, provide additional information, or to highlight

services. Just select the text or object that you want to link from and press Control-K to open the Insert Hyperlink dialog. Next, type the URL in the Address field at the bottom of the dialog and click OK. You can test your hyperlink in Slide Show view by pressing F5 on the keyboard. Now, click the hyperlink to launch your Web browser, which will launch your website.

SIZE DOWN

By default, if you open multiple presentations, they're displayed in Normal view, one on top of the other, forcing you to close each presentation to view the others—that bites! I want to view all of my open presentations at once…and you can. Here's how: First, open several presentations (File>Open), then press Control-F5 on your keyboard. This sizes down all of your presentations within the PowerPoint window. Now maximize any presentation you want. Repeat this keyboard shortcut to quickly minimize any open presentation.

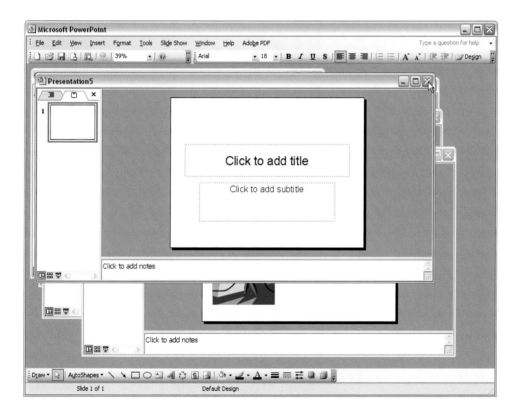

▣ TAKE A PICTURE

Here's a really slick trick for saving an entire slide as a graphic. It's great for when you need to create screen shots of your presentations to use on the Web. First, switch your view to Notes Page by clicking View>Notes Page in the menu bar, then right-click anywhere on the slide and click Copy in the shortcut menu. Now switch back to Normal view (View>Normal), right-click anywhere on a slide, and click Paste in the shortcut menu. Next, right-click the pasted picture and click Save as Picture in the shortcut menu. Using the Save as Picture dialog, select a location to save the picture on your hard drive and select your image's format using the Save as Type drop-down menu (e.g., JPEG or GIF for the Web), then click Save.

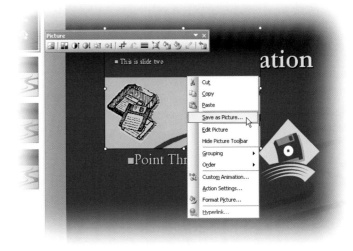

CONTROL THE SHADOWS

Shadowed text just looks cool! I personally think all text should have a drop shadow, but that's just me. Unfortunately, PowerPoint's default text shadowing isn't great, but that doesn't mean you shouldn't use drop shadows for your text—you just have to find a better way. To apply drop shadows to text, never use the text shadow formatting command. Instead, do this: Select the text you'd like to add a drop shadow to, click the Shadow Style button on the Drawing toolbar, then click Shadow Settings to display the Shadow Settings toolbar, and click any Nudge Shadow button to create a drop shadow for your text. Now you have complete control over your drop shadow: You can move the shadow in any direction by clicking the Nudge Shadow buttons or give it any color you like by pressing the Shadow Color button in the Shadow Settings toolbar.

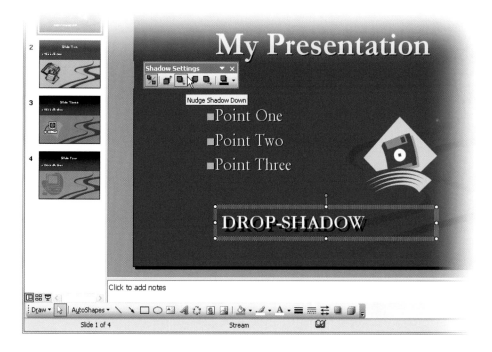

⊟□☒ SUPER-FAST SYMBOLS

There are three characters that you're going to use repeatedly in presentations, especially when giving corporate presentations: They're the ©, ™, and ® symbols. Fortunately, there are quick keyboard shortcuts for inserting each of them. Next time you need to use one of these symbols, try these shortcuts: Type "(c)" for ©, "(tm)" for ™, and "(r)" for ® (all without the quote marks). PowerPoint will immediately replace the text with the symbols.

⊟□☒ KIOSK COOL

Presentations don't have to always be in person. You can create a self-running presentation, complete with voice recordings—ideal for kiosk presentations. To add voice recordings to your presentation, select the slide to which you want to add voice recordings, then click Insert>Movies and Sounds>Record Sound in the menu bar. Name your recording in the Name field, then click the Record button (the button with a red circle) in the Record Sound dialog. When finished, click the Stop button, then click OK. A small speaker icon will appear on your slide. To preview your recording, double-click the speaker icon on the slide in Normal view (View>Normal) or right-click the icon for more options.

 **MIX IT UP**

If you're giving a presentation and need to skip ahead to a slide or jump back to a previous slide, this is how to do it—all the while looking like a PowerPoint pro: While you're in Slide Show view (press F5), type the number of the slide that you want to open (making sure that the Number Lock key is on), then press Enter on your keyboard. This opens the slide, making you look magical and even a little better looking. You can of course always right-click any slide during a presentation and click Go to Slide and select your slide's number on the shortcut menu, but that won't look magical or better looking at all.

 CAN'T MISS THAT LOGO

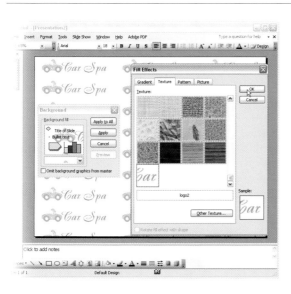

If you want people to remember your company logo, put it where they can't miss it: Tile it on the background of your presentation. To do this, right-click your slide and click Background on the shortcut menu, then click the drop-down menu under Background Fill and click Fill Effects. Next, click the Texture tab on the Fill Effects dialog and click Other Texture. Now browse your hard drive for your logo, click Insert, and then OK on the Fill Effects dialog. Now, click Apply to All to tile your logo on every slide in your presentation or click Apply to add your logo to the current slide only. Now that's a hard-to-miss logo.

IT'S GOOD TO TAKE NOTES

When giving an informational presentation, you may find it useful to provide handouts for note-taking. While you can create hand-outs (aka: speaker's notes) in PowerPoint, there's a better option: Export your handouts to Word, which gives you greater control of the handout's formatting and design. To do this, open the Power-Point presentation for which you want to create handouts, then click File>Send To>Microsoft Office Word. Select the page layout for your notes ("Blank lines next to slides" works best for note-taking), then click OK in the dialog. Word will launch, showing your slides in tables, which you can quickly edit and print (File>Print).

GIDDYAP

You can save a PowerPoint presentation so that it starts automatically when opened, bypassing the program window. This only works when you haven't launched Power-Point yet. First, save your presentation as a Power-Point Show (.pps). Click File>Save As in the menu bar, select PowerPoint Show from the Save as Type drop-down menu on the Save As dialog, and then click Save. Now, whenever you double-click the document's icon to open the presentation, it will automatically launch PowerPoint and begin to play.

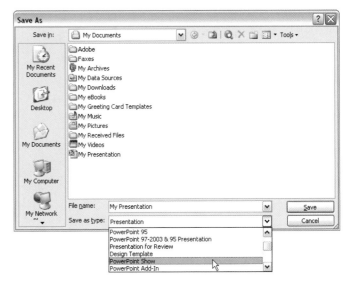

DON'T JUST FLIP, TRANSITION

Don't just flip slides, add a little flair to your presentations with transitions. To add a transition to any slide, make sure you're in Normal view (View>Normal), then right-click a slide in the Slides tab, and click Slide Transition in the shortcut menu. This opens the Slide Transition task pane. Next, choose a transition from the list. Select the transition's speed (how quickly it displays) by using the Speed drop-down menu, then select any sound to accompany the transition in the Sound drop-down menu. To apply the transition to just the selected slide, simply close the Slide Transition task pane; to apply the transition to all slides, click the Apply to All Slides button. Click the Play button to preview your transitions.

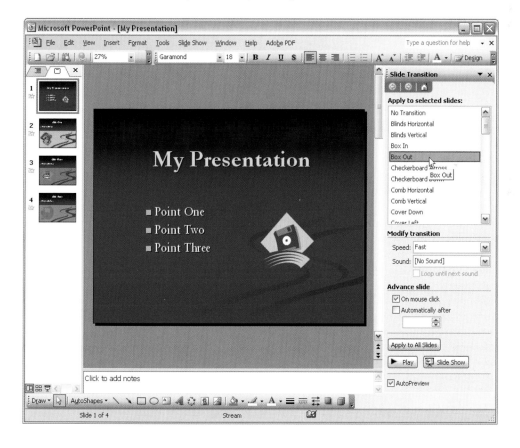

PIXEL PUSHING

Do you need to move your object a single pixel or just 1/12th of an inch? When you need to be exact, you need to be exact, and when you need to be that exact, remember this: By default, you can nudge your objects 1/12th of an inch—with or without the rulers visible (View>Ruler) —by using the arrow keys on your keyboard. But if you live in a pixel world, press-and-hold the Control key, then press the Left or Right Arrow keys to move your object a single pixel in either direction (as I did here with the computer logo).

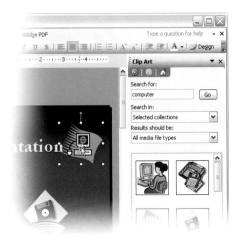

POWER ALBUMS

PowerPoint is perfect for sharing your digital photo albums. What, you haven't used PowerPoint to create digital photo albums and then sent them to your family and friends? I'm shocked! Well, you will now, once you learn how to do it. Click Insert>Picture>New Photo Album in the menu bar, which opens the Photo Album dialog. Next, click File/Disk to browse your hard drive or click Scanner/Camera to import your pictures from a digital camera

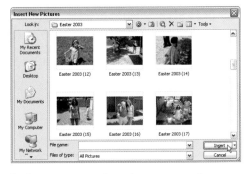

or scanner. Continue to click File/Disk to insert all of your images, then choose your album layout options from the Picture Layout drop-down menu, and click Create when finished. PowerPoint creates your photo album and lays it out in a new presentation window. To update your album, click Format>Photo Album in the menu bar.

 **SUMMARY SLIDE**

To create a summary slide of your PowerPoint presentation, Control-click to select the slides in the Slides pane that you want to include in your summary, then press Alt-Shift-S on your keyboard. This will create a summary slide and place it at the top of the slide order. Creating a summary slide can be used effectively to highlight topics that will be covered during your presentation or to recap your presentation at the closing.

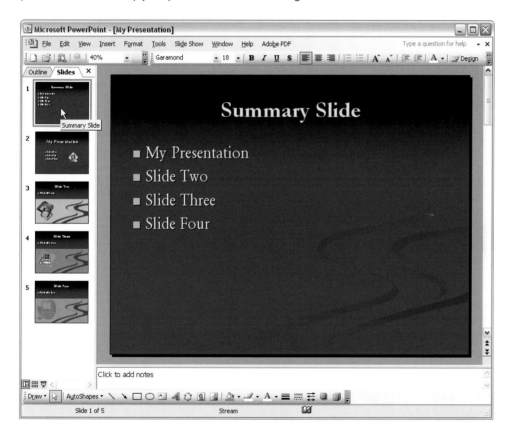

BLACKOUT

There will be times during a presentation when you'll want to "black out" your display—useful before beginning a presentation or when pausing to answer questions. To black out your display while in Slide Show view (press F5), press the "b" key on your keyboard. Press the "b" key again to show your display again.

 OBJECTS TOO SMALL?

We probably all have too much stress in our lives, and selecting objects in PowerPoint really shouldn't push anyone into having a psychotic episode, but trying to select small objects that are buried by a pile of other objects can just about do that. Here's a tip to help you avoid freaking out at your desk. First, press the Escape (Esc) key on your keyboard to ensure that nothing is selected. Next, repeatedly press the Tab key to jump from object to object until you've selected the freakishly small object, then press the Backspace key to delete it. You really shouldn't be using freakishly small objects anyway.

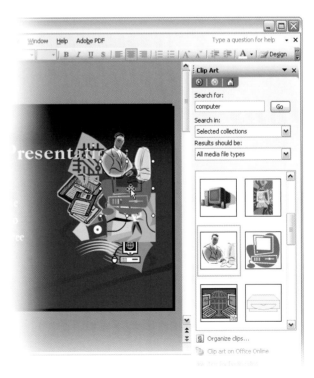

 GIVE CREDIT

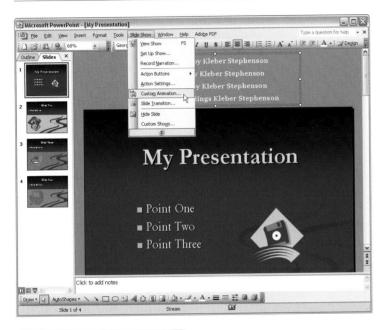

Want to throw in some closing credits? Here's how: Create a text box on your final slide by selecting your slide in the Slides tab and clicking Insert>Text Box in the menu bar. Click-and-drag to create your text box and then type your credits (names and titles). Next, select the text box and drag it off the top of the slide. Now, click Slide Show>Custom Animation in the menu bar and, with the text box still selected, click the Add Effect drop-down menu in the Custom Animation task pane. Now click Entrance>More Effects and select Crawl In, then click OK. Click Play to preview your credits. To edit your effect, click the down-facing arrow next to your effect in the Custom Animation task pane and choose Effect Options in the shortcut menu. *Note:* You may need to change the color of your text to ensure that it doesn't blend in with your slide's background by selecting the text and clicking the Font Color button in the Formatting toolbar.

▣◻◻ CAN YOU SPELL BUSINESS?

There's nothing worse than poor spelling in a presentation. Honestly, if you can't spell business, then you're probably not going to get mine. So, do yourself a favor and always check
your spelling before you give a presentation. You have no excuse not to—PowerPoint makes it
easy. Press F7 on the keyboard and PowerPoint will check the spelling on each slide. If any misspellings are found, PowerPoint will open the slide, launch the Spelling dialog, and highlight
the incorrect text so you can fix it.

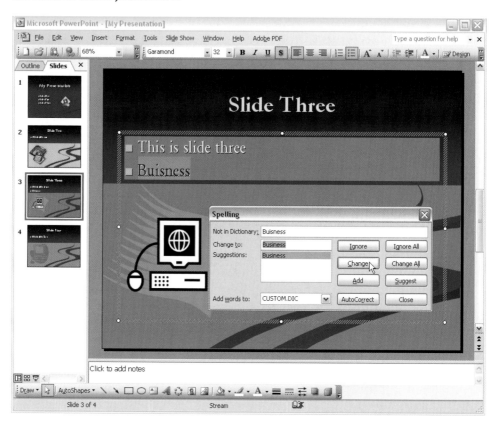

BECOME A TEMPLATE DESIGNER

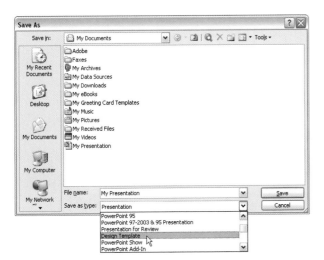

Creating really good presentations takes time and effort, and once you've completed your work of art, be sure to put it to good use by making it into a design template so you can use it again. To save your presentation as a template, click File>Save As in the menu bar, select Design Template from the Save as Type drop-down menu in the Save As dialog, then click Save. To use your design template, click File>New in the menu bar, then click the From Design Template link on the New Presentation task pane. Your saved templates will appear at the top of the Available for Use category in the Slide Design task pane. Click your template icon to apply it to your new presentation. *Note:* If your design template doesn't show up in the Slide Design task pane, try re-launching PowerPoint.

DON'T CUT, CROP INSTEAD

Sometimes the whole picture just won't do; maybe you just want to emphasize a portion of a picture. Well, you can hide a portion of a picture in PowerPoint by using the Crop tool. To crop a picture, first select the object and then click the Crop button in the Picture toolbar. (If you don't see the Picture toolbar, right-click any toolbar or menu and click Picture.) Next, click-and-drag any resize handle to crop the picture. If you crop too much of your picture, don't worry, it's not deleted. Simply drag the handle out while using the Crop tool to reveal cropped portions of the picture.

WE'RE CONNECTED

When I was a kid, I loved to play connect-the-dots—actually, I rocked at connect-the-dots. If there had been a connect-the-dots circuit, I'd have a different career. Unfortunately, not everyone shares my love of dots, but I'm pretty sure there's a fellow connect-the-dotter on the Office development team, because they dedicated an entire AutoShapes collection to connecting things. If you have two or more objects that you'd like to connect in PowerPoint—such as a text box to a graphic—do this: Click AutoShapes>Connectors in the Drawing toolbar to select a style for your connector line. Next, place your mouse pointer over one of the objects and click any anchor point that you'd like to connect to. Then, move your mouse pointer to the second object and click any anchor point to create the connector line. You can customize your connector line by double-clicking on the line (avoiding the line's anchor points) to open the Format AutoShape dialog.

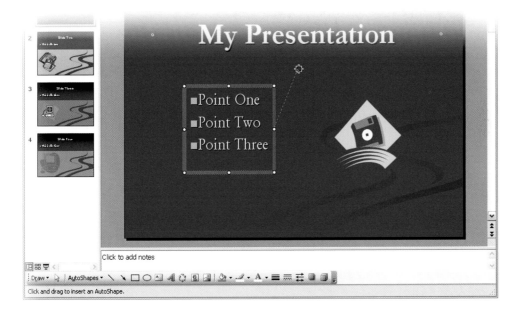

 I'D LIKE TO COMMENT

Adding comments to your presentations is a perfect way to remind yourself of ideas or to offer suggestions when designing a presentation with others. To insert a comment, first make certain you're in Normal view by clicking View>Normal in the menu bar, then click Insert>Comment. This will insert a comment into your slide. Type your comments in the text box, then click anywhere outside the comment box to close it. Simply click the comment's icon to view it again. To delete a comment, right-click the comment's icon and click Delete in the shortcut menu.

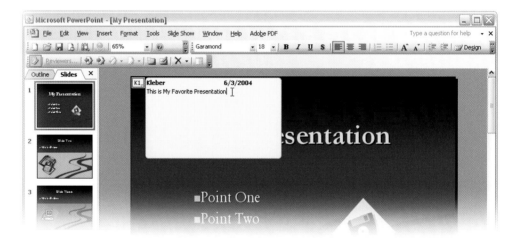

⬛◻❎ QUICKLY ANIMATE OBJECTS

Adding animations to text and objects is what PowerPoint is all about. Yep, it's all about the animations. To add animations to just about anything (text blocks, graphics, shapes, etc.), first select the object, then right-click it and click Custom Animation in the shortcut menu. Now click the Add Effect drop-down menu in the Custom Animation task pane to choose an effect. PowerPoint will preview the effect when the AutoPreview checkbox is selected. When finished, click Play at the bottom of the Custom Animation task pane to preview your animation.

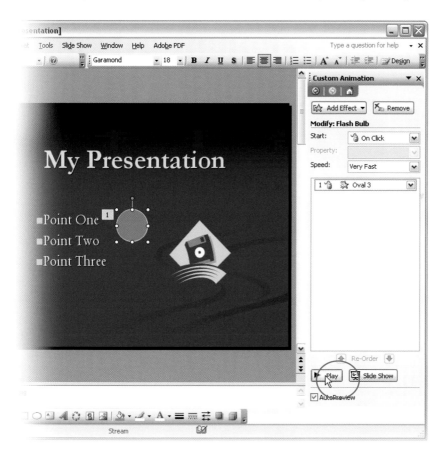

▭▢▣ MORE TEMPLATES

About the only thing that's better than PowerPoint's design templates are more templates. And you can get a ton for free, if you know where to look. Open PowerPoint's Startup task pane by pressing Control-F1. Then click the down-facing arrow to the left of the Close button on the task pane's header and choose Site Design to display the Site Design task pane. Scroll to the bottom of the available templates and click the last thumbnail, named Design Templates on Microsoft Office Online. This will launch your Web browser and take you to PowerPoint template heaven. Go nuts, there's a ton of 'em.

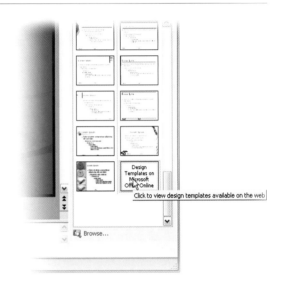

▭▢▣ I'M COMPRESSED!

It's time to knock PowerPoint down to size— PowerPoint's graphics anyway. Graphics can really add up in a presentation, especially if you're using stock photography. And, if you're not able to save your presentation to CD because it's the size of your MP3 collection, then you may have a problem. You could try to compress your graphics one at a time, but that would take way too long. Try this instead: Right-click the Standard toolbar and click Picture to open the Picture toolbar, then click the Compress Pictures button. Select the All Pictures in Document option in the Compress Pictures dialog, choose a Resolution, and whether or not to "Delete cropped areas of pictures," then click OK. Now, you can save your presentation to a disc. *Note:* This may alter the way graphics print or look onscreen.

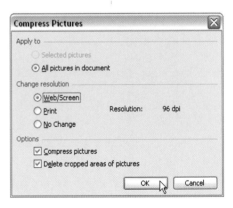

PREVIEW AND EDIT

Viewing your presentation in Slide Show view has its limitations—most obviously, you can't edit your presentation. Unless of course you know this trick: Press-and-hold the Control key on your keyboard and click View>Slide Show in the menu bar. This opens a mini preview window. Now you can compare your presentation in Slide Show view and Normal view (although you may have to adjust your PowerPoint window to see both views, as I did here). Make any changes to your presentation in Normal view while you're viewing the presentation in Slide Show view. To close the mini Slide Show view, click on it to make it active and press the Escape key. Pretty cool!

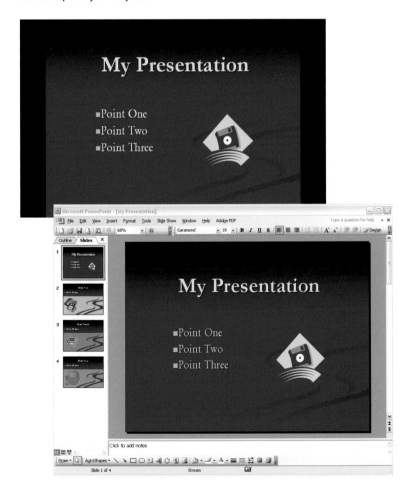

QUICK NOTES

I typically take a lot of notes, simply because I can't remember anything. Hold on, what was I writing about?…see, it's bad. Fortunately, PowerPoint comes to the rescue for all of us memory-challenged folks. As I'm designing a slide for a presentation, I may have several great ideas (and even more bad ones) that I want to share, or I may want to record some comments (called speaker notes) to help during my presentation. To save your ideas and comments for any particular slide, type them into the Notes pane located directly beneath your slide in Normal view (View>Normal). This is your notes page. If you need more room for your notes, place your cursor over the divider bar until the cursor changes to the horizontal move tool and just drag the bar upward to expand the Notes pane. Now you won't forget a thing, I think…I can't remember.

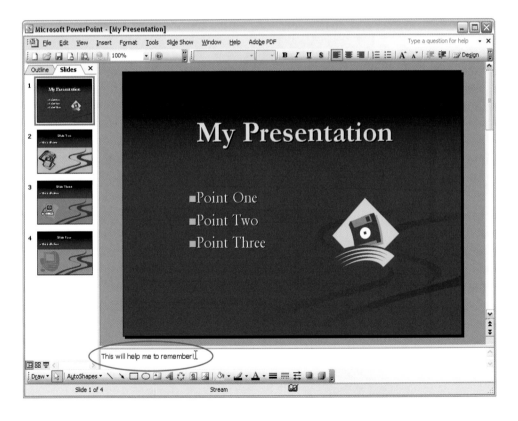

CUSTOMIZE YOUR CUSTOMERS

You've created the perfect presentation, worked weeks on getting it just right, and now you just have to figure out how to make it work for all of your potential customers. Well, you don't have to create a new presentation for each customer; create a custom show instead. Open your presentation, then click Slide Show>Custom Shows in the menu bar. Next, click the New button in the Custom Shows dialog, name your custom show, then select which slides to add by selecting them in the left column and clicking Add in the Define Custom Show dialog. When finished, click OK, then click the Show button to see what your presentation will look like. Use the Custom Show feature to create as many variations of your presentation as you want. When you're ready to use your custom shows, click Slide Show>Custom Show in the menu bar, click a saved custom show in the dialog, and then click the Show button.

DON'T HAVE TRANSITIONS FOR THE WEB?

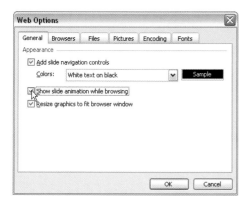

Transitions and animations are really cool, but if you've ever saved a presentation for the Web, you might have noticed that your transitions and animations weren't included. For whatever reason, you've got to tell PowerPoint to include these when saving for the Web. Here's how: Click Tools>Options in the menu bar, then click the General tab in the Options dialog. Next, click Web Options and in the dialog, check "Show slide animation while browsing." Now when you save your presentation for the Web (File>Save As Web Page), your transitions and animations will be included.

QUICK DEFAULTS

PowerPoint's default colors for shapes just don't work. Have you ever seen the default light-blue shapes in any PowerPoint presentation? Probably not. To avoid the light-blue blues, create a shape (I used the Oval tool from the Drawing toolbar), then click the down-facing arrow next to the Fill Color button, and change its stroke color by clicking the down-facing arrow next to the Line Color button (both found in the Drawing toolbar). Next, right-click the shape and click Set AutoShape Defaults in the shortcut menu. Now anytime you draw the shape, it'll be created using your new default colors.

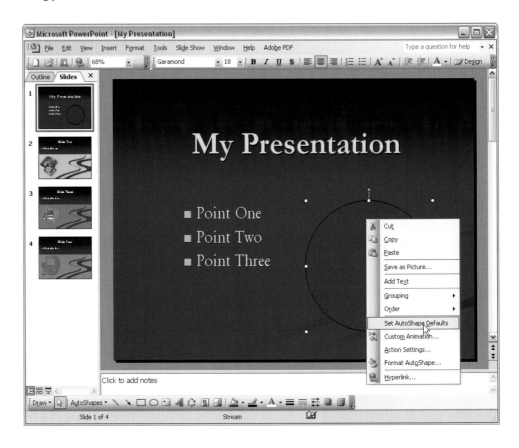

Time to
Excel

WORKING WITH EXCEL

My chapter description for Word contained an inaccuracy. I stated that Word finally gave computer users something to do with their computers. Well, that's not entirely

Time to Excel

working with excel

true. Believe it or not, the program that gave rise to the computer was a spreadsheet application. Yeah, a spreadsheet application. It was named VisiCalc and was created by Dan Bricklin and Bob Frankston in 1979. People who never had a use for computers finally did. Although I hate to admit it, Excel is my favorite Office application. I hate to admit it because I get so geeky with it. The true computer geek comes out in me when I'm using Excel. It's just so powerful, and when mastered, it's amazing what you can make it do. So, let's get geeky and jump right in. Turn the page.

 ☐☐☒ **STOP FLINCHING**

Let's face it, Excel's an ugly program; it just is (please don't email me about this, you won't change my mind). Every time I open it, I flinch. It could be the mass of gray grid lines…yeah I'm pretty sure it's the mass of gray grid lines. Gray is an ugly color. So let's change the color. Click Tools>Options in the menu bar, then click the View tab in the Options dialog. Next, select a new color from the Gridlines Color drop-down menu (anything other than gray will do), and click OK. That's slightly better!

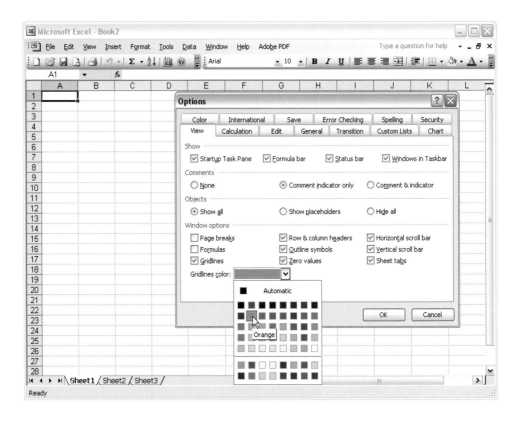

GETTIN' CRAZY WITH BACKGROUNDS

Now, I know that coloring your grid lines might be about all the excitement the average Excel user can take, but let's push the envelope and get really daring. Let's add a little more personality to your worksheets by adding a background picture. I know, take a couple deep breaths and we'll start when you're ready. Ready? Good! Click Format>Sheet>Background in the menu bar. Next, browse your hard drive using the Sheet Background dialog to locate a picture, and then click Insert. To remove the image, go to Format>Sheet>Delete Background. It's almost more than you can handle, isn't it?

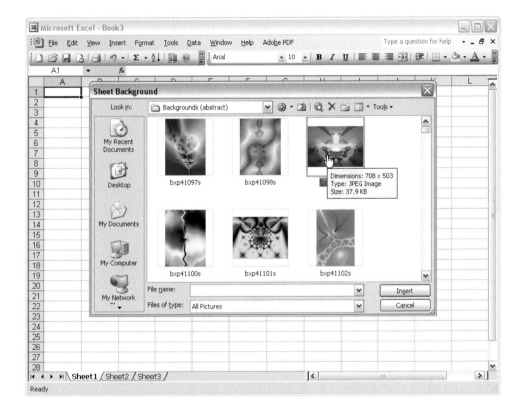

WHOA, THAT'S A DIFFERENT WORKSHEET

If you're really sick of looking at Excel's grid lines—regardless of their color—then get rid of 'em. You think I'm getting carried away…well, maybe, but I can't stop doing it. I'm this close to getting comfortable with working in Excel with no grid lines and headers. Try it; maybe it'll catch on. Click Tools>Options in the menu bar, then click the View tab in the Options dialog. Next, in the Window Options category, uncheck Gridlines, Row & Column Headers, and anything else that you can live without, and then click OK. Whoa, that's different!

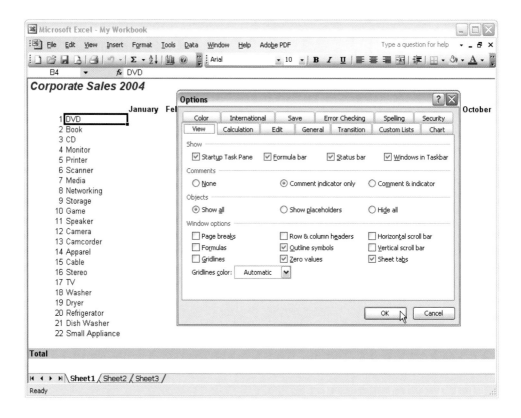

CENTERING TEXT

Excel may not offer Word's formatting capabilities, but you can still get your worksheets to look good. Centering a row's text inside columns to create a page header is a start. On line 1 type a heading, then click-and-drag to select as many cells as necessary in line 1, which will create headings over the worksheet's data (and if you use a month, as I did here, Excel will automatically enter the following months in the selected cells as you drag). Next, right-click a selected cell and click Format Cells in the shortcut menu. Then, click the Alignment tab in the Format Cells dialog, select Center Across Selection in the Horizontal drop-down menu, and click OK. Your text will now be centered in the selected cells.

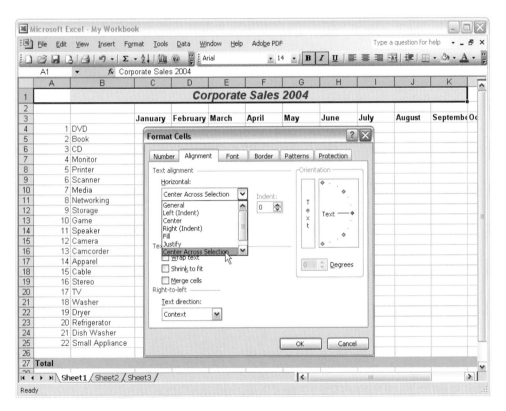

A QUICKER CALCULATOR

The tool that you'll probably use most frequently in Excel is the calculator, and when you get tired of going to your Start menu in Windows Taskbar every time you need it, you can add it to any Excel toolbar or even add it to the menu bar. Here's how: Click Tools>Customize in the menu bar and click the Commands tab in the Customize dialog. Next, select Tools under Categories, then drag-and-drop the Custom Calculator command from the Commands list onto the menu bar or any toolbar, and click Close. Now, anytime you need a calculator it's only a click away.

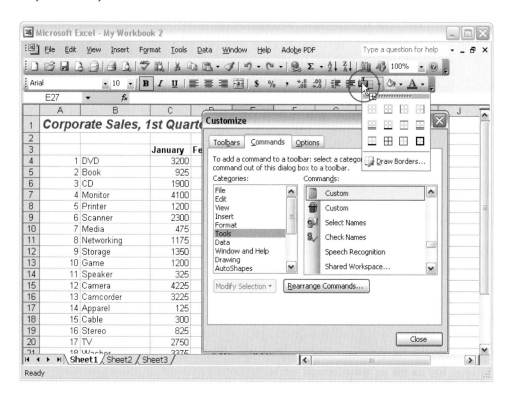

⊟ ⊡ ⊠ IT'S PICTURE TIME

Excel has the ultimate camera. It allows you take pictures of data on any worksheet then place the picture onto any other workbook's worksheet. Not impressed yet? You're about to be. What makes Excel's camera so cool is that the picture is live, meaning that whenever you make any changes to the photographed worksheet's data, the picture is updated simultaneously. Told ya you'd be impressed. To do this, first add the camera to your toolbar by clicking Tools>Customize in the menu bar and click the Commands tab in the Customize dialog. Next, select Tools under Categories, then drag-and-drop the Camera from the Commands list onto any toolbar, and then click Close. Now, Shift-click or click-and-drag to select the cells that you want to take a picture of, and then click the Camera button on the toolbar—the cells will be outlined by "marching ants" (an animated dashed line). Open any worksheet and click anywhere with your mouse pointer to paste the picture automatically. Now the data is always available to you. Anytime the data is changed on the original worksheet, it will be updated in the "picture" as well. To remove the picture, simply select it, then press Delete on your keyboard.

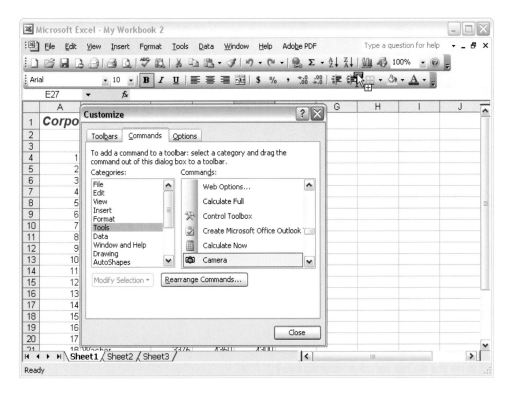

TAKE A (REAL) PICTURE

Okay, I'm sure you're thoroughly impressed with Excel's Camera tool (see previous tip). But maybe you're wondering if it's possible to actually take a picture of your data that you can then paste into other Office applications, such as Word, PowerPoint, or Publisher. Boy, we really think alike (scary). You can, and here's how: Select the data that you want to create a picture of, then press-and-hold the Shift key on your keyboard and click Edit>Copy Picture in the menu bar. Select As Shown on Screen in the Copy Picture dialog, then choose a format, and click OK. This copies the picture to the Office Clipboard. Now, open Word, PowerPoint, Publisher, or any application that will accept Picture and Bitmap file formats, and press Control-V to paste the picture.

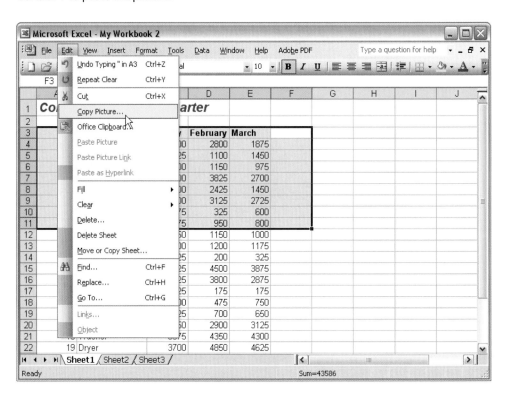

▣ MY FAVORITE WORKBOOK, RIGHT AWAY

Did you know that you could automatically open your favorite workbook each time you launch Excel? You can! Do this: Open your workbook, then click File>Save As in the menu bar. Next, use the Save In drop-down menu in the Save As dialog to navigate to the XLSTART folder (don't you just love how Microsoft names stuff?) that's typically located in C:\Program Files\Microsoft Office\OFFICE11\XLSTART if you installed Office 2003 using the default setup (if not, perform a search for "XLSTART" by going to Start>Search from the Windows Taskbar). Now click Save. Now each and every time you open Excel, it will automatically open your favorite workbook. If you want to restore Excel to its default setup, simply remove the workbook from the XLSTART folder, and Excel will once again open a new, blank spreadsheet when launched.

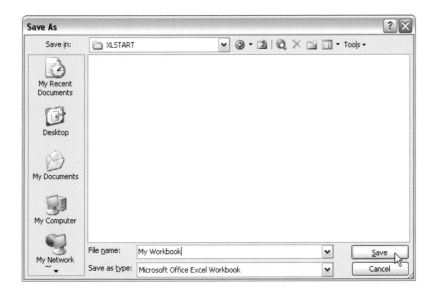

◨◨◨ ABC'S TO 123'S

You don't have to use letters as your worksheet's column headings. Oh, Microsoft would like you to think that you have to because they named the option to change this "R1C1 reference style"—huh? Anyway, you can change your ABC's to 123's—despite Microsoft's attempts to deter you—by clicking Tools>Options in the menu bar and clicking the General tab in the Option dialog. Next, check "R1C1 reference style" (baffling) in the Settings category and click OK. Now your ABC's are 123's. *Note:* This may alter the way Excel performs functions.

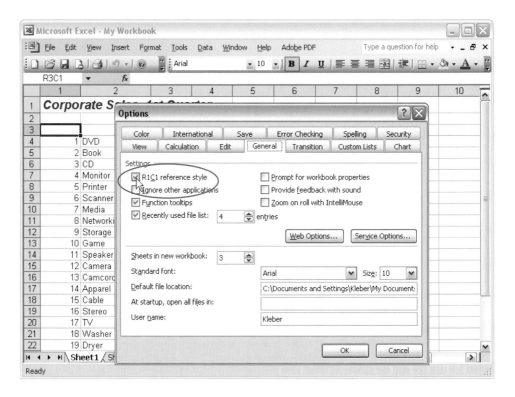

BETTER PRINTS

By default, Excel prints workbook data starting from the top-left margin of each page, which is fine—I guess you have to set something as the default. But this doesn't always look best when distributing printouts. For instance, you may want to center your data, and I wouldn't blame you. Here's how to do it: Click File>Page Setup in the menu bar and click the Margins tab in the Page Setup dialog. In the Center on Page category, check Horizontally to print data centered at the top of the page or choose Vertically to print data centered along the left side of the page. Check both to center printed data directly in the center of the page.

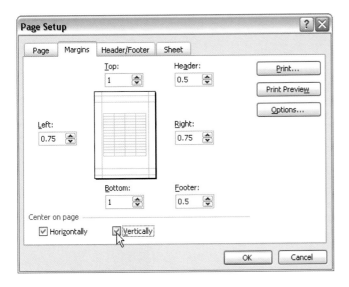

CONTROL YOUR PRINTS

If you need even greater control over how your worksheets print, then you're a control freak—you have issues, and you should seek counseling. But until you get help, you can use Excel's Print Preview to get your printed worksheets to look just right. Click the Print Preview button on the Standard toolbar, then click the Margins button at the top of the Print Preview window. Now, place your mouse pointer on any margin line and click-and-drag the margin line to any location on the worksheet. When finished, click Print.

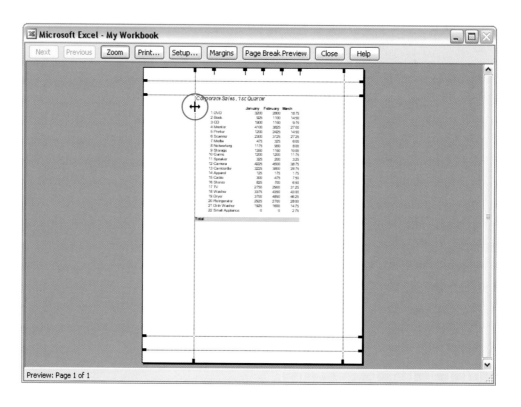

⊟ ⊡ ☒ IT'S TIME TO BREAK UP

By default, Excel automatically creates page breaks for your worksheets, which break it into sections that will print on your printer's default paper size (typically 8.5"x11"). You can view a worksheet's page breaks by scrolling until you see a black dashed line, which indicates a page break. (*Note:* If you still don't see page breaks, go to File>Page Setup, then click the Sheet tab, check Gridlines, and click OK. This option prints your gridlines. If you don't want to print your gridlines but still want to see the page breaks, return to the Page Setup dialog and uncheck Gridlines under the Sheet tab. Your page breaks will still appear.) But, what do you do if you want to break your 8.5"x11" worksheet into two or more sections that will print on individual sheets of paper? You need to insert manual page breaks. To do this, select the cell at the bottom-right of the last cell that you want to appear on your page, and then click Insert>Page Break in the menu bar. A page break will appear above the selected cell. Now, click the Print button to print the pages. To remove the page break, select the same cell and click Insert>Remove Page Break in the menu bar.

	Microsoft Excel - My Workbook								

File Edit View Insert Format Tools Data Window Help Adobe PDF   Type a question for help

Arial   ▾ 10 ▾ **B** *I* <u>U</u>

F12   *fx*

	A	B	C	D	E	F	G	H	I	J
3			January	February	March					
4	1	DVD	3200	2800	1875					
5	2	Book	925	1100	1450					
6	3	CD	1900	1150	975					
7	4	Monitor	4100	3825	2700					
8	5	Printer	1200	2425	1450					
9	6	Scanner	2300	3125	2725					
10	7	Media	475	325	600					
11	8	Networking	1175	950	800					
12	9	Storage	1350	1150	1000					
13	10	Game	1200	1200	1175					
14	11	Speaker	325	200	325					
15	12	Camera	4225	4500	3875					
16	13	Camcorder	3225	3800	2875					
17	14	Apparel	125	175	175					
18	15	Cable	300	475	750					
19	16	Stereo	825	700	650					
20	17	TV	2750	2900	3125					
21	18	Washer	3375	4350	4300					
22	19	Dryer	3700	4850	4625					
23	20	Refrigerator	2925	2700	2800					
24	21	Dish Washer	1925	1600	1475					
25	22	Small Appliance	0	0	275					

I◄ ◄ ► ►I \ **Sheet1** / Sheet2 / Sheet3 /

Ready

⊟⊡☒ A FAMILIAR PRINT

Have you ever noticed that
a printed worksheet doesn't
read as well as an onscreen
worksheet? Do you know
why? It's because Excel
doesn't print gridlines. You
get so used to seeing them
that when they're not there,
your printout almost looks
confusing. You can, how-
ever, tweak Excel so that it
prints the gridlines, which is
a good thing because I really
don't like being almost
confused. Click File>Page
Setup in the menu bar and
click the Sheet tab in the
Page Setup dialog. Next,

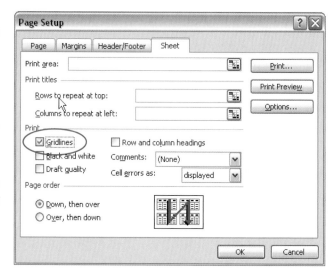

check Gridlines under the Print category and click OK. Now when you print your workbook, Excel will also print the familiar grid lines.

⊟▣☒ PRINT A WORKBOOK RANGE

If you need to print a selected range of several or all worksheets in a workbook, here's how: First, select the worksheets that you want to print the same range for by pressing-and-holding the Control key on your keyboard, then click each worksheet's tab at the bottom-left corner of the Excel window. Next, select your print range on Sheet 1, then click File>Print in the menu bar. Now, choose Selection listed under Print What in the Print dialog and click OK. Each worksheet will now print only the selected range from Sheet 1.

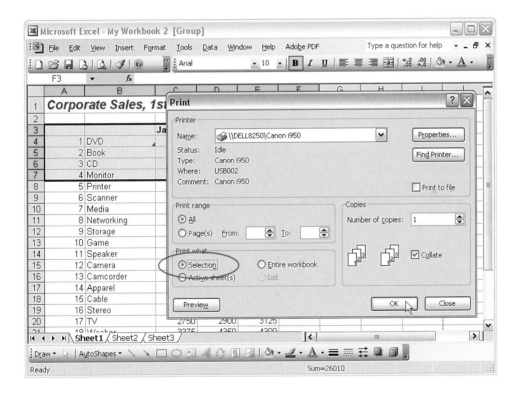

AM I RICH YET?

I love things that are live: football games, fireworks, Limp Bizkit (small venue), and adding live data to my Excel worksheets. I can't help you with football games, fireworks, or Limp Bizkit, but I can show you how to liven up your worksheets with live data. Excel uses Smart Tags to insert live stock quotes into your worksheets. All you need is an active Internet connection and your favorite stock symbol. By default, Smart Tags are not turned on, so let's do that first. Click Tools>AutoCorrect Options in the menu bar and click the Smart Tags tab in the AutoCorrect dialog. Next, check Label Data with Smart Tags, and under the Recognizers category check Financial Sym-

bol (Smart Tag Lists) and any other Recognizers you wish, then click OK. Now, type your stock symbol into any cell using all capital letters, and then press Enter on your keyboard. You'll notice a small triangle in the bottom-right corner of the cell. Move your pointer over it to show the cell's Smart Tag, click the Smart Tag, and click Insert Refreshable Stock Price. Next, select where to insert the stock quote using the Insert Stock Price dialog (either on a new worksheet or starting in a particular cell on the current worksheet) and click OK. And, there it is—your favorite stock quote courtesy of MSN MoneyCentral. To control when the stock quote is refreshed, right-click anywhere over the stock quote and click Data Range Properties in the shortcut menu. In the dialog, check Refresh Every and change the minutes to any number you'd like or choose to Refresh Data on File Open, then click OK.

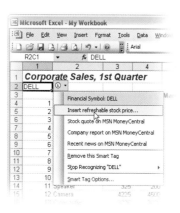

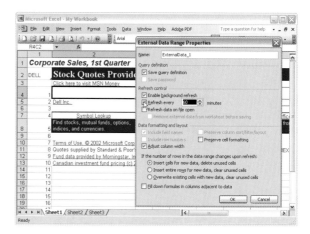

⊟⊡⊠ YOU COULD SAVE A PENCE

That previous tip was fun, wasn't it? Live data always gets me going. So, let's keep the adrena-
line pumping and add other live data without using Smart Tags. It just gets better and better,
doesn't it? Anytime I travel overseas, I watch the currency exchange rates (I'll wait days to
save a penny). And, with my laptop, Excel, and Wi-Fi, I'm always on top of what the dollar's
doing at any given time. Do this: Select any cell on an existing or new worksheet and click
Data>Import External Data>Import Data in the menu bar. Then, select MSN MoneyCentral
Investor Currency Rates from the My Data Sources folder and click Open. Choose where to
insert the data on your existing worksheet or choose a new worksheet in the Import Data
dialog, and then click OK. Oh yeah, I'm a master of money.

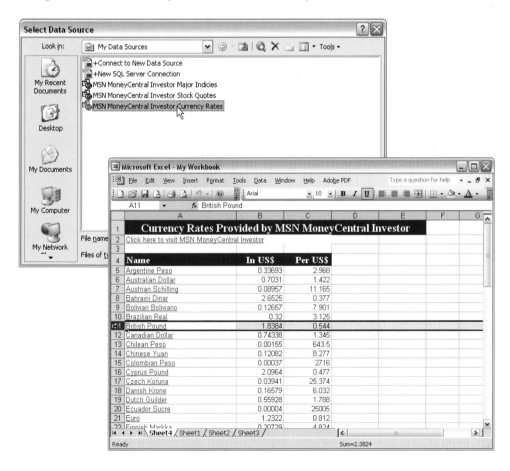

⬛ ◻ ☒ **IT'S A RANDOM THING**

There are good random things (hugs, gifts, winning the lottery) and bad random things (violence, bee stings, hair loss), but adding random numbers to an Excel worksheet is somewhere in between. To add random numbers to your worksheets, select the cell that you want to add a random number function to, then type =rand()*50 (use any number you want), and press Enter on your keyboard. This places random numbers zero to 50 into the formula field. Now drag the field's fill handle (its bottom-right handle) to expand your random numbers to as many cells as you'd like (as I did here). By default, Excel will use the General number format to generate the numbers. If you want to display only whole numbers, Shift-click to select all of your cells, right-click the selection, click Format Cells in the shortcut menu, and then click the Number tab on the Format Cells dialog. Next, select Number under Category, choose 0 (zero) in the Decimal Places drop-down menu, and then click OK. Now, you'll see only whole numbers.

	A	B	C	D	E	F	G	H	I	J
5	2	Book	925	1100	1450	4.547345	44.0751	25.64151		
6	3	CD	1900	1150	975	35.44887	24.62832	48.20423		
7	4	Monitor	4100	3825	2700	45.52643	0.53639	26.91065		
8	5	Printer	1200	2425	1450	7.534828	25.73961	15.12388		
9	6	Scanner	2300	3125	2725	41.31406	0.761965	4.159164		
10	7	Media	475	325	600	20.42733	32.04052	47.06695		
11	8	Networking	1175	950	800	9.287081	43.0901	28.92261		
12	9	Storage	1350	1150	1000	25.58892	29.30255	19.87352		
13	10	Game	1200	1200	1175	28.99266	32.52093	43.2724		
14	11	Speaker	325	200	325	10.03996	24.69657	7.959079		
15	12	Camera	4225	4500	3875	17.03413	10.23941	47.44989		
16	13	Camcorder	3225	3800	2875	49.3616	24.75804	49.66472		
17	14	Apparel	125	175	175	34.71285	28.38495	0.213509		
18	15	Cable	300	475	750	13.9209	22.64069	28.14285		
19	16	Stereo	825	700	650	34.21343	36.58277	46.28459		
20	17	TV	2750	2900	3125	16.26047	18.07141	20.65016		
21	18	Washer	3375	4350	4300	35.99612	28.06984	4.738346		
22	19	Dryer	3700	4850	4625	42.89456	20.79691	1.94924		
23	20	Refrigerator	2925	2700	2800	1.075767	12.09476	46.29169		
24	21	Dish Washer	1925	1600	1475	41.84987	45.21441	14.00736		
25	22	Small Appliance	0	0	275	2.997971	10.24669	47.75954		

⬛⬜❎ .2989345?

Do your cells or range have too many decimal spaces? If there are more than two, then yes they do—at least they do for me. I don't even know what three decimals represent, much less 20 of them. Decimals make me feel stupid, so I delete them as quickly as possible. You can too by selecting your cell or range and clicking the Decrease Decimal button on the Formatting toolbar. If you're a freak, you can click the Increase Decimal button on the Formatting toolbar.

Microsoft Excel - My Workbook

File Edit View Insert Format Tools Data Window Help Adobe PDF   Type a question for help

Arial   10   B I U

F4   fx =RAND()*50

Decrease Decimal

	A	B	C	D	E	F	G	H	I	J
1	**Corporate Sales, 1st Quarter**									
2										
3			January	February	March	April	June	July		
4	1	DVD	3200	2800	1875	11.74				
5	2	Book	925	1100	1450	45.98				
6	3	CD	1900	1150	975	45.91				
7	4	Monitor	4100	3825	2700	18.65				
8	5	Printer	1200	2425	1450	11.47				
9	6	Scanner	2300	3125	2725	9.98				
10	7	Media	475	325	600	24.65				
11	8	Networking	1175	950	800	23.45				
12	9	Storage	1350	1150	1000	2.70				
13	10	Game	1200	1200	1175	0.70				
14	11	Speaker	325	200	325	23.78				
15	12	Camera	4225	4500	3875	15.87				
16	13	Camcorder	3225	3800	2875	3.92				
17	14	Apparel	125	175	175	26.81				
18	15	Cable	300	475	750	39.64				
19	16	Stereo	825	700	650	38.20				
20	17	TV	2750	2900	3125	19.93				
21	18	Washer	3375	4350	4300	31.67				
22	19	Dryer	3700	4850	4625	24.48				

Sheet1 / Sheet2 / Sheet3 /

Ready   Sum=470.72

 SHARE YOUR FORMATTING

To add the same page formatting to multiple worksheets, press-and-hold the Control key on your keyboard, then click to select each worksheet's tab (along the bottom-left corner of the Excel window) that you want to apply the same page setup to. Next, click File>Page Setup in the menu bar and click the Page tab in the Page Setup dialog. Make any changes to the page setup, and then click OK. The settings are applied only to the selected worksheets. I use this tip when setting up pages within a workbook that should print landscape instead of the default portrait orientation. When finished, press the Shift key and click the current tab to deselect the grouped worksheets.

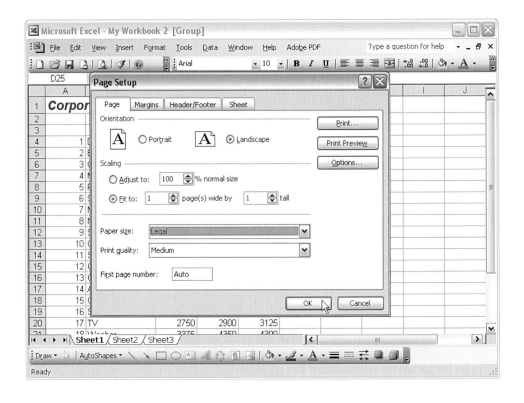

▬ ▢ ☒ THE TITLE'S THE SAME

I often give each worksheet within a workbook the same title. Each worksheet may hold different data, but the report's title doesn't typically change from worksheet to worksheet. Giving each worksheet the same title manually can be a real chore, but you don't have to type or paste the title onto each worksheet; use this shortcut instead: First, group your worksheets by pressing the Control key on your keyboard and clicking each worksheet's tab (along the bottom of the Excel window) that you want to have the same title. Then click Sheet 1, select cell A1, and type your title (my title is "Corporate Sales 1st Quarter"). The title now appears on each worksheet in the same location. Repeat this to share any type of data among your worksheets. When finished, press the Shift key and click the current tab to deselect the grouped worksheets.

		January	February	March					
1	DVD	3200	2800	1875					
2	Book	925	1100	1450					
3	CD	1900	1150	975					
4	Monitor	4100	3825	2700					
5	Printer	1200	2425	1450					
6	Scanner	2300	3125	2725					
7	Media	475	325	600					
8	Networking	1175	950	800					
9	Storage	1350	1150	1000					
10	Game	1200	1200	1175					
11	Speaker	325	200	325					
12	Camera	4225	4500	3875					
13	Camcorder	3225	3800	2875					
14	Apparel	125	175	175					
15	Cable	300	475	750					
16	Stereo	825	700	650					
17	TV	2750	2900	3125					
18	Washer	3375	4350	4300					
19	Dryer	3700	4850	4625					

Corporate Sales 1st Quart

⊟ ⊡ ☒ HOW LONG TIL MY BIRTHDAY?

Counting the number of days between two dates is harder than you might think. It's almost impossible to remember which months have 30 or 31 days (February's easy, unless it's a leap year, then it gets crazy). Even if you think you know, you're probably wrong. Well, you can use Excel to take the guesswork out of counting days. For example, if you need to know how many days there are between now and your next birthday (mine's January 21st), do this: Select any cell, then type: ="your next birthday's date"-"today's date". It should look something like this: ="1/21/05"-"5/6/04". Now press Enter on your keyboard. The number that appears represents the number of days between now and the blessed event—in this case, my birthday.

⊟☐☒ QUICK CALCULATIONS

The previous tip works great for calculating the days between two dates; however, what if you want to calculate the days between two existing dates? For example, cell A9 already contains the date of your next birthday (1/21/2005) and cell B9 contains today's date (5/6/2004). Do this: In cell C9, type =A9-B9, then press Enter on your keyboard. Next, right-click the cell containing the results (C9) and click Format Cells in the shortcut menu. Click the Number tab in the Format Cells dialog and click General listed under Category, and then click OK. Cell C9 displays the results—260. That's quick!

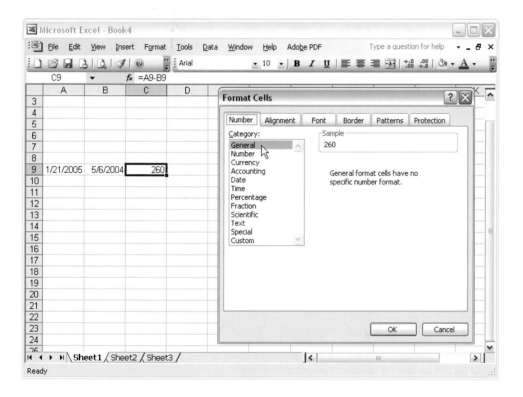

TOTAL YOUR WORKSHEETS

There are certain circumstances that require adding sums from several worksheets to compare data. This is very common when comparing monthly, quarterly, and annual sales reports. And, you can do this easily as long as each worksheet shares the same layout. To demonstrate this, open a new Excel workbook (File>New and click Blank Workbook in the New Workbook task pane). Next, type "Sales" in cell A3, and type "10,000" in cell B3 (both without the quotes). Then type "10,000" in cell B3 on both Sheet 2 and Sheet 3. Now, type: =SUM(Sheet1:Sheet3!B3) into cell A5 on Sheet 1, and then press Enter on your keyboard. Cell A5 on Sheet 1 displays the result of 30,000.

ANOTHER QUICK CALCULATION

This is the best quick sum tip, and it's so obvious I bet you've never noticed it. Select several cells on your worksheet containing numbers that you'd like to sum, then look at the bottom of Excel's window. The sum of the selected cells (SUM="total") appears along the bottom-right side of the status bar. Now, right-click anywhere on the status bar for additional options. Very quick!

Microsoft Excel - My Workbook

File Edit View Insert Format Tools Data Window Help Adobe PDF   Type a question for help

Arial   10   B I U

E4   fx 1875

	A	B	C	D	E	F	G	H	I	J
1	*Corporate Sales, 1st Quarter*									
2										
3			January	February	March					
4	1	DVD	3200	2800	1875					
5	2	Book	925	1100	1450					
6	3	CD	1900	1150	975					
7	4	Monitor	4100	3825	2700					
8	5	Printer	1200	2425	1450					
9	6	Scanner	2300	3125	2725					
10	7	Media	475	325	600					
11	8	Networking	1175	950	800					
12	9	Storage	1350	1150	1000					
13	10	Game	1200	1200	1175					
14	11	Speaker	325	200	325					
15	12	Camera	4225	4500	3875					
16	13	Camcorder	3225	3800	2875					
17	14	Apparel	125	175	175					
18	15	Cable	300	475	750					
19	16	Stereo	825	700	650					
20	17	TV	2750	2900	3125					
21	18	Washer	3375	4350	4300					
22	19	Dryer	3700	4850	4625					

Sheet1 / Sheet2 / Sheet3 /

Ready   Sum=7875

None
Average
Count
Count Nums
Max
Min
✓ Sum

▄□☒ QUICK LISTS

To create a numbered list in Excel, first select the cell that you want to be your first numbered cell and type the numeral one (1). Now, press-and-hold the Control key on your keyboard and drag the fill handle downward to create a numbered list that increases by one number for each cell selected.

	A	B	C	D	E	F	G	H
1	**Corporate Sales, 1st Quarter**							
2								
3			January	February	March			
4	1	DVD	3200	2800	1875		1	
5	2	Book	925	1100	1450		2	
6	3	CD	1900	1150	975		3	
7	4	Monitor	4100	3825	2700		4	
8	5	Printer	1200	2425	1450		5	
9	6	Scanner	2300	3125	2725		6	
10	7	Media	475	325	600		7	
11	8	Networking	1175	950	800		8	
12	9	Storage	1350	1150	1000		9	
13	10	Game	1200	1200	1175		10	
14	11	Speaker	325	200	325		11	
15	12	Camera	4225	4500	3875		12	
16	13	Camcorder	3225	3800	2875		13	
17	14	Apparel	125	175	175		14	
18	15	Cable	300	475	750		15	
19	16	Stereo	825	700	650		16	
20	17	TV	2750	2900	3125		17	
21	18	Washer	3375	4350	4300		18	
22	19	Dryer	3700	4850	4625			

Microsoft Excel - My Workbook. Cell G4, fx 1. Sum=171. Ready.

MORE QUICK LISTS

The previous technique works great for creating numbered lists, but don't stop there. Try this: Select a cell and type "Sunday" (without the quotes), drag the fill handle downward to create a daily calendar. This also works for months, years, and other sequential data. Go nuts! If the list doesn't appear sequentially, then click the Auto Fill Options Smart Tag that appears at the bottom of the last cell selected and click Fill Series.

Microsoft Excel - My Workbook							
File Edit View Insert Format Tools Data Window Help Adobe PDF							
G4		fx Sunday					
	A	B	C	D	E	F	G
1	Corporate Sales, 1st Quarter						
2							
3			January	February	March		
4	1	DVD	3200	2800	1875		Sunday
5	2	Book	925	1100	1450		Monday
6	3	CD	1900	1150	975		Tuesday
7	4	Monitor	4100	3825	2700		Wednesday
8	5	Printer	1200	2425	1450		Thursday
9	6	Scanner	2300	3125	2725		Friday
10	7	Media	475	325	600		Saturday
11	8	Networking	1175	950	800		Sunday
12	9	Storage	1350	1150	1000		Monday
13	10	Game	1200	1200	1175		Tuesday
14	11	Speaker	325	200	325		Wednesday
15	12	Camera	4225	4500	3875		Thursday
16	13	Camcorder	3225	3800	2875		Friday
17	14	Apparel	125	175	175		Saturday
18	15	Cable	300	475	750		Sunday
19	16	Stereo	825	700	650		Monday
20	17	TV	2750	2900	3125		Tuesday
21	18	Washer	3375	4350	4300		
22	19	Dryer	3700	4850	4625		

Sheet1 / Sheet2 / Sheet3 /

Ready

MY OWN QUICK LISTS

The previous few tips work great for adding lists to Excel, but it gets better. If you have your own sequential list that Excel doesn't recognize (such as your products listed in alphabetical order), add them to Excel's custom list, then you can quickly create entire lists of your products by simply dragging them onto your worksheet. Click Tools>Options in the menu bar and click the Custom Lists tab in the Options dialog. Next, select NEW LIST in the Custom Lists category and add your list in the List Entries field. Separate each entry with a comma and space (or simply press Enter after each entry) and then click Add. Click OK to close the dialog. Now your custom list is ready to be inserted at any time—just type the first word or number of your custom list and drag the cell's fill handle. If the list doesn't appear sequentially, click the Auto Fill Options Smart Tag that appears at the bottom of the last cell selected and click Fill Series.

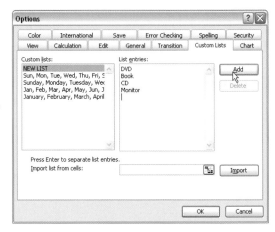

I WANT MORE

At the bottom of the File menu, Excel displays the four most recent documents you've worked on, which is helpful, but it's not enough. I'd like to see my last 10 or 15 files that I've worked on. To change this, click Tools>Options in the menu bar and click the General tab on the Options dialog. Type 10, 15, or whatever you prefer into the Recently Used File List, and then click OK. Now click File in the menu bar to view the new list of most recently viewed files.

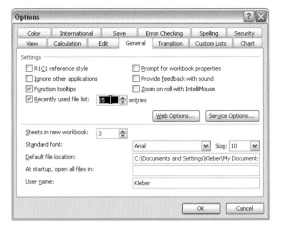

▄ ▄ ☒ MOVABLE DATA

Here's a slick trick to show field data in text boxes. This allows you to move data anywhere you'd like on your worksheet without affecting your fields. To do this, open the Drawing toolbar by right-clicking any toolbar and selecting Drawing. The Drawing toolbar appears at the bottom of the Excel window. Click the Text Box button and click-and-drag on your worksheet to draw a text box. Now, type "=" (without the quotes) in the Function bar, click the cell that contains the data you want to display in the text box, and then press Enter on your keyboard. The data appears in the text box. Now you can move the text field anywhere on the worksheet.

 PROTECT YOUR WORKSHEETS

Protecting your worksheet's data in Excel is very difficult, so follow along closely. First, click Tools>Protection>Protect Sheet, and then type a password in the Password to Unprotect Sheet field. Next, select the various tasks that you want to allow users to perform without your permission and click OK. Reenter your password when prompted and click OK again (this isn't the hard part). Now for the hard part: Don't save your password to an Outlook sticky note and then email the note along with the worksheet to practically everyone in your address book (a pathetic, true story).

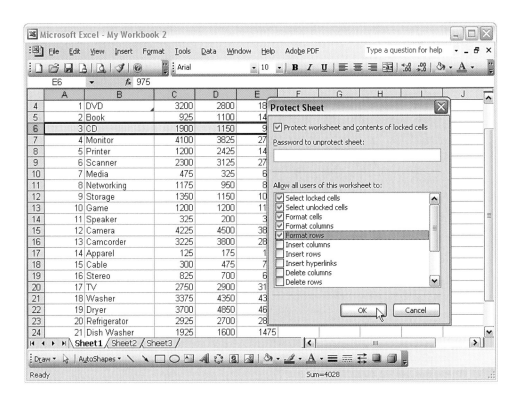

BE IMPATIENT

I've always been told that I'm impatient. It's true—traffic and low batteries on my TV remote freak me out—but sometimes impatience pays off. For example, I found a nice little trick to speed up AutoCorrect. When you begin typing in a cell, you'll notice that after a while, AutoCorrect begins to offer suggestions to complete your text. If you want to speed up this handy feature, right-click the cell and click Pick from Drop-Down List in the shortcut menu. A little pop-up menu listing available AutoCorrect words will appear directly beneath your cell. Now, find your choice and click it to place it in your document.

	A	B	C	D	E	F	G	H	I	J
7	4	Monitor	4100	3825	2700					
8	5	Printer	1200	2425	1450					
9	6	Scanner	2300	3125	2725					
10	7	Media	475	325	600					
11	8	Networking	1175	950	800					
12	9	Storage	1350	1150	1000					
13	10	Game	1200	1200	1175					
14	11	Speaker	325	200	325					
15	12	Camera	4225	4500	3875					
16	13	Camcorder	3225	3800	2875					
17	14	Apparel	125	175	175					
18	15	Cable	300	475	750					
19	16	Stereo	825	700	650					
20	17	TV	2750	2900	3125					
21	18	Washer	3375	4350	4300					
22	19	Dryer	3700	4850	4625					
23	20	Refrigerator	2925	2700	2800					
24	21	Dish Washer	1925	1600	1475					
25	22	Small Appliance	0	0	275					
26		Cam								
27	Total									

Cam
Camcorder
Camera
CD
Dish Washer
Dryer
DVD
Game
Media

⊟ ☐ ☒ FREEZE!

This is a real problem for me. I can't remember the names of my column headings. It doesn't matter if I have 20 columns or just one—if it's out of sight, it's out of mind. But, I found a fix…I freeze my column headings. To do this, select the first cell on the left directly below the column headings and click Window>Freeze Panes in the menu bar. A thin black line appears directly below the column headings. Now, scroll your worksheet. The headings don't move; they're always in sight. To unfreeze your headings, click Window>Unfreeze Panes in the menu bar.

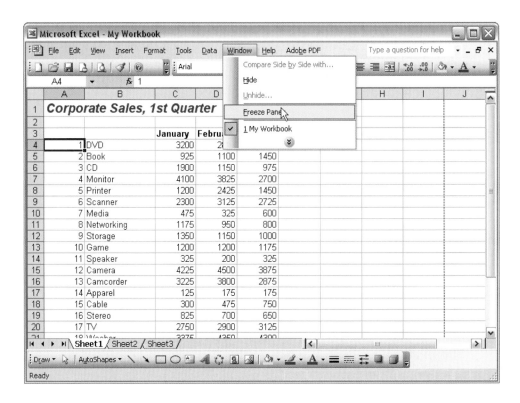

 **IN THE RED**

Get back the red—as in "in the red." By default, negative currency numbers are displayed in black. But, when I'm in the red, I want to see it. If you do too, select your cells that use currency, click Format>Cells in the menu bar, and click the Number tab in the Format Cells dialog. Click Currency listed under Category, and then select a red format in the Negative Numbers field to display negative currency numbers in red. Now all negative currency numbers will be shown in red.

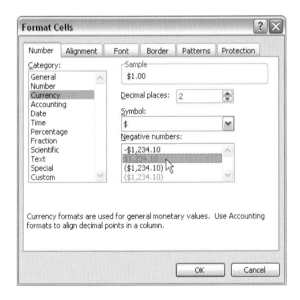

▬ ▢ ☒   WRAP TEXT

For formatting's sake, wrap your text. By default, you can type text into a cell until your fingers fall off and all your text will still appear on one line. This wreaks havoc on your columns. You can avoid this, however, by wrapping your text within a cell. To do this, right-click any cell where you want to wrap the text, click Format Cells in the shortcut menu, and then click the Alignment tab in the Format Cells dialog. Next, check Wrap Text under the Text Control category and click OK. The text is now wrapped in the cell.

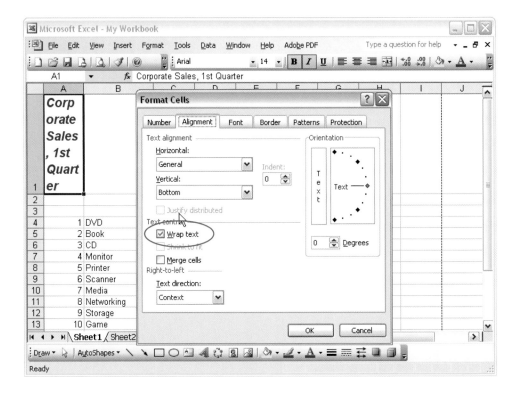

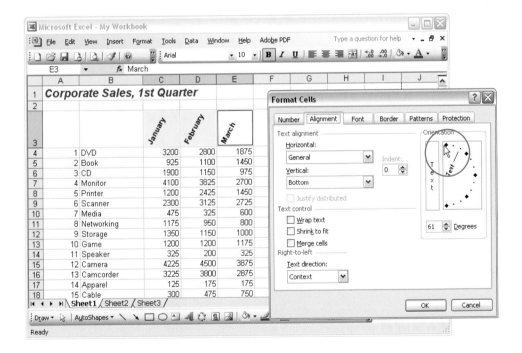

IT LOOKS COOL, SO IT MUST BE DONE

Here's a completely useless tip, which serves absolutely no purpose. But it looks cool and anything that looks cool in Excel must be done—because as we all know: Nothing in Excel looks cool (except for this). Select your column headings by pressing-and-holding the Control key on your keyboard and clicking each heading's cell. Next, click Format>Cells in the menu bar and click the Alignment tab in the Format Cells dialog. Be sure that the Horizontal drop-down menu in the Text Alignment category is set to General. Now, click any angle in the Orientation window to slant the column headings and click OK. Your text is now slanted to the orientation you selected. Hmm, a little flair. This is just so unexpected of Excel.

⊟ ⊡ ⊠ SHARE (KIND OF)

Want to share just a little? I love to share just a little. I've never been an especially good sharer. In my family, I was the only boy and I had four sisters, so I never had to share anything. My sisters, on the other hand, had to share everything…they still resent me to this day (kidding, my sisters are wonderful, really). Anyway, here's a way to share your workbooks with others but prevent them from making changes (kind of like sharing). Open the workbook that you want to protect and click File>Save As in the menu bar. Next, click Tools in the top-right corner of the Save As dialog and click General Options. In the Save Options dialog, leave the Password to Open field blank (this allows anyone to open the workbook), but type a password in the Password to Modify field, and then click OK. You'll be asked to confirm your password. Click Save on the Save As dialog and you're finished. Now when anyone opens the workbook, they'll have the option to provide a password for unlimited access to your workbook or to open the workbook as Read Only. It feels good to share a little. To remove password protection, simply delete the password from the Save Options dialog, click OK, and then click Save in the Save As dialog.

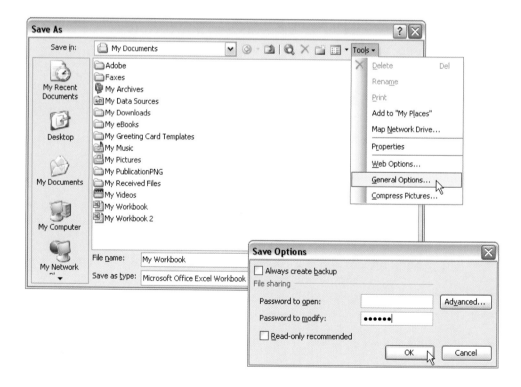

DO YOU VALIDATE?

It's always a good idea to assign data validation to cells that require very specific information. For instance, you may be gathering information about someone's shoe size (I'm sure shoe size is very important to someone out there), which requires a number. Well, if the person accidentally types "really big," that's not giving you the info you need. So, you can force the person to enter a number range. Here's how: Select the cell to which you want to add data validation, then click Data>Validation in the menu bar and click the Settings tab on the Data Validation dialog. Next, select Whole Number from the Allow drop-down menu and select Between from the Data drop-down menu. Type a Minimum number (e.g., 5) and a Maximum number (e.g., 14), and then click OK. Now the cell will only accept a number between 5 and 14. To remove validation from a cell, select the cell and click Data> Validation in the menu bar. Select the Settings tab, click the Clear All button, and click OK.

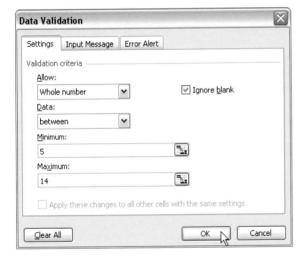

GIVE ME FRACTIONS

Go ahead—type a fraction into a cell (e.g., 1/12) and press Enter on your keyboard. Didn't work? Try it again. Still didn't work? Try it again. Hmm, you must be doing something wrong. Oh wait, it's not you, it's Excel. Excel interprets fractions as dates. Nice, huh? Actually you can make Excel recognize your fractions. Here's how: Type a zero followed by a space in front of your fraction (e.g., 0 1/12). I bet that'll work.

CHECK ALL OF MY SPELLING

Yes, even Excel users need to check their spelling, and here's a quick trick to check the spelling for your entire workbook. Press-and-hold the Control key on your keyboard, then click each sheet's tab in your workbook to group them. Now, press F7 on your keyboard and the Spelling Checker will check each selected worksheet for misspellings, not just the current worksheet.

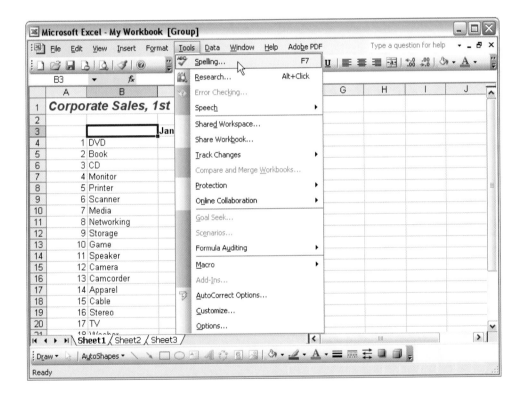

 THE FORMULA TO COMMENTS

When developing workbooks with others, you may want to attach comments directly to your formulas as reminders, ideas, or explanations. To do this, click the cell containing the formula that you want to add a comment to, and then type: +N("your comment") (including the quotation marks) in the Formula bar. Press Enter on your keyboard when you're finished. This command applies the comment to the formula without affecting its results. To view the comment, just click the cell and look in the Formula bar.

	A	B	C	D	E	F	G	H		J
8	5	Printer	1200	2425	1450					
9	6	Scanner	2300	3125	2725					
10	7	Media	475	325	600					
11	8	Networking	1175	950	800					
12	9	Storage	1350	1150	1000					
13	10	Game	1200	1200	1175					
14	11	Speaker	325	200	325					
15	12	Camera	4225	4500	3875					
16	13	Camcorder	3225	3800	2875					
17	14	Apparel	125	175	175					
18	15	Cable	300	475	750					
19	16	Stereo	825	700	650					
20	17	TV	2750	2900	3125					
21	18	Washer	3375	4350	4300					
22	19	Dryer	3700	4850	4625					
23	20	Refrigerator	2925	2700	2800					
24	21	Dish Washer	1925	1600	1475					
25	22	Small Appliance	0	0	275					
26										
27	**Total**				2150					
28										

Formula Bar: E27 — fx =SUM(E4+E25)+N("March was a great month keep up the good work")

WINGDINGIN' IT

Comments are useful but they're not cool; you'd have to be able to place pictures into comments for them to be cool and you can't. But wait—Wingdings are kind of like pictures. Actually, they're exactly like pictures (type pictures), and we can place type into text boxes. Let's see if it works. Select any cell where you want to add a comment, then click Insert>Comment in the menu bar, and a comment box appears. Now highlight the text and change the Font field in the Formatting toolbar to Wingdings. Type until you find a character that expresses your comment (I pressed Shift-J to get a smiley face). You can also make the character as large as necessary by highlighting it and using the Font Size drop-down menu in the Formatting toolbar. Comments are now officially cool!

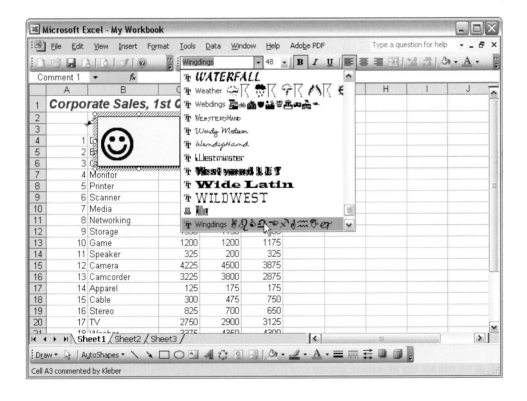

⬛◻️❌ EXCEL CAN BE LONELY

Creating Excel worksheets is a lonely business. Most people avoid Excel users (our brilliance intimidates them). Well maybe your colleagues won't talk to you, but Excel will. First, open the Text to Speech toolbar by right-clicking any toolbar and clicking Text to Speech. Next, select the cells that you want Excel to read, then press the By Rows or By Columns button on the Text to Speech toolbar to tell Excel the order in which your cells should be read, then click the Speak Cells button. I feel so loved! To stop Excel from talking to you, click the Stop Speaking button on the Text to Speech toolbar.

⬛⬜❎ LET'S HOOK UP

If you need to join separate cells into a single text string, use the Concatenate function; =CONCATENATE(first cell," ",second cell). For example, you want to join the text from cell A4 through E4 into G4. To do this, type into cell G4 =CONCATENATE(A4," ",B4," ",C4," ",D4," ",E4,"") and then press Enter on your keyboard. The text from each field appears in G4. You can add any cell from your worksheet or add as many cells as you want to appear in the selected cell. You can also add formatting to separate the text—simply replace the space between the quote marks with commas, periods, hyphens, or whatever.

⊟ ⊡ ☒ QUICK GRAPHS

The only thing better than graphs are quick graphs, and you can make one by first selecting a data range on your worksheet and then pressing the F11 key on your keyboard. Your new graph appears on its own worksheet. You can also change the chart type: Simply click the Chart Type button on the Chart toolbar (which opens automatically anytime a chart is created) and select a chart style in the Chart Type drop-down menu.

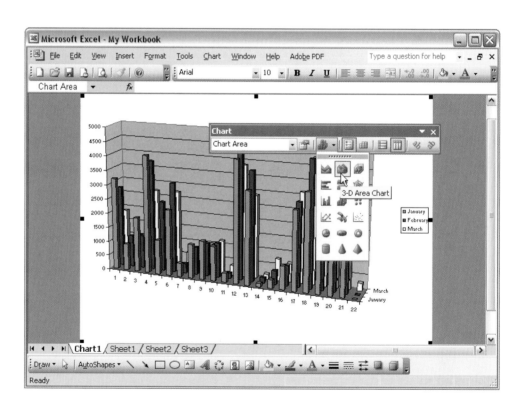

JUMPIN' HERE, JUMPIN' THERE

I'm always jumping back and forth between worksheets and I've found the quickest way to do this is by pressing Control-Page Down on the keyboard to move to the next worksheet to the right (as shown) or pressing Control-Page Up to jump to the next worksheet to the left.

 SMART NAVIGATION

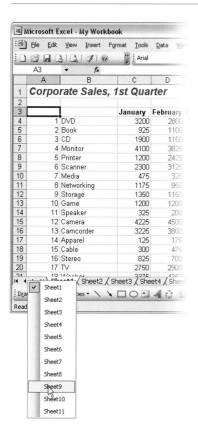

You may think you have to use the four arrow buttons at the bottom-left corner of your Excel workbook's window to jump to a worksheet in a large workbook. Well, you'd be right, but you don't actually have to click the arrows—you can right-click the arrows. This gives you a shortcut menu of all worksheets in your workbook. Now, simply click the worksheet in the shortcut menu that you want to view to instantly jump to it.

CHAPTER 5 • Working with Excel   **193**

POWER SHARING

Excel makes sharing workbooks painless and even gives you the final "say-so" to any conflicting changes. This means that if two other users have a different idea about a formula or whatever, you'll be asked to determine who "wins." To share your workbook, click Tools>Share Workbook in the menu bar and click the Editing tab in the Share Workbook dialog. Next, check "Allow changes by more than one user at the same time. This also allows workbook merging." Now, click the Advanced tab and select Automatically Every and type 15 to save update changes every 15 minutes. This allows you to compare your changes with others'. Then click OK. You can tell when a workbook is shared by looking at the workbook's title bar—the word Shared appears in brackets: "[Shared]". To stop sharing your workbook, click Tools>Share Workbook in the menu bar and under the Editing tab uncheck "Allow changes by more than one user at the same time. This also allows workbook merging." Then click OK.

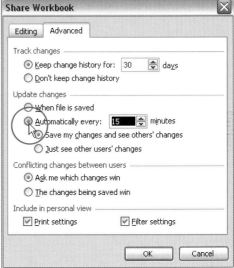

HIDE WORKSHEETS

Workbooks can get stupidly large, making them a little difficult to navigate. Many of mine are stupid and large. So, to make large workbooks a little easier to navigate, hide worksheets that you don't regularly use or that contain static data that very seldom (if ever) changes. To hide a worksheet, first select the worksheet you want to hide, then click Format>Sheet>Hide in the menu bar. It's gone! When you want to unhide your worksheets, click Format>Sheet>Unhide in the menu bar. Now, select the worksheet that you want to view using the Unhide dialog and click OK. It's back!

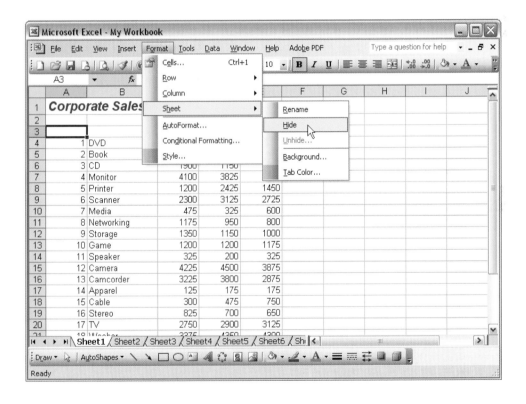

▣▣☒ DON'T FORGET THE PIXELS

The Web is a world of pixels. Resolution is measured in pixels: 800x600, 1280x1024, and so on. So, when optimizing a worksheet for the Web, you should use this scale of measurement—and Excel's ScreenTips can help. When pressing-and-holding your mouse pointer to adjust column widths and row heights, check out the measurement ScreenTip—not only does it show Excel's standard measurements but also the pixel measurement to the right. As you adjust columns and rows, the pixel distance is also displayed.

▣▣☒ CASE-SENSITIVE SORTS

By default, when sorting data in Excel, it doesn't distinguish between upper- and lowercase letters, which may be a problem, especially if you want to sort by words using capital letters, for example. We can change this, though. Select your range, then click Data>Sort in the menu bar and click the Options button in the Sort dialog. Next, check Case Sensitive in the Sort Options dialog and click OK. Now Excel will recognize letter case when sorting.

SELECT LARGE RANGES

There are many ways to select ranges in Excel, but the one I use most is the Shift-click short-cut. This shortcut really comes in handy when you have to select columns that don't appear onscreen. When this happens to you, click the first cell in your range (top-left cell) and use the scroll bar to navigate to the bottom-right cell of the range. Now, press-and-hold the Shift key on your keyboard and click the last cell in your range (bottom-right cell). Your range is now selected. Now delete it, ranges shouldn't be that big (just kidding).

	A	B	C	D	E	F	G	H	I	J
7	4	Monitor	4100	3825	2700					
8	5	Printer	1200	2425	1450					
9	6	Scanner	2300	3125	2725					
10	7	Media	475	325	600					
11	8	Networking	1175	950	800					
12	9	Storage	1350	1150	1000					
13	10	Game	1200	1200	1175					
14	11	Speaker	325	200	325					
15	12	Camera	4225	4500	3875					
16	13	Camcorder	3225	3800	2875					
17	14	Apparel	125	175	175					
18	15	Cable	300	475	750					
19	16	Stereo	825	700	650					
20	17	TV	2750	2900	3125					
21	18	Washer	3375	4350	4300					
22	19	Dryer	3700	4850	4625					
23	20	Refrigerator	2925	2700	2800					
24	21	Dish Washer	1925	1600	1475					
25	22	Small Appliance	0	0	275					
26										
27	Total				2150					

Microsoft Excel - My Workbook

File Edit View Insert Format Tools Data Window Help Adobe PDF

Type a question for help

Arial 10 B I U

A3

Sheet1 Sheet2 Sheet3

Draw AutoShapes

Ready Sum=128228

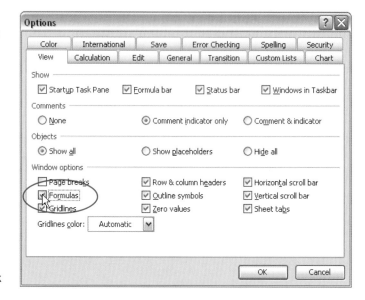

⊟⊡☒ SHOW OFF YOUR FORMULAS

Are you a show-off? I am! It's so bad that I'm always catching myself trying to impress me. It's really very distracting. Here's a way to show off your formulas onscreen, or even print and share your formulas. Hold on, I know what you're thinking; you're thinking that Excel only displays and prints formula results, not the formula itself. Well, it does by default, but we don't believe in defaults. Click Tools>Options in the menu bar and click the View tab in the Options dialog. Next, check Formulas under the Window Options category, and then click OK. All your formulas are displayed, not the formula results. Now, display 'em, print 'em, and share 'em. It's fun to be a show-off!

REMEMBER TO COLOR CODE

We all need reminders and here's a great way to remind yourself of work that you need to complete on a worksheet or to highlight worksheets that contain special or important data. Right-click a sheet's tab at the bottom-left corner of the Excel window, then click Tab Color in the shortcut menu. Select a color (anything but gray) and click OK…instant reminder.

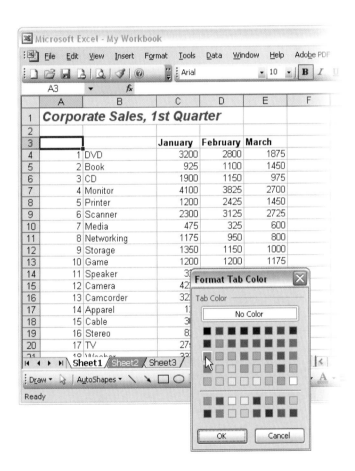

"WATCH" YOUR WINDOW

Excel's Watch Window is a clever idea and it's very useful. If you're not using it, you should be. As your worksheet becomes longer and longer, important data is shifted out of view in Excel's window. The Watch Window keeps important data always in view. To add a Watch Window, right-click a cell that you always want to view and click Add Watch in the shortcut menu. A Watch Window dialog appears listing your cell. To add additional cells to your Watch Window, select the cell and click Add Watch on the Watch Window dialog. The Watch Window dialog will sit on the worksheet's foreground as you work, always keeping your favored cells in view.

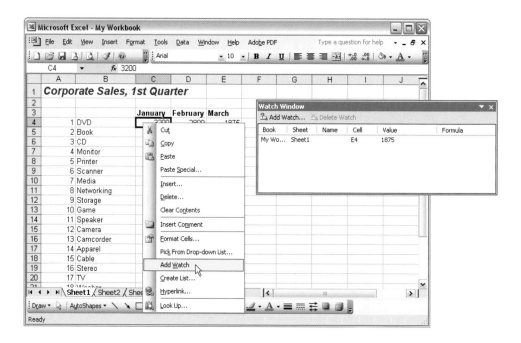

DON'T SAVE THE GEEK-SPEAK

Most Excel users don't give a great deal of thought to naming their workbooks. It's usually something like "Q1604R"—they're very creative people. Well, this may be effective geek-speak, but remember, when saving workbooks to the Web, most people don't understand geek-speak. So when saving, be sure to change the workbook's title to something that helps users to identify it. To change a workbook's title for the Web, click File>Save as Web Page in the menu bar, then click the Change Title button on the Save As dialog. Name your file in the resulting dialog, click OK, and then click Save in the Save As dialog. By default, if you don't change the workbook's title, the file name will appear as the webpage's title.

⊟□☒ PAINT COLUMNS AND ROWS

To copy a row's or column's formatting and apply it to other rows or columns, use Excel's Format Painter. Select the row or column with the formatting that you want to copy by clicking the row or column heading and then click the Format Painter button (it looks like a paintbrush) on the Standard toolbar. Next, click the row or column heading that you want to copy the formatting to (your mouse pointer will appear as a paintbrush). Your formatting is applied to the row or column. To apply the same formatting to multiple rows or columns, double-click the Format Painter. Now you can continue to apply the formatting to as many rows or columns as you'd like. When finished, click the Format Painter button again to turn it off.

		January	February	March
1	DVD	3200	2800	2575
2	Book	925	1100	1450
3	CD	1900	1150	975
4	Monitor	4100	3825	2700
5	Printer	1200	2425	1450
6	Scanner	2300	3125	2725
7	Media	475	325	600
8	Networking	1175	950	800
9	Storage	1350	1150	1000
10	Game	1200	1200	1175
11	Speaker	325	200	325
12	Camera	4225	4500	3875
13	Camcorder	3225	3800	2875
14	Apparel	125	175	175
15	Cable	300	475	750
16	Stereo	825	700	650
17	TV	2750	2900	3125

Corporate Sales, 1st Quarter

Easy Access

WORKING WITH ACCESS

I used to think that "database" was the worst sound I'd ever heard until I started my car with a cat on the manifold. That's the worse sound I've ever heard! After that

Easy Access

working with access

happened, I thought I'd give databases another shot. And once I figured 'em out, I fell in love with 'em (not literally, that would be weird). I began making databases for just about anything and everything. The first one I created was for tracking the members of my "the-terrors-of-starting-your-car" therapy group (it took me a while). After that, it was off to the races. And to think, I owe my love of databases all to a cat. It's funny how things happen. It's not funny about the cat, that's sad.

KillerTips

Microsoft Office 2003

▬ ▢ ☒ YOUR VERY OWN TOOLTIPS

Aren't ToolTips sweet? They're very helpful and just plain fun. Really, I love 'em. So, you can only imagine how excited I was when I discovered how to make my own when I'm using a form in Access (File>New>Blank Database>Forms). Let me share how to do this: Open any form in Design View (View>Design View), then right-click the control that you want to add a ToolTip to. (In case you didn't know—a ToolTip [sometimes called a ScreenTip] is a tiny window that

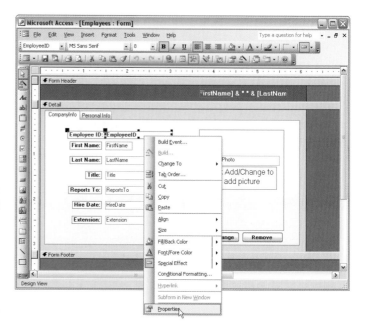

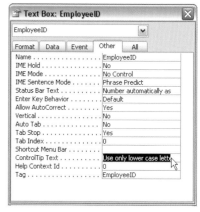

pops up when you position your mouse pointer over a control. It explains the control's function or offers help. You can turn these on and off by choosing Tools>Customize and selecting Show ScreenTips on Toolbars.) Anyway, once you've right-clicked the control, then click Properties in the shortcut menu. See if the control you've selected has the option to create a ToolTip by clicking the Other tab in the control's dialog and type your ToolTip in the Con-trolTip Text field, then close the dialog. Now, switch your form's view by choosing Form View from the View menu, then place your pointer over the control and there it is…your very own ToolTip.

IT'S YOUR DEFAULT

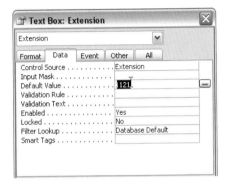

If a field generally will have the same data for each record, you can save time for users by changing the field's default value to display the data automatically for each new record created. Here's how: Open your form in Design View (View>Design View), right-click the control that you want to assign a default value to, and then click Properties in the shortcut menu. Next, click the Data tab on the control's dialog and type the recurring data in the Default Value field. Close the control's dialog when finished. Now, switch your form to Form View (View>Form View) and create a new record. You can now see your default value in that control's field. This will be the default value for each record until the user changes it.

I'M IMPORTANT!

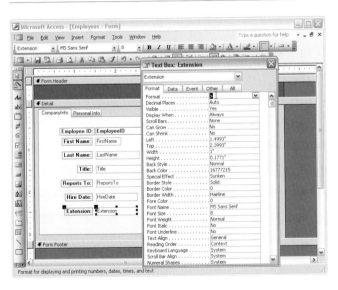

Here's a great way to bring attention to a field containing important data: Automatically show all text for a control's field in uppercase letters. To do this, make sure you're in Design or Form View by choosing either view from the View menu, then right-click the field where you want to apply this formatting and click Properties in the shortcut menu. Next, click the Format tab on the control's dialog and type ">" (press Shift-period) in the Format field, then close the dialog. Now all text for that control will be displayed in uppercase letters. You can't miss it. To display all text in lowercase letters, type "<" (Shift-comma) into the Format field.

▬ ▢ ☒ SAY NO TO SNAP TO GRID

Grids are good; Snap to Grid is
not. So, don't use it. You can
turn off Snap to Grid by clicking Format>Snap to Grid in the
menu bar. If you insist on using
Snap to Grid, however, there
will be times when you'll want
to move your controls freely to
place them in the correct positions. You can do this without
turning off Snap to Grid: While in
Design View (View>Design), just
press-and-hold the Control key on
your keyboard as you reposition
the control. This will allow you to
resize or place the control any-

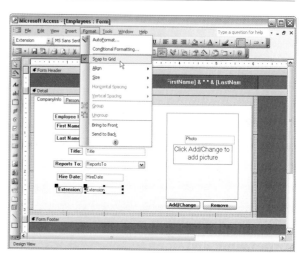

where on your forms or reports without the controls snapping to your grid. If you decide
that you want to snap a control to your grid after all, simply release the Control key before
you release your mouse button.

▬ ▢ ☒ INSTANT FIT

Instead of trying to resize your
image box manually to fit your
picture, use the To Fit command to adjust your image
box to the exact dimension
of your image. To resize an
image box so that it fits your
image, select the image box,
then click Format>Size>To Fit
in the menu bar. Your image
box will expand or shrink to fit
your image perfectly. This tip
also works for fitting controls
(e.g., text boxes, etc.) to text.

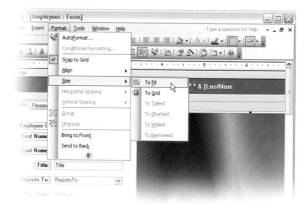

⊟ ⊡ ☒ CAN YOU PICTURE IT?

Pictures just make things better, and this is very true for databases because databases are boring. They just are, and you should do anything that you can do to spice 'em up. Actually, images are fairly essential for any database. They can be your logo to help identify your company, photos of employees, or pictures that relay a message about the form being used. Fortunately, Access makes it easy to add these gems to your forms or reports. First, view your form or report in Design View by clicking View>Design View in the menu bar. Next, right-click any toolbar or menu and select Toolbox in the shortcut menu. Then, click the Image button on the Toolbox toolbar that appears and click-and-drag an image box to where you want the image to appear on your form or report, or simply click your mouse where you want the image to appear on the form. Now, using the Insert Picture dialog, browse your hard drive to locate the image, and then click OK when finished. Your image will appear in the image box. To add a caption, click the Label button on the Toolbox toolbar, click-and-drag to create a label box, then type your caption, and press Enter on your keyboard. Lastly, move the caption to arrange it within your image.

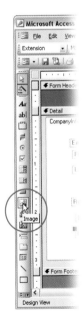

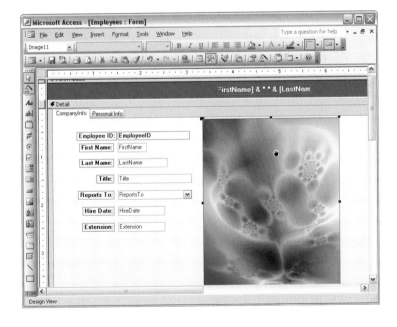

THE OBJECT OF SHORTCUTS

Typically, I work with the same object in a database or at the very least, I always use the same object when first opening a database. Well, you can speed up this process by actually creating a desktop shortcut to your favorite database object—a form, a report, etc. Here's how: Open the object you want to create a shortcut to (I used a form here) and in the object's Database window, right-click the object's icon, then click Create Shortcut in the shortcut menu. Next, click Browse to navigate to your desktop, and then click OK in the Create Shortcut dialog. Now you can close out of Access, go to your desktop, and there's your object's new shortcut. Double-click the shortcut to launch Access and go directly to your object, bypassing the default database window.

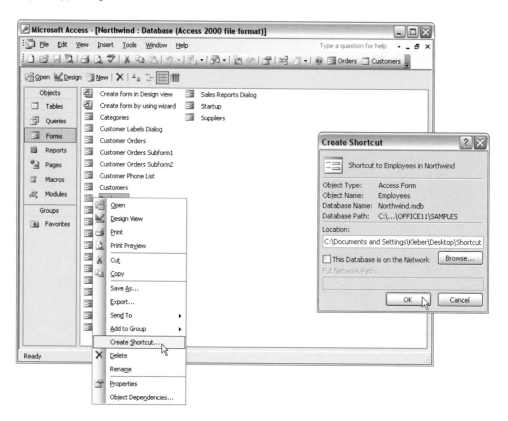

ACCESS SPECIFICATIONS

Have you ever wondered what Access is capable of, such as the maximum possible size of any database or the maximum possible number of records in a table? If so, then you can find out. In the "Type a question for help" field (in the top-right corner of the menu bar), type "Access Specifications" and then press Enter on your keyboard. This opens the Help pane. Click the Access Specifications link at the top of the task pane, which will display Access's capabilities for databases and projects.

 ## ALL I SEE ARE ASTERISKS

If you need to protect sensitive or confidential information when entering data into a field, you should set the control's Input Mask property to Password. To do this, open your form in Design View (View>Design View), then right-click the control's field that you want to protect, and click Properties in the shortcut menu. Next, click the Data tab in the control's dialog and click the Input Mask field to select it. Type "Password" in the Input Mask field (as in the first example) or click the Build button to the right of the field (it looks like an ellipsis) and choose Password from the Input Mask Wizard dialog (as in the second example), then click Finish. Now when you switch to Form View from the View menu, all data in that field will appear as asterisks (*).

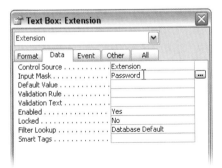

 DON'T IMPORT—LINK

You don't always have to import your text files for use in your database; you can link to them instead. Here's how: From the menu bar, click File>Get External Data>Link Tables. Next, use the Link dialog to browse your hard drive to locate the text file you want to import (be sure to choose Text Files in the Files of Type drop-down menu in the Link dialog), and then click Link. Follow the Link Text Wizard to choose your import options, and then click Finish. Your file will appear in your object's Database window.

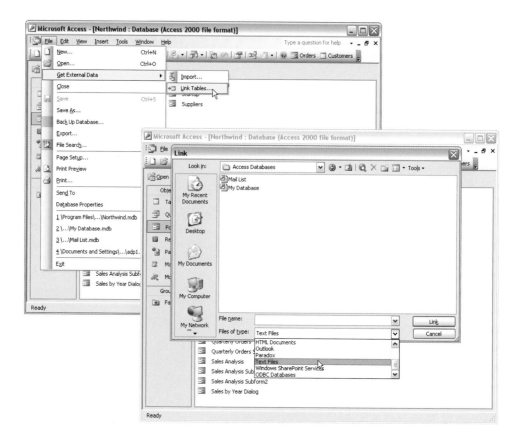

▣▣▣ TAKE IT TO THE WEB

One of the coolest features of Access 2003 is its ability to convert forms and reports into webpages. I do it all the time for no reason at all and you can too. First select the form or report that you want to convert into a webpage by choosing Select Record or Select All from the Edit menu, and then click File>Save As in the menu bar. (*Note:* If you're using a report, make sure you're in Design View.) Type a name for your page in the Save Report/

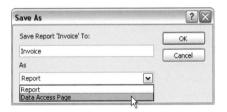

Form To field and choose Data Access Page from the As drop-down menu, and then click OK. This opens the New Data Access Page dialog. Next, choose a location on your hard drive to save your page and click OK. You've just created a webpage from your form/report. Double-click the page's icon saved on your hard drive to open it in your Web browser.

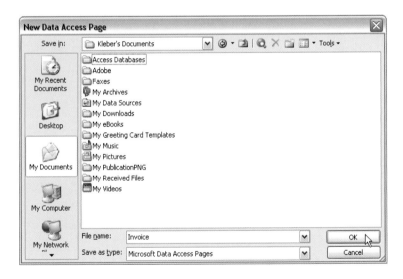

▣◻▣ MENU BAR OBJECTS

I'm working in the same database 90% of the time, and I'm constantly switching back and forth between several database objects, which slows things down. To speed things back up, you can place objects on any toolbar or even in the program's menu bar: Simply drag-and-drop any database object from the Database window onto the program's menu bar (or toolbar of your choice). Now your favorite objects are always just a click away.

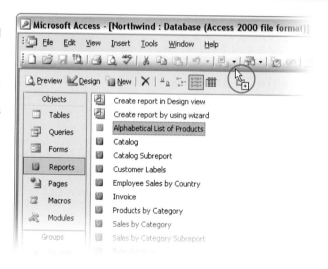

▣◻▣ DON'T DOUBLE-CLICK

Anytime you can do anything faster, you should. So, why double-click to open an object when you can single-click instead? Click Tools>Options in the menu bar, and then in the View tab on the Options dialog, check Single-click Open, then click OK. I have no idea why this isn't the default option. It just makes sense to change it.

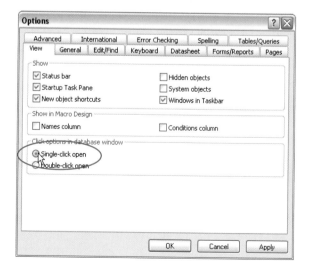

 **ZOOM ZOOM**

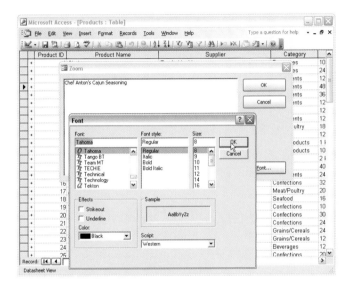

Let's face it—the old eyes just aren't what they used to be, and at higher monitor resolutions, your database's text can look something like alien hieroglyphics, making it almost impossible to edit. Fortunately, you can give your eyes a break. Click anywhere in the field that you want to edit and press Shift-F2 on your keyboard. Now, make any changes you'd like to the field's text. To change the font size or style, click the Font button. Click OK when finished.

 INSTANTLY LAUNCH A FORM

To instantly launch a form from the Database window, click Tools>Startup in the menu bar, then click the Display Form/Page drop-down menu on the Startup dialog and select the form you want to automatically open when you open your database, then click OK. Now close your database and reopen it. The form you specified in Startup automatically opens.

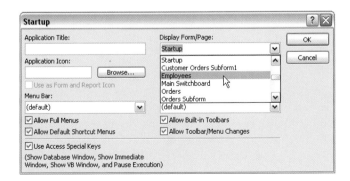

INSTANTLY LAUNCH A RECORD

If you want to open a specific record automatically when opening a form, try this: First open the form in Design View (View>Design View), then click View>Properties in the menu bar. In the Event tab on the Form dialog, click the On Open field, and then click the Build button to the right (it looks like an ellipsis). Choose Code Builder in the Choose Builder dialog and click OK. This opens the Visual Basic window. Now, on a new line directly beneath Private Sub Form Open(Cancel As Integer), type: DoCmd. GoToRecord acForm, "your form name", acGoTo, #, (replacing # with the number of the record that you want to open first). Close the Visual Basic window, then save the changes (File>Save) and close the form. Now, open your form, and the designated record will appear first.

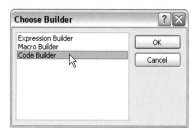

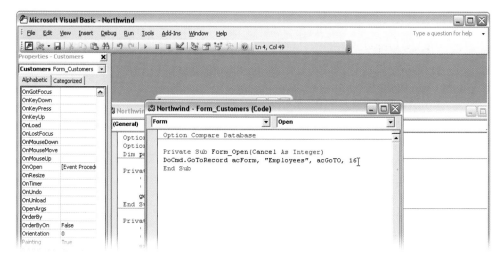

GET YOUR TABS IN ORDER

The tab order of any form is very important because pressing the Tab key on your keyboard jumps you to the next field to be completed. The sequence in which the Tab key selects a field can be important when navigating a form. To make your forms user-friendly, you should design your tab order to follow a logical progression, such as address, city, state, zip, and so on, and put product codes and other information at the bottom. This doesn't happen automatically, you have to assign your database's tab order; otherwise, Access will assign the tab order as your fields are created.

To change your tab order, first switch your form to Design View (View>Design View), then click View>Tab Order in the menu bar. Now, put your controls into any order by dragging-and-dropping the selector boxes to the left of the controls in the Custom Order list. When finished, click OK. Now click Form View in the View menu, and press the Tab key. Your fields will highlight according to your new tab order.

HIDIN' OUT

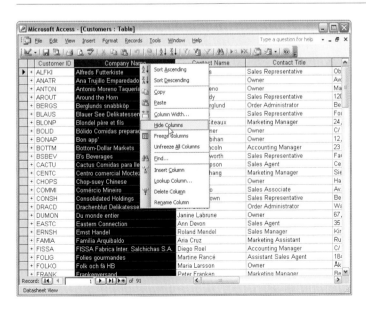

To quickly hide table columns, right-click the column header you want to hide and click Hide Columns in the shortcut menu. To view the column again, click Format>Unhide Columns in the menu bar, turn on the hidden column's checkbox in the Unhide Columns dialog, and click Close.

A BETTER VIEW

Tables can get ridiculously long, and this can make entering new data in tables tedious. Well, there's a way to make working in a table while in Datasheet View much easier—hide existing records before entering new ones. To do this, first open the table that you want to work with, then click Records>Data Entry in the submenu. Access hides all of the records, leaving only a new blank record. Now, go crazy. Each new record is added to your table. When you're done, click Records>Remove Filter/Sort.

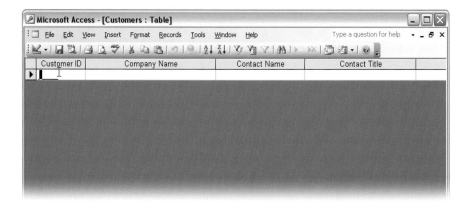

HOW'S YOUR RELATIONSHIP?

Trying to decipher the relationship between tables is impossible so don't ever try it (kidding).
Actually, it's almost impossible to build an effective database without understanding the relationships between tables. Fortunately, Access offers a way to help with this: You can print a table
relationships map. In Access's Database window, click Tables in the Objects list in the left column
of the window. Now click Tools>Relationships in the menu bar. This will open the Relationships
dialog and the Show Table dialog (if the Show Table dialog doesn't appear, right-click in any
blank space in the Relationships dialog and choose Show Table in the shortcut menu). In the
Show Table dialog, select the tables that you want in the Tables tab and click the Add button.
When you're finished, click Close. Next, click File>Print Relationships in the menu bar, which

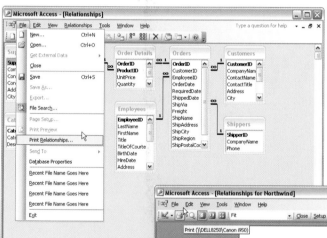

opens the database's
relationships layout in
Print Preview. Click the
Print button on the Print
Preview toolbar, then click
Close. Next, close the relationships Report window
that appears and you'll
be prompted to save the
report. Click Yes to save or
No to close without saving.

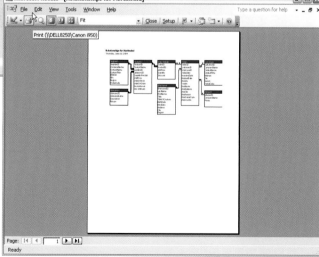

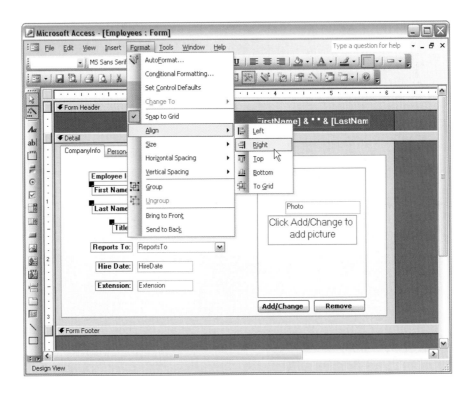

LINE 'EM UP

To align multiple controls on a form, first switch to Design View by clicking View>Design View in the menu bar, then select the controls and the control fields by pressing the Shift key as you click on each control that you want to align. Next, click Format>Align and select an alignment direction in the submenu (e.g., Left, Right, etc.). All of your controls will instantly align.

⊟⊡☒ QUICK CALENDAR

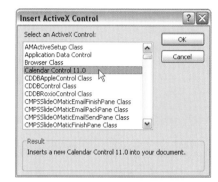

Adding a calendar to a form is easy. First, open your form in Design View (View>Design View). Then, click Insert>ActiveX Control in the menu bar, select Calendar Control 11.0 in the Insert ActiveX Control dialog, and click OK. Now, click-and-drag the calendar to any location on your form.

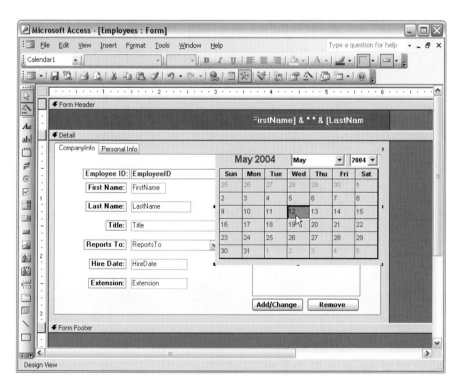

A BETTER PREVIEW

Layout Preview is better than Print Preview, but don't take my word for it: Open a report that contains a query or two, then click View>Print Preview. Are you still waiting for it to open? Still waiting? Reports with queries can sometimes take a while to generate a print preview; however, you don't experience such processing downtime when using Layout Preview. To view your report in Layout Preview, start off in Design View (View>Design View), then click View>Layout Preview in the menu bar and there it is. This is the same view as Print Preview, only faster in some cases. The only drawback to Layout Preview is that you can't edit your document as you can in Print Preview, but if you're like most users on the planet, you don't edit your reports in Print Preview anyway.

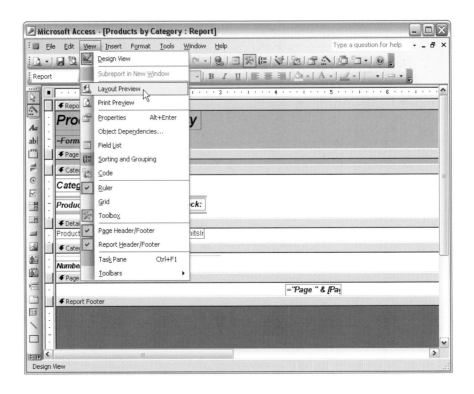

SHIFT SIZE

Adjusting the size of your controls is fairly straightforward: You grab a resize handle and drag it to resize; however, it's pretty tricky to be accurate when using the resize handles. Try this instead: While in Design View (View>Design View), click to select your control, press the Shift key on your keyboard, then use the arrow keys to increase or decrease the size of your control. Each press of an arrow key changes the control's size by 1/24th of an inch in any direction.

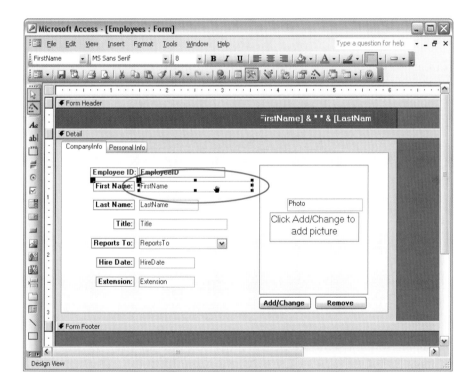

▢▢☒ TITLE PAGES MADE EASY

Did you know that you could design and print a title page for your reports directly within Access? Bet you didn't. If you've ever gone through the hassle of creating one, then you'll love this tip. To create a title page from your existing report, first open your report in Design View (View>Design View), then lay out your title page in the report's header, adding any images and text. Next, right-click any blank space in the header and click Properties in the shortcut menu. Now, click the Format tab in the Section dialog and click the Force New Page field to select it, then choose After Section from the field's drop-down menu and close the dialog. Your report's header will now print on a separate sheet of paper.

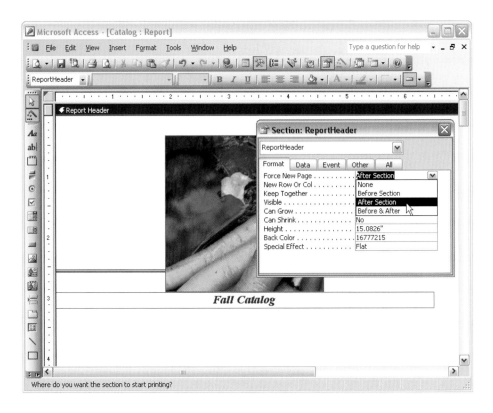

CAN'T CLOSE

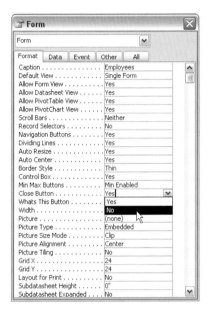

Want to make it harder for users to close forms? Of course you do, messing with people is half the fun of databases. Well, you can disable the form window's Close button so that users can't easily close your form. To do this, open your form in Design View by choosing Design View in the View menu. Then click View>Properties in the menu bar and click the Format tab in the Form dialog. Next, click the Close Button field to select it and choose No from the field's drop-down menu, and then close the dialog. Now users won't be able to use the Close button in the form's window. To return the Close button's function to its default state, repeat this tip but choose Yes in the field's drop-down menu. It's fun to mess with people.

 ## CAN'T ADD

If you want to allow users to access data but don't want them to add new data, then do this: Open your form in Design View (View>Design View), select View>Properties in the menu bar, and click the Data tab in the Form dialog. Next, click the Allow Additions field and choose No from the field's drop-down menu, and then close the dialog. Now when you access the form in Form View (View>Form View), the New Record button will appear dimmed, indicating that this option is disabled.

SET THE TIMER

If you really want to see a look of confusion on people's faces, then automatically close your forms on 'em. If you time it just right, you can make 'em cry. Just kidding—we don't want to make anyone cry. There's actually a practical use for automatically closing a form. This is perfect for giving someone a limited amount of time to complete a form, perhaps in the form of a test or quiz. To do this, first open the form in Design View (View>Design View), click View>Properties in the menu bar, and then click the Event tab in the Form dialog. Next, click the Timer Interval field and type the number of seconds to leave the form visible once opened (1000 = 1 second). Next, click the On Timer field and click its Build button (it looks like an ellipsis) to the right. Choose Code Builder in the Choose Builder dialog and click OK. This opens the Visual Basic window. Now on a new line directly beneath Private Sub Form_Timer (), type: DoCmd.Close, "" (with a space between the comma and double quotation marks). Close the Visual Basic window, save the changes, and close the form. Now, open your form to test your timer. To change your timer setting back to its default, repeat this tip but enter a zero in the Timer Interval field, and delete any command in the On Timer field.

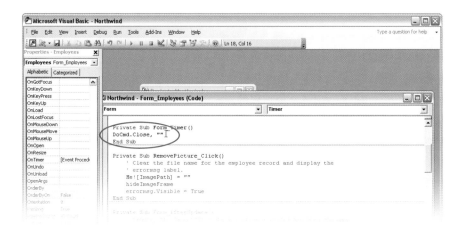

WHAT'S THIS?

I'm not sure how many of you will actually use this tip, but I'm sure it's going to be exactly what someone was hoping to find. If you're secretive or just want to baffle people using your forms, don't give them titles. I know you're thinking, "You can't do that!" But you can. By default, your form has to have a title and it does, but you can change it. Here's how: Open your form in Design View (View>Design View), click View>Properties in the menu bar, and then click the Format tab in the Form dialog. Next, delete the form title from the Caption field, then type a single space into the Caption field, and close the dialog. Choose View>Form View in the menu bar, and your title's gone. Baffling isn't it? To see the title again, repeat this tip but enter your title in the Caption field instead of deleting it.

GETTIN' AROUND

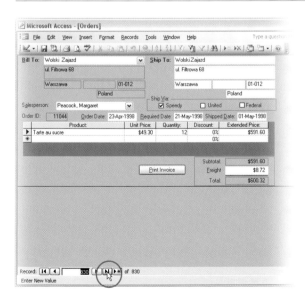

To quickly navigate your records in Access, try these handy keyboard shortcuts. To jump from field to field, press the Left and Right Arrow keys on your keyboard (instead of scrolling through records by clicking the Next Record or Previous Record buttons, as shown here). To advance to the next record in a database, press the Page Down key or press the Page Up key to advance to the top of your data list. You can get to the last record in a database by pressing Control-End, or press Control-Home to go to the first record in your database.

SUPER-FAST APPEND

To append data records from the Database window, click Tables in the Objects list on the left-hand side of the window, then right-click the table that contains the records that you want to append to another table and click Copy in the shortcut menu. Next, right-click any blank space in the Database window and click Paste in the shortcut menu. This opens the Paste Table As dialog. Now, in the Table Name field, type the name of the target table to which you want to append the copied records, then select Append Data to Existing Table, and click OK. Your records are instantly added to the table you specified. *Note:* Your target table must have the same fields (headers) as the table you've copied.

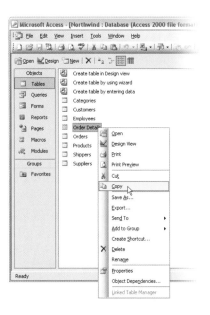

REPORT SNAPSHOT

There's a much better way to distribute reports than printing them—unless of course you're a tree killer, then go ahead (just kidding). Actually, the environment has nothing to do with this; it just makes good sense to share your reports in a digital format that allows the recipients greater control over storing, retrieving, and yes, even printing the report once they receive it. To do this, send a snapshot of your report. To create a snapshot of your report, select the report by clicking Reports in the Objects list on the left side of the Database window and clicking once on the report's icon to select it. Then click File>Export in the menu bar. Select Snapshot Format from the Save as Type drop-down menu in the Export Report As dialog. Select a location to save your snapshot, name it in the File Name field, and then click Export. Now, locate your saved snapshot report on your hard drive and double-click to open it. Cool, huh? Now, save it to disk or attach it to emails for distribution.

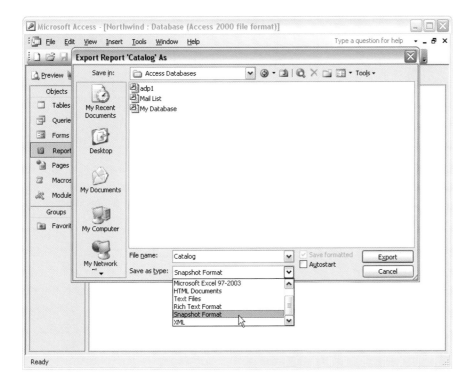

ANALYZE THIS!

Access databases are great, but you'll probably find that Access can't always give you the kind of data-crunching power that you want. I mean, it's not Excel. Well, maybe not, but it doesn't have to be. We can export our reports to Excel and data-crunch away anytime we want. Try this: In the Reports pane (which you open by clicking Reports in the Objects list of the Database window), select a report that you want to export to Excel, then, in the menu bar, click Tools>Office Links>Analyze It with Microsoft Office Excel. This launches Excel and opens your report. To save the report in Excel, click File>Save As on Excel's menu bar.

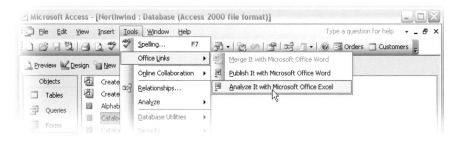

QUICK DATES

Here's a handy shortcut for entering dates into forms. You don't have to go to the trouble of typing the entire date into a field (for example, 21-July-2004). Simply type 7/21 instead. Access interprets this as a date and appends the current year to the end of your date (depending on the date settings for that field). Once you exit the field, 7/21 will automatically change to 21-July-2004.

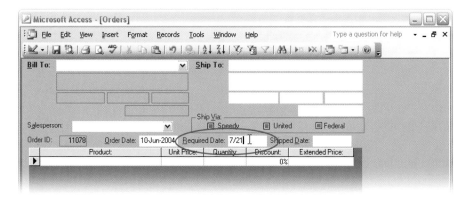

⊟ ⊡ ⊠ ONE-CLICK EXCEL

I always use Excel and Access together (especially when working with forms). They just go together…kind of like cookies and milk or pencil and paper. And, to make it easier to get to Excel, I place a command button directly on my form that launches Excel with a single click of my mouse. You can too. Open any form in Design View (View>Design View), right-click any menu or toolbar and select Toolbox, then click the Command Button tool on the Toolbox toolbar (it looks like a solid gray bar). Then, click on the form where you want to place the Command Button. This opens the Command Button Wizard. Click Application from the Categories window, then choose Run MS Excel from the Actions window, and click Finish. Return to Form View (View>Form View), and click the Excel Command Button to launch Excel anytime you'd like.

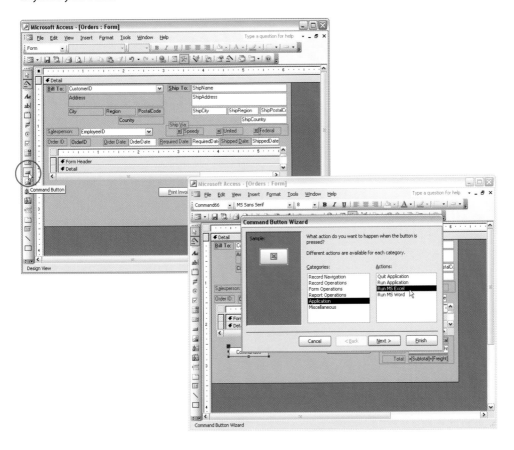

Get Published

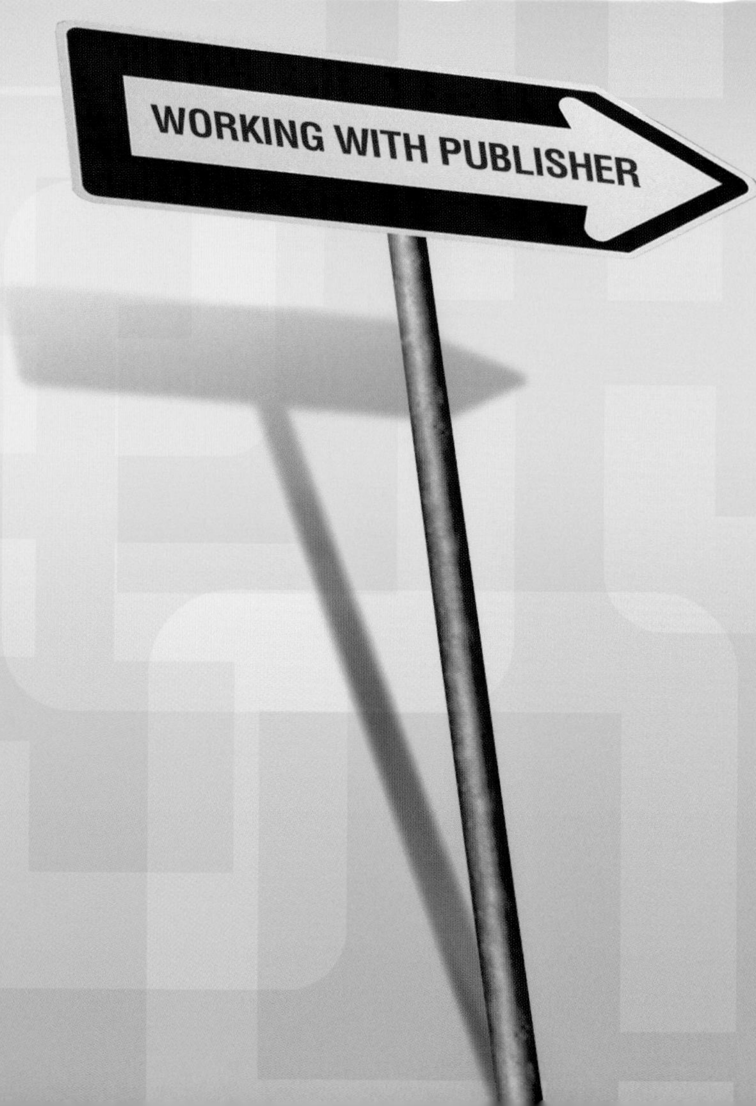

I know what you use Microsoft Publisher for: You use it for exactly the same thing that everybody else uses Microsoft Publisher for…creating greeting cards. Hands-down, it's

Get Published
working with publisher

the best program available for creating greeting cards, but that really is the tip of the iceberg, so to speak. Publisher is also perfect for creating newsletters, advertisements, flyers, brochures, and more. Now, while "professional" layout designers may smirk when you tell them that you created your brochure in Microsoft Publisher, there's always one thing that you'll have on Adobe InDesign and QuarkXPress users. You didn't drop 700 bucks for your software. That'll stick it to 'em. Honestly, there are few things that you can't do in Publisher, so before you take a withdrawal from your children's college fund for "professional" software, give Publisher a try. You'll be surprised at what you can do.

EDIT IN WORD

If you're going to edit text in Publisher (or any Office application), it's best to do it in Word. Word simply provides the best tools and capabilities for the task. And you can easily edit your Publisher text using Word. To do this, first select your text, then right-click it with your mouse, and click Change Text>Edit Story in Microsoft Word in the shortcut menu. This opens the selected text in Word. Now, make any changes, and when finished, click

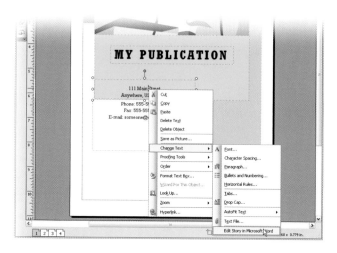

File>Close & Return to *<your document's title>* in Word's menu bar. Your edited text now appears in your publication.

DELETE THE WHOLE THING

When you select a text box in Publisher and press Backspace on your keyboard, sometimes only the character to the right of the insertion point is deleted, not the entire text box, which probably isn't what you intended. You probably wanted to delete the entire text box. You still can—just press Control-Shift-X on your keyboard and the text box is gone.

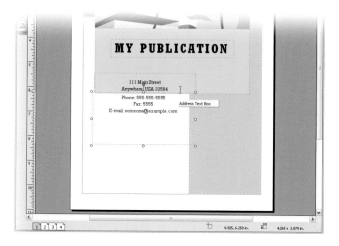

NAVIGATE WEB PUBLICATIONS

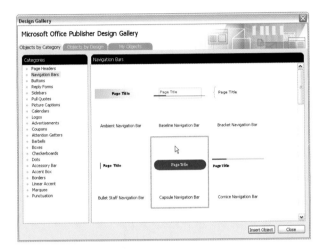

You can add navigation buttons to any Web publication by clicking Insert>Design Gallery Object in the menu bar. In the Objects by Category tab in the Design Gallery dialog, click Navigation Bars (this option only appears for publications saved as Web publications) in the Categories window, then select a button in the Navigation Bars window, and click Insert Object. This will open the Create New Navigation Bar dialog, where you can choose on which pages to insert the bar and choose to update navigation bar links automatically. Click OK when finished. Now click-and-drag your new navigation bar to position it in your document.

 CUSTOMIZE COLOR SCHEMES

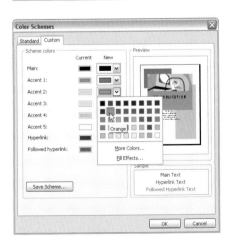

Keep this in mind when choosing any of Publisher's default publication designs: Don't worry about their colors. That's right, don't think twice about 'em. The colors don't matter because you can quickly change the entire color scheme. Here's how: Open any publication design from the New Publication task pane (File>New), then click Format>Color Schemes in the menu bar. Click the "Custom color scheme" link at the bottom of the Color Schemes task pane, then click the Custom tab on the Color Schemes dialog. All colors represented in the design are shown in the Current color column. To change any Current color, click the New color drop-down menu to the right and select a new color. You'll see your changes in the Preview window. When finished, click OK to apply your new color scheme.

GET PERSONAL

A real time saver in Publisher is its ability to automatically insert your personal information into publications. First, set up your info by clicking Edit>Personal Information in the menu bar, then update your information in the Personal Information dialog, and click Update when finished. To create a publication that includes your personal infor-mation, create a new document (File>New), then open the Quick Publication Options task pane by clicking the down-facing arrow to the left of the Close button on the New Publication task pane. Select the Personal Information With Picture icon in the Layout category (it's the last icon in the last row). You can also insert single fields of personal information by clicking Insert>Personal Information in the menu bar and selecting any of the available personal info tags.

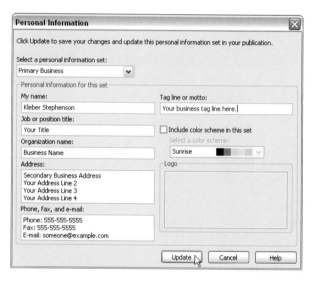

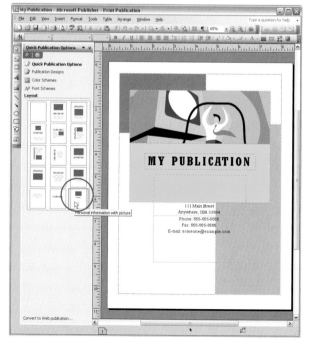

CONTROL GROUPS

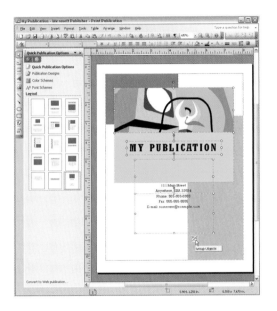

To group objects so they move together when laying out your publication, press-and-hold the Control key on your keyboard and click each object with your mouse—this selects each object. Anytime you select more than one object, the Group Objects icon will appear. Click this icon to group your selected objects and now you can move the group to any location on your layout. To ungroup your objects, simply click the Ungroup Objects Icon while your group is selected.

THAT SHOULD BE A PICTURE

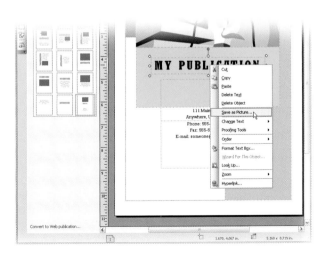

You can save just about any object—even text—as a picture in Publisher. To save objects as pictures, right-click an object and click Save as Picture in the shortcut menu. Choose a location on your hard drive to save your picture, choose the picture's format in the Save as Type field in the Save As dialog, and then click Save.

THE KEY TO THE WEB

What's the point of posting your Web publication to the Web if no one can find it—probably no point at all. So, you're going to want to include keywords, or metatags, in your publication's HTML. Search sites such as Google and Yahoo index websites by the site's keywords. If your site doesn't have keywords, it won't be indexed by many search engines…so, make certain that you add keywords. Here's how: Open the title page of your Web publication, then click the Web Page Options button in the Web Tools toolbar (if you don't see the Web Tools toolbar, right-click the Standard toolbar in your Web document and click Web Tools). Next, complete the Web Page Options dialog, providing a Page Title and File Name. Now, under the Search Engine Information category, provide a description of your website, then in the Keywords field, enter keywords that will help to identify your website when someone searches for your products or services. Click OK when finished.

 ## HEADIN' TO THE PRINTERS

If you've created a business pub-lication, such as a brochure or other informational literature, then you should consider having it profession-ally printed to get the best possible quality. Most Publisher users wouldn't know where to begin to do this but fortunately, Publisher makes getting your publication ready for a printer extremely easy. When you're ready to have your publication printed, click File>Pack and Go>To a Commercial Printing Service, then follow the Pack and Go Wizard to prepare your print job. When you're finished, simply take your publication's Pack and Go folder and its contents to your printer.

PUBLISHER-FRIENDLY PRINTERS

Okay, you're all excited about taking your files to the local printer, but when you get there and tell him that you have Microsoft Publisher files, he looks at you as if you were the "dumbest of a dumb, dumber, and dumbest trio." Believe it or not, not every printer appreciates the growing number of designers using Publisher to create publications. Well, you don't have to take it—you can take your business somewhere else. To find a local printer who will be happy to take your Publisher files, press F1 on your keyboard to open the Publisher Help task pane, then click Connect to Microsoft Office Online (that is, as long as you're connected to the Internet). This will launch your Web browser and take you to the Microsoft Office website. Click the Publisher link under the Microsoft Office category to the left and on the resulting webpage, click the "Find a local printer" link under the Browse Publisher category.

I'VE BEEN FRAMED

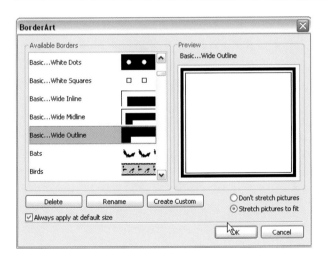

Know what makes pictures better? Frames! You can add frames or borders to your pictures by first selecting the picture that you want to apply a frame to, then clicking the Line/Border Style button in the Formatting toolbar, and clicking More Lines. Next, in the Colors and Lines tab in the Format Picture dialog, click BorderArt, select a border from the Available Borders category in the BorderArt dialog, and then click OK. In the Format Picture dialog, click OK again to apply the border to your picture.

FLOWING TEXT

You probably think that text boxes are boring, don't you? Well, you're wrong. You can create some very cool effects using text boxes, such as flowing text from one text box to another. Here's how: Create at least two text boxes (Insert>Text Box), then select the first text box. Next, click the Create Text Box Link button on the Connect Text Boxes toolbar (if you don't see the Connect Text Boxes toolbar, right-click the Standard toolbar and click Connect Text Boxes). Now click the second text box that you want the text to flow into (your mouse pointer will turn into a tiny pitcher). Repeat the steps as many times as necessary to link as many text boxes as you want. Now when you type your text, it will flow from text box to text box. You can even move the text boxes to any location on your page or resize your text boxes and the text will continue to flow into them.

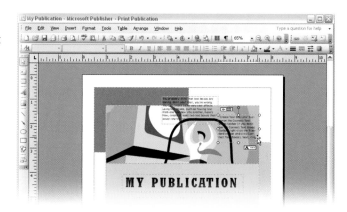

TRANSPARENT SHAPES

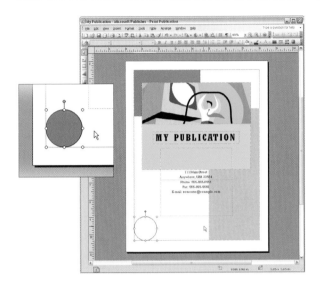

To make a shape transparent, try this: Click any shape (I used a red circle with a black border by clicking the Oval tool in the Drawing toolbar), then press Control-T on your keyboard. This will make the shape transparent (remove its fill color), but leave the shape's line color untouched.

 ## PAINT YOUR FORMATTING

I like to play around with my text formatting in Publisher; for example, I'll apply different text formatting attributes to different boxes of text on a page just to get a feel for what looks best. When I find the text formatting that I want to use, I use Format Painter to apply it to all the text. Try this: Highlight the text with the formatting that you want to copy, then double-click the Format Painter button in the Standard toolbar to copy the text's formatting (your mouse pointer will change to a paintbrush). Next, simply click inside any additional text blocks where you want to apply the formatting. When finished, click the Format Painter button once more to turn it off. You can also use the Format Painter button to apply similar formatting to shapes.

DON'T STRESS OVER FONTS

If you're like me, you have about 30,000 fonts on your computer, and finding just a few that look good together can be a real chore. Well, don't stress—Publisher can help. To find just the right fonts for your presentation, click Format>Font Schemes in the menu bar, then select any font scheme in the Font Schemes task pane to instantly apply it to your publication.

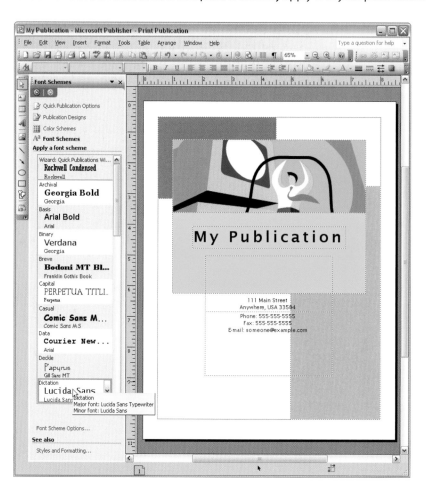

WHAT ARE YOUR MEASUREMENTS?

Do you need to know the exact measurements of your objects? If you do, you're in luck—it's easy. Select any object, then look at the bottom-right corner of Publisher's program window. There it is—the exact measurement of your object.

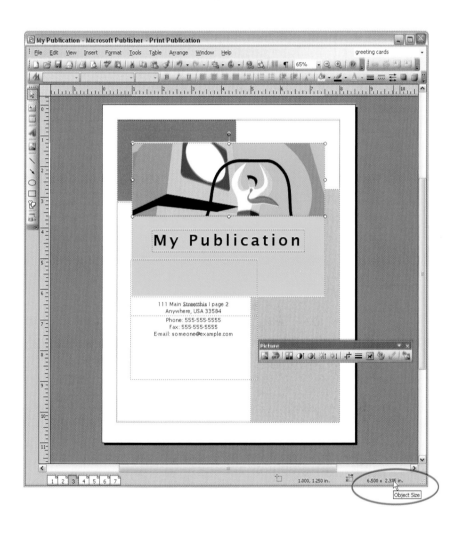

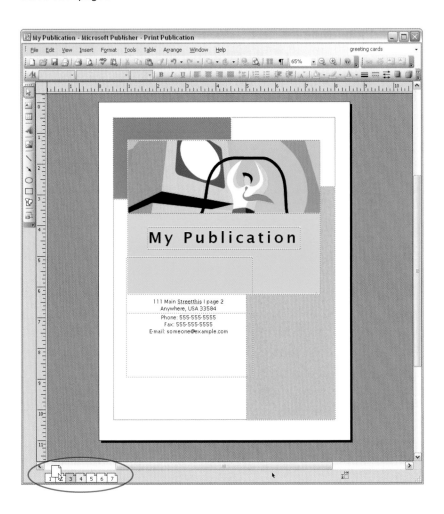

DRAG, DROP, MOVE

To move or rearrange your publication's pages, simply grab a page number's icon on the Page Sorter, located at the bottom-left corner of Publisher's view window, and drag-and-drop it into any order you'd like. *Note:* If you have two-page spreads, dragging-and-dropping will move both pages.

▭ ▢ ☒ DRAG-AND-DROP DUPLICATES

In the previous tip, I showed you how to use the Page Sorter to move pages quickly, but you can also use it to create duplicates of pages. To do this, drag-and-drop any page that you want to duplicate while pressing-and-holding the Control key on your keyboard. This instantly creates a duplicate of the page and places it into your publication. *Note:* If you have two-page spreads, dragging-and-dropping will duplicate both pages.

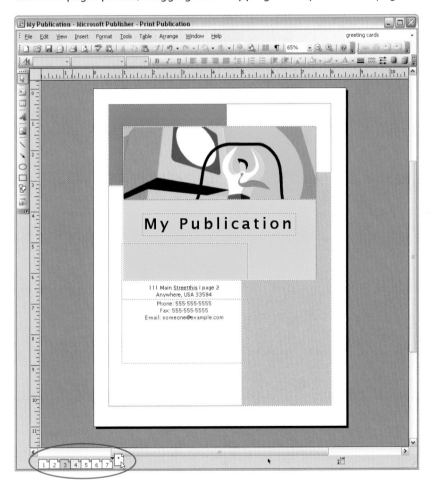

FAUX FRAME

When creating the layout for a publication, it can be useful to create empty picture frames to help with your design. For instance, you may not know exactly which picture you want to use yet, but you do know how large it will be and where it's going to be placed. When this happens, use an empty picture frame to lay out the page's elements until you find the right picture. To do this, click the Picture Frame button in the Objects toolbar (if you don't see the Objects toolbar, right-click any toolbar and click Objects) and click Empty Picture Frame. Then, drag out a frame with your mouse pointer onto the current presentation page. Now, resize and move it to where you want. Notice that the frame works exactly as a picture would: You can wrap text around it, rotate it, or anything that you could do with a picture. When you're ready to replace the frame with your picture, right-click the frame and on the shortcut menu, click Change Picture> From File (or select Clip Art to use Office's images), and browse for your image. Then click Insert, which inserts your picture into your frame. *Note:* You may have to resize your image frame once it's placed.

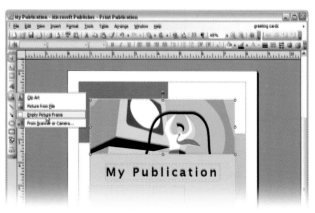

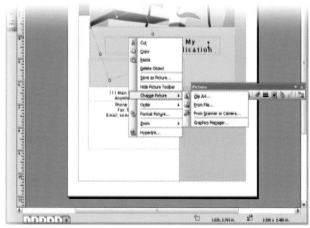

 **LINE UP**

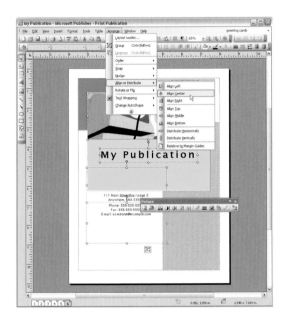

To line up your objects on a page, press-and-hold the Control key on your keyboard and click to select each object that you want to line up. Next, click Arrange>Align or Distribute and choose an alignment for your objects.

 EXACT ROTATION

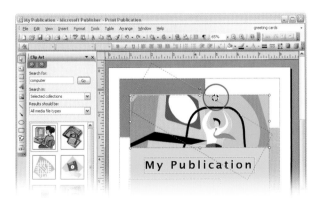

Rotating an object is easy: Just select the object, then pull the rotate picture handle at the top of the picture's frame to the left or right to rotate the object freely. But what if you want to be a little more exact with your rotation? If you need a little more precision when rotating your objects, hold the Shift key on your keyboard as you rotate an object. This rotates the object in 15° increments.

FIND THE RIGHT WORDS

If you're struggling to find the perfect quote or sentiment for your greeting cards, don't! Publisher offers an enormous collection of verses for just about any occasion. Open the New Publication task pane (File>New), click the Publications for Print folder, click Greeting Cards, select a category, then click on the card you want to create. To view the selection of verses for your new card, click the "Select a suggested verse" link at the bottom of the Greeting Card Options task pane, which opens the Suggested Verse dialog. Now, choose an occasion from the Category drop-down menu and click a verse in the Available Messages window to preview them.

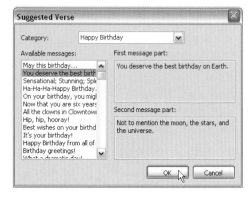

 RULERS ANYWHERE

Sometimes guides just won't do it— you need rulers (View>Rulers), but you need them in the middle of your page. What now? Move the rulers! Press-and-hold the Shift key on your keyboard and then grab the rulers and drag-and-drop them wherever needed. To put them back, press-and-hold the Shift key and drag them back to the window's edge.

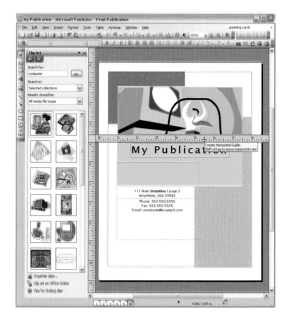

WRAP TEXT

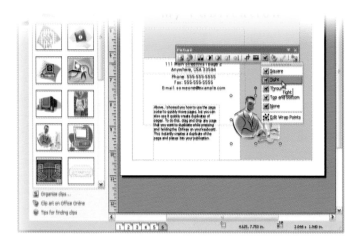

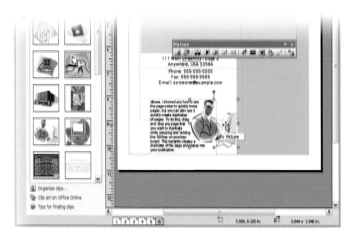

Publisher wraps text like a pro—it makes Word envious. To wrap text around pictures or objects, select the picture (this opens the Picture toolbar) that you want to wrap text around, and click the Text Wrapping button on the Picture toolbar. Choose the type of text wrap to apply. Now, move your picture over a text box (depending on how the objects are ordered—the picture is positioned in front of the text box by right-clicking the image and choosing Order>Bring to Front), and the text wraps automatically around the picture.

⬛⬜❎ RECOLOR PICTURES

If you need to quickly recolor a picture to match your publication's color scheme, try this: Right-click the picture then click Format Picture in the shortcut menu. Next, click the Picture tab on the Format Picture dialog and click Recolor. Now, click the Color drop-down menu and select a color that more closely matches your color scheme. After you choose a replacement color, you can then choose to "Recolor the whole picture" or "Leave black parts black." When finished, click OK and your picture's new colors are applied.

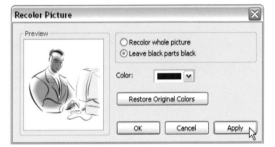

COLOPHON

The book was produced by the author and the design team using Dell and Macintosh computers, including a Dell Precision M60 2-GB 1.7-GHz Pentium M Processor, a Dell PWS650 1-GB 3.06-GHz, a Power Mac G5 Dual 2-GHz, a Power Mac G5 1.8-GHz, a Power Mac G4 1.25-GHz, a Power Mac G4 733-MHz, and a Power Mac G4 Dual 500-MHz. We used Sony Artisan, LaCie Electron Blue 22, and Apple Studio Display monitors.

Page layout was done using Adobe InDesign CS. The headers for each technique are set in Adobe MyriadMM_565 SB 600 NO at 11points on 12.5 leading, with the horizontal scaling set to 100%. Body copy is set using Adobe Myriad MM_400 RG 600 NO at 9.5 points on 11.5 leading, with the horizontal scaling set to 100%.

Screen captures were made with SnagIt and were placed and sized within Adobe InDesign CS. The book was output at 150 line screen, and all in-house printing was done using a Xerox Phaser 7700 DX.

Index

- (minus sign), 41
* (asterisk), 211
+ (plus sign), 41

A

abbreviations, 38
accented characters, 50
Access, 205–231
  Excel and, 230–231
  fields in. *See* **fields, Access**
  forms in. *See* **forms, Access**
  grids in, 208
  Layout Preview vs. Print
    Preview, 222
  records in. *See* **records,
    Access**
  reports in. *See* **reports, Access**
  tables in. *See* **tables, Access**
  toolbars, 214
  ToolTips, 206
  zooming in, 215
Access databases
  analyzing with Excel, 230
  linking text files to, 212
  object shortcuts, 210
  passwords, 211
  pictures in, 209
  relationships in, 219
  specifications, 211
  tab order, 217
Access Specifications option, 211
alignment
  form controls, 220
  Publisher objects, 247
  worksheet column
    headings, 183
**Always Show Full Menus
  checkbox,** 3
animation, 131, 141, 145
applications. *See also* **specific
  applications**

copying "pictures"
    between, 156
  crashed/hung, 12
  menus in, 3–4, 29
appointments, 106
archiving email messages, 80
asterisk (*), 211
AutoCorrect feature
  Excel, 179
  Word, 38
AutoFit to Contents feature, 47
Automatic Color feature, 56
AutoPreview feature, 99
AutoRecovery feature, 21
AutoShapes. *See also* **shapes**
  PowerPoint, 139, 146
  Word, 63
AutoSummarize feature, 49
AutoText entries, Word, 26

B

backgrounds
  color, 56
  Word documents, 56
  worksheets, 151
Bcc button, 90
bookmarks, Word, 35
borders, picture, 239
bullets
  customizing in Word, 44
  slides, 114
buttons
  assigning hyperlinks to, 6
  Bcc, 90
  command, 231
  Format Painter, 241
  Recolor, 112
  Recover Application, 12
  Shrink to Fit, 42
  Speak Cells, 190
  toolbar, 7
  Undo, 92

C

calculator, Excel, 154
calendars, Access, 220
calendars, Outlook, 107–109
camera, Excel, 155–156
captions
  Access forms, 227
  graphics, 62
  Word documents, 62
case, changing in Word, 52
CDs, packaging, 113
cells, Excel worksheets
  adding to Watch Window, 200
  assigning data validation
    to, 185
  AutoCorrect feature, 179
  centering text in, 153
  concatenating, 191
  decimal spaces in, 167
  fractions and, 186
  joining into single text
    string, 191
  negative currency
    numbers, 181
  reading with Text to
    Speech, 190
  red numbers in, 181
  selecting, 197
  wrapping text in, 182
cells, Word tables, 39
characters
  accented, 50
  tab, 39
  Word, 50
Chart toolbar, 192
charts
  in Excel, 192
  in Word, 20
Click and Type feature, 58
clip art, slides, 112, 115
Clipboard, 10, 24

color
> background, 56
> changing for gridlines, 150
> email messages, 90
> in Excel, 150, 199
> fonts, 135
> in PowerPoint, 112, 135, 146
> in Publisher, 235, 250
> recoloring pictures, 250
> shapes, 146
> text, 56, 135
> in Word, 56
> worksheets, 199

columns, Access, 217

columns, Excel worksheets
> formatting, 202
> freezing headings, 180
> headings, 158, 180, 183
> removing gridlines, 152
> selecting, 197

columns, Word documents, 42, 47

Command Button tool, 231

Command Button Wizard, 231

commands
> adding to menus, 4
> assigning hyperlinks to, 6
> AutoFit to Contents, 47
> buttons for, 231
> To Fit, 208
> shortcut keys for, 12

comments
> Excel documents, 188
> formulas, 188
> PowerPoint, 140, 144
> presentations, 140, 144
> slides, 144
> voice, 54
> Word documents, 30

Compare Side by Side With option, 8

compression, PowerPoint graphics, 142

Concatenate function, 191

contacts, Outlook
> activities, 101
> adding names, 103
> adding to Safe Senders list, 97
> categories, 104
> displaying address map, 102
> groups of, 102
> instant messaging, 104
> nicknames, 101
> picture of, 103
> printing, 100, 105
> printing addresses on envelopes/labels, 105
> sending email to, 96
> vCards, 105

control groups, 237

Control key, 23

Control-Spacebar, 43

controls, Access, 223

copying
> all items in Clipboard, 10
> paragraph formatting in Word, 44
> "pictures" between applications, 156
> slides, 116
> text in Office documents, 10

cropping pictures in PowerPoint, 138

currency
> exchange rates, 165
> negative numbers, 181

customization
> bullets in Word documents, 44
> charts in Word, 20
> dictionary in Word, 19
> menus, 4
> My Places bar, 8
> toolbars, 4

D

data, Access, 225

data, worksheets
> comparing, 172
> live, 164–165

> moving between worksheets, 177
> protecting in Excel, 178
> validating, 185

Data Access Page command, 213

database objects, 210, 214

databases, Access
> analyzing with Excel, 230
> linking text files to, 212
> object shortcuts, 210
> passwords, 211
> pictures in, 209
> relationships in, 219
> specifications, 211
> tab order, 217

dates
> current, Word, 22
> entering in forms, 230
> number of days between, 170–171

decimals, 167

deleting Publisher text, 234

Delivery Point Bar Code option, 27

desktop alerts, 99

Detect and Repair dialog, 13

dictionaries, Word, 19

Document Scraps, Word, 50

documents, Excel. *See* worksheets

documents, Office. *See also* files
> comparing, 8
> copying text, 10
> corrupted, 13
> password protecting, 10
> pasting text, 10
> recovering, 12
> repairing, 13
> saving, 9
> sending via email, 95
> sharing, 95
> using hyperlinks in, 14
> Web publications, 238

documents, Word
> closing all, 33

columns in, 42
comments, 30
comparing, 35
creating from existing, 37
exporting PowerPoint
    handouts to, 130
formatting. *See*
    formatting, Word
line numbers, 49
lines in, 38, 45, 49
merging, 35
moving text objects
    between, 55
navigating, 34
opening last-used, 19
page numbers, 46
passwords, 30
previewing, 34
protecting, 30
quick summary of, 49
saving all, 33
saving as templates, 41
selecting entire document, 57
sharing, 30
shrinking to fit, 42
splitting, 31
tables in. *See* **tables, Word**
text in. *See* **text, Word**
drag-and-drop
Document Scraps, Word, 50
email attachments, 72
Outlook Notes, 74
in Publisher, 244–245
text objects, Word, 55
drawing in PowerPoint, 118–121
drop shadows, text, 127
dummy text, Word
    documents, 53

E

editing
email messages, 87
multiple pages, 33
in Print Preview, 52
Publisher text in Word, 234

recalling last three edits, 57
toolbar buttons, 7
in Word, 33, 52, 57
email. *See also* **Outlook**
addressing, 69
archiving, 80
attachments, 72, 93, 96
auto-sorting, 83
automatically checking for, 94
Bcc option, 90
blocking senders, 88, 97
choosing account, 74
color coding, 90
contacts, 96–97
delivery receipts, 91
desktop alerts, 99
on different computers, 67
editing, 87
flagging, 89
folders. *See* **mail folders**
hyperlinks in, 73
Inbox, 68, 70, 78, 92
junk, 76, 82, 88, 97–99
multiple accounts, 74
Note documents, 73–74
notification of, 87, 94
notification sounds, 87
polling recipients about, 100
previewing, 99
printing contacts, 100
reading, 85
recalling sent email, 92
receiving, 66
replying to, 91
saving as text files, 71
saving stationery, 80
searching in, 77
sending, 66
sending webpages, 93
sharing Word documents
    via, 30
shortcuts, 69
signatures, 88
sorting, 68, 83
spell checking, 76

text format, 72
turning appointments
    into, 106
vCards, 105
zipped files, 93
emoticons, 87
envelopes
in Outlook, 105
printing, 59
in Word, 27, 59
Envelopes and Labels feature
Outlook, 105
Word, 27, 59
Excel, 149–202
Access and, 230–231
analyzing databases with, 230
AutoCorrect feature, 179
calculator in, 154
camera tool, 155–156
case sensitivity and, 196
cells. *See* **cells, Excel**
    worksheets
changing gridline color, 150
charts in, 192
color, 150, 199
Compare Side by Side With
    option, 8
currency exchange rates, 165
fonts in, 189
formatting in. *See* **formatting,**
    Excel
formulas in, 188, 198
fractions and, 186
graphs in, 192
gridlines in, 150, 152, 162
numbered lists, 174
passwords in, 178, 184
pixel measurements, 196
printing in. *See* **printing, Excel**
quick lists in, 174–176
random number function, 166
recently viewed files, 176
removing gridlines, 152
Screen Tips, 196
selecting ranges in, 197

Excel *(continued)*
    Smart Tags, 164
    sorting in, 196
    spell checking in, 187
    Text to Speech toolbar, 190
    Watch Window, 200
    workbooks. *See* workbooks
    worksheets. *See* worksheets
Excel worksheets. *See*
    worksheets

F

F8 keys, 57
fields, Access. *See also*
    forms, Access
    default values for, 207
    displaying data in
        uppercase, 207
    font size, 215
    highlighting data in, 207
    passwords, 211
fields, Word, 22–23
files. *See also* **documents**
    attaching to email, 72
    linking to databases, 212
    links to, 212
    recently viewed, 176
    zipped, 93
Find and Replace feature,
    Word, 24
finding
    email, 77
    repeating searches in Word,
        18
    replacing text in Word, 24
    similarly formatted text in
        Word, 47
folders
    email. *See* **mail folders**
    favorite locations, 8
    My Documents, 9
    in Outlook, 69
    Personal Folders, 75
fonts. *See also* **text**
    color, 135

database fields, 215
    in Excel, 189
    in PowerPoint, 117, 119, 135
    presentations, 117, 119, 135
    in Publisher, 242
    Wingdings, 189
Format Painter, 202, 241
formatting
    email text, 72
    Publisher text, 241
    shapes, 241
formatting, Excel
    columns, 202
    rows, 202
    workbooks, 168
    worksheets, 168
formatting, Word
    columns, 42
    copying, 44
    finding/replacing, 48
    preserving, 40
    text boxes, 62
Formatting Toolbar, 5
forms, Access
    adding calendar to, 220
    adding ToolTips to, 206
    aligning multiple controls
        on, 220
    automatically closing, 226
    captions, 227
    closing, 225
    controls, 223
    converting to webpages, 213
    entering dates into, 230
    instantly launching, 215
    modifying data in, 225
    pictures in, 209
    records in. *See* **records**
    tab order of, 217
    timer setting, 226
    titles, 227
    using Access with, 230–231
    using Excel with, 230–231
formulas, Excel, 188, 198

fractions, in cells, 186
frames, in Publisher, 239, 246
Full Screen mode, 32

G

graphics, PowerPoint
    compression, 142
    logos, 129
    saving entire slide show
        as, 126
graphics, Word
    AutoShapes, 63
    captions, 62
    dimensions, 61
    picture placeholders, 59
    resizing, 60–61
graphs, in Excel, 192
Greeting Cards option, 248
gridlines, Excel
    changing color, 150
    printing, 161–162
    removing, 152
grids
    in Access, 208
    snapping to, 208
    in Word, 61
grouping
    contacts, 102
    mail folders, 77
    Publisher objects, 237
    worksheets, 168–169
groups, control, 237
guides, 122. *See also* **rulers**

H

handouts, presentation, 130
hard drive, 8
headings
    column, 158, 180, 183
    freezing, 180
    worksheets, 158
help
    Office, 11
    Outlook, 82

hiding
  Access table columns, 217
  records, 218
  slides, 116
  Word text, 55–56
  worksheets, 195
home pages, mail folders, 78
hyperlinks
  assigning to buttons, 6
  assigning to commands, 6
  in email messages, 73
  in Office documents, 14
  in PowerPoint
    presentations, 124
  text files to databases, 212
  to Webpages, 14
  in Word documents, 23

I

icons, on My Places bar, 9
image boxes, in Access, 208
images. *See* graphics; photos;
    pictures
Inbox folder, 68, 70, 78, 92
insertion point, 58
instant messaging, 104

J

"J" symbol, 87
Junk E-mail folder, 76, 82
junk email, 76, 82, 88, 97–99

K

keyboard shortcuts, Office, 11.
    See also **Shortcut Keys**
keyboard shortcuts, Word
    documents
  accented, 50
  Print Preview, 37
  Symbol dialog, 51
  Word, 18
kiosk presentations, 128

L

labels
  Outlook, 105
  printing, 27
  Word, 27, 59
languages, translating, 25
lines
  numbers, 49
  in PowerPoint, 118
  spacing, 45
  in Word, 38, 45, 49
links
  assigning to buttons, 6
  assigning to commands, 6
  in email messages, 73
  in Office documents, 14
  in PowerPoint
    presentations, 124
  text files to databases, 212
  to Webpages, 14
  in Word documents, 23
lists
  in Excel, 174–176
  numbered, 174
  Safe Senders, 97
logos
  in databases, 209
  in presentations, 129

M

mail folders
  adding home pages to, 78
  archive folders, 80
  auto-sorting email into, 83
  comparing, 81
  creating, 69
  grouping messages, 77
  Inbox, 68, 70, 78, 92
  Junk E-mail, 76, 82
  moving email to, 71
  naming, 75
  organizing email in, 69, 71
  password protecting, 66

  personal, 75
  starting up in, 79
MapPoint website, 102
maps, 102
measurements, objects, 243
menu bar objects, Access, 214
menus, Office applications
  adding commands to, 4
  customizing, 4
  expanding, 3
  renaming, 4
  Word menus, 29
Microsoft Messenger, 104
Microsoft Office, 11. *See also*
    Office documents;
    specific applications
Microsoft Office Application
    Recovery tool, 12
minus sign (-), 41
MSN MoneyCentral, 164–165
My Documents folder, 9
My Places bar, 8–9

N

navigation
  database records, 227
  presentations, 123, 129
  slides, 129
  Web publications, 235
  Word documents, 34
  worksheets, 193
nicknames, 101
notes
  drag-and-drop, 74
  emailing, 73–74
  Outlook Notes, 73–74
  speaker, 130, 144
  sticky, 74
numbered lists, Excel, 174
numbers
  negative currency, 181
  page, Word, 46
  random, 166
  totaling in Excel, 172–173

O

objects
    animating in
        presentations, 141
    database, 210, 214
    grouping in Publisher, 237
    lining up in Publisher, 247
    measurements, 243
    moving in slides, 132
    opening, 214
    rotating in Publisher, 247
    selecting in PowerPoint, 134
    wrapping text around, 249
Office, 11. *See also* **Office**
    documents; specific
    applications
Office Assistant, 11
Office Clipboard, 10, 24
Office documents. *See also* **files**
    comparing, 8
    copying text, 10
    corrupted, 13
    password protecting, 10
    pasting text, 10
    recovering, 12
    repairing, 13
    saving, 9
    sending via email, 95
    sharing, 95
    using hyperlinks in, 14
    Web publications, 238
outlines, Word, 124
Outlook, 65–109. *See also* **email**
    contacts. *See* **contacts,**
        Outlook
    email folders, 69
    emailing office documents, 95
    help, 82
    launching at startup, 79
    printing in. *See* **printing,**
        Outlook
    Reading pane, 85
    receiving mail, 66
    reminders, 85
    searching in, 77

    sending email, 66
    shortcuts, 86
    sound in, 87
    web browsing with, 84
Outlook calendar, 107–109
Outlook Notes, 73–74

P

Package for CD feature, 113
pages, Word documents
    editing multiple, 33
    numbered, 46
    shrinking Word documents to
        fit, 42
paragraph marker, 44
paragraphs, Word documents
    copying formatting, 44
    selecting, 57
passwords
    databases, 211
    email folders, 66
    in Excel, 178, 184
    fields, 211
    Office documents, 10
    Word documents, 30
    workbooks, 184
    worksheets, 178
pasting items, 10
Personal Folders, 75
Personal Information
    option, 236
Photo Album feature, 132
photos, 132. *See also* **pictures**
picture placeholders, Word, 59
pictures. *See also* **graphics;**
    photos
    borders for, 239
    captions, 209
    contacts, 103
    cropping in PowerPoint, 138
    in databases, 209
    Excel Camera tool, 156
    Excel data, 155–156
    in forms, 209

    frames for, 239, 246
    in presentations, 123
    in Publisher, 237, 250
    recoloring, 250
    in reports, 209
    saving text as, 237
    in slides, 123
    Wingdings, 189
    wrapping text around, 249
pilcrow, 44
pixels, 132, 196
placeholders, Word
    documents, 59
plus sign (+), 41
PowerPoint, 111–146. *See also*
    presentations; slides
    AutoShapes, 139, 146
    color in, 112, 135, 146
    drawing in, 118–121
    exporting handouts to
        Word, 130
    fonts in, 117, 119, 135
    graphics in. *See* **graphics,**
        PowerPoint
    hyperlinks, 124
    Package for CD feature, 113
    Photo Album feature, 132
    shapes, 118–121, 139, 146
    spell checking in, 136
    templates, 137, 142
    text in. *See* **text, PowerPoint**
    Word and, 124, 130
PowerPoint Viewer, 113
presentations. *See also*
    PowerPoint; slides
    adding voice recordings
        to, 128
    animation in, 131, 141, 145
    blacking out display, 134
    comments, 140, 144
    converting Word outlines
        into, 124
    custom, 145
    fonts, 117, 119, 135
    guides in, 122

handouts, 130

hyperlinks, 124

inserting slides from existing presentations, 112

jumping to end of, 113

kiosk, 128

logos in, 129

navigating in, 123, 129

opening multiple, 125

Package for CD feature, 113

photo albums, 132

pictures in, 123

repeating objects on, 115

saving as templates, 137

shadowed text, 127

sharing on Web, 117

size of, 125

slide transitions, 131, 145

sound in, 128

spell checking, 136

starting automatically, 130

summary slides, 133

symbol shortcuts, 128

variations of, 145

viewing, 123, 143

previewing

AutoPreview, 99

email, 99

in Outlook, 99

Print Preview mode, 37, 52

in Word, 34, 37, 52

worksheets, 160

Print Preview mode, 37, 52

printers, 238–239

printing, Excel

formulas, 198

gridlines and, 161–162

page breaks and, 161

Publisher documents, 238–239

workbook data, 159–160, 162–163

worksheets, 159–160, 162–163

printing, Outlook

contact addresses, 105

contacts, 100

Outlook calendars, 107

printing, Publisher, 238–239

printing, Word

envelopes, 59

labels, 27

multiple pages on one sheet, 21

portion of Word document, 28

postal zip codes, 27

in reverse order, 28

problems. *See* troubleshooting

programs. *See* applications

Publisher, 233–250

arranging pages, 244

color pictures in, 250

color schemes, 235

deleting text in, 234

duplicating pages, 245

editing text in Word, 234

fonts and, 242

formatting in, 241

greeting cards, 248

grouping objects in, 237

lining up objects in, 247

moving pages, 244

navigating Web publications, 235

object measurements, 243

Personal Information option, 236

picture frames, 239, 246

printing documents, 238–239

rotating objects in, 247

rulers, 248

saving items as pictures, 237

text boxes, 240

text in. *See* text, Publisher

transparent shapes, 241

verses, 248

Web publications, 235, 238

wrapping text in, 249

R

Reading Layout mode, 36

Recolor button, 112

records, Access. *See also* forms, Access

appending to tables, 228

default values for, 207

hiding, 218

instantly launching, 216

navigating, 227

Recover Application button, 12

recovering Office documents, 12

reminders, Outlook, 85

reports, Access

analyzing with Excel, 230

converting to webpages, 213

pictures in, 209

snapshots, 229

title pages for, 224

Research task pane, 13

resolution, worksheets, 196

rotating Publisher objects, 247

rows, Excel worksheets

formatting, 202

removing gridlines, 152

rows, Word tables

adding to tables, 39

calculating numbers in, 40

rulers. *See also* guides

in Publisher, 248

in Word, 29

S

saving

all open Word documents, 33

calendars as webpages, 108

default location for, 9

documents, Office, 9

email as text files, 71

new documents, 9

slide show as graphics, 126

stationery, 80

text as pictures, 237

ScreenTips, 196. *See also* ToolTips

search feature
email, 77
repeating searches in Word, 18
search and replace text, Word, 24
similarly formatted text, Word, 47

sections, selecting in Word, 57

shadows, drop, 127

shapes
AutoShapes, 63, 139, 146
color, 146
formatting, 241
in PowerPoint, 118–121, 139, 146
transparent, 241
in Word, 63

sharing
digital photo albums, 132
formulas, 198
Office documents, 95
Outlook calendars, 108
presentations on Web, 117
via email, 30
Word documents, 30
workbooks, 184, 194

shortcut keys, 12. *See also* keyboard shortcuts

shortcuts
database objects, 210
email, 69
Outlook, 86

Shrink to Fit button, 42

signatures, email, 88

Single-click Open option, 214

Slide Master, 114–115

Slide Show view, 143

slide shows, 123, 143

slides. *See also* **PowerPoint; presentations**
animations, 131, 141, 145
bullets, 114

clip art, 112, 115
closing credits, 127, 135
comments, 140, 144
copying, 116
cropping pictures on, 138
hiding, 116
inserting from existing presentations, 112
moving objects in, 132
navigating between, 129
pictures in, 112, 115, 123, 138
saving as graphics, 126
selecting objects on, 134
spell checking, 136
summary, 133
tabs, 114
text on, 127, 135
transitions, 131, 145

Smart Tags
Excel, 164
Outlook, 104
Word, 26

Snap to Grid feature, 208

snapshots, reports, 229

sorting, in Excel, 196

sound
email notification, 87
presentations, 128
Speak Cells button, 190
Text to Speech toolbar, 190

spam, 82, 88, 97–99

Speak Cells button, 190

speaker notes, 130, 144

spell checking
email, 76
in Excel, 187
in Outlook, 76
in PowerPoint, 136

Spike feature, Word, 26

spreadsheets. *See* worksheets

Standard toolbar, 5

Startup task pane, 2

stationery, 80. *See also* templates

sticky notes, 74

style, resetting for text (Word), 43

Symbol dialog, 51

symbols
in presentations, 128
in Word, 51

synonyms, in Word, 48

T

Tab character, 39

table of contents, Word, 36

tables, Access
appending records to, 228
hiding columns in, 217
relationships between, 219
target, 228
viewing, 218

tables, Word
adding rows to, 39
calculating numbers in, 40
placing text above, 54
plus/minus signs, 41
selecting in Word, 25
size, 46

tabs
bulleted lists, 114
forms, 217
Word documents, 39

target tables, 228

task panes, 2

tasks, 2–3, 84

templates
email, 80
PowerPoint, 137, 142
saving presentations as, 137
in Word, 41

text, Excel
centering in worksheet cells, 153
wrapping in worksheet cells, 182

text, Office documents. *See also* fonts
copying, 10

pasting, 10
saving email as, 71

text, PowerPoint
color, 135
drop shadows, 127
on slides, 127, 135

text, Publisher
deleting, 234
formatting, 241
saving as pictures, 237
wrapping, 249

text, Word
changing case of, 52
color, 56
dummy, 53
hidden, 55–56
increasing/decreasing size
of, 51
placing above tables, 54
resetting style, 43
selecting, 51, 53, 57
selecting blocks of, 51
Smart Tags, 26
translating, 25

**text blocks, selecting in
Word,** 53

text boxes
Excel, 177
Publisher, 240
showing field data in, 177
Word, 62

**text files, linking to
databases,** 212

Text to Speech toolbar, 190

time, current (Word), 22

time zones, 109

timer setting, forms, 226

title pages, reports, 224

titles
forms, 227
reports, 224
workbooks, 201
worksheets, 169

To Fit command, 208

toolbar buttons, 7

toolbars
Access, 214
closing, 5
customizing, 4
displaying, 5
Formatting, 5
Full Screen mode and, 32
opening, 5
resetting to defaults, 6
splitting, 5
Standard, 5
Word, 32

ToolTips, 206

transitions, presentations,
131, 145

Translation window, 25

transparent shapes, 241

troubleshooting
crashed/hung programs, 12
Detect and Repair dialog, 13
repairing corrupted
documents, 13

U

Undo button, sent email, 92

undo feature, in Word, 43

URLs, linking to, 14

V

vCards, 105

voice comments, Word, 54

W

Watch Window, 200

Web
optimizing worksheets for,
196
sharing presentations on, 117
slide animations, 131, 141, 145
slide transitions, 131, 145

Web browsing, 84

Web publications, 235, 238

webpages
converting forms/reports
into, 213
emailing, 93
linking to, 14
saving calendars as, 108

Wingdings, 189

Word, 17–63
AutoCorrect feature, 26, 38
AutoFit to Contents
command, 47
Automatic Color feature, 56
AutoRecovery feature, 21
AutoShapes, 63
AutoSummarize feature, 49
AutoText entries, 26
bookmarks, 35
Click and Type feature, 58
columns, 47
Compare Side by Side With
option, 8
creating lines in, 38
customizable charts, 20
dictionary, 19
Document Scraps, 50
editing multiple pages in, 33
editing Publisher text in, 234
fields in, 22–23
finding/replacing
formatting, 47
finding/replacing words, 24
Full Screen mode, 32
graphics in. *See*
graphics, Word
grids in, 61
line spacing, 45
menus in, 29
opening last-used
document, 19
outlines, 124
PowerPoint and, 124, 130
preserving formatting, 40
printing in. *See* **printing,
Word**

Reading Layout mode, 36
repeating find operation, 18
resetting text style to
    normal, 43
rulers in, 29
search feature, 18, 24, 47
shortcuts, 18
Smart Tags, 26
Spike feature, 26
stationery, 80
table of contents, 36
tables in. *See* **tables, Word**
templates, 41
translation feature, 25
undos in, 43
Word documents. *See also* **files;**
    Office documents
closing all, 33
columns in, 42
comments, 30
comparing, 35
creating from existing, 37
dummy text in, 53
editing multiple, 33
exporting PowerPoint
    handouts to, 130
formatting. *See*
    formatting, Word
line numbers, 49
lines in, 38, 45, 49
merging, 35
moving text objects
    between, 55
navigating, 34
opening last-used, 19
page numbers, 46
passwords, 30
previewing, 34

protecting, 30
quick summary of, 49
saving all, 33
saving as templates, 41
selecting entire document, 57
sharing, 30
shrinking to fit, 42
splitting, 31
tables in. *See* **tables, Word**
tabs in, 39
text in. *See* **text, Word**
words, in Word documents
automatically repeating, 45
changing case of, 52
finding/replacing, 24
jumping between, 32
selecting, 53
synonyms, 48
Work menu, 24
workbooks. *See also* **Excel;**
    worksheets
automatically opening, 157
favorite, 157
formatting, 168
hiding worksheets in, 195
jumping between worksheets
    in, 193
naming, 201
password protection, 184
printing, 159–160, 162–163
sharing, 184, 194
spell checking, 187
titles, 201
worksheets. *See also* **Excel;**
    workbooks
adding live data to, 164–165
adding picture to
    background, 151

adding random numbers, 166
adding sums in, 172–173
cells in. *See* **cells, Excel**
    worksheets
color coding, 199
columns in. *See* **columns,**
    Excel worksheets
comments, 188
data in. *See* **data, worksheets**
data "pictures," 155–156
formatting, 168
formulas in, 188, 198
grouped, 168–169
hiding, 195
jumping between, 193
moving data between, 177
numeric headings, 158
optimizing for Web, 196
page breaks, 161
passwords, 178
previewing, 160
printing, 159–160, 162–163
protecting, 178
reading with Text to
    Speech, 190
recently viewed, 176
removing gridlines from, 152
resolution, 196
rows in, 152, 202
sharing page formatting, 168
spell checking, 187
titles, 169

Z

zipped files, 93
zoom feature, Access, 215